THE UNITED STATES IN THE GLOBAL ECONOMY

Challenges and Policy Choices

John J. Accordino

The Last Quarter Century:
A Guide to the Issues and
the Literature, no. 2
Edited by John H. Whaley, Jr.

American Library Association
Chicago and London 1992

Cover designed by Harriett Banner

Text designed by Ray Machura

Composed by Impressions, a Division of Edwards Brothers, Inc.
in Times Roman and Melior on an
Autologic μ-5 phototypesetter

Printed on 50-pound Glatfelter, a pH-neutral stock,
and bound in 10-point C1S cover stock
by Edwards Brothers, Inc.

The paper used in this publication meets the minimum requirements of American National Standard for Information Sciences—Permanence of Paper for Printed Library Materials, ANSI Z39.48-1984. ∞

Library of Congress Cataloging-in-Publication Data

Accordino, John J., 1954–
   The United States in the global economy : challenges and policy choices / John J. Accordino.
     p. cm.— (The Last quarter century ; no. 2)
   Includes bibliographical references and index.
   ISBN 0-8389-0591-9
   1. Industry and state—United States. 2. United States—Foreign economic relations. 3. United States—Economic policy. 4. United States—Commercial policy. I. Title. II. Series.
HD3616.U47A54 1992
337.73—dc20   92-11399
                                                                         CIP

Copyright © 1992 by the American Library Association. All rights reserved except those which may be granted by Sections 107 and 108 of the Copyright Revision Act of 1976.

Printed in the United States of America.

96 95 94 93 92   5 4 3 2 1

For Mac, Joey, and Mario

Contents

FIGURE	ix
TABLES	ix
FOREWORD	xi
ACKNOWLEDGMENTS	xiii
INTRODUCTION	xv

Chapter 1
SYMPTOMS AND MAGNITUDES OF CHANGE 1

THE GOLDEN AGE IN AMERICA: 1948–1973	2
The U.S. Role in a New International Order	2
Stabilizing the Domestic Economy	6
Demand-Side Fiscal Policy	6
Workforce Education and Labor Relations Policy	10
An Age of Prosperity	13
THE ERA OF DISLOCATION AND TRANSITION: 1973–PRESENT	16
The Rise of Foreign Competition	16
The Global Restructuring of Production and Trade	18
Demise of the Bretton Woods Monetary System	20
After Bretton Woods: International Economic Instability	21
Domestic Impacts of the Changing International Economy	23
Stagflation: The Unraveling of Demand-Side Fiscal Policy	23
Effects of Foreign Competition on Workers and Communities	25
The Rise of Services and Income Polarization	27
Crisis in Workforce Education and Labor Relations Policy	28
Plan of This Book	29

Chapter 2
PERSPECTIVES ON ECONOMIC POLICY: CONSERVATIVE, LIBERAL, AND RADICAL 43

    Foundations and Frameworks 43

    THE CONSERVATIVE PARADIGM 45
    Intellectual Antecedents 45
    Framework and Philosophical Foundation 45
    The Role of Government 47
    The Limits of Government 48
    Policy Prescriptions 50

    THE LIBERAL PARADIGM 51
    Intellectual Antecedents 51
    Framework and Philosophical Foundation 52
    The Role of Government 54
    Policy Prescriptions 56

    THE RADICAL PARADIGM 57
    Intellectual Antecedents 57
    Framework and Philosophical Foundation 58
    Marxist Economic Analysis 60
    The Role of Government 65
    Policy Prescriptions 66
    A Spectrum of Views 67

    Summary 68

Chapter 3
THE MACROECONOMIC FRAMEWORK 85

    DOMESTIC STABILIZATION AND GROWTH POLICY DILEMMAS 86
    The Supply-Side Revolution 86
    Results of Supply-Side Fiscal Policy and Monetarism 88
    The Budget Deficit 90
    Growing Disparities of Income and Wealth 92
    Conservative Views 94
    Liberal Views 95
    Radical Views 98

    TOWARD INTERNATIONAL COOPERATION? 102
    Liberal Views 103
    Radical Views 105
    Conservative Views 107

    Conclusion 108

Chapter 4
INDUSTRIAL AND TRADE POLICIES — 124

INDUSTRIAL POLICY — 127
Liberal Proposals — 127
Radical Proposals — 135
Conservative Critiques — 140
The Policy Record — 144

TRADE POLICY — 145
Liberal and Progressive Views — 145
Marxist Views — 150
Conservative Views — 151

Conclusion — 154

Chapter 5
EDUCATION AND TRAINING POLICY — 182

PRIMARY AND SECONDARY EDUCATION AND
WORKFORCE TRAINING — 185
Conservative Critiques and Reforms — 185
Radical Responses to Conservative Reforms — 191
Liberal Responses to Conservative Reforms — 195

HIGHER EDUCATION POLICY — 201
Curriculum Content and Achievement Standards — 201
Higher Education and Economic Development — 202

Summary — 204

Chapter 6
STATE AND LOCAL RESPONSES TO GLOBAL ECONOMIC RESTRUCTURING — 223

Ideology, Pragmatism, and Policy — 226
The Evolution of State and Local Economic Development Policy — 227

FEATURES OF STATE AND LOCAL INDUSTRIAL POLICY — 231
Business Recruitment and Its Critics — 231
Managing the War Between the States — 236
Business Retention — 238
Business Formation and Expansion — 240
Export Promotion — 242
The "Third Wave" in Economic Development — 244
The Rise of Strategic Planning — 245
Global Restructuring and American Federalism — 247

Summary — 252

Chapter 7
CONCLUSION 275

Appendix
A GUIDE TO RESOURCES 281
   Guides to Bibliographic Reference Works 284
   Indexes and Abstracts 288
   Journals 290
   Government Publications 293
   Other Periodic Sources 297

Author-Title Index 303

Subject Index 00

Figure

1   A Spectrum of Views   68

Tables

1	Distribution of Employment by Sector, 1947–1984	15
2	Distribution of Total Income by Population Quintile	26
3	Summary of Conservative, Liberal, and Radical Paradigms	70
4	State and Local Economic Development Tools and Strategies	232

Foreword

With distressing regularity we are reminded that the engine that drives our economy malfunctions. John Accordino's treatise explores the factors that help to explain how the emerging global economy affects domestic economic health and defines a number of policy choices available to the United States as it attempts to cope with a rapidly changing world. By placing these debates within the conservative, liberal, and radical frameworks, he shows how the philosophical positions of contending views have shaped definitions of the problems and thus the prescriptions for dealing with them. Does the United States need to concentrate on education or on training its workforce? Is a national industrial policy possible or necessary? How will economic policy decisions play out at the state and local levels? The options chosen by our policymakers will affect us all. This book provides an overview that will help us to understand better the terms and concepts of the ongoing debate about our economic future.

The United States in the Global Economy is the second title in the series The Last Quarter Century. Like the other books in the series, it provides a synthesis of recent scholarship, supported by an annotated bibliography for each chapter, and an appendix that guides subsequent research in the library. Most of the citations in the bibliography are to books and articles published within the last decade. The appendix will help students and other researchers use library sources to update their knowledge of topics covered in the book. Briefly annotated reference tools and journals will guide the reader to sources found in most academic and many public libraries.

John H. Whaley, Jr.
Series Editor

Acknowledgments

I am very grateful to Jay Whaley for helping to shape the book's scope and contents and for his patient and painstaking editing, especially his ruthless purges of most of my passive voice constructions. Annalee Saxenian provided helpful advice on the book's scope, as well as useful sources. Robert Holsworth and William Hellmuth advised me on the book's issue coverage and reviewed several chapters. Their suggestions improved the book substantially. I am also very grateful for the support and encouragement of my colleagues in the Department of Urban Studies and Planning at Virginia Commonwealth University, especially John Moeser and Chris Silver, who provided helpful comments on two chapters. It was Chris who first suggested that I write the book and who almost convinced me that the task would be an easy one.

I also wish to thank my graduate instructors at MIT, especially Joshua Cohen and Michael Piore, whose lectures on political and economic theory inspired me and nurtured my interest in this subject, as well as Michael Lipsky, whose critique of an earlier effort to compare political-economic paradigms haunted me as I wrote this book.

Most of all, I thank my wife, Anne-Marie McCartan, who helped me plan the book, who reviewed each chapter at least twice, and who gave me countless hours of loving support and encouragement as I plodded along.

Introduction

Tremendous changes are shaking the foundations of the U.S. economy and challenging our welfare and way of life. Although many causes and factors contribute to these changes, the single most important one, and the one to which most others are tied, is the global restructuring, or globalization, of production and trade. Global restructuring refers to changes in the division of labor among countries—who makes what goods and services and who buys them. As international trade has evolved over the centuries, restructuring has taken place. But since World War II, revolutions in transportation, communications, and corporate organization have accelerated the pace of restructuring, transforming the economic roles of the United States, Europe, Japan, and several newly industrializing countries. In a few short decades, these revolutions have shrunk the world.

While changes of appreciable magnitude generally bring both threats and opportunities, Americans have some reason to perceive more of the former than of the latter in the globalization of production and trade. For the first decades after World War II, the United States enjoyed a position of virtual economic, political, and military dominance. Americans looked upon the world with a sense of confidence. They shared values, or at least compromise positions, on a broad range of fundamental domestic and international economic issues. They believed that the members of each generation would live better than their parents.

Events in the 1970s and 1980s shook that sense of confidence. The economic revitalization of Europe and Japan, and the development of modern production facilities in the newly industrializing countries—Taiwan, Singapore, South Korea, and others—challenged American supremacy in world markets. As this tremendous increase in world production capacity helped to satisfy demand for consumer durables (autos, refrigerators, and so forth), it caused a slowdown in economic growth in the 1970s. Coupled with the inflationary OPEC (Organization of Petroleum Exporting Countries) oil crises of 1973 and 1979, the slowdown produced a rare malady in the postwar world known as stagflation—persistent inflation plus slow growth and high unemployment.

In the early 1980s, stagflation became economic strangulation for many American communities, as the United States slipped into its worst recession since the Great Depression. The ensuing recovery seemed robust on the surface, but in the new global economy, life is complex. The recovery was purchased, in part, at the price of huge foreign trade deficits. By the early 1990s, the United States had lost its once-dominant position in a number of industries, including automobiles, consumer electronics, semiconductors, machine tools, textiles, shoes, and garments. To satisfy consumer demand for imports and to service a record-breaking and growing public debt, the United States began to borrow money from Japanese and other foreign investors, thus becoming the world's largest net debtor nation. Despite reform efforts, both the foreign trade deficit and the federal budget deficit remain stubbornly high.

The global restructuring of production and trade and its many side effects have undermined our confidence about our place in the world economy as well as our postwar consensus on domestic economic policies. National spending priorities, business-government relations, minimum wages, labor unions, education and training policies, tariffs and trade policy, federal aid to states and localities—these and other policy areas now are the subjects of intense debate. We must, of course, construct a new consensus on domestic and international economic policies, but the task is a difficult one. Global restructuring has transferred economic power from the United States to other countries and increased the economic interdependence of all nations. Hence we no longer can control many of the forces that vitally affect the success of our efforts. Our domestic and international economic policies must take into account the policies of other nations.

The issues are complex and difficult, especially for those who seek to understand the problems behind the news stories and the assumptions behind the pronouncements of pundits and policymakers. This book is a response to the complexities. Its purpose is to help librarians, students, and other concerned citizens understand policy alternatives that address America's domestic and international economic problems caused by global economic restructuring.

The issues include macroeconomic stabilization policy and international monetary and fiscal policy coordination, the pros and cons of industrial policy and trade policy, education reform and training policy, and state and local government responses to global restructuring. For each topic, the policy alternatives are arranged according to the major schools of thought in which they originate—conservative, liberal, and radical.

Each chapter includes an extensive annotated bibliography of current sources, grouped by issue and school of thought. Numbered endnotes following each chapter contain additional explanatory material as well as citations. The appendix provides information to help the reader use library sources and update the information presented in this book. It contains an extensive list of government documents and other sources of primary economic data as well as a description of the major think tanks that frequently publish economic policy proposals.

The presentation format followed here should provide the reader with a firm foundation of knowledge of the major policy questions facing the United States. In addition it will give the reader an understanding of the sources of disagreement among the proponents of different policy alternatives, which he or she may then apply in studying more specific economic policy issues. Chapter 1 sets the stage for the rest of the book by describing significant events in the development of the domestic and international economies from World War II to the present. Chapter 2 explains the distinguishing features of the three major traditions in political economy—conservative, liberal, and radical. Chapters 3, 4, and 5 discuss domestic and international macroeconomic policy issues, industrial and trade policies, and education and training policies. Chapter 6 discusses the responses of states and localities to global economic restructuring and their implications for the future of American federalism.

CHAPTER 1

Symptoms and Magnitudes of Change

The United States emerged from World War II as the strongest economic and military power in the world—a giant towering over the rubble of the Japanese and European economies. Only 45 years later, it finds itself groaning under the weight of record trade and budget deficits, and with a diminished ability to compete in world markets against the Japanese, the Europeans, and the newly industrializing Third World countries, especially Hong Kong, Taiwan, South Korea, Singapore, and Brazil. How is it that a nation so recently the preeminent world power is now losing ground in a dynamic and changing world?

The complete story of declining U.S. economic power cannot be told here, but the major events in that story must be described to set the stage for the survey of economic policy alternatives that follows. For these purposes, postwar American economic history can be divided into two periods. The first period began with the end of the war or shortly thereafter, and ended about 1973. During this time, the United States assumed the role of world leader, stimulating reconstruction of the war-torn industrial economies, fostering the resurgence of world trade, and maintaining world peace. Domestic economic policies, such as demand-side fiscal policy, social welfare spending, workforce education and training policy, and labor relations policy, stabilized the economy and thus bolstered the U.S. role abroad. These policies also helped to spread the wealth that the economy generated, so that, for many Americans, the quarter century following the Second World War was a "golden age."

The reconstruction of the European and Japanese economies by the late 1960s and the rise of the newly industrializing countries undermined the United States' dominant position and ultimately destroyed the postwar international monetary system, leaving economic instability and growing international tension in its place. As U.S. economic performance lagged, the nation questioned the wisdom of its fiscal stabilization and welfare policies, as well as the education, training, and labor relations systems that had seemed to work so well before. During the 1980s, the United States adopted new economic policies, but by decade's end, it was not clear that the country was better off as a result. Thus from 1973 to the present, America has struggled through a period of economic dislocation, attempting to find its way in a changing world order.

The Golden Age in America: 1948–1973

The U.S. Role in a New International Order

In 1946, the United States had over 50 percent of the world's productive capacity.[1] Because of its economic and military might, it played the dominant role in shaping and maintaining the institutions of the postwar international order. The assumption of this role necessitated a change in America's self-conception from that of an isolated nonparticipant in world entanglements to a world leader. Changes in attitude on the part of the other victorious powers, particularly England and France, were also required. Previous conflicts involving the European powers, such as the First World War, had ended in heavy and punitive peace settlements. In the Versailles Peace Treaty of 1919, for example, England and France assessed Germany for such harsh reparations payments that the country's economy was seriously crippled. The resentment engendered by this economic oppression was effectively used by the Nazis in their rise to power. By the end of the Second World War, the leaders of the industrialized world were ready to accept the view that neither isolationism nor harsh economic punishment of any of the belligerents would bring lasting peace. Rather, they would have to find a way to rebuild the world's economies and link them through peaceful trade for mutual advantage. This new attitude made good economic sense. As the great English economist John Maynard Keynes had said in his opposition to the vindictive terms of the Versailles Treaty, international political relations are founded upon economic relations; nations who are at war economically may soon be shooting each other.[2]

Political economists and policymakers seldom have agreed on the best way to achieve the benefits of international economic cooperation while avoiding the conflicts that arise from competition.

Indeed, this debate lies at the heart of current policy dilemmas. Throughout history, nations have sought, more often than not, to improve their economic welfare at the expense of others, by amassing gold or specie during the mercantilist era, or by establishing a dominant position in key industries today.

The classical economists Adam Smith (1776) and David Ricardo (1817) articulated an alternative to the beggar-thy-neighbor practices of mercantilism. They argued that specialization and the assignment of tasks to those most skilled or best equipped to perform them was the key to increasing productivity and, therefore, wealth. The principle is applicable on both the single factory scale and on a global scale. Each country has distinctive resources, proclivities, and skills that enable it to produce some goods and services more efficiently than others. If each country specializes in producing the goods and services that it can produce most efficiently and trades the excess of these goods for those that it does not make as efficiently, all will be wealthier than if each tried to produce everything it needs. Taken to its logical conclusions, this "theory of comparative advantage" promises a world of increasing wealth, with no economic warfare.[3]

Despite the apparent reasonableness of this principle, nations often slide into economic warfare. Why? One reason is that no central authority tells a nation where its comparative production advantages lie or exactly how much it should produce of this or that good. Nations learn this as their firms succeed or fail in the competitive marketplace. But since innovation, entrepreneurship, and other factors can change comparative advantages, governments find it difficult to ignore the demands of business leaders for assistance in establishing or maintaining competitive advantages. Acting alone, nations often perceive their interests to lie in establishing comparative advantages in as many markets as possible, using subsidies to assist their own firms and tariffs and other barriers to keep out imports. While this strategy can be quite costly in the short run, its proponents argue that it can benefit the nation in the long run. As a country comes to dominate the markets for certain goods, it can raise its prices on those goods and thus afford to purchase more of the exports of other countries, improving its standard of living at their expense. It can also purchase the productive assets of other countries, thus expanding its capacity to control the sources of global wealth in the long run.

The pursuit of economic supremacy by all countries at once easily degenerates into economic warfare. This is the situation that prevailed from 1914 through the Second World War. The little world trade that occurred was confined to "trading blocs," which, to a large degree, prefigured the military blocs of the Second World War.[4]

In the history of capitalism, nations have been able to avoid economic warfare only when one was powerful enough to establish and enforce an international monetary system that preserved stability and allowed at least the most powerful nations to prosper. In the nineteenth century, Great Britain played this hegemonic role. By the 1940s, the United States had become the obvious candidate for this job. As early as December 1941, the United States and Britain began discussing a set of rules that would serve as a foundation for economic peace when the war ended. These discussions culminated in the Bretton Woods Agreement of July 1944. The most important features of the agreement were the following.

First, the exchange rates of all national currencies were fixed in relation to the value of the U.S. dollar. Thereafter, if the value of a country's currency on the private currency exchange markets varied from its agreed-upon value, that country's central bank was obligated to buy or sell enough of its currency to reestablish it at that fixed value. The framers of the agreement believed that stable relative currency values were necessary to promote stable world trade. An International Monetary Fund (IMF) was established to support the fixed exchange rate system by helping to stabilize currency values.[5]

Second, to assure the world of the dollar's stability, the United States agreed to redeem dollars for gold at $35 per ounce. Given the large supply of gold in Fort Knox, this was a credible promise, especially while there was great demand for dollars.

Third, the dollar became the world's international reserve currency. Henceforth much world trade would take place in dollars, especially between countries with weak currencies. Central banks in every country would now hold dollars in reserve, as a hedge against unforseen events. With the dollar as the international currency, it became the responsibility of the United States to supply the world with the right amount of dollars to support economic growth, but not such a large amount as to cause inflation.[6]

In addition to its efforts to create a stable international monetary system, the United States sought to eradicate the high tariff barriers that had reduced world trade to a trickle during the 1930s. In 1948, the United States helped to establish the General Agreement on Tariffs and Trade (GATT), a multinational forum whose purpose is to reduce tariff barriers through reciprocal concessions. Forty years and seven rounds of multilateral discussions later, the GATT system had cut tariffs on industrial products from an average of 40 percent to 5 percent.[7]

Of equal or greater importance to the United States' role as stabilizer and facilitator of international trade was its role as world economic engine. As the only nation with a viable industrial economy at the end of the war, it fell to the United States to supply Europe, Japan, and the rest of the world with food and manufactured goods, as well as investment capital to rebuild their productive capacities. In order to be able to buy American goods and rebuild their economies, Europe and Japan needed American dollars. Several mechanisms were developed to transport dollars from the United States overseas:

1. Direct aid, through such programs as the Marshall Plan and Point Four Aid for Greece and Turkey, channeled over $12 billion to Europe and Japan between 1948 and 1952, to rebuild infrastructure and production facilities.[8]
2. In its role as guarantor of the postwar political order, the United States spent $675 billion (in current dollars) on defense between 1951 and 1965. These expenditures paid for 375 major military bases and 3,000 minor installations around the world, as well as major wars in Korea and Vietnam.[9] These operations were (and are) financed with dollars that found their way into local economies.
3. From 1950 to 1980, American corporations invested over $192 billion in plants and other subsidiary facilities in Europe, Japan, and other countries, sometimes in partnership with Marshall Plan projects. These investments contributed substantially to the reconstruction and development of the affected economies, as well as to the development and growth of American transnational corporations.
4. The huge American market, with the wartime savings of American consumers, constituted an important outlet for foreign manufactured goods, as it does to this day.

For the first quarter century after World War II then, the United States played the roles of world economic engine and guarantor of economic stability. Cohen and Rogers sum up this dual role well:

> U.S. economic power was founded upon agricultural self-sufficiency, massive export strength, great domestic energy reserves, domination of the crucial international oil business, supremacy in most of the key industries that would shape the postwar world (aircraft, automobiles, computers, electronics, and others), and the enormous growth of its investment and commercial banking sectors that permitted it to replace

England as the world's banker. The huge U.S. domestic market permitted the absorption of goods from other countries, while the technological and cost superiority of U.S. goods generated tremendous demand from other countries for American products. This great economic power was the final guarantee both of the dollar's value and of the global U.S. military superiority essential to keeping the postwar institutional arrangements intact.[10]

Stabilizing the Domestic Economy

While the Bretton Woods system assured international stability and growth, a number of corresponding domestic arrangements were established. They added stability to the domestic economy that made it possible for the United States to play its role of economic engine and to share the benefits of economic supremacy more equally among Americans. Chief among these arrangements were demand-side fiscal policy, social welfare spending, and workforce education and labor relations policy.

Demand-Side Fiscal Policy

Throughout its history, capitalist development has been prone to cycles of boom and bust, known as the business cycle. The business cycle, a natural feature of capitalism, sometimes exacts a toll in human suffering and dislocation that has incited criticism and protest over the centuries. In his attempts to reverse the Great Depression of the 1930s, President Roosevelt adopted an approach that, over the next half century, was to become the method of choice for smoothing out the business cycle and thus avoiding the extremes of boom and bust. A brief analysis of the business cycle will help to clarify this point.

Profits, or more accurately, the expectation of profits, drive a capitalist economy. The entrepreneur who ploughs her life's savings into her computer software business and the commercial banker or investor who makes loans or invests equity capital in this software company both expect to get their money back, plus a profit, as compensation for risking their money in the business. They may have other motivations as well, but the capitalist system could not exist if investors were not motivated to make profits. When profit expectations fall below a level acceptable to investors, they cease investing their capital and production slows considerably. This is called a recession, or, if the slowdown is more severe and long-lasting, a depression.

The opposite of depression or recession in the business cycle is inflation. Inflation occurs when prices rise without a proportionate increase in production. This happens when production levels strain existing capacity. As demand for its product increases, for instance, a business will hire more workers or ask existing employees to work overtime. In order to induce them to do so, the employer may have to pay an overtime differential. Unless the employer is willing to accept lower profits (which may be the case in a very competitive industry), he or she will pass the higher labor cost through to the consumer in the form of higher prices. Moreover, as the overall level of production in the economy increases, unemployment rates decline, and workers begin to demand more money, knowing that there are other employment opportunities if their demands are not met. Other costs of production also increase as capacity limits are strained. Machinery may begin to break down more often and waste more material. Materials supplies become more expensive as they are depleted. At this point, the economy is at its peak in the business cycle.

Eventually the rise in prices and the saturation of markets begin to depress consumption levels. Meanwhile, the increased demand for money to finance consumption and investment causes banks to raise interest rates on their loans, which, eventually, reduces the demand for money. Businesses now adjust their profit expectations downward and curtail investment plans. Production falls and workers are eventually laid off. Since the unemployed have little or no money, they spend little, which further depresses the demand for goods and services in the economy.

At some point the economy reaches a trough, or low point in the business cycle. With labor and other production costs now very low and inventories depleted, expected profits once again rise to a level that is acceptable to investors and entrepreneurs, and the economy begins another round of expansion. Yet, as the case of the Great Depression illustrates, the economy does not always correct itself so easily. Moreover, even when the downturn is less severe than a depression—a mere recession—the adjustment process can be quite painful for businesses and workers and for governments relying on tax revenues.

Until the Great Depression of the 1930s, few economists outside of the Marxist tradition considered the prospect of a permanent or protracted decline in profit expectations and business investment very likely. But the Depression opened the door to new explanations of economic forces and policy prescriptions. John Maynard Keynes and his followers focused on the expected level of consumer demand as a key determinant of business profit expectations and of business investment and economic growth. After Keynes, most economists and policymakers came to believe that the Depression lasted as long as it did because of the expectation by investors and manufacturers that goods produced would not be sold. Hence they hired no workers to produce goods, so workers did not earn the money they needed to *buy* goods. To end the vicious circle, the federal government "created" demand, first by hiring workers to build public facilities, and then by purchasing armaments and paying soldiers in World War II. As worker purchasing power rose, investor confidence rebounded, and the market economy began working again.

The success of President Roosevelt's New Deal policies, and especially of wartime production, convinced many economists that the solution to the inherent problems of the business cycle was at hand. Demand-side fiscal policy, or Keynesian stabilization policy as it is called, envisioned a continuous role for the national government in monitoring and fine-tuning the macroeconomy to avoid the extremes of both inflation and unemployment, the peaks and troughs of the business cycle. Demand-side fiscal policy uses the federal government's taxing and spending powers to raise or lower aggregate (total) demand for goods and services, so as to smooth the ups and downs of the business cycle. If the government raises (income) taxes, consumer expenditures on private goods and services will fall. As expenditures fall, businesses lower their prices and eventually produce fewer goods. Thus, raising taxes can have a dampening effect that may be useful if the economy is suffering from inflationary pressures. Conversely, if the economy is in recession, the federal government can stimulate consumer demand by lowering taxes, or by borrowing and spending money itself, or both.

Since the 1930s, the U.S. government has used both taxing and spending to stimulate demand. Examples of the latter include military expenditures during World War II, the Korean War, the Vietnam War, and the Cold War. The U.S. interstate highway system, begun in the 1950s, also stimulated demand by pumping money directly into the economy to finance highway construction. During the 1960s, demand-side fiscal policy reached its heyday as the tool of choice for economic stabilization and growth management. The salubrious effects of the tax cut of 1964, in particular, convinced many observers that economists and economic policymakers were the architects of a permanently healthy economy. Between 1960 and 1972, the economy grew by over 3.7 percent annually, while unemployment averaged only 4.9 percent annually.[11]

Even before the advent of fiscal policy, the federal government used monetary policy to intervene indirectly in the economy by controlling and adjusting the supply of money. The Federal Reserve

Act of 1913 established a system of Federal Reserve Banks and a board of governors, whose primary task is to provide enough liquidity to the system to avoid financial panics, while keeping the money supply from growing so fast as to cause high inflation. The "Fed" adjusts the supply of money by buying or selling government bonds, raising or lowering the discount rate (the interest rate that banks must pay to borrow money from the Federal Reserve), or raising or lowering the fractional reserve requirement (the percentage of deposits that banks must keep on hand and therefore cannot lend out). As the supply of money is increased, the price charged by lenders to business and consumer borrowers (the interest rate) declines. At lower interest rates, more businesses can afford to borrow money to expand production, and more consumers can borrow money to buy homes, appliances, and other durable goods. Consequently, increasing the money supply, since it lowers interest rates, is a tool that can be used to stimulate business investment and consumer spending, and thus counter recessions. Conversely, decreasing the money supply raises interest rates and slows consumer spending and business investment, so it is a tool to counteract inflation.

In addition to demand-side fiscal policy and monetary policy, the United States adopted other demand stabilization measures in the 1930s and 1940s. The Davis-Bacon Act of 1931 and the Walsh-Healy Act of 1936 required the government to pay "prevailing wages" on government public works projects and supply contracts. The Fair Labor Standards Act of 1938 established national guidelines for minimum wages and maximum hours. The Social Security Act of 1935 guaranteed income for retired persons. Unemployment insurance and welfare assistance made it possible for many people to survive during periods of unemployment. With the Employment Act of 1946 the federal government established the President's Council of Economic Advisers and required the president to deliver an annual economic report to Congress, in order to supply the information and guidance needed to promote a high level of employment and low unemployment. By promoting full employment, placing a floor under wages, and establishing an income-support system, these arrangements sought to keep the economy from falling into deep troughs in the business cycle. In so doing, however, they also built inflationary tendencies into the system that would plague it later.

Government regulation of business also added stability to the economy. To maintain public confidence in the banking system and thus forestall bank failures, even during economic downturns, the Federal Deposit Insurance Corpration was created in 1934 to insure bank deposits. Interest payments on insured deposits were disallowed. Government regulation of the stock market (through the Securities and Exchange Commission), interstate commerce (through the Interstate Commerce Commission), the aviation industry (through the Federal Aviation Administration and Civil Aeronautics Board), and consumer goods (through the Food and Drug Administration), mitigated the risks of the competitive marketplace for the consumer and public at large, and sometimes for the businesses being regulated. The federal government created price supports to reduce the risk of failure for farmers and made subsidized loans available to small businesses.

Workforce Education and Labor Relations Policy

Smoothing out the extremes of the business cycle and regulating business helped in the effort to create a more stable economy. Equally important was the establishment of appropriate workforce education policies and a framework for adjudicating labor-management conflict. America's system of free and compulsory primary and secondary public education—through which all students, at least in theory, received a basic foundation of knowledge and skills—provided a pool of human capital necessary for economic growth. At the same time, a "tracking" system that began in subtle ways at the primary level and became more explicit at the secondary level, provided workers with levels of knowledge and skill as well as work-life expectations suited to various levels in the job skill hierarchy. "Bright" students were set on the fast track and given college preparatory courses for careers in management, research and development, or a profession. "Slow" students were set on the slow track and advised to take vocational-technical courses to prepare themselves for skilled craft jobs. Students who dropped out or did poorly found themselves in unskilled or semiskilled jobs. Second-chance opportunities to move up the ladder existed, however. The two-year community college provided a stepping stone to a four-year college for the high school graduate with low grades or insufficient funds for college. Alternatively (and increasingly) in the majority of cases, the community college provided students with technical certificates that qualified them for skilled production jobs, clerical work, or lower-level supervisory positions.[12]

Postwar federal policies—such as the G.I. Bill, which provided free education for returning soldiers, and the Truman Commission recommendation for the expansion of open-door, tuition-free community colleges—promoted the value of an educated workforce. In the same spirit, the federal government established the United States Employment Service, designed to link unemployed workers with training and job opportunities. In 1961, it initiated job training programs for disadvantaged and structurally unemployed workers. It expanded this commitment through numerous acts passed in the next two decades, including the Comprehensive Employment and Training Act of 1973 (CETA), the Targeted Jobs Tax Credit program of 1978, and the Job Training Partnership Act, which was established in 1983 as the successor to CETA.

For the most part, this education and training system produced workers who had both the skills necessary to perform the different types of jobs available in the labor market and personal career expectations that corresponded to different levels in the wage and skill hierarchy. While this was a necessary condition for peaceful labor-management relations, it was not a sufficient one. The first three decades of the twentieth century had seen particularly bloody battles between labor and management, as the introduction of the assembly line and increasing scale and centralization of production destroyed many highly paid, skilled craft jobs and replaced them with less skilled jobs in which workers had little control over the production process. By the 1930s, the incumbents of these low-skill jobs formed industrial unions that staged effective strikes and stopped production.[13]

Two national laws eventually established the terms of a "labor-management accord" to achieve industrial peace. Through the Wagner Act of 1935 and the Taft-Hartley Act of 1947, the government recognized the right of workers to form unions, and established the National Labor Relations Board to oversee union certification elections in workplaces and to adjudicate grievances by labor or management. The new laws also gave the states the power to enact closed- or open-shop regulations as they saw fit. In closed-shop states, all workers in plants that vote to have union representation must join and pay dues to the union. In "right-to-work" states, on the other hand, the open shop prevails. Here, no one is required to join a union, even if he or she works in a plant that has union representation.[14]

Although the national labor legislation recognized the right of workers to strike, employers could seek court injunctions to end strikes. Moreover, unions were restricted from engaging in general strikes or "secondary boycotts" against firms or industries connected to the one experiencing labor-management conflict. The legislation accorded unions the right to bargain over the "terms and conditions of employment," which was usually interpreted to mean wage levels, job descriptions, work rules, and seniority ladders. In areas such as the development and deployment of new tools or technology, which products should be produced, or where and how much profit or debt should be invested in the business, management retained unilateral decision-making powers.[15]

Through these arrangements, American organized labor became a sort of business organization whose primary purpose was to secure as large a piece of the growing profits pie as possible. Unions also sought to ensure that all workers were treated fairly in the exercise of company personnel practices—hiring, firing, layoffs, work rules, and disciplinary procedures. They insisted upon detailed descriptions of work rules and procedures in labor-management contracts, and they monitored management compliance. "Management acts and the union grieves" became the motto of this new unionism. With the economy booming, wage raises were frequent, and American workers became content. Between 1947 and 1972, real (after inflation) average weekly earnings increased by an average of almost 2 percent annually.[16] Over the same period, the after-tax corporate profits rate averaged over 7 percent per year.[17] Apparently, the labor-management accords were working.

Not every industry became unionized, of course. At its peak in 1954, union membership stood at about 35 percent of the nonfarm labor force.[18] Unions were confined, for the most part, to large, bureaucratic, mass production goods industries dominated by a few firms, such as steel, automobiles, rubber, transportation, communications, machinery, some food processing, oil and chemicals, and, by the mid-1970s, government agencies.[19] For the first 25 years after World War II, these capital-intensive, mass-production industries endured the extra costs of size and multiple levels of management and supervision, as well as the higher wages that union workers demanded, because strong demand for their products enabled them to achieve economies of scale over long production runs. Also, the higher costs could usually be passed on to consumers, because most of these industries were dominated by a few large firms that did not compete on the basis of price. Under these conditions, the most desired features of the labor-management relationship, at least from the management perspective, were peace and stability, which the new labor legislation secured.

While wages and working conditions continually improved in unionized industries, wages remained low and working conditions poor in nonunion firms in competitive industries such as textiles, poultry dressing, consumer services, and clerical work. In short, unionization reinforced the development of a two-tiered structure of American industry: a core made up of large, bureaucratic firms that controlled significant shares of their respective product markets and paid high wages, and a periphery of competitive, nonunion firms paying lower wages.[20]

Unionization also fit into, and clearly influenced the emergence of, three distinct and separate labor market segments:

1. An independent primary segment of doctors, lawyers, managers, and other professionals, as well as skilled craftspersons. Although most of these workers do not belong to unions, they have considerable control over their work, as well as high skills and high wages. They make decisions, plan production and marketing, and carry out other tasks requiring thought and judgment. Considerable formal education and training are required to perform these jobs.
2. A subordinate primary segment of semiskilled workers. Through their unions or by means of their job-specific knowledge, these persons manage to exert some control over their worklives and they command moderate to high wages. But their jobs require little formal education and they are subject to "de-skilling" (the breakdown of complex jobs into discrete, low-skill tasks) and automation.
3. A secondary segment of unskilled workers, such as restaurant workers, janitors, hospital orderlies, unskilled laborers, and fast-food workers. They have no union protection or job security, and they earn low wages. Their jobs require little or no formal education or training.[21]

An Age of Prosperity

As the new institutions and practices of demand-side fiscal policy and workforce policy succeeded, they affirmed a growing American belief in the possibility of continuous economic growth and improving living standards for everyone. In the quarter century following the Second World War, the United States achieved the greatest steady economic expansion in the history of capitalism. The creation of dollar purchasing power through U.S. aid, military installations, and direct investment by American companies fueled demand for American products abroad. From 1946 to 1970, average annual U.S. merchandise exports exceeded imports by over a third (a factor of 1.37).[22] More significant than exports was the economic stimulus that American consumers themselves created through purchases of durable goods that wartime production and rationing had put out of reach. Although wartime savings financed many of these expenditures, private consumer debt increased sixfold between 1950 and 1970, from $164.8 billion to $975.3 billion.[23] By the mid-1970s, over three-fourths of American households owned radios, televisions, vacuum cleaners, and washing machines.[24]

The period between 1947 and 1968 saw a 107 percent increase in the real net value of capital plant and equipment in manufacturing, a more than doubling of output per worker, and a 70 percent increase in real income per capita.[25] Real gross national product grew 3.7 percent per year from 1948 to 1972.[26]

During the same period, the U.S. unemployment rate averaged only 4.8 percent annually.[27] From 1930 to 1941, by contrast, unemployment had averaged 17.2 percent per year.[28] Throughout the postwar period and particularly during the 1950s, household diets improved in both nutritional content and diversity.[29] These were truly golden years for many Americans.

Of course, there were problems in the domestic economy. Capital investment in the manufacturing sector brought increasing worker productivity but also automation, which led to some worker displacement and hardship. But job losses in one manufacturing industry were more than offset by gains in others, so that overall, employment in manufacturing grew at the same rate as employment in the nation as a whole (see table 1). Moreover, unemployment insurance made it easier to suffer the pains of temporary unemployment.

Automation in the agricultural sector had far more serious impacts, however. The mechanization of farming, particularly the introduction of machine harvesting of cotton and corn on a large scale in 1950, as well as the expansion of acreage devoted to soybeans (which use little labor), rendered many farm hands and small-scale farmers redundant. Between 1947 and 1969, the number of Americans employed in farming declined by over one-half, from 6.5 million to 3.1 million.[30] Some areas of the South were particularly hard hit. For example, "from 1949 to 1952, the use of unskilled agricultural labor in twenty Mississippi delta counties fell by 72 percent, and five years later it was down to only 10 percent of the 1949 level."[31]

The mechanization of agriculture caused a dramatic increase in the decades-long migration of black families from southern farms to northern cities in the 1950s. Between 1950 and 1960, about 1.5 million blacks moved to the North.[32] For several reasons, however, these newcomers did not easily find roles in the urban economy.[33] Thus poor, black ghettos appeared in central cities throughout the

Table 1
Distribution of Employment by Sector, 1947–1984

	1947	1959	1969	1979	1984
Persons Employed* (in thousands)	57,320	63,770	78,478	94,332	100,502
Food and Goods Production					
Agriculture	11.3%	7.4%	4.0%	3.3%	3.0%
Mining	1.7	1.2	0.8	0.9	1.0
Construction	5.6	5.5	5.4	5.8	5.5
Manufacturing	26.5	25.6	25.5	22.1	19.2
Services					
Transportation, Communication, and Public Utilities	7.4	6.4	5.7	5.5	5.2
Wholesale Trade	4.6	5.2	5.1	5.6	5.7
Retail Trade	14.6	13.9	13.3	14.6	15.3
Finance, Insurance, and Real Estate	3.3	4.2	4.6	5.5	6.1
Personal, Business, Professional, and Health Services	13.0	14.6	16.8	19.5	22.7
Government	11.8	16.2	18.7	17.1	16.4
Total	99.8%	100.2%	99.9%	99.9%	100.1%

Numbers may not add to 100 percent due to rounding.
* Number of persons employed equals all full-time equivalent employees plus self-employed persons.
Sources: U.S. Department of Commerce, Bureau of Economic Analysis, *National Income and Product Accounts of the United States, 1929–76* (1981), Table 6.11B; *Survey of Current Business*, vol. 63, no. 7 (July 1983), Table 6.11B and vol. 66, no. 7 (March 1986), Table 6.10B, reported in Levy, *Dollars and Dreams*,0 Table 5.2: "Distribution of Full-Time Equivalent Employment by Sector and Industry, 1947–1983."

United States. During the 1960s, these ghettos exploded in revolt against their harsh conditions.

Yet Americans eventually responded with a certain confidence that these and other related problems could be solved. With the passage of the Economic Opportunity Act of 1964, the federal government, under the Lyndon Johnson presidency, declared a War on Poverty. Initiatives included public expenditures for job training, counseling, and, eventually, public employment; a dramatic growth in income-support programs, such as food stamps, Medicaid, Medicare, AFDC (Aid to Families with Dependent Children), and aid to elementary and secondary education; and a commitment to macroeconomic demand stimulation that brought the country to nearly full employment by 1965.[34] These programs contributed to an increase in government expenditures of 56.6 percent between 1959 and 1969, as well as increased taxes.[35] But with the economy booming and real incomes rising, increasing numbers of Americans supported public spending to share the wealth and improve society.

Between 1959 and 1969, the percentage of Americans in poverty was cut in half, from 22.4 percent to 12.1 percent.[36]

Thus, as Gilpin and others have observed, the postwar economic system was based upon the theories of Keynes at home and Smith abroad. In their domestic economic policies, the United States and other countries promoted full employment and stabilized demand through fiscal and monetary policies, labor-management accord, and social welfare policies. International economic relations, however, were based upon the premise that markets should be allowed to determine economic outcomes without discretionary government intervention, although government actions had obviously been necessary to set the system in motion.[37]

These seemingly incompatible economic arrangements worked well together for over two decades, in part because the global economy did not yet impinge, to a great extent, upon the domestic economy. By the 1970s, however, international economic interdependence had grown considerably, and the postwar international agreements and institutions had either crumbled or come under severe stress. Other nations now challenged American economic supremacy. As the global economy changed, and American power declined, the Keynesian domestic policies suddenly appeared unequal to the task of promoting full employment and stabilizing the economy.

The Era of Dislocation and Transition: 1973–Present

The Rise of Foreign Competition

America's dominance of the world economy in the postwar years rested upon its tremendous productive capacity, the superiority of its manufactured goods, and its abundant food surplus. Indeed, the underlying premise of the Bretton Woods arrangements was that America was the only country capable of revitalizing the world economy. The United States played its role well. By providing Europe and Japan with dollars to buy American food and manufactured goods, both through direct aid programs and through military expenditures abroad, the United States stimulated the reconstruction of these war-torn economies.

Of equal or greater significance than these public expenditures was the vast amount of private capital invested overseas by American corporations during the postwar era. From 1950 to 1980, direct foreign investment by American corporations in plants and other subsidiary facilities increased 16 times, from about $12 billion to over $192 billion (in current dollars).[38] Indeed, it is largely through these investments that the transnational corporation came of age. With Europe and Japan in ruins, American corporations found themselves with almost no competition in world markets for the better part of two decades. They used this opportunity to establish worldwide operations whose annual sales revenues now dwarf the gross national products of most nations.

> During the decade of 1957–67 alone, a third of all U.S. transportation equipment plants were located abroad. For chemicals, the ratio was 25 percent; for machinery, it was 20 percent. By the end of the 1970s, overseas profits accounted for a third or more of the overall profits of the hundred largest multinational producers and banks in the United States.[39]

This tremendous flow of U.S. capital overseas produced impressive results in the countries where it was invested, but it also undermined the dominant position of production facilities located in the United States. Within the space of a few short years, U.S. plants lost their competitive edge to modern production facilities in Europe, Japan, and elsewhere.

> In the late 1940s, the United States produced 60 percent of the total manufactures in the industrialized West, and 40 percent of the total goods and services. By the late 1970s, both shares had been chopped in half. U.S. export dominance was also eroding. Of Western industrialized countries' manufactured exports, the United States claimed nearly a 30 percent share in 1953. By 1976, the U.S. share had dwindled to a mere 13 percent. The change in the relative position of the United States reflected the growing strength of the economies devastated by the war, particularly West Germany and Japan. By virtually every conventional measure, those economies vastly outperformed the United States during the postwar era. Between 1953 and 1960, the rate of growth of gross domestic product in the United States was 2.4 percent, in Japan 9.4 percent, in Germany 7.0 percent. Between 1950 and 1976, industrial productivity in the United States grew at an annual rate of 2.8 percent, in Japan 8.3 percent, in Germany 5.4 percent. Between 1950 and 1970, the annual growth rate of total fixed capital stock (excluding housing) was 3.8 percent in the United States, 8.8 percent in Japan, and 6.2 percent in Germany. During the 1956 through 1976 period, the American share of world exports in manufactures dropped from 25.5 percent to 17.3 percent. Germany grew from 16.5 percent to 20.6 percent. Japan grew from 5.7 percent to 14.6 percent.[40]

While American investment clearly played a significant role in rebuilding the Japanese and West European economies, one should

18   *Symptoms and Magnitudes of Change*

not underestimate the importance of these countries' existing skills and organization, and their conscious policies of growth through exports to the United States. These industrial policies, as they are called, will be discussed in Chapter 4.

The Global Restructuring of Production and Trade

The rise of Japanese and European competition marks a profound change in the world situation from that which prevailed in the late 1940s, but it is only one aspect of a much larger and far more fundamental transformation of the world economy that has taken place in the postwar era—the globalization of production, trade, and capital markets. Prior to the 1950s, trade among nations consisted mostly of food, raw materials, and finished products. Production processes were started and completed within single nations, often within single plants. To produce an automobile, for example, a country might have to import a few raw materials, but all or almost all of the components of the car would be built and assembled in that country. In the past 30 years, however, the number and types of goods traded across national borders have increased dramatically. For example, the Ford Motor Company's European Escort contains parts that are made or assembled in 15 countries on three continents.[41]

> National boundaries no longer act as fairly "watertight" containers of the production process; rather they resemble sieves through which extensive leakage occurs.... Each one of us is more fully involved in a *global* economic system than were our parents and grandparents. Few, if any, industries now have much ... "natural protection" from international competition, whereas in the past, of course, geographical distance created a strong insulating effect. Today, in contrast, fewer and fewer industries are oriented towards local, regional or even national markets. A growing number of economic activities have meaning only in a global context.... And because of the increasingly complex ways in which production is organized *across* national boundaries, rather than contained within them, the actual origin of individual products may be very difficult to ascertain.... What these developments imply is the emergence of a *new international division of labour—a change in the geographical pattern of specialization at the global scale.*[42]

Under a global production system, a company may be controlled from its headquarters in Tokyo, New York, or Düsseldorf, while product design and engineering take place in the United States, and production takes place in low-wage countries such as Singapore and Taiwan. The electronics industry provides an example of the new international division of labor:

Circuits are printed on silicon wafers and tested in California; then the wafers are shipped to Asia for the labor-intensive process in which they are cut into tiny chips and bonded to circuit boards; final assembly into products such as calculators, video games or military equipment usually takes place in the United States.[43]

Why is global production taking place? In a capitalist market economy, production facilities locate where profits—the difference between sales revenues and production costs—are maximized. Production costs include labor, land, raw materials, energy, transportation of raw materials and finished goods, and machinery. Much of the relocation of production facilities throughout the world over the past few decades has been driven by the lower labor costs of developing countries. These labor cost differences are significant. In 1986, for example, average hourly compensation for manufacturing workers was $13.44 in (West) Germany, $13.09 in the United States, $9.50 in Japan, $1.87 in Hong Kong, $1.71 in Taiwan, $1.55 in South Korea, and $1.28 in Brazil.[44]

For the most part, it is the unskilled jobs that are farmed out to low-wage countries; most of the skilled work is still performed in industrialized countries. Only after complex production jobs, such as skilled craft jobs, have been broken down into simple, routine parts can the simple parts be farmed out to low-skilled, low-wage workers.[45]

But these de-skilling processes, as some economists call them, have been taking place at least since Adam Smith's day. Global production has emerged only recently, however, because the technological prerequisites for it did not exist until after World War II. Since then, the development of wide-bodied cargo jets, satellites, and computers—in short, the transportation/communications revolution—has made it possible to transport people, products, and information around the globe in fractions of the time and cost required only a couple of decades ago. Even tasks such as data entry, which a few years ago were considered vital back-office functions, now can be contracted out to workers in say, Puerto Rico, and sent via satellite back to corporate headquarters in New York or elsewhere. Global production requires not only feasible technology but also the financial resources and organizational capacities that today's huge transnational corporations only developed after World War II.[46]

The rise of the transnational corporation and the practice of global production have blurred the traditional lines of national economic interest. Previously, if General Motors reported profits, that was good news for American shareholders and for workers in communities throughout the United States. Now, the same profit may mean good news for American shareholders and for workers employed by GM in West Germany or Mexico, but not for American workers employed by Japanese auto makers.[47] In fact, much of what Americans experience as "foreign competition" is nothing more than one company's *internal* transactions. "Twenty-nine percent of all U.S. imports in 1971 came from the output of overseas plants and majority-owned subsidiaries of American multinational corporations."[48]

By the 1980s, the resurgence of the Japanese and West European economies, the global restructuring of production and trade, and the more recent rise of the newly industrializing countries (NICs)— Brazil, Hong Kong, South Korea, Singapore, and Taiwan—had undermined the stability of state and local economies in the United States as well as in Western Europe. In some cases, low-wage foreign competition forced less competitive companies out of business; in others, multinational corporations closed plants as they restructured operations and sought lower-cost locations for certain parts of their production and assembly processes.

Demise of the Bretton Woods Monetary System

As the balance of economic power shifted from the United States to Europe, Japan, and the NICs, it undermined the monetary system that had made that very shift in economic power possible. The Bretton Woods monetary regime supported the expansion of U.S. corporations overseas and the rapid postwar reconstruction of the Japanese and European economies. By using the dollar as the reserve currency and setting the values of all other currencies in relation to the dollar, the Bretton Woods system established the trust and stability necessary for world trade and prosperity.

As they rebuilt their economies and began to export goods to the United States, the Japanese and Europeans had less need for American dollars to finance imports. Yet U.S. worldwide military installations, expenditures for the wars in Korea and Vietnam, and American corporate investments kept up a steady flow of dollars overseas. As early as 1959, the central banks of foreign countries found themselves holding many more dollars than they wanted. In most markets, when the quantity supplied greatly exceeds the quantity demanded, the price falls until the excess supply is absorbed at a lower price.[49] Hence central bankers and investors holding dollars began to fear that the value of the dollar would fall—despite the pledge to pay $35 per ounce of gold—and that they would be caught holding dollars of depleted value. Their response was to cash in their excess dollars for gold at the $35-per-ounce price. Beginning in 1959, and during the mid- and late 1960s, a series of such "runs" on the dollar rapidly depleted the U.S. gold stock.

When in August 1971, the value of U.S. gold reserves fell below $10 billion, President Nixon unilaterally ended conversion of dollars for gold, thus uncoupling the dollar's value from that of gold and loosening the glue that held the world's currencies together. The major industrialized countries rushed to patch up the damage and reached agreement on a new fixed currency exchange rate system, but by 1973, this attempt had failed. The Bretton Woods system was dead. In its place were wildly fluctuating exchange rates and currency values that undermined the stability of the world trading system. The rigid exchange rate structure, tied to the U.S. dollar, which had seemed necessary to reestablish international trust and commerce after the war, had proved too inflexible to respond when the changing balance of trade caused the demand for dollars to fall.

After Bretton Woods: International Economic Instability

In theory, a free-floating exchange rate system is good because it allows currency values to reflect the relative desirability of a nation's goods and services in foreign markets. If the French start buying more American goods, for example, their demand for dollars, which they need so that they can buy the goods, will increase. This will raise the exchange value of the dollar against the franc. Of course, as the dollar's value rises, American goods become more expensive in France, until the French demand for American goods eventually stops increasing. By fixing the dollar's value, the Bretton Woods system prevented this adjustment process from taking place for transactions between the United States and other countries. Thus conservatives, who believe that market forces should be allowed to adjust economic relations, criticized the Bretton Woods system, while liberals argued that the fixed dollar rate was necessary for any trade to take place in the aftermath of the war.

Since the demise of the Bretton Woods system, trade in goods and services has become a relatively small percentage of total international capital flows; thus the traditional arguments for fixed or floating exchange rates are now somewhat beside the point. Now the chief concern is international lending and currency speculation. The vast outflow of dollars from the United States during the 1950s, 1960s, and 1970s, found its way into foreign banks, including foreign subsidiaries of American banks, whose lending policies the U.S.

Federal Reserve cannot control. Because they are not subject to fractional reserve requirements (which regulate the amount of deposits that banks may lend), these banks have been free to loan their so-called eurodollars over and over, thus dramatically increasing the supply of dollars in the world. By 1984, there were $1 trillion eurodollars in the world—dollars beyond the control of U.S. banking regulatory authorities.[50] Just as global production supersedes national boundaries and controls, so too does global banking supersede national regulations.

Unregulated international lending and speculation in currency markets by multinational corporations and other holders of large amounts of currency now account for most international transactions. Some economists believe that this causes wide and unpredictable fluctuations in exchange rates. This is a problem, because as the value of a country's currency shifts, the prices of its exports and imports change accordingly. Exchange rate uncertainty may cause producers and traders to diminish their activity or to trade with fewer countries.

Speculation in currency markets can have even more deleterious effects, however. Suppose the supply of dollars increases because the Federal Reserve raises the money supply or because international banks increase their lending of eurodollars. The effect of this rise in the supply of dollars could well be a precipitous fall in the dollar's value against other currencies, as speculators rush to be the first to unload their dollars before their value declines. A likely consequence of such a rapid fall in the dollar's value would be an increased demand for American exports and a reduction in imports, but it would also cause foreign and domestic investors to trade their dollars for other currencies, causing a shortage of capital for investments in the United States and a shortage of capital for U.S. government borrowing.

Such a dramatic fall in the value of the dollar seemed to be taking place in 1978–79. Concerned about the likelihood of massive capital flight to currencies with higher values, and under pressure by European banks to stabilize the dollar's value, the Federal Reserve tightened the money supply in 1979. This resulted in interest rates of 21.5 percent and plunged the United States economy into its deepest recession since the 1930s. The high interest rates attracted investors, whose purchases of dollars soon bid up the value of the dollar. The strong dollar made U.S. exports more expensive and made imports cheaper, which, in conjunction with the decline in American competitiveness discussed previously, resulted in an annual foreign trade (current account) deficit of $141.4 billion by 1986.[51]

In short, the demise of the Bretton Woods monetary system rendered the United States and all countries more vulnerable to fluctuating and unpredictable international economic forces beyond the control of any single nation. Chapter 3 discusses alternative interpretations of, and responses to, this problem.

Domestic Impacts of the Changing International Economy

The demise of the Bretton Woods system in 1971 had little immediate impact on most Americans. But they soon felt the changes taking place in the international economy. First, they experienced the dramatic rise in oil prices that followed the formation of the OPEC cartel.[52] In ensuing years, they witnessed the unraveling of demand-side fiscal policy. By 1980, the major features of postwar social welfare policy had come under attack. By the early 1980s, communities across the country had felt the pain of closed plants and lost tax revenues due to foreign competition and global production restructuring. By the mid-1980s, the American education and training systems had come under attack, and the labor-management accord had broken down. Although the institutions of the postwar welfare state remained in existence, the consensus of public support for them had dissipated, leaving only interest group conflict in its wake.

Stagflation: The Unraveling of Demand-Side Fiscal Policy

As discussed previously, demand-side fiscal policy uses taxes and government expenditures as tools to stimulate demand and therefore production, employment, and investment, or, in times of inflation, to dampen demand, production, employment, and prices. But national fiscal policy is not so powerful in an open, interdependent economy. Since 1973, Americans often have confronted this reality. The oil price shocks of 1973 and 1979, as well as increases in the prices of other raw materials from abroad, were passed into the American economy as price increases that resulted in widespread inflation.[53] The annual average rate of inflation between 1973 and 1982 was 8.6 percent, as opposed to 3 percent from 1948 to 1972.[54] Yet this inflation was not accompanied by economic growth and full employment, as economists had come to expect. Instead, from 1973 to 1988, average annual growth was only 2.7 percent, as compared to 3.7 percent from 1948 to 1972. Civilian unemployment averaged 7.1 percent per year from 1973 to 1988, as compared to

4.8 percent annually from 1948 to 1972.[55] While average hourly earnings increased steadily from World War II through 1973, by 1987 they had fallen to only 94 percent of the 1973 level.[56]

In addition to the rise in oil prices (and the prices of other raw materials), two other factors contributed to slow world growth and rising unemployment after 1973. One was the saturation of consumer durables markets by the late 1960s. High levels of American, Japanese, and European investment and production since World War II eventually absorbed the effective demand for durable goods that had developed during the 1930s and 1940s and created excess production capacity. Also important was the tremendous slowdown in U.S. productivity—the amount of output per labor hour—after 1973.[57] Such a situation, with slow or no growth and high inflation, is called stagflation—economic stagnation plus inflation.

Faced simultaneously with the two problems that, according to accepted macroeconomic theory, were not supposed to occur at the same time, economists soon lost the aura of omnipotence they had enjoyed in the 1960s. Using conventional tools to attack either inflation or unemployment aggressively would risk losing control of the other problem. As a result, no clear policy direction emerged in the 1970s. Throughout the decade, businesses and workers continued to push for higher prices and wages to recoup their losses from the higher energy costs, despite unemployment rates consistently in excess of 5 percent. Given sluggish productivity growth, this simply increased prices without raising the level of production; that is, it added to the inflationary pressures created by the raw materials' price rises. Federal government expenditures for the military and the welfare state—Medicare, Medicaid, Social Security, and AFDC—also added to the inflationary pressures.[58] Measures such as unemployment insurance and the minimum wage, once deemed necessary to stabilize aggregate demand, also fueled inflation. Unemployment insurance kept wages high by making it possible for workers to remain idle for longer periods without having to accept low-paying jobs. These factors helped to keep the inflation rate well above 5 percent, even during the 1974–75 recession.

By the end of the 1970s, Americans were sick of inflation and worried about declining U.S. economic power. Many blamed these problems on government spending, government regulations, high union wages, and expensive social welfare policies.[59] Ronald Reagan promised to "get the government off the backs of the people" by slashing taxes and federal spending for social welfare programs, thus hoping to end inflation and stimulate economic growth simultaneously.

The monetary contraction initiated by the Federal Reserve Board in 1979 and the collapse of the OPEC cartel in 1986 substantially reduced inflation during the 1980s. In the meantime, President Reagan cut taxes and social welfare spending from 28 percent of federal outlays to 22 percent (excluding Social Security and Medicare). Nevertheless, overall government spending grew, due to an increase in military spending from 23 to 28 percent of federal outlays, and interest payments on the growing national debt.[60] This resulted in huge budget deficits, which the Treasury financed by borrowing dollars at high interest rates, from both foreign and domestic investors. The great demand for dollars by the federal government exacerbated the effects of monetary tightness initiated by the Federal Reserve in 1979. This helped to drive up the value of the dollar and contributed to the soaring foreign merchandise trade deficit, which reached $159 billion in 1987.[61]

From the trough of the recession in 1982 through 1988, however, the U.S. economy grew at the rate of about 3.9 percent per year, and before-tax corporate profits increased by 92 percent between 1982 and 1986. Total employment expanded by 13 percent, leading some economists and policymakers to celebrate the dynamism of the "American job machine" and to advocate continuation of the Reagan administration's policies.[62]

Other economists point to the alarming growth of foreign trade and federal budget deficits, the loss of American firms' competitive shares of world markets, the continuing decline of the U.S. share of world production and wealth, unemployment rates averaging over 7.5 percent from 1980 through 1988; and declines in the minimum wage and AFDC benefit levels, which contributed to growing income inequality during the Reagan years. Indeed, as table 2 indicates, the trend toward greater income inequality, which began as early as 1974, accelerated during the 1980s, especially for middle and lower-middle income persons.[63] In light of these trends, many policymakers and economists argue that the Reagan policies and the policies of Reagan's successor, George Bush, should be discontinued. This debate will be taken up in chapter 3.

Effects of Foreign Competition on Workers and Communities

By the late 1970s, the rise of foreign competition and global production had begun to cause hardship for many American workers and communities. For example, from 1969 to 1976, over 44.3 million jobs were created, but almost 35.5 million jobs disappeared.

Table 2
Distribution of Total Income by Population Quintile

	Percentage of Money Income Received by Each Quintile				
Year	Lowest Quintile	2nd Quintile	Middle Quintile	4th Quintile	Highest Quintile
1969	5.6	12.4	17.7	23.7	40.6
1974	5.5	12.0	17.5	24.0	41.0
1979	5.2	11.6	17.5	24.1	41.7
1980	5.1	11.6	17.5	24.3	41.6
1981	5.0	11.3	17.4	24.4	41.9
1982	4.7	11.2	17.1	24.3	42.7
1983	4.7	11.1	17.1	24.3	42.8
1984	4.7	11.0	17.0	24.4	42.9
1985	4.6	10.9	16.9	24.2	43.5
1986	4.6	10.8	16.8	24.0	43.7
1987	4.6	10.8	16.9	24.1	43.7
1988	4.6	10.7	16.7	24.0	44.0

Source: U.S. Census Bureau, cited in Phillips, Kevin: *The Politics of Rich and Poor: Wealth and the American Electorate in the Reagan Aftermath.* New York: Random House, 1990, Chart 2: "Rising U.S. Income Inequality," p. 13.

While some regions, particularly the South Atlantic, Western Pacific, West South Central, and East North Central gained more jobs than they lost, the New England and Middle Atlantic states were net losers and the East South Central and Western Mountain regions came close to breaking even:

> Between January 1975 and January 1984, 11.5 million workers (over 10 percent of all U.S. workers) were fired or laid off because of plant closings or employment cutbacks.

Of the 5.1 million of these workers who were displaced between 1979 and 1983 and who had worked at least three years at their jobs,

> about 3.1 million, or 60 percent of these workers were reemployed by January 1984, but about half of those were earning less than they had in their previous jobs.... About 1.3 million, or 25 percent of these workers were still looking for work in January 1984 (the other 15 percent left the labor force).[64]

While the permanent earnings losses of displaced workers can be substantial, the nonpecuniary costs are even more disturbing. Researchers have found statistically significant correlations between long-term unemployment and the incidence of deaths—particularly cardiovascular deaths, suicides, homicides, and deaths caused by cirrhosis of the liver.[65]

The impacts of lost wages and increased social problems ripple through local and regional economies. Workers making less money spend less money. This slows economic activity and dampens sales tax revenues, which depletes state and local treasuries. As the number of well-paying jobs in a community decreases, people leave. As plants and homeowners leave, property values decline, and this results in lower property tax yields for local governments (which derive a third of their revenues from the real property tax). At the same time, unemployment and increased health problems add to the costs of state and local governments. The result is fiscal stress and, in some cases, fiscal crisis. During the 1970s and 1980s, many state, and especially, local, governments suffered various degrees of fiscal stress caused by plant closings.[66]

State and local governments scrambled to replace the lost jobs and tax bases. Initially, their efforts consisted mainly of attracting capital and firms from each other—the traditional method of state and local economic development. As the shortcomings of this beggar-thy-neighbor approach became more obvious, however, states and localities also began to pursue increasingly sophisticated strategies designed to build their economies from within. Nevertheless, some observers believe that states and localities cannot sustain an effective response to the global restructuring of production and trade without federal assistance and federal regulation of the interstate war for jobs and dollars. These issues are discussed in chapter 6.

The Rise of Services and Income Polarization

The disappearing manufacturing jobs have been replaced with new jobs, mostly in the personal, business, and health services industries, as well as in government (see table 1). Until the late 1970s, most observers of the U.S. economy saw the rise of service jobs as a natural and beneficial development from an industrial to a postindustrial economy. Yet by the early 1980s, it was becoming clear that while many of the new service jobs require high skills and pay high wages, many others are undesirable "secondary labor market" jobs (described earlier), such as restaurant, hotel, and fast-food workers, clerks, and tourism workers.[67] These jobs typically pay only minimum wages and offer few or no benefits, little job security, and minimal opportunities for career advancement.

Some economists and policymakers view the growth of low-wage service jobs and high-wage professional jobs at the expense of middle-wage manufacturing jobs with great concern.[68] Some have called for industrial policies that would retain manufacturing jobs, as will be discussed in chapter 4. Some observers believe that the greatest cause for concern is the growing polarization of jobs and wages within industries and within occupations, which they ascribe to new management policies to create more flexible, lower-cost labor forces. They have called for new labor laws and education policies to protect workers and achieve flexibility in other ways, as will be discussed in chapters 4 and 5.[69]

Crisis in Workforce Education and Labor Relations Policy

The rise of foreign competition and global production restructuring, and the partial replacement of manufacturing jobs with service jobs undermined the postwar labor-management accord based on bureacuratic corporate organization, union workrules, and annual wage increases. It also called into question the time-honored practices of America's education and training systems. As U.S. net exports declined and plants closed, Americans asked: "Whose fault is it?" Observers on all sides of the political spectrum cited sagging productivity growth as a chief cause, but they disagreed about the reasons for this problem. Aside from macroeconomic determinants (taxes, interest rates, and the rate of savings), conservatives and business leaders pointed to high union wages and rigid workrules as the primary causes of declining productivity growth and loss of competitiveness. They also claimed that workers increasingly lacked the education, training, and workplace attitudes to do the jobs needed by management.

Liberals maintained that sluggish productivity growth was due to management decisions to move production facilities overseas rather than invest in new equipment and technology for American factories. They blamed high production costs on the growth of unproductive corporate bureaucracy—the use of middle management and supervisors to make decisions and monitor product quality, rather than giving line workers the training and authority to do so. Thus they criticized the hierarchical division of labor in American companies and the education and training systems that support it.

During the 1980s, the continued loss of blue-collar manufacturing jobs due to corporate restructuring and low-cost foreign competition depleted the ranks of organized labor. Attempts to organize the new service workers were only partially successful. By 1986, union membership, which stood at 35 percent of the nonfarm workforce in 1954, had skidded to 18 percent, including the newly organized public sector workers.[70]

While the postwar labor-management accord has crumbled, it is not yet clear what type of labor-management relationship will replace it, and whether "accord" will be an appropriate label. On the one hand, some unionized industries, such as automobile manufacturing, have indeed created what may be a new accord. Auto companies have closed plants to reduce capacity and trimmed the ranks of production workers, supervisors, and middle managers. From the remaining workers, they have demanded wage reductions and workrule changes to increase their flexibility in deploying the workforce, and they have broadened production worker tasks and responsibilities.[71] They have given most workers assurances of employment security, and they have introduced year-end, profit-sharing bonuses. Also, business leaders and conservative and liberal political economists have called for improved education and training to meet the demands of a competitive global economy. One might interpret such developments as evidence that American managers are seeking new roles in the global economy and crafting a new labor-management accord to support them.

Yet many analysts contend that the evidence does not support such a conclusion. While corporations may be nurturing a small core of permanent, loyal workers, increasingly they are turning to subcontractors, part-time, and temporary workers (to whom they have no loyalty and pay no fringe benefits) to absorb the fluctuations of the global economy.[72] Other critics claim that most companies are not creating jobs that require more highly skilled workers or reforms in the education and training systems. Rather, they continue to de-skill and simplify the labor process. In this view, the new management policies will require workers to bear the brunt of global economic change and uncertainty through low-wage, irregular jobs, unless government responds with new labor legislation that establishes the terms of a new accord.

While economists and educators of different political ideologies debate the extent of demand for more highly skilled, technical workers, the appropriate focus of primary and secondary curricula, and the roles of government and business in fostering educational improvements, the notion that job skill requirements are outstripping workers' skills and that America can regain its competitive edge only if worker knowledge and skills improve has profoundly shaken the education field since the mid-1980s. Ambitious education experiments and reforms are on virtually every state legislative agenda. These debates and reforms are discussed in chapter 5.

Plan of This Book

The United States has yet to sort out the tremendous changes that have taken place in the world economy since 1973. The dramatic increase in global economic interdependence makes this job much more difficult than it was in 1945. The combination of Keynesian demand stabilization policies at home and Smithian free trade abroad may no longer work. One thing is certain—whatever policies are chosen to promote international growth and trade, they will affect domestic affairs, and domestic economic policies will exert unprecedented effects on the global economy.

Chapters 3 through 6 discuss the major proposals to solve the current policy dilemmas. Chapter 3 addresses issues of macroeconomic stabilization policy—the framework and context for economic activity. How important are the national budget and trade deficits, and what should we do about them? What about the rising incidence of poverty? What should national spending priorities be? To what extent should the United States coordinate its fiscal and monetary policies with those of other nations in order to maintain an appropriately stable international financial and trading system?

Chapter 4 discusses the role of government in production and trade. It analyzes alternative views on the competitive position of American industries and on government intervention to alter industrial trends and trade relations. Is the United States deindustrializing, as some economists claim? Should it pursue an industrial policy to bolster the competitive position of American firms in world markets? Do we need federal programs to speed adjustment out of declining industries into competitive ones? Does the United States need a strategic trade policy to rationalize and limit growing protectionism in world markets or to assure that it maintains a worldwide presence in so-called key industries and sectors?

Chapter 5 addresses questions about the American labor force. Does global competitiveness require changes in the American education and training systems? Would such changes conflict with other important education values, such as equal opportunity and education for democratic citizenship? What institutional structures would best serve the nation's education and training needs?

Chapter 6 surveys the state and local response to global economic restructuring, describing the growing sophistication of state and local efforts, as well as the problems that continue to undermine their effectiveness. The chapter also considers the effect of these efforts, as well as the effects of global production generally, on the American federal system.

Thus the book focuses on certain fundamental features and determinants of economic prosperity—the macroeconomic context, capital, management, labor, and intergovernmental relations. Specific issues, such as poverty and income distribution; or subsystems of the economy, such as infrastructure; or specific sectors or industries, such as agriculture, finance, steel making, or automobile manufacture, are mentioned as examples, but they are not singled out for special treatment. It is hoped that the reader will find the exposition of the major issues sufficiently clear that he or she can then extend the analysis to more specific ones.

Each chapter discusses the alternative policy proposals put forth by scholars working in the major political economic paradigms, or ideological perspectives—conservative, liberal, and radical. The intent of this method of presentation is to give the reader not only a synopsis of particular policy proposals but an understanding of the systems of thought in which they originate. This classification system will help the reader to understand and interpret subsequent literature in this field as well. Chapter 2 provides an introduction to the conservative, liberal, and radical traditions of political economy.

Notes

1. "The Decline of U.S. Power." *Business Week*. March 12, 1979.
2. Wachtel, Howard M.: *The Money Mandarins: The Making of a Supranational Economic Order*. New York: Pantheon Books, 1986, p. 39.
3. Smith, Adam: *The Wealth of Nations*. R.H. Campbell and A.S. Skinner (eds). London: Oxford University Press, 1976 (1776); Ricardo, David· *The Principles of Political Economy and Taxation*. New York: Penguin Publishers, 1971 (1817).
4. Wachtel, *The Money Mandarins*, p. 33.
5. Since a currency's value basically reflects the relative desirability of that country's goods in world markets, falling currency value might signal fundamental economic problems in that country. In such cases, a country can borrow dollars from the IMF to stabilize its currency's value, if it is willing to implement economic policies set by the IMF. If even these efforts are not sufficient to stabilize the currency's value, the IMF may approve an official change in the exchange rate for that currency.
6. This is similar to the way that money functions in a domestic economy. A growing money supply is necessary to support increased investment and consumption for economic growth. But if the supply of money grows faster than investment and consumption can absorb it, the result will be too much money chasing too few goods, or inflation. See Wachtel, *The Money Mandarins*, pp. 36–37, for an explanation of the dollar's role in greasing the wheels of the world economy.
7. Kelly, Margaret, Naheed Kirmani, Miranda Xafa, Clemens Boonekamp, and Peter Winglee: *Issues and Developments in International Trade*

Policy. Washington, D.C.: International Monetary Fund, December 1988, p. 29.

8. The Bretton Woods Agreement also established a public international institution to play this role—the World Bank (the International Bank for Reconstruction and Development). The World Bank sold bonds on Wall Street to raise capital for reconstruction loans to European countries. With the advent of the Cold War, however, U.S. congressional support for such multilateral initiatives waned, to be replaced with bilateral lending and direct investment through the Marshall Plan, U.S. military installations, and corporate investment. Between 1948 and 1952, the United States provided over $12 billion in aid for development projects in Europe and Japan through the Marshall Plan and other aid, while during the same period, the combined loans of the World Bank and International Monetary Fund totaled less than $3 billion. See Wachtel, *The Money Mandarins*, pp. 40–52 and Potter, George Ann: *Dialogue on Debt: Alternative Analyses and Solutions*. Washington, D.C.: Center of Concern, 1988.

9. Cohen, Joshua and Joel Rogers: *On Democracy: Toward a Transformation of American Society*. New York: Penguin Books, 1983, p. 108, and Wachtel, *The Money Mandarins*, p. 44.

10. Cohen and Rogers, *On Democracy*, p. 90.

11. *Economic Report of the President*. U.S. Council of Economic Advisors. Washington, D.C.: U.S. Government Printing Office, 1989, Table B-2: "Gross national product in 1982 dollars, 1929–88" and Table B-39: "Unemployment rate, 1948–88."

12. Although the tracking system and its products certainly seemed to meet business needs for different types of labor, it was often criticized, particularly by radical political economists. See the annotated bibliography in chapter 5, especially Karabel, Jerome and A.H. Halsey (eds): *Power and Ideology in Education*. New York: Oxford University Press, 1977.

13. U.S. Department of Labor: "Trend of Strikes, 1933 to November 1939." *Monthly Labor Review*. Vol. 50, No. 1, January 1940, p. 154; Bowles, Samuel and Richard Edwards: *Understanding Capitalism: Competition, Command, and Change in the U.S. Economy*. New York: Harper and Row, 1985, pp. 215–218.

14. The rationale generally given for the closed shop is that all workers benefit from union representation and wage bargaining services, hence all should pay. The rationale for the open shop is that no one should be required to join or pay dues to an organization against his or her will.

15. Bowles and Edwards, *Understanding Capitalism*, pp. 216–218.

16. *Economic Report of the President*, 1973, Table C-31: "Average weekly earnings in selected private nonagricultural industries, 1947–72," p. 229.

17. U.S. Department of Commerce, Bureau of Economic Analysis: *Survey of Current Business*, January 1986, Vol. 66, No. 1, Table 2: "Current-dollar net stock of fixed private capital, nonresidential and residential, by industry, 1947–84;" *Economic Report of the President*, 1987, Table B-84:

"Corporate profits with inventory valuation and capital consumption adjustments, 1929–86."

18. Center for Popular Economics: *A Field Guide to the U.S. Economy.* New York: Pantheon Books, 1987, Table 2.16: "The decline of union membership."

19. Wallihan, James: *Union Government and Organization in the United States.* Washington, D.C.: The Bureau of National Affairs, 1985, p. 54.

20. Political economists dispute the actual causes of the core-periphery split among industries. Bowles and Edwards, in *Understanding Capitalism,* claim that it arose from the structure of markets and corporate power, while others, such as Friedman, in *Free to Choose,* claim that unionization, by raising wages and thus stimulating investment in capital-intensive production, caused the split.

21. Bowles and Edwards, *Understanding Capitalism,* chapter 8.

22. *Economic Report of the President,* 1982, Table B-101: "U.S. international transactions, 1946–81."

23. Federal Reserve Board: *Flow of Funds Accounts,* various issues, cited in Cohen and Rogers, *On Democracy,* p. 96.

24. Levy, Frank: *Dollars and Dreams: The Changing American Income Distribution.* New York: W.W. Norton and Company, 1988, p. 51.

25. Cohen and Rogers, *On Democracy,* p. 96.

26. *Economic Report of the President,* 1989, Table B-2: "Gross national product in 1982 dollars, 1929–88."

27. *Economic Report of the President,* 1982, Table B-31: "Selected employment and unemployment data, 1948–81."

28. *Economic Report of the President,* 1949, Table C-7: "Labor force, 1929–48."

29. Levy, *Dollars and Dreams,* chapter 4: "Income, Consumption and Government Economic Policy," especially p. 49.

30. Ibid., p. 87, Table 5.2: "Distribution of Full-Time Equivalent Employment by Sector and Industry, 1947–1983."

31. Fusfeld, Daniel R.: *The Basic Economics of the Urban Racial Crisis.* New York: Holt, Rinehart and Winston, 1973, p. 16.

32. This migration wave was not much larger than the one which occurred during the Second World War, but the earlier migrants were *pulled* by the jobs created through wartime production, rather than *pushed* off the land by mechanization of farming methods. See Fusfeld, *Urban Racial Crisis,* pp. 16–21.

33. Some of the reasons black migrant families were not easily absorbed into the northern urban economies are the following: First, they lacked the education and skills needed by manufacturers. Second, automation was also displacing workers from unskilled and semiskilled manufacturing jobs, so there was no shortage of labor in most urban labor markets. Third, the brunt of the migration of the 1950s took place during a period of relatively modest economic growth (2.7 percent per year between 1952 and 1960). Fourth, racist employment practices ensured that displaced white farm-

workers would be hired before blacks. Finally, new production technologies, the increasing use of truck transport, and for some companies, union-avoidance strategies, resulted in the relocation of manufacturing jobs from the central cities to the suburbs. Exclusionary zoning and housing development practices kept blacks from moving into these suburbs, and without private transportation, they had no access to suburban jobs. See Fusfeld, *Urban Racial Crisis*, pp. 16–23 and U.S. Council of Economic Advisors, *Economic Report*, 1989, Table B-2, "Gross national product in 1982 dollars, 1929-88."

34. Heilbrun, James: *Urban Economics and Public Policy.* Third Edition. New York: St. Martin's Press, 1987, pp. 260–262 and Levy, *Dollars and Dreams*, p. 55.

35. The federal budget also increased by about 56.6 percent during the 1950s, but there was more emphasis on military spending than on social welfare programs during those years. See Levy, *Dollars and Dreams*, pp. 57–59.

36. Levy, *Dollars and Dreams*, pp. 57–59.

37. Gilpin, Robert: *The Political Economy of International Relations.* Princeton: Princeton University Press, 1987, especially chapters 9 and 10. For an insightful discussion of the role of governments in establishing and maintaining markets see Polanyi, Karl: *The Great Transformation: The Political and Economic Origins of Our Times.* Boston: Beacon Press, 1957.

38. Bluestone, Barry and Bennett Harrison: *The Deindustrialization of America: Plant Closings, Community Abandonment, and the Dismantling of Basic Industry.* New York: Basic Books, 1982, p. 42.

39. Bluestone and Harrison, *Deindustrialization of America*, p. 42. As Wachtel notes in *The Money Manadarins*, pp. 44–45, American corporate investment often occurred in conjunction with project financing through the Marshall Plan.

40. Cohen and Rogers, *On Democracy*, pp. 100–101.

41. U.S. Department of Transportation. Washington, D.C.: U.S. Government Printing Office, 1980, p. 57, cited in Dicken, Peter: *Global Shift: Industrial Change in a Turbulent World.* London: Harper and Row, 1986, p. 304. See also Knox, Paul and John Agnew: *The Geography of the World Economy.* London: Edward Arnold, 1989.

42. Dicken, *Global Shift*, pp. 3–4 (emphases in original).

43. Fuentes, Annette and Barbara Ehrenreich: *Women in the Global Factory.* Boston: South End Press, 1984, p. 7.

44. Center for Popular Economics: *A Field Guide to the U.S. Economy.* New York: Pantheon Books, 1987, Table 10.4: "Wages around the world."

45. The geographical location and movement of production facilities is determined by a variety of factors that are external to the production process, including transportation costs, raw materials availability, energy costs, and labor costs and skills. Location is also determined by internal factors, especially the dynamics of product and production process development, known as the product-process cycle. In the early stages of product development, production and design are closely linked, and skilled persons

are needed to produce the product. During this innovative stage of the cycle, facilities are generally located in large cities and, increasingly, near university research and development centers. As the bugs are worked out, the production process becomes routine. It is now possible to separate the routine aspects of production from the more difficult aspects of design and testing. The routine operations can now be farmed out to low-skilled, low-wage rural areas or developing countries. See Utterback, J. and W. Abernathy: "A Dynamic Model of Process and Product Innovation." *Omega, The Journal of Management Science.* Vol. 3, No. 6, 1975, pp. 639–656 and Sabel, Charles F.: *Work and Politics.* Cambridge: Cambridge University Press, 1981. It is important to note, however, that low-wage no longer necessarily means low-tech. The rapid growth of the South Korean economy, for example, is partly attributable to its production of ships, cars, and electronic equipment at low wages. See Magaziner, Ira C. and Mark Patinkin: *The Silent War: Inside the Global Business Battles Shaping America's Future.* New York: Random House, 1989.

46. Cavanagh, John and Frederick Clairmonte: *The Transnational Economy: Transnational Corporations and Global Markets.* Washington, D.C.: Institute for Policy Studies, 1982.

47. Reich, Robert B.: "As the World Turns." *The New Republic.* Vol. 200, No. 18, Issue 3,876, May 1, 1989, pp. 23–28.

48. Bluestone and Harrison, *The Deindustrialization of America*, p. 44.

49. In most markets, as the price falls, producers also supply less of the good until quantity supplied falls so low that a "shortage" occurs and the price begins to rise again. The United States could have responded to the dollar glut as a producer of dollars in a normal market would have, by tightening the money supply. Yet for the most part, the United States did not pursue such a course during the 1960s as it would have slowed economic growth and made it difficult to pay for military expenditures and the social programs that were initiated in that decade. Had the United States been able to shut off the flow of dollars during the 1960s, it might have been able to postpone or perhaps avoid the collapse of the Bretton Woods system. On this point, see Wanniski, Jude: *The Way the World Works.* New York: Touchstone Books, 1978, chapter 10 and Wachtel, *The Money Mandarins*, chapter 4.

50. Wachtel, *The Money Mandarins*, p. 92.

51. Finally, in 1985, the United States reached agreement with the other major Western industrial countries to sell dollars to reduce the dollar's value. The result was a very rapid decline in the value of the dollar.

52. OPEC, the Organization of Petroleum Exporting Countries, is a cartel formed for the purpose of regulating world oil output so as to control its price. In 1973, OPEC raised oil prices from $2.59 to $11.59 per barrel. In 1979, it raised the price from $13.34 to $24.00 per barrel.

53. As Cohen and Rogers point out in *On Democracy*, pp. 98–99, oil was not the only raw material to increase in price during the early 1970s:

Upward pressures on resource prices significantly reflected the long period of steady growth itself. Differential rates of inflation in the United States for raw materials and finished products between 1972 and 1974 illustrate these pressures. Wholesale prices for raw materials inflated at an annual rate of more than 28 percent from 1972 to 1974, while the comparable rate for finished products was only 12 percent. In the raw materials category, prices for food and feedstuffs and for nonfood-nonfuel raw materials inflated at a faster rate than fuel prices until the recession of 1974–75. Between 1970 and 1973, even before the major oil price increases that would later mark the decade, the composite index of raw materials increased some 300 percent.

See also Levy, *Dollars and Dreams*, p. 61.

54. By contrast, the collapse of the OPEC cartel in 1986 helped to reduce the U.S. inflation rate to less than 2 percent for that year. *Economic Report of the President*, 1989, Table B-58: "Consumer price indexes, major expenditure classes, 1946–88."

55. Ibid., Table B-2: "Gross national product in 1982 dollars, 1929–88" and Table B-39: "Unemployment rate, 1948–88."

56. Baumol, William J. and Alan S. Blinder: *Economics: Principles and Policy, Macroeconomics*. Fourth Edition. New York: Harcourt Brace Jovanovich, 1988, Appendix: "Selected U.S. Macroeconomic Data, 1929–1986."

57. Economists differ in their views on the importance of the productivity slowdown and its causes. These arguments are reviewed in Chapter 4. For present purposes, note that two probable causes are the slowdown in business investment in capital equipment and innovation, and the labor supply glut caused by the movement of the baby boom generation into the labor market. See Levy, *Dollars and Dreams*, pp. 60–68.

58. Ibid.

59. See for example, Freeman, Roger A.: *The Wayward Welfare State*. Stanford University, Stanford, Calif.: Hoover Institution Press, 1981. Americans were not alone in their frustration with social welfare policies. Most Western European countries also responded to the global economic slowdown and growth of foreign competition with attacks on the welfare state. With the exception of Great Britain, however, these attacks were generally less severe than in the United States. See Brown, Michael K. (ed): *Remaking the Welfare State: Retrenchment and Social Policy in America and Europe*. Philadelphia: Temple University Press, 1988.

60. Phillips, Kevin: *The Politics of Rich and Poor: Wealth and the American Electorate in the Reagan Aftermath*. New York: Random House, 1990, pp. 87–88.

61. U.S. Department of Commerce, Bureau of Economic Analysis: *Survey of Current Business*, March 1988, cited in Mansfield, Edwin: *Economics: Principles, Problems, Decisions*. New York: W.W. Norton and Company, 1989, pp. 351–352.

62. *Economic Report of the President*, 1989, Table B-2: "Gross national product in 1982 dollars, 1929–88." See also Phillips, *Politics of Rich and*

Poor, chapter 5; also McKenzie, Richard B.: *The American Job Machine*. New York: Universe Books and the Cato Institute, 1988.

63. Levy, *Dollars and Dreams*, pp. 60–68; also Phillips, *Politics of Rich and Poor*, pp. 115–125.

64. Center for Popular Economics, *A Field Guide*, Table 2.14: "Plant closings and displaced workers."

65. Brenner, Harvey: "Estimating the Social Costs of National Economic Policy: Implications for Mental and Physical Health and Clinical Aggression." A report prepared for the Joint Economic Committee, U.S. Congress (Washington, D.C.: U.S. Government Printing Office, 1976), cited in Bluestone and Harrison, *Deindustrialization of America*, p. 65.

66. The increasing number and devastating impacts of plant closings provoked strong reactions in affected communities. Throughout the 1980s, labor unions and community organizations fought to keep plants open and lobbied state and Congressional representatives for legislation to control or mitigate the effects of plant closings. In 1988, Congress passed a national plant closing law, called the Worker Adjustment and Retraining Notification Act, despite objections from the business community and the Reagan administration. The Act requires businesses with 100 or more employees to provide written notification 60 days in advance of a plant closing or mass layoff. See the discussion of this issue in chapter 4.

67. U.S. Census Bureau: *County Business Patterns*, 1985, Table 1B: "United States—establishments, employees, and payroll by industry by employment-size class: 1985."

68. Steinberg, Bruce: "The Mass Market Is Splitting Apart." *Fortune*. November 28, 1983, pp. 76–82, cited in Levy, *Dollars and Dreams*, chapter 5: "The Industrial Structure."

69. Some economists maintain that the most significant causes of growing income inequality are changes in the structure of work and organization within all industries and existing job categories. In this view, the use of two-tier wage structures, and part-time and temporary workers lowers labor costs and gives management increased labor flexibility, at workers' expense. See Bluestone, Barry and Bennett Harrison: *The Great U-Turn: Corporate Restructuring and the Polarizing of America*. New York: Basic Books, 1988. See also note 71.

70. Center for Popular Economics, *A Field Guide*, Table 2.16: "The decline of union membership."

71. "A Revolution in Work Rules: New Job Flexibility Boosts Productivity." *Business Week*. May 16, 1983, pp. 100–110, and Walton, Richard E. and Paul R. Lawrence (eds): *Human Resource Management: Trends and Challenges*. Boston: Harvard University Press, 1985.

72. Parker, Mike: *Inside the Circle: A Union Guide to QWL*. Boston: South End Press, 1985. See also Harrison, Bennett: "The Return of the Big Firms." *Social Policy*. Vol. 21, No. 1, Summer 1990, pp. 7–19 and Lozano, Beverly: *The Invisible Work Force: Transforming American Business with Outside and Home-Based Workers*. New York: The Free Press, 1989.

Bibliography

Background

Baumol, William J. and Alan S. Blinder: *Economics: Principles and Policy, Macroeconomics.* Fourth Edition. New York: Harcourt Brace Jovanovich, 1988.
    A thorough introduction to macroeconomic principles and policies that is frequently updated.

Bowles, Samuel and Richard Edwards: *Understanding Capitalism: Competition, Command and Change in the U.S. Economy.* New York: Harper and Row, 1985.
    See the annotated bibliography in chapter 3.

Eggert, Jim: *What Is Economics?* Los Altos, Calif.: William Kaufmann, Inc., 1987.
    A short (205 pages) and very accessible introductory economics text for those with no economics background.

Mansfield, Edwin: *Economics: Principles, Problems, Decisions.* Sixth Edition. New York: W.W. Norton and Company, 1989.
    A comprehensive and up-to-date text that covers economic theory and public policies.

Ricardo, David: *The Principles of Political Economy and Taxation.* New York: Penguin Publishers, 1971 (1817).
    See the annotated bibliography in chapter 2.

Smith, Adam: *The Wealth of Nations.* R.H. Campbell and A.S. Skinner (eds). Vols. 1 and 2. London: Oxford University Press, 1976 (1776).
    See the annotated bibliography in chapter 2.

International Monetary Relations

Gilpin, Robert: *The Political Economy of International Relations.* Princeton: Princeton University Press, 1987.
    A thorough introduction to the study of international economic relations, from a nontechnical policy perspective. The author discusses the recent development of international trade policies, finance and monetary policy, multinational corporations, and developing countries. He compares conservative, liberal, and Marxist perspectives on most policy issues.

Polanyi, Karl: *The Great Transformation: The Political and Economic Origins of Our Times.* Boston: Beacon Press, 1957.
    An anthropological account of the development of modern international trade and monetary relations. Polanyi argues that a market system cannot function according to principles of government nonintervention (laissez faire). In fact, the very creation and maintenance of a market system requires significant government action.

Wachtel, Howard M.: *The Money Mandarins: The Making of a Supranational Economic Order.* New York: Pantheon Books, 1986.

A detailed and accessible, liberal analysis of the evolution of the international monetary system, from the Bretton Woods Agreement in 1944 through 1984. Wachtel's major concern is that the rise of "stateless money"—the eurodollars and other eurocurrencies—make the international monetary system very unstable.

Foreign Competition, Global Production, and Trade

Cavanagh, John and Frederick Clairmonte: *The Transnational Economy: Transnational Corporations and Global Markets*. Washington, D.C.: Institute for Policy Studies, 1982.

This monograph traces the rise of the world's transnational corporations and their role in creating a global production and trading system.

"The Decline of U.S. Power." *Business Week*. March 12, 1979.

An analysis of shifts in competitive advantages and trading relations between the United States and other countries since World War II.

Dicken, Peter: *Global Shift: Industrial Change in a Turbulent World*. London: Harper and Row, 1986.

An analysis of the globalization of production since World War II. The author begins by analyzing the origin and growth of transnational corporations and the transportation/communications revolution that enable global production systems to function. Next, he describes how various industries have been restructured to facilitate global production, specifically, textiles and clothing, iron and steel, motor vehicles, and electronics. Finally, Dicken examines the impacts of global production on both industrialized and newly industrializing countries and alternative policies for adjusting to global production.

Fuentes, Annette and Barbara Ehrenreich: *Women in the Global Factory*. Boston: South End Press, 1984.

This monograph describes and criticizes features of the new global production systems, focusing on working conditions in factories in the newly industrializing countries.

Kelly, Margaret, Naheed Kirmani, Miranda Xafa, Clemens Boonekamp, and Peter Winglee: *Issues and Developments in International Trade Policy*. Washington, D.C.: International Monetary Fund, December 1988.

See the annotated bibliography in chapter 4.

Knox, Paul and John Agnew: *The Geography of the World Economy*. London: Edward Arnold, 1989.

A very accessible introduction to economic geography. The authors describe the historical development of the world economy, focusing on the current period of the globalization of production and trade and particularly, issues arising from the relationships between "core" (industrialized) countries and "periphery" (non-industrialized or newly industrializing) countries.

Magaziner, Ira C. and Mark Patinkin: *The Silent War: Inside the Global Business Battles Shaping America's Future*. New York: Random House, 1989.

See the annotated bibliography in chapter 4.

Reich, Robert B.: "As the World Turns." *The New Republic.* Vol. 200, No. 18, Issue 3,876, May 1, 1989, pp. 23–28.

    Reich discusses the policy dilemmas facing countries in the new age of global production, in which companies may thrive even when the workers in their "home" or headquarters country do not.

Sabel, Charles F.: *Work and Politics.* Cambridge: Cambridge University Press, 1981.

    See the annotated bibliography in chapter 4.

Utterback, J. and W. Abernathy: "A Dynamic Model of Process and Product Innovation." *Omega, The Journal of Management Science.* Vol. 3, No. 6, 1975, pp. 639–656.

    The authors explain the theory of product and production process evolution through three distinct cycles, or stages.

Domestic Economic Trends and Policies

Bluestone, Barry and Bennett Harrison: *The Deindustrialization of America: Plant Closings, Community Abandonment, and the Dismantling of Basic Industry.* New York: Basic Books, 1982.

    See the annotated bibliography in chapter 4.

_____: *The Great U-Turn: Corporate Restructuring and the Polarizing of America.* New York: Basic Books, 1988.

    See the annotated bibliography in chapter 4.

Brown, Michael K. (ed): *Remaking the Welfare State: Retrenchment and Social Policy in America and Europe.* Philadelphia: Temple University Press, 1988.

    See the annotated bibliography in chapter 3.

Center for Popular Economics: *A Field Guide to the U.S. Economy.* New York: Pantheon Books, 1987.

    A collection of easily readable tables and graphs depicting trends in the U.S. economy, including macroeconomics, labor issues, foreign trade, and income distribution. Sources for each table and methods for conducting research are also clearly explained.

Cohen, Joshua and Joel Rogers: *On Democracy: Toward a Transformation of American Society.* New York: Penguin Books, 1983.

    See the annotated bibliography in chapter 2.

Freeman, Roger A.: *The Wayward Welfare State.* Stanford University, Stanford, Calif.: Hoover Institution Press, 1981.

    See the annotated bibliography in chapter 3.

Friedman, Milton and Rose Friedman: *Free to Choose: A Personal Statement.* New York: Harcourt Brace Jovanovich, 1980.

    A contemporary statement of the conservative philosophy of government and the market economy, with a critique of government intervention in the 1970s and a call for less government in the 1980s.

Fusfeld, Daniel R.: *The Basic Economics of the Urban Racial Crisis.* New York: Holt, Rinehart and Winston, 1973.

    See the annotated bibliography in chapter 6.

Harrison, Bennett: "The Return of the Big Firms." *Social Policy.* Vol. 21, No. 1, Summer 1990, pp. 7–19.
  See the annotated bibliography in chapter 4.
Heilbrun, James: *Urban Economics and Public Policy.* Third Edition. New York: St. Martin's Press, 1987.
  A comprehensive and relatively accessible introduction to urban economic theory and policy. For additional references see the annotated bibliography in chapter 6.
Levy, Frank: *Dollars and Dreams: The Changing American Income Distribution.* New York: W.W. Norton and Company, 1988.
  Using a nontechnical style and clear tables and graphs, Levy examines U.S. economic performance from the 1940s to the present. He explains these trends by analyzing changes in American family structure and birth rates, occupations and earnings of workers, worker productivity and management strategy, federal budgetary expenditures, interregional migration, and international economic events.
Lozano, Beverly: *The Invisible Work Force: Transforming American Business with Outside and Home-Based Workers.* New York: The Free Press, 1989.
  Through extensive interviews with workers and firms in the San Francisco Bay area, the author uncovers the motives for, and specific arrangements involved in, "informal work," whereby an increasing number of persons work at home, on a temporary or contract basis, achieving some of their goals for independence and also providing firms with a more flexible, cheaper labor force.
McKenzie, Richard B.: *The American Job Machine.* New York: Universe Books and the Cato Institute, 1988.
  See the annotated bibliography in chapter 4.
Parker, Mike: *Inside the Circle: A Union Guide to QWL.* Boston: South End Press, 1985.
  See the annotated bibliography in chapter 4.
Phillips, Kevin: *The Politics of Rich and Poor: Wealth and the American Electorate in the Reagan Aftermath.* New York: Random House, 1990.
  See the annotated bibliography in chapter 3.
"A Revolution in Work Rules: New Job Flexibility Boosts Productivity." *Business Week.* May 16, 1983, pp. 100–110.
  See the annotated bibliography in chapter 4.
Wallihan, James: *Union Government and Organization in the United States.* Washington, D.C.: The Bureau of National Affairs, 1985.
  A description of the nature, structure, and governance systems of American unions.
Walton, Richard E. and Paul R. Lawrence (eds): *Human Resource Management: Trends and Challenges.* Boston: Harvard University Press, 1985.
  See the annotated bibliography in chapter 4.
Wanniski, Jude: *The Way the World Works.* New York: Touchstone Books, 1978.
  See the annotated bibliography in chapter 3.

U.S. Government Documents

Economic Report of the President. U.S. Council of Economic Advisors. Washington, D.C.: U.S. Government Printing Office.

    The annual report transmitted to Congress that reviews the state of the economy and presents the president's economic policy agenda.

U.S. Department of Commerce, Bureau of Economic Analysis: *Survey of Current Business.*

    A monthly statistical guide to the U.S. economy that includes reviews and articles.

U.S. Department of Labor: *Monthly Labor Review.*

    A report of labor conditions with statistics, regular features, and articles on current issues.

CHAPTER 2

Perspectives on Economic Policy: Conservative, Liberal, and Radical

One of the first things that strikes the student of economic policy is that the experts often disagree. Indeed, throughout this book, the reader will confront conflicting views on almost every economic policy issue. In order to understand and make sense of these disagreements, one must dissect and analyze them to discover the major concerns at stake. Fortunately, there is a logic to the disagreements, so they can be grouped into three more or less distinct schools of thought, or paradigms: the conservative, liberal and radical.[1]

Before plunging into the economic policy debates, it will be useful to consider the main features of each of the paradigms. Knowing something about the paradigm or school of thought within which an economic policy analyst develops her views helps one to understand, critique, and learn from the views, just as knowing something about a foreign country's history and culture helps one to understand the behavior of its citizens and interact with them more effectively.

Foundations and Frameworks

Paradigms are ways of looking at the world. They are an integral part of human reason, and every aspect of our lives—from the public or social aspects, to our private, interpersonal lives—is lived and experienced through a sort of paradigm. Each of us has a political-economic paradigm, but our own paradigms tend to be much less developed, articulate, and internally consistent than those of the great political-economic traditions.[2]

Each paradigm consists of a *framework* for the world we experience. Within the framework are all of the elements of experience that the paradigm-holder (implicitly or explicitly) considers relevant for understanding and acting effectively in the world. Those things that fall outside of the framework are, by definition, irrelevant. For example, the conservative political-economic paradigm differs from the liberal and radical paradigms on the issue of individual preference formation. Conservatives take individuals' wants and desires as given and do not concern themselves with questions of why or how they came to want those things. Liberals and radicals, on the other hand, regard the institutions and social processes that shape preferences as important aspects of political-economic analysis.

Another feature of a political-economic paradigm is its *philosophical foundation*. Every paradigm within the social sciences rests upon a more or less explicit foundation of beliefs about human nature, which include notions about human behavioral tendencies and the social arrangements that promote human happiness. The conservative view stresses individualism and the need to be free of external constraints, while the liberal and, especially, the radical views believe that human behavioral tendencies are largely determined by the structure of society and its economic institutions.

A third important feature of a paradigm is its set of *causative theories* and its *research program*. Each paradigm consists of a theory, or set of theories, about how everything within its framework is organized and interrelated. To demonstrate the validity of their theories, political economists conduct empirical research. Over time, each of the major theories and propositions of a paradigm is subjected to research, whereby it is eventually refuted, accepted, or retained as an unsettled issue.

Fourth and finally, each set of theories or propositions in a political-economic paradigm has implications for the best course of human action, that is, for *public policy*. Although each of the three paradigms discussed here rests upon a somewhat different philosophical foundation, includes somewhat different facts in its framework of analysis, and studies issues through different research programs, all three usually offer policy proposals for the same set of economic problems.

It is easy to see why political economists and policy experts disagree so often. They may disagree over fundamental philosophies of human nature or over which facts of human experience to include in their frameworks. This is where many of the disagreements begin, and this is why distinctly different political-economic paradigms exist. Yet even when experts agree on the philosophical fundamentals and frameworks, they may disagree about specific issues or research results. They may interpret current economic statistics and trends differently, or they may want to apply their paradigm to public policy issues differently. This is why we speak of liberal, conservative, and radical views; within each paradigm, there is room for disagreement and debate.

Political-economic paradigms gain and lose popularity over time, as their analyses of economic life and prescriptions for public policy are perceived to be more or less accurate and useful. Although the liberal paradigm has had a dominant influence on public policy for much of this century, conservative views held sway in the nineteenth century and have made a comeback in the last two decades. Radical views have never achieved this level of popular acceptance in capitalist countries, but they have always found adherents, especially at the turn of the century and during the 1930s, 1960s, and 1970s.

The Conservative Paradigm

Intellectual Antecedents

The contemporary conservative political-economic paradigm has a rich and extensive history. Its two most significant precursors are John Locke, whose *Two Treatises of Government* (written about 1680) laid the philosophical foundations of the democratic capitalist state, and Adam Smith, whose *Wealth of Nations* in 1776 described the basic principles of a capitalist, free market economy. Other political economists, especially David Ricardo, Alfred Marshall, Joseph Schumpeter, and Friedrich Hayek, have made significant contributions to the field of economics and to the world views and research approaches of contemporary conservatives.[3]

Framework and Philosophical Foundation

In the conservative paradigm, the most important category and the primary unit of analysis is the individual person, who is, as Milton Friedman puts it, "the ultimate entity in society."[4] In his most natural state, the individual is free from constraints imposed by any other person, free to do as he wishes. In the conservative view, humans are naturally motivated to seek pleasure and avoid pain, and all human actions can be classified as the result of one of these two basic motivations. Being perfectly capable of advancing his own welfare as he defines it, the free individual does not need the guiding hand of a nurturing government. Indeed, the best form of government and society is the one that imposes as few constraints upon individual behavior as possible.

A key feature of such a good society is the private ownership of property, both personal property (such as clothing) and productive property (such as factories, land, and capital). It is property of the latter sort that is generally the subject of political-economic debate. Writers in the conservative tradition have justified the argument for private property ownership in two ways: (1) As a matter of entitlement, that is, a basic, natural right of free individuals; and (2) as a means to other ends, such as diffusion of power (which is itself a means to the goal of human freedom) and economic growth and development.

John Locke's entitlement view is perhaps the most well known. He argues that because each individual owns his own person and his own labor, whatever he or those whom he has employed remove out of "the state of nature" (for instance, undeveloped land, mineral resources), belongs to him, so long as "there is enough and as good left in common for others."[5] Hence private property—that which has been removed from the earth or created through the work of the individual—is a natural and morally legitimate product of a society of free individuals supporting themselves by the produce of their own labor, or that of their workers.[6]

Most conservative political economists justify the institution of private property ownership as a means to other ends. Adam Smith believed that the desire to accumulate private property, so long as it was channeled through competitive markets, was the primary motive force behind national economic growth and development. Don Lavoie provides a contemporary statement of this view:

> It is precisely because the scientist has his reputation (and self-esteem)—and the capitalist his wealth—*at stake* that he is impelled to make his commitments for or against any particular direction of scientific or productive activity. Thus both the property rights that permit separate owners to use their resources as they see fit and the intellectual freedom that permits scientists to adhere to the theories of their choice play the same role. To the extent that either form of personal commitment is undermined—when scientific reputation or economic wealth depends on loyalty to a party line rather than to a personal devotion to truth or a pursuit of anticipated profit opportunities—each of these achievements of civilization, science and our advanced economy, is to that degree sabotaged.[7]

Friedrich Hayek, Milton Friedman, and others believe that private property ownership promotes additional important ends, such as the decentralization of power and, particularly, the separation of political from economic power. In the conservative view, concentrations of power pose the greatest threats to individual freedom.

Thus it can be said that private property ownership promotes the goal of human freedom because it separates political from economic power.[8]

Adam Smith observed that individuals also have a natural propensity to "truck, barter and exchange" the goods that they can more easily produce for those that they cannot easily produce. Indeed, as individuals become increasingly specialized in the production of goods and services for which they are most talented or have the most resources, production as a whole becomes more efficient and national wealth grows.[9] So long as exchanges between individuals are completely voluntary, both sides benefit. Hence a natural outgrowth of free individuals peacefully interacting is a market system. To sum up, the "good society," because it is a natural one, is characterized by individuals freely pursuing their own good, through their own specialized work (or that of their workers), through the accumulation and use of their property, and through voluntary exchanges in the marketplace.

The Role of Government

In most respects, a society composed of self-interested individuals can function quite well with no government. But for several reasons, some amount of government is necessary. First, because some persons are good and some are not, government is needed to protect private property and to enforce voluntary contracts and exchanges. Stated more broadly, in a capitalist market society, government is the rule maker and umpire. It determines the precise nature of property rights and enforces them.[10]

Second, there is a certain class of goods, which economists call public goods, that the market cannot easily provide. Examples of such public goods are national defense, roads, and police and fire protection. Even though everyone wants to consume these goods, no single individual wants to pay for them. The reason is that it is impossible to exclude anyone from consuming such goods, even those who have not paid for them. Moreover, the costs of these goods far outweigh the benefits that any single individual would receive from paying for them alone. Hence forced payment through taxes is needed to provide public goods.[11]

Third, governments can regulate or tax market exchanges that produce unwanted effects on third parties. Such negative side effects are called externalities or neighborhood effects. They are either so diffuse or so difficult to specify clearly that it is impossible to identify and compensate all of the individuals who are adversely affected.

An excellent example of such neighborhood effects is air pollution, which arises from the production and exchange of, say, steel between a company and a certain number of buyers. The effects of pollution are experienced by countless numbers of persons who are not the buyers or sellers of steel, over entire regions and several generations. Hence government regulations or taxes on pollution are necessary to curb it. However, as conservatives point out, government action also creates neighborhood effects, because it alters the natural (market) allocation of resources. Thus the government should only act to curb a neighborhood effect when the benefits of such action are clearly greater than all costs of new, government-generated neighborhood effects.[12]

Fourth, conservatives believe that government should maintain competitive markets for goods, services, and labor, particularly by preventing the establishment of monopolies that arise from collusive agreements among firms or from the government's own regulatory actions. Such prevention is necessary because monopolies restrict consumer choice and thus constrain individual freedom.

Fifth and finally, government should provide a stable monetary framework to facilitate free exchanges of goods and services through money. Without stable money, the relative values of commodities become uncertain. This hampers exchange unnecessarily and limits individual choice and freedom.[13]

The Limits of Government

Although some conservatives may tolerate more government action than is entailed in this list, the principle of laissez-faire and of "that government governs best that governs least" is at the heart of the conservative world view. Government is at best a necessary evil, since any government action strains "the delicate threads that hold society together" and constrains individual freedom.[14] Why? Conservatives believe that individual preferences are formed outside of, and logically prior to, the collective decision-making processes of government, and they are not altered by collective decision-making processes. This differs from the liberal and radical views, which claim that individual perspectives become broader and their preferences change during the process of democratic decisionmaking.

In the conservative view, all that government can do is to sum up the already formed preferences of parties to the decision-making process. But since everyone's experiences and preferences are different, if not conflicting, it is impossible to reach a decision that is completely satisfactory to everyone through the collective decision-making apparatus of government; some must submit to the will of others. Hence when we use government to make decisions, all we can get is conformity without unanimity, but through the free market, we get unanimity without conformity—everyone gets what he or she is willing and able to pay for, no more and no less.[15] In the words of Milton Friedman, the market "is a system of effectively proportional representation."[16]

How does this work? In the marketplace, individual consumers express their relative preferences—the relative values that they place on goods and services—through the prices at which they are willing to buy goods and services. Likewise through the market, producers announce the prices at which they wish to sell their products; these prices include both the costs of production and profits. In a well-functioning market, there is a price at which all of the goods that were produced can be sold—the market-clearing price. But prices are not just the outcome of the act of exchange. They are the glue that holds the entire market exchange system together. They transmit information about the supply and demand of resources and thus facilitate the adjustment of relative consumer preferences and production costs. For example, I now prefer coffee to tea, but if the price of coffee triples and the price of tea does not change, I may switch to tea.

The beauty of the market system is that it obviates the need for a governmental authority to determine what goods and services need to be produced. Consumers and producers determine this through a process of continual, mutual adjustment of relative consumption preferences with production costs. Prices are an indispensable part of this system. They provide producers and consumers with incentives to use the least costly materials and resources for the most highly valued end products or purposes. Ultimately, prices also determine the distribution of income—labor services that are more highly valued fetch higher wages.[17]

Through our choices in the marketplace of how much to work, what skills to learn, where to live, and so forth, we determine our incomes and other life outcomes. But chance also plays a role—we may be born into a poor family or suffer poor health. We may devote time and resources to train ourselves for a certain occupation, only to find after several years that our skills have become obsolete or that someone else's have become less costly. But embedded within the conservative view of human nature is the belief that individuals are risk takers; they prefer to live in a society in which they have an opportunity to earn a high income, even if that means that they risk achieving only a low income.[18]

Government interventions into the market system (above and beyond the five types listed previously) almost always have baleful, if unintended, effects. If government regulates prices, or redistributes incomes, or redirects resources from one use to another (say, through taxing and spending), it creates static that interferes with the price system, distorting individual preferences and leading to inefficient and unfair outcomes. When government attempts to correct these problems through further interventions, it only makes matters worse.[19]

The negative consequences of government intervention in the market are generally not apparent in the short run. Indeed, in the short run, it often appears that government can solve problems that the market cannot, such as unemployment, poverty, discrimination, or international trade imbalances. But such interventions invariably engender human behavior that is worse than the problem that government meant to solve. To take a simple example, liberals clamor for increases in the minimum wage, arguing that the existing minimum wage is not enough to support a family, or in many places, even a single person. Raising the minimum wage would appear to solve the problem, but this, say conservatives, is only a short-term solution. In the longer term, businesses will pass the costs of the higher minimum wage through to consumers in the form of higher prices. In turn, consumers (who are also workers) will demand wage increases, which will result in a general price inflation that leaves the minimum wage workers exactly where they started. To the extent that businesses cannot pass the higher wages through to consumers, they will hire less labor, thus raising the unemployment rate and making some people *worse* off than before the minimum wage was raised. The solution to the minimum wage problem, conservatives maintain, lies *not* in a futile attempt to redistribute shares of the existing pie, but to increase everyone's share, by lifting the dead weight of government intervention from the market, thus stimulating economic growth.[20]

Policy Prescriptions

A major focus of conservative research and policy analysis concerns the attempt to show that government intervention in the market undermines efficiency and ultimately makes goods and services more expensive for the consumer. Conservatives have argued for many years that the Keynesian demand management policies described in chapters 1 and 3 undermined the long-run performance of the economy. Conservatives advocate fiscal policies to stimulate the supply side, not demand. During the 1980s, the conservative Reagan administration implemented many supply-side policies in an effort to stimulate economic growth and American competitiveness.[21] Some conservative political economists, particularly Milton Friedman, argue that fiscal policy of any sort is an unwarranted intrusion of government into the marketplace. Friedman and other economists of the "monetarist" school believe that a slowly and steadily growing supply of money is all that is needed to ensure long-term, healthy growth of the economy.[22]

Conservatives oppose liberal proposals for strategic trade or industrial policies, which would require the government to help targeted industries become more competitive on world markets. They believe that education reforms are necessary to enhance U.S. competitiveness, and they advocate the introduction of market competition among public schools to achieve this goal.

The Liberal Paradigm

Intellectual Antecedents

The contemporary liberal and conservative paradigms both spring from the same intellectual origins in classical and neoclassical political economy, and they still share many views. Both believe in the value of individual freedom and in the right of individuals to own private productive property. Both believe that the capitalist market system is the form of social organization most capable of ensuring individual freedom and producing wealth and prosperity. Hence one must count among the intellectual precursors of the contemporary liberal paradigm the classical and neoclassical political economists whose views underlie those of contemporary conservatives—John Locke, Adam Smith, David Ricardo, and Alfred Marshall, in particular.

At the same time, it must be recognized that the contemporary liberal paradigm arose as a reaction to, and critique of, classical and later, neoclassical political economy. John Stuart Mill (1806–1873) and John Maynard Keynes (1893–1946) are perhaps the most well known of those political economists who shared the conservative support for the capitalist system but who deplored the gross inequalities of income and living standards that the system seemed to generate. In *Principles of Political Economy* in 1848 and other works, Mill argued for government intervention in the economy to adjust the distribution of income toward greater equality. He also championed a shorter working day, the legalization of unions, and other causes that he believed would humanize the capitalist system.

Keynes believed that the capitalist market system is prone to collapse from within and that government intervention is therefore necessary to keep the system afloat. Writing during the Great Depression of the 1930s, Keynes provided an economic rationale for government intervention through demand stabilization policies that soon became standard practice in Western capitalist countries.

This view of the proper role of government is what most sharply distinguishes the liberal paradigm from the conservative. Liberals are far more optimistic about the potential for government to improve human conditions than are conservatives, because liberals subscribe to a philosophy of government that differs somewhat from that of John Locke and others in the conservative tradition. The philosophers Rousseau, Kant, and Hegel, in particular, put forth a concept of human nature that supported a far more powerful role for government than that of Locke or other conservative theorists.[23]

Framework and Philosophical Foundation

Liberals and conservatives agree that the best form of social organization allows individuals to pursue their own self-interest, free of constraints. The institutions of private property and free markets achieve this goal better than any others known to us. Both traditions believe that government should enforce property rights and voluntary exchanges, provide public goods, control externalities, and regulate the money supply.

There the agreement ends, however. Whereas conservative economic analysis views humans only as self-centered individuals, liberals believe that humans also are *social* creatures. They have natural proclivities to live in communities and to organize their lives through norms and values that are not reducible to a common denominator of individual self-interest or the simple calculus of pain and pleasure. These values include loyalty, patriotism for one's community or society, love, compassion, pride, guilt, social cooperation, the pursuit of excellence, and a sense of justice.[24]

Whether persons display these so-called civic values in their behavior or act only in the pursuit of their individual self-interest depends upon the nature and strength of the society's political, social, and economic institutions. In a healthy society, these institutions integrate civic values with the pursuit of individual self-interest, resulting in wealth and prosperity, as well as harmonious social relations and a high quality of life throughout the society. If, on the other hand, the institutions and social practices that call upon the exercise of civic values are weak or nonexistent, these capacities will atrophy, and the pursuit of individual self-interest alone will direct the course of human events. As this happens, however, life becomes increasingly brutal for everyone, a war "of every one against every one."[25]

Consider next the workings of the market system and the place of government in the economy. Liberals since John Stuart Mill have believed that, while the competitive market is an efficient vehicle for the *creation* of wealth, it does a very poor job of distribution, so that many are forced to live in poverty, while others live in splendor. Government intervention is therefore necessary to redistribute incomes and, more importantly, to ensure that everyone has an opportunity to earn a decent living.

The capitalist market system is also inherently unstable. The decisions of individual capitalists, entrepreneurs, and households, each of which is rational from the perspective of the individual actor, lead to collective irrationality, as the system lurches through cycles of boom and bust, and sometimes slides into deep depressions that destroy the livelihoods of many people. Since the Great Depression and the work of John Maynard Keynes, liberals have believed that government intervention is necessary to stimulate demand during troughs in the business cycle and to fight inflation during peaks in the business cycle.

Conservatives believe that the liberal faith in government to correct market problems is misplaced. Left to itself, the market will produce the most optimal social outcomes, in the long run. But as Keynes said,

> In the long run we are all dead. Economists set themselves too easy, too useless a task if in tempestuous seasons they can only tell us that when the storm is long past the ocean is flat again.[26]

Liberals regard government intervention in the marketplace as necessary because, unlike conservatives, they believe that most people are somewhat risk averse—they are willing to trade the chance for very high incomes for the security of at least a decent standard of living.[27] Moreover, liberals believe that government can solve the problems generated by the market system because they do not share the conservative pessimism about the possibility for non-coerced agreement and collective action through government. Because persons have the capacity for compassion and a sense of social justice, they are able to understand the legitimate needs of others and to respond to those needs through concerted, public action. Through their participation in public decision-making processes, citizens develop perspectives that lead them to make and support decisions that promote the good of the society as a whole, rather than just their own individual self-interest. Hence in the liberal view, citizen preferences can change in the process of democratic decision making, whereas in the conservative view, it is assumed that such changes do not take place.[28]

The Role of Government

The task for the liberal policymaker, then, is to create policies and institutions that preserve both individual freedom *and* community. For some "centrist" liberals, such as Arthur M. Okun, this means simply balancing the goal of equality of wealth and income with the goal of efficiency, in the creation of wealth and income. In Okun's view, there is a conflict between efficiency, produced through the competitive market, and equality, which is the product of government intervention in the economy. Too much efficiency brings poverty and social pathology; too much equality brings bureaucracy and the stifling of individual initiative. In Okun's view, the task of government in a democratic capitalist system is to balance the two desiderata.[29]

Other contemporary liberals, such as Lester Thurow, see efficiency, distributive justice, and social cooperation as complementary values:

> America is more than a simply statistical aggregation of individuals. It is a community, a society, where socially organizing to help each other leads to a more attractive society, a more equitable society, *and a more efficient society than one where each individual is left to make it on his or her own*. In a good society, social organization is central.[30]

Similarly, Davidson and Davidson regard government in a democratic capitalist society as

> the process by which we combine self-interest and civic values into institutions. These institutions, when properly designed, protect civic values from the corrosive effects of self-interest. At the same time, institutions make use of productive forms of self-interest, enabling people to enjoy the products of both.[31]

An example of an economic policy issue that sharply distinguishes the liberal and conservative conceptions of human nature, government, and the economy is the payment of individual income taxes. Both liberals and conservatives believe that some amount of government is necessary to make and enforce laws and to furnish public goods, such as national defense. But the collective nature of government goods and services makes payment problematic. All individuals will receive the goods, even if some, called free riders, do not pay for them. The task for society is to ensure that everyone pays for the public goods. The income tax is the single most important source of revenue for both the federal and state governments. Yet for much of the past two decades, American taxpayers have increasingly avoided paying some or all of the income taxes that they owe.[32] The norm of paying one's taxes has grown weak.

Conservatives generally regard weak income tax payment norms as a predictable response to government's effort to take individuals' hard-earned money. As discussed in chapter 3, supply-side economists argue that income taxes also stifle the incentive to work. Hence the conservative solution would be to lower income taxes, thereby reducing the incentive to cheat, as well as increasing hours worked and hence, production. To raise needed revenues, conservatives advocate the use of sales taxes, which are difficult to evade.[33]

Liberals see two problems with this approach. They see it as unfair to lower-income people, since sales taxes take a larger percentage of their incomes than they do of wealthier persons' incomes. Income taxes, on the other hand, can easily be set so as to take larger percentages of income from wealthier persons. Moreover, unless consumption taxes are set at an extremely high rate, they cannot raise the amount of revenues that even moderate income tax rates generate. Hence total tax payments are likely to fall under a conservative tax system, which will undermine government's ability to provide public goods, and thus undermine citizen satisfaction with government. As their satisfaction decreases, citizens may become progressively alienated from government and hence *more* inclined to avoid paying their taxes and to press for tax reductions.[34]

The liberal solution to the tax avoidance problem is to institute policies that tap human motives in addition to individual self-interest. Through policies that call upon the human sense of justice, or fairness—as well as guilt, gratitude, and fear—liberals would strengthen taxpaying compliance on a *voluntary* basis. In the liberal view, citizens will voluntarily comply with a tax system that they believe charges everyone a fair tax, and from which they believe that no one escapes through loopholes or outright cheating. Initially, broad public consensus must be achieved on the question of what constitutes a fair tax rate. Thereafter, other actions must be taken to maintain the integrity and fairness of the system.[35]

As described by Davidson and Davidson, the Massachusetts REAP (Revenue Enforcement and Protection Program) initiative of 1983, illustrates the kinds of policies that can strengthen voluntary taxpaying norms:

1. Framing the issue as one of fairness—The state revenue department informed the public that tax evasion totalled $640 million in 1983, and that everyone's taxes could be lowered by 10 percent if everyone paid his or her share. The state also published lists of the major tax delinquents, so as to shame them into paying their fair shares.
2. Establishing credibility through well-publicized seizures of the assets of tax delinquents—This action was designed to evoke fear among tax cheaters and to convince honest taxpayers of the system's integrity, despite the limited nature and cost of the enforcement actions.
3. Altering the costs and benefits of cheating—The state simplified taxpaying forms and provided more assistance to taxpayers, but it also passed legislation making tax evasion a felony with stiff fines and prison sentences.
4. Evoking the gratitude of taxpayers through a widely publicized, one-time amnesty program before punitive measures went into effect.

The REAP initiative won widespread acclaim although, predictably, liberals and conservatives disagree about the reasons for its success.[36] In any case, the tax compliance issue illustrates how the liberal approach to economic policy seeks to build institutions and practices that integrate human motives and values of self-interest with civic values of social cooperation and fairness. If they are well crafted, claim liberals, such institutions provide the basis for both individual wealth and a high quality of life for the entire society.

Policy Prescriptions

From the 1930s to the 1970s, the liberal paradigm dominated economic policymaking throughout the Western capitalist world. As Keynesian economist Alvin Hansen jubilantly declared in 1957:

> This society is committed to the welfare state and full employment. The government is firmly in the driver's seat. In such a world, practical policy problems became grist for the mill of economic analysis. Keynes, more than any other economist of our time, has helped to rescue economics from the negative position to which it had fallen to become

once again a science of the Wealth of Nations and the art of Political Economy.[37]

In a similar vein, Paul Samuelson maintained that "a community can have full employment, can at the same time have the rate of capital formation it wants, and can accomplish all this compatibly with the degree of income-redistributing it ethically desires."[38]

But the stagflation of the 1970s and other dislocations caused by the rise of foreign competition, the globalization of production and trade, and the dissolution of the Bretton Woods monetary framework undermined support for the liberal world view. This paved the way for the conservative resurgence of the late 1970s and 1980s. Nevertheless, many liberals have continued to advocate a strong role for government in the economy. They attacked the supply-side fiscal policies of the Reagan and Bush administrations as harmful to the poor, the middle class, and the economic health of the nation. They call for national economic policies in which the federal government would play an active role, enhancing the competitiveness of American industries in world markets, educating and training all citizens for more productive roles in the new global economy, and providing health insurance, housing, and other necessities for those who need them. These positions will be described in the chapters that follow.

The Radical Paradigm

Intellectual Antecedents

Like the liberal and conservative paradigms, the radical paradigm has a long lineage of insightful thinkers. Nevertheless, one person has done far more than any others to shape the questions and approach of radical political economy—Karl Marx (1818–1883). While radical thought has evolved considerably since Marx wrote, Marx's writings remain its foundation. As explained at the end of this section, it is often necessary, when discussing radical policy views, to distinguish Marxist from so-called progressive thinkers.

Contrary to popular belief, Marx did not develop theories of socialism or communism. Indeed, Marx made only a few vague remarks about how such societies might function—certainly not enough to serve as a blueprint for a real socialist society. Rather, Marx developed a theory of capitalism—how it came to be, how it functions, and why it will end one day. In so doing, Marx drew upon some of the same sources that have inspired liberal and conservative thinkers—the classical economists Adam Smith and, especially, David Ricardo; the political philosophers Rousseau, Kant, and, especially, Hegel; as well as the French utopian socialists, Fourier and St. Simon.

Framework and Philosophical Foundation

Marx adopted Hegel's philosophy of historical progress—a dialectical process in which each epoch is characterized by a dominant organizing principle or idea, the thesis, that naturally begets its own antithesis, or opposing idea. Through the conflict of the two, a synthesis emerges that eventually begets its own antithesis, and so on. Marx turned Hegel's system on its head.[39] Rather than view forms of society as the manifestations, through history, of ideas, Marx placed economic, or productive, relations at the center of his theory of society and social development. In Marx's view, human history is to be understood first and foremost as the development of different economic systems, or "modes of production," as he called them. This material life that people experience determines, in large part, the ideas and principles that they invent to explain it, as well as the forms of law, education, and government they construct for themselves.

Marx used Hegel's dialectic to analyze how one mode of production changes to another. He described how the feudal mode of production was transformed into the capitalist mode via the conflict between the feudal aristocracy (the thesis) and the bourgeoisie (the antithesis). He then developed a theory of how the conflict in capitalism between capitalist and worker would work its way through to a new synthesis—socialism. In this "historical materialist" system, as Marx called it, socialism comes about naturally and inevitably through a transformation of the entire economic system, and not through the spread of utopian socialist colonies or experiments such as those of the French and English utopian socialists of the nineteenth century.[40]

Capitalism's transformation into socialism was all to the good, in Marx's view, because while he admired the amazing human productive powers unleashed by capitalism, he decried what he considered to be its brutal exploitation of the working class and the unplanned, anarchic nature of the market system that frequently caused crises of overproduction, depression, and hardship for many. Under socialism and, eventually, communism, workers acting through government would own the "means of production" (factories, machines, finance capital) and would plan and control production. Each person would work according to his or her ability and receive according to his or her needs; this was a system that would succeed by drawing upon human capacities for compassion and cooperation—capacities that are important in the liberal paradigm also. With the rational planning of production and the equitable distribution of wealth, the working day could be shortened considerably, making it possible for men and women to pursue activities that would allow for the full flowering of their potentials as creative human beings.[41]

It should be noted that while radicals and liberals share many beliefs about the *social* nature of the person and human capacities for cooperation, mutual aid, and democratic governance, there is an important difference between the two paradigms. Liberals believe that humans can develop and manifest their social, cooperative side within a thriving capitalist order. Marx and most radicals, on the other hand, believe that such human capacities can only be consistently manifested within a supportive economic structure, such as that afforded by socialism. In the competitive world of capitalism, on the other hand, humans tend to act as self-centered individualists. Hence, in the Marxist view, efforts to promote general social cooperation by drawing upon "civic values" at best serve as temporary Band-Aids to paper over the fundamental problems of capitalism and at worst obfuscate and prevent a clear understanding of the real relations of individualism and domination that characterize the system. Indeed, throughout history, capitalist development has destroyed cohesive communities and replaced them with impersonal, consumerist societies—a clear illustration of how the basic economic structure of society determines human behavioral tendencies. The liberal attempt to temper individualism with civic values is therefore doomed to frustration and failure as long as capitalism is the mode of production.

Liberals and radicals also share a belief in the role of government as a natural and inevitable force in the economy and society. Yet here too, the parallel soon breaks down. Liberals believe that the role of government is to mitigate and solve the negative side effects of what is fundamentally a good capitalist market system. Marxists believe that the capitalist economic system is fraught with fundamental contradictions and problems that render it but a way station on the road to a better economic system. In every type of society, according to Marxists, the role of government is to support and legitimate the existing economic system. Hence it follows that government in a capitalist market society cannot solve the problems of capitalism. It can at best paper them over so as to put off the ultimate transformation of the system and, with it, the solution to its problems.

Marxist Economic Analysis

In describing the capitalist system, liberals and conservatives take the market—the act of exchange—as their point of departure. Marxists begin with the mode of production—the way in which production is organized and carried out. In the capitalist mode of production, one class, the capitalists, owns the means of production—the factories, offices, machines, and capital necessary to produce goods and services—and this class or its representatives (upper-level management) plans and controls the production process and the disposition of the product. The other class, the workers, owns no means of production, only its labor power. In order to live, workers must sell their labor time to capitalists for a wage. Having purchased this labor time, the capitalist is more or less free to organize it with machines and materials to produce goods and services.[42]

Although the exchange of labor time for a wage appears on the surface to be a free and equal one, and is so understood by liberals and conservatives, in fact this exchange masks the real relations of domination and exploitation of workers by capitalists. It is the capitalists who own the means of production and who direct the production process. Workers have far fewer choices and alternatives than do capitalists, so they must submit, more or less, to the will of the capitalists. Yet this submission is not necessarily complete. A capitalist can only purchase a worker's *time* (except under a piece-rate remuneration system) through the labor contract. Although the capitalist wants as much work as possible from the worker, the worker may want to work less. The worker may wish to organize his work in a way that he deems most efficient, whereas the capitalist has her own ideas on the subject. Most important, the capitalist wants to pay the worker as low a wage as possible; the worker wants just the opposite. In short, most of the important interests of capitalists and workers conflict, and this gives rise to a more or less continuous struggle between them, in which the capitalist, as the owner of the means of production, is by far the more powerful party.

What are they fighting over? Under the capitalist mode of production, the production process is so efficient that it yields more product, or value, than is needed to support workers and capitalists at their customary standard of living. A surplus is produced.

Capitalists and workers fight over the size of the surplus, insofar as workers want shorter hours and less intensive work than do capitalists. They also fight over how the surplus will be used—for higher worker wages and a higher standard of living, or for higher capitalist profits.

Profits are the engine of the capitalist system. Indeed, capitalism is the first economic system ever in which production takes place *not* to fulfill a specific consumption need, but to fill the expectation by the capitalist, that after production is over and the goods are sold, and everyone, including the capitalist herself, has received an average wage, she will have more money than she invested to produce the goods in the first place. The extra, the profit, comes from the surplus just described.[43]

Yet capitalism is also the first economic system ever in which the dominant class cannot simply consume all of the surplus in luxurious living. Capitalists who consume all of their profits do not remain capitalists for long because other, competing capitalists are reinvesting their profits to make their production processes more efficient, to cut prices so as to drive competing capitalists out of the market, and to develop new goods and services for new markets. Hence to remain a capitalist, every capitalist must do everything possible to increase profits, including paying the lowest wages possible, increasing the amount of labor done by increasing work speed and supervision, using the least costly materials and machines, and investing in new machinery and production methods.

These attempts by the capitalist to increase profits and stay in business have several effects. At the level of the firm, one significant effect is the increasingly detailed division of labor. As Adam Smith observed in his analysis of pin making, specialization through the division of labor is the source of increased efficiency and economic growth:

> A workman not educated to this business ... could scarce, perhaps, with his utmost industry, make one pin in a day.... But in the way in which this business is now carried on, not only the whole work is a peculiar trade, but it is divided into a number of branches.... One man draws out the wire, another straightens it, a third cuts it, a fourth points it, a fifth grinds it at the top for receiving the head; to make the head requires three distinct operations; to put it on is a peculiar business, to whiten the pins is another; it is even a trade by itself to put them into the paper.... I have seen a small manufactory of this kind where ten men only were employed.... Those ten persons, therefore, could make among them upwards of forty-eight thousand pins in a day.[44]

As Smith also pointed out, and as Marx and his successors have sought to illustrate, the *detail* division of labor also stunts the intellectual and often the physical development of the worker, ultimately transforming him into a mere appendage of a machine. Hence the worker becomes progressively more dependent upon employment by the capitalist to support himself, as he loses the skills that made his ancestors self-sufficient.

The process of dividing a craft into ever more specialized tasks and assigning each task to a different worker is called de-skilling.[45] Many of the jobs in our contemporary economy are the results of de-skilling processes that have taken place over the course of several generations. The data entry job, for instance, is one that was once performed as part of the skilled craft of research, management, or a secretary's or research assistant's job. Similarly, the paralegal is a semiskilled job that was formerly one of many tasks performed by a skilled lawyer.

The division of labor generally improves production efficiency and therefore increases the surplus and, potentially, profits. But the *detail* division of labor may increase the costs of coordination and supervision, and because the skill levels required to do many tasks are lower after de-skilling takes place, it may result in more mistakes, waste, and lower product quality. Still, the detail division of labor may also result in higher profits for the capitalist, because de-skilled jobs command lower wages. Why pay a lawyer to do work that can be done tolerably well by a cheaper paralegal? The strategy of separating skilled from unskilled tasks, so as to pay lower wages, is known as the Babbage Principle, after Charles Babbage, who first advocated it as a management strategy.[46]

In the radical paradigm then, the nature of jobs and tasks and, more generally, the nature and application of technology, are not the results of autonomous market forces to which capitalists respond. Rather, technology, which entails both machines and organization, is the result of conscious choices made over time by capitalists to further their interests. If workers had the power to make such choices, many production processes would be different from the way they are now. In particular, we would not see the increasing polarization of job-skill levels and wages that characterizes capitalist development.[47]

The capitalist competition for profits also has significant effects at the level of the industry and the economy as a whole. Despite all of the planning and organization that individual capitalists carry out for their own firms, the capitalist market economy as a system is unplanned and anarchic. Hence what seems rational from the point of view of the individual capitalist often has deleterious effects on the economy as a whole. One such effect is the periodic "crisis of overproduction," which liberal and conservative economists call the business cycle. Since no central coordinator tells capitalists how much to produce, they can only estimate the amount of demand for their products. Since no capitalist can forego the possibility for earning profits from greater sales, all capitalists as a group produce more than will clear the market. As markets become saturated, consumer demand falls, which in turn leads to a decline in prices and a squeeze on profits. From the standpoint of the individual capitalist, the rational response to the decline in profits is to lay off workers and attempt to reduce their real wages. But, as all capitalists do this, unemployment grows and demand falls further, undermining first one industry and then others. Since falling demand results in further declines in prices, capitalists become pessimistic about the prospect for future profits, so they cease investing, producing, and employing workers. A recession or depression ensues.

During the early stages of a country's development under capitalism, economic downturns generally cure themselves (as conservatives maintain), albeit at the cost of considerable misery and impoverishment of workers and failed capitalists. As increasing numbers of workers become unemployed, their real-wage demands decline substantially, leading capitalists to perceive greater profit opportunities and to reinvest and rehire accordingly.

Over time, however, the capitalist economy grows increasingly unable to survive business cycle downturns. The key source of the difficulty is the falling rate of profit. As capital accumulates—that is, as a country builds up its stock of plant and equipment, infrastructure, and durable goods—the opportunities for profitable new production diminish. The result is not simply a business cycle downturn, but ever deeper and longer lasting downturns. Declines in wages or other supply costs no longer suffice to stimulate new investment, since the problem is a lack of profitable investment opportunities. Moreover, with each downturn, more people fall from the capitalist class to the working class, and more people become impoverished.[48] Gradually, they become ready to discard the anarchic market system in favor of a democratic alternative—socialism.

Capitalism can forestall its inevitable demise, however. It can expand into undeveloped regions where opportunities for profit making are greater. Indeed, the history of capitalism is one of continual expansion into undeveloped areas. Capitalism can also gain a new lease on life through government intervention in the form of demand stimulation policies, such as those practiced by capitalist countries since the 1930s. War is an occasion for such government intervention. Through war, the government typically employs the entire population in fighting and making armaments. If the war destroys plant, equipment, infrastructure, and durable goods, it will create new opportunities for profitable investment. World War II provided just such a stimulus to the capitalist economy (see chapters 1 and 3).

In addition to the falling rate of profit and resultant economic stagnation, another developmental trait of capitalism is the increasing concentration of control over capital in a few hands. Through competition, the stronger, smarter, more hardworking, or more ruthless capitalists drive the others out of business. The successful capitalists become the only sources of supply in their respective industries, which makes it possible for them to limit production and charge much higher prices than they could in a competitive market. As this occurs, it changes the capitalist system. Radicals call the current stage of capitalism "monopoly capitalism," as distinguished from the "competitive capitalism" of Marx's day.[49] Several of the most important industries in the economy, such as steel, automobiles, breakfast cereal, pharmaceuticals, and oil refining, now are dominated by a few "core" companies—companies that do not compete on the basis of price. Rather, they maintain prices well above what they would be under competitive conditions. They compete through expensive advertising and by conquering new markets overseas. Because of their high and stable profits, core companies are able to pay workers more than average wages, and they are able to grow into giant multinational corporations by using their profits from one industry to buy companies in other industries. To cite but one example, Philip Morris USA has used its tremendous profits from cigarettes to purchase and build the market shares of companies such as Miller Beer, General Foods, and Kraft.[50] Today, about 1,200 core companies account for half of all sales in the American economy, 65 percent of all nonfinancial corporate assets, and 70 percent of all profits earned in the United States. The remaining 16 *million* periphery companies constitute the rest of the American economy.[51]

Marxists interpret the development of monopoly capitalism as a clear refutation of the conservative model that sees the capitalist economy as one made up of many producers who compete on the basis of price.[52] They also view it as an inevitable step in the transformation of capitalism to socialism, because under monopoly capitalism, the number and economic clout of individual entrepreneurs decreases, and gradually almost everyone becomes a worker. As this happens, it becomes increasingly difficult to sustain the myth of the self-made man that legitimizes the great disparities of wealth and income under capitalism. Moreover, under monopoly capitalism, the capitalist economy begins to lose some of its anarchic character, as multinational corporations engage in extensive, long-range planning that affects the lives of millions of persons around the globe. In short, Marxists believe that multinational corporations are building the technical apparatus of planning that is vital to the functioning of a socialist society, without the systemic rationality or public participation and accountability that would be the basis of socialist planning.[53]

The Role of Government

In the Marxist historical materialist view of society, the form of government is determined largely by the nature of the prevailing economic relations, the mode of production. In all societies, government acts to maintain these relations, or, in other words, to maintain the hegemony of the class that dominates in the production process. Under capitalism, the government carries out this function in two ways. One way is through direct intervention in the economy to protect capitalist interests. Perhaps the clearest example of such intervention is the role played by the government in suppressing strikes, sometimes with the justification that it is acting in the interest of the general welfare, and sometimes with the open admission that it is acting to protect private property. The latter justification is especially illustrative of the Marxist view of government, since the "private" property that "belongs" to the capitalist is nothing more than the surplus value that was created by workers over the years, which was expropriated by the capitalist as profit and reinvested in plant and equipment, rather than being paid to workers in wages.[54]

The second way in which the government helps to maintain capitalist domination is by stabilizing the system so as to preserve its legitimacy in the eyes of workers. The government responds to strong popular pressure to make the capitalist system palatable for the great mass of workers—through public spending to stimulate demand and investment opportunities, through antitrust policy to regulate the growth of monopolies, and through the various stabilization policies discussed in chapter 1, such as unemployment insurance, welfare, and social security. Although such policies often do not serve the short-run interests of capitalists, they do maintain the political legitimacy of the capitalist system.[55]

Yet many government policies benefit capitalists in both the short and the long runs. An example of such a policy that highlights the differences between the liberal and radical paradigms is "incomes policy." One by-product of the stabilized capitalist economy since World War II is a tendency toward inflation. To dampen inflation, liberal economists have proposed, and some capitalist countries have adopted, incomes policies. Incomes policies limit annual wage increases to a percentage equal to the inflation rate or inflation plus productivity increases. In effect, they freeze worker incomes at their current levels, ensuring, in the liberal view, "maximum production and the highest standard of living possible for the community."[56]

Such a policy, in the Marxist view, is clearly biased in favor of capitalists and against workers, since it is only during the peak of the business cycle—when the economy is at full employment—that conditions are favorable to wage increases. At other times, when unemployment is higher, workers have great difficulty securing wage raises. A fair incomes policy would not only hold wage increases equal to productivity increases during business cycle peaks, it would also increase wages during business cycle troughs to stimulate the economy. Also, if worker incomes are frozen during inflationary times, so too should be profits, and this demands "as a prerequisite *workers' control of production, opening up of company books,* and *the abolition of banking secrets,* if for no other reason tha[n] to establish the *exact* income of the capitalists, and the *exact* increases in productivity."[57]

Policy Prescriptions

Contemporary radical critiques of capitalism and proposals for change all begin with the capital-labor relationship. Radicals believe that major decisions concerning the nature and purpose of investment and production, including the location of economic activity, should not be made in the boardrooms of multinational corporations, but by workers and their communities, within the context of supportive national policies and institutions. Until workers and the government have larger roles in steering the economy, the worst problems of capitalism—persistent poverty and gross inequalities of opportunity and outcomes, the development of some regions at the expense of others with dislocation and hardship caused by rapid disinvestment from some regions and rapid capital investment into others—will continue to plague our society.[58]

Since the nineteenth century, however, radicals have disagreed about how to achieve their goals. For this reason, there are two distinct traditions within this paradigm. One is the revolutionary socialist-communist tradition most often associated with Marx, Engels, Lenin, and Mao. Contemporary heirs include Ernest Mandel, Paul Sweezy, and Harry Magdoff. This tradition will be referred to as "Marxist" throughout this book, since its adherents call their views Marxist.

The other tradition is evolutionary socialism, whose early proponents include the German Social Democrats Eduard Bernstein and Karl Kautsky. Adherents of this tradition believe that the goals of socialism can be achieved through democratic reforms within the existing structure of capitalism. They advocate a mixed economy, in which both markets and governments play active roles, as in the social democracies of Sweden, Germany, and other West European countries. In the United States, contemporary adherents of social democracy generally label their views "progressive," so that term will be used throughout this book to designate those views.

Contemporary American Marxists and progressives share the radical philosophical foundation and framework just presented. When it comes to research focus and policy alternatives, however, they sometimes part company. Being skeptical of the efficacy of reforms from within the capitalist system, Marxists focus on explaining how contemporary economic and social problems are produced by the capitalist mode of production itself. They exhort the victims of capitalist oppression to organize and transform the system.

Progressives focus less on critical analysis and more on policy alternatives, such as national and regional economic planning, legislation to expand and protect worker rights on the job, and worker ownership and control of enterprises. On many issues, such as strategic trade policy and macroeconomic policy, progressives advocate reforms that are similar to liberal proposals. Yet the two positions are not identical. Whereas liberal proposals seek to reestablish social harmony and progress within the existing system, radical proposals seek to change the structure of the system to move decision making and control away from capitalists and their advocates in government, and toward working class interests.

Throughout this book, the term "radical" is used as a label where Marxist and progressive views are sufficiently similar that they can be discussed together. Where the two traditions differ substantially, that difference is noted.

A Spectrum of Views

Just as there are two distinct traditions within the radical paradigm, the conservative paradigm also has a less conservative,

Figure 1
A Spectrum of Views

CONSERVATIVE	LIBERAL	RADICAL
Libertarian Moderate	Centrist Liberal	Progressive Marxist

moderate tradition and a more conservative tradition associated with libertarianism and monetarist economic policies (see chapter 3). These distinctions will be noted, where appropriate, throughout the book. Likewise, in a few places, a distinction will be drawn between mainstream liberals and the somewhat conservative centrists or neoliberals. Figure 1 depicts the spectrum of conservative to radical views.

Summary

Although they share many intellectual roots, the contemporary conservative, liberal, and radical paradigms hold qualitatively different views of human nature, markets, government, and public policy. Conservatives take individuals as their unit of analysis and assume that individuals are interested in maximizing their own welfare, free of constraints. The market is the only vehicle that can facilitate this human interest. Government is necessary to perform a few functions that the market cannot perform. Government policies should be used sparingly, as they diminish individual freedom. Macroeconomic stabilization policies should be limited to maintaining a slowly growing money supply and, at most, stimulating the economy through supply-side tax cuts. Although liberals call for international macroeconomic coordination, conservatives see no need for such an extra layer of government (see chapter 3). They regard industrial policies and strategic trade policies as technically and politically infeasible and generally undesirable (see chapter 4). Improvements in primary and secondary education are necessary, and they can be achieved if market incentives are introduced into the public education system (see chapter 5). State and local government actions to develop their economies should focus on supply-side tax cuts, deregulation of the labor market, and the abolition of welfare (see chapter 6).

Liberals take the individual as the primary unit of analysis, but they regard human nature as not only self-interested, but also socially motivated to uphold and adhere to civic values. Markets are the most effective vehicle for organizing economic activity, especially wealth creation, but they suffer from numerous limitations. Government is necessary to shape and temper market mechanisms in accordance with broader civic values. Macroeconomic policies should focus on demand management and an activist monetary policy to achieve full employment with stable prices. Due to the increasing interdependence of national economies and policies, formal international coordination agreements are needed (see chapter 3). If the United States is to compete in the global economy, it must adopt industrial and trade policies that develop and support its key industries, as other countries are doing (see chapter 4).

Liberal economists believe that if we are to compete in the global economy, the United States must strengthen its education and training systems and link them closely to a policy of industrial revitalization. Liberal educators argue that we must focus on providing a humanistic education for everyone (see chapter 5). State and local government actions to develop state and local economies should be well-planned, strategic efforts that use a variety of targeted, supply-side tax incentives, export promotion tools, and local capacity development measures (see chapter 6).

Radicals take economic classes as their primary units of analysis. They believe that human nature varies, depending upon the structure of society's economic institutions. Under capitalism, humans tend to maximize their own individual welfare, as claimed by conservatives. But they have the capacity to promote social interests, which they would manifest to some degree under a socialist society and completely under a communist society. The market as a vehicle for the distribution of resources is anarchic in nature, and thus prone to collapse. Because it is not a democratically planned system, the market allows capitalists to dominate the working class. Marxists believe that government facilitates the continued operation of the current economic system. Under capitalism, therefore, government functions in such a way that it ultimately supports the continuation of capitalism. Social democrats, or progressives, believe that a democratically structured government allows for reforms of the capitalist system that benefit the working class and move the system toward socialism.

Progressives support macroeconomic policies that stimulate demand and expand the money supply. Marxists do not object to these policies, but they do not agree that such policies constitute solutions to the problems of capitalism. Progressives support liberal calls for international economic coordination, but Marxists do not believe that such schemes can work (see chapter 3). Radicals support industrial and trade policies to the extent that they entail democratization of economic decision making at the national, local, and company levels (see chapter 4). Radicals believe that education and training should not focus on narrow skills for business needs, but should teach critical thinking, problem solving, and humanistic knowledge and values. To the extent that education and training focus on vocational skills for business needs, they should be organized by workers through their unions (see chapter 5). State and local economic development policies should promote economic democracy (see chapter 6).

Table 3 provides a shorthand summary of the chapter's major points.

Table 3
Summary of Conservative, Liberal, and Radical Paradigms

	Conservative	Liberal	Radical
Framework of analysis	Individual	Individual and society	Economic classes
Philosophy of human nature	Self-interest	Self-interest and social interest	Self-interest or social interest
Role of market	Organize free choice, prosperity	Organize free choice and wealth creation	Allow capitalist domination of working class
Role of government	Shore up a few market gaps	Organize society and economic activity	Facilitate economic system, e.g., capitalism
Policies:			
Macroeconomy, domestic	Supply-side and monetarism	Demand-side and expand money supply	Demand-side and expand money supply
Macroeconomy, international	International coordination not needed	International coordination necessary	*Progressives:* coordination necessary *Marxists:* it won't work
Industrial policy	Infeasible and unnecessary	Feasible and necessary	Yes, if democratic
Trade policy	Infeasible and unnecessary	Feasible and necessary	*Progressives:* yes, if democratic *Marxists:* it won't work
Education	Privatize, improve	Increase funding, humanize	Worker control, humanize
State and local development policy	Tax cuts and deregulation	Target tax cuts and plan	Democratize and plan

Notes

1. The terms conservative, liberal, and radical are not the only ones that one might use to label the major traditons in Western political economy. Most economists would find these labels a bit vague, because they tend to confound distinct schools of economic thought and methods with policy positions. Most economists would probably prefer the term neoclassical economics to describe much of what one encounters in conservative views, Keynesian and neoclassical economics to describe what we generally find in liberal views, and Marxian political economy, rather than radical. (The reader interested in studying these paradigms from an economic methods point of view should consult the works listed in the bibliography, especially Harry Landreth's *History of Economic Theory: Scope, Method and Content*, and Marc Blaug's *Economic Theory in Retrospect*). I have chosen the broader, less precise terms, however, because I will be focusing not on the fine points of the economic theories and methods, but on the broader, public policy implications of the views and the theories of government that are generally associated with them. For these purposes, the less precise terms are more appropriate.

    The reader should also be aware of other, less well-known political-economic paradigms, such as the institutionalist and neo-Ricardian paradigms. With the exception of a few well-known institutionalists, notably John Kenneth Galbraith, these views have remained at the periphery of public policy debates. Hence they will not be addressed in this book. The reader interested in studying these views should consult Randy Albelda, Christopher Gunn, and William Waller: *Alternatives to Economic Orthodoxy*, as well as the appropriate chapters of Robert Heilbroner's *The Worldly Philosophers* and Landreth's *History of Economic Theory*.

2. Note that the description here refers to political economic, or social science paradigms, not natural science paradigms. Thomas Kuhn's *The Structure of Scientific Revolutions*, which popularized the term paradigm, deals solely with natural science paradigms. Many writers have applied Kuhn's work to social science paradigms, including Blaug in *Economic Theory* and David Gordon in *Problems in Political Economy*.

3. Two important qualifications are in order. First, while the works of Smith and Locke are most frequently cited in support or elucidation of contemporary conservative economic views, it is not appropriate to label these thinkers as conservatives or to assume that all of their views coincide with those of contemporary conservatives. For example, a close reading of Smith's entire *Wealth of Nations*, as well as his *The Theory of Moral Sentiments*. Indianapolis: Liberty Classics, 1976 (1759), reveals that he probably did not think markets would produce desirable results without government intervention and strong norms of social cooperation. Likewise, one can interpret Locke in ways consistent with somewhat different political ideologies. Nevertheless, Locke is an important source of ideas for contemporary conservative political economy.

A second qualification concerns the label conservative itself. Some contemporary political economists reject this descriptor. Milton Friedman, a leading spokesperson of this tradition, maintains that its proper label is liberalism, in the sense in which the term was used in the nineteenth century. A related point is that many so-called social conservatives advocate positions on family policy, criminal justice, religion, and education that call for a relatively strong government role in maintaining traditional standards—views that might conflict with the general laissez-faire market philosophy of conservative political economists, such as Friedman. We can avoid most of the confusion surrounding the term by noting that this book deals solely with economic policy (chapter 5 is a partial exception). In the realm of economic policy, the terms conservative, liberal, and radical do denote distinctly different views of the nature of markets and the proper role of government in the economy.

4. Friedman, Milton: *Capitalism and Freedom.* Chicago: University of Chicago Press, 1962, p. 5. Conservatives and particularly neoclassical microeconomists, generally treat the *household* as the primary unit of analysis, but for analytical purposes, individuals and households are equivalent, since relationships *within* the household fall outside of the scope of their analysis. George Gilder's *Wealth and Poverty.* New York: Bantam Books, 1982—which treats the family as an important factor in economic growth—is an exception to this rule. The notion that human behavior can be understood as individuals maximizing their utility owes much to the utilitarian philosopher, Jeremy Bentham. See his *An Introduction to the Principles of Morals and Legislation* (1780).

5. Locke, John: *The Second Treatise of Government,* 1698, in *Two Treatises of Government,* paragraphs 27 and 28. New York: Cambridge University Press, 1963. The interested reader should also consult *The First Treatise of Government* (in the same volume), especially paragraph 28, in which Locke appeals to human charity to mitigate the harmful effects of the system of private property through appropriation.

6. For a contemporary application of Lockean entitlement theory see Nozick, Robert: *Anarchy, State and Utopia.* New York: Basic Books, 1974.

7. Lavoie, Don: *National Economic Planning: What Is Left?* Cambridge, Mass: Ballinger Publishing Co., 1985, p. 84 (emphasis in original). See also Adam Smith: *The Wealth of Nations.* London: Oxford University Press, 1976 (1776), Book I, chapter 2; Schumpeter, Joseph: *Capitalism, Socialism and Democracy.* New York: Harper and Row, 1975; and Gilder, *Wealth and Poverty,* especially chapter 3: "The Returns of Giving"

8. Hayek, Friedrich: *The Road to Serfdom.* Chicago: University of Chicago Press, 1944, and Friedman, Milton and Rose Friedman: *Free to Choose: A Personal Statement.* New York: Harcourt Brace Jovanovich, 1980.

9. Smith, *Wealth of Nations,* Book I, chapter 1.

10. Friedman, *Capitalism and Freedom,* pp. 12, 25, and 27, and Smith, *Wealth of Nations,* Book IV, chapter 9.

11. Friedman, *Capitalism and Freedom*, pp. 23-24, and Smith, *Wealth of Nations*, Book IV, chapter 9.
12. Friedman, *Capitalism and Freedom*, p. 32, and McKenzie, Richard B. *Competing Visions: The Political Conflict over America's Economic Future*. Washington, D.C.: The Cato Institute, 1985, p. 201.
13. Friedman, *Capitalism and Freedom*, p. 27.
14. Ibid., p. 24.
15. Friedman and Friedman, *Free to Choose*, pp. 64-69.
16. Friedman, *Capitalism and Freedom*, p. 23.
17. Friedman and Friedman, *Free to Choose*, pp. 13-24.
18. Ibid., pp. 128-149, and Gilder, *Wealth and Poverty*: chapter 3: "The Returns of Giving," and Smith, *Wealth of Nations* Book 1, chapter 10.
19. Friedman and Friedman, *Free to Choose*, pp. 13-24
20. See McKenzie, Richard B.: *The American Job Machine*. New York: Universe Books and the Cato Institute, 1988, chapter 9.
21. Evans, Michael K.: *The Truth about Supply-Side Economics*. New York: Basic Books, 1983; Federal Reserve Bank of Atlanta: *Supply-Side Economics in the 1980's: Conference Proceedings*. Westport: Quorum Books, 1982; Niskanen, William A.: *Reaganomics: An Insider's Account of the Policies and the People*. New York: Oxford University Press, 1988; Roberts, Paul Craig: *The Supply-Side Revolution: An Insider's Account of Policymaking in Washington*. Cambridge, Mass.: Harvard University Press, 1984.
22. Friedman, *Capitalism and Freedom*, chapter 3, and Friedman and Friedman, *Free to Choose*, pp. 70-88. See also chapter 3 of this book.
23. The most in-depth contemporary synthesis of liberal thought on the nature of the person, society, and government is John Rawls's *A Theory of Justice*. Cambridge, Mass.: Harvard University Press, 1971.
24. Selections from Aristotle's *Politics*, in Kaplan, Justin D. (ed): *The Pocket Aristotle*. New York: Pocket Books, 1958. For an excellent discussion of the contemporary liberal perspective on social values, see Davidson, Greg, and Paul Davidson: *Economics for a Civilized Society*. New York: W.W. Norton and Company, 1988; also Rawls, *A Theory of Justice*. As discussed in note 3, "social conservatives" also subscribe to a concept of human nature that has a capacity for expressing civic values such as loyalty and patriotism. The social conservative's list of civic virtues differs from that of the liberal, however. More importantly, few thinkers have tried to integrate the concepts of human nature propounded by social and economic conservatives, whereas an integration of social and economic theory is a pillar of modern liberal thought.
25. Hobbes, Thomas: *Leviathan*. C.B. Macpherson (ed). New York: Penguin Books, 1968 (1651), Part I, chapter 13. Hobbes, a founder of modern political theory, advocated authoritarian rule as a way to solve the problem of political legitimacy and order. Modern liberals, radicals, and even conservatives have placed more faith in democratic governance than this.
26. Keynes, John Maynard, *The General Theory of Employment, Interest and Money*, 1936, cited in Davidson and Davidson, *Civilized Society*, p. 57.

27. Rawls explains this assumption in *A Theory of Justice*.

28. Perhaps the clearest and most explicit modern statement of this view that participation in democratic governance stimulates human compassion and social learning is in Rousseau, Jean Jacques: *Of the Social Contract*. A useful companion piece is Mill, John Stuart: "Representative Government," in *Utilitarianism, On Liberty and Considerations on Representative Government*. H.B. Acton, (ed). New York: E.P. Dutton and Company, Inc., 1972. For a contemporary explication and application of these views, see Pateman, Carole: *Participation and Democratic Theory*. London: Cambridge University Press, 1970.

29. Okun, Arthur M.: "Equality and Efficiency: The Big Trade-Off." *The New York Times Magazine*. July 4, 1976.

30. Thurow, Lester: *The Zero-Sum Solution*. New York: Simon and Schuster, 1985, p. 24 (my emphasis).

31. Davidson and Davidson, *Civilized Society*, p. 196.

32. Ibid., pp. 69–80.

33. "Supply-side" fiscal conservatives believe that lowering tax rates itself can increase tax revenues, by removing the disincentive to work created by taxes. See the discussion of supply-side economics in chapter 3.

34. Davidson and Davidson, in *Civilized Society*, pp. 80–83, also maintain that a conservative solution to the tax evasion problem would be to increase expenditures for monitoring compliance and punishing offenders.

35. Ibid., pp. 83–95. See also Aronson, J. Richard and Eli Schwartz: *Management Policies in Local Government Finance*. Washington, D.C.: The International City Management Association, 1987, especially Parts 1 and 3, for discussions of taxes and fairness issues.

36. Davidson and Davidson, *Civilized Society*, pp. 86–87.

37. Hansen, Alvin: *The American Economy*. New York: McGraw-Hill, 1957, p. 175.

38. Samuelson, Paul A.: "The New Look in Tax and Fiscal Policy," in *Federal Tax Policy for Economic Growth and Stability*, Joint Committee on the Economic Report, Washington, November 9, 1955, p. 234, cited in Gordon, David: *Problems in Political Economy: An Urban Perspective*. Second Edition. Lexington, Mass.: D.C. Heath and Company, 1977, p. 35.

39. Perhaps the clearest statements of these views are "The German Ideology" and "Contribution to the Critique of Hegel's Philosophy of Right," in Tucker, Robert C. (ed): *The Marx-Engels Reader*. New York: W.W. Norton and Company, 1972.

40. The most complete statement of Marx's and Engels's views on this matter is Engels's "Socialism: Utopian and Scientific," in Tucker, *Marx-Engels Reader*. In this view, both utopian and scientific socialism arise as a reaction to the inhuman consequences of capitalist development. Utopian socialism, however, is an abstract blueprint for an ideal society concocted by an individual, such as Robert Owen's famous New Lanark experiment in the early nineteenth century. While such communes may give the world an idea of alternative economic arrangements, they themselves can only exist in isolation from the rest of society and therefore are doomed to short

lives. By scientific socialism Marx and Engels meant the analysis of the nature and development of capitalism: understanding how contradictions within the mode of production (conflict between capital and labor) and contradictions between the capitalist mode of production and the developing forces of production (technological capacities) undermine the system itself and thus lead to a general, system-wide revolution, not just the establishment of an isolated utopian commune. The task for the scientist who understands these laws of capitalist development is to explain them to everyone else and to lend a hand in bringing about socialist revolution by working with the key agents of change. Since scientific (historical materialist) analysis reveals that the industrial working class is the key agent to lead the overthrow of capitalism, the appropriate role for the scientific socialist is to assist in organizing the working class.

41. The famous passage "from each according to his ability, to each according to his needs," is from Marx, Karl and Friedrich Engels: "Critique of the Gotha Program," in Tucker, *Marx-Engels Reader*, p. 388. Marx's views on human nature and, particularly, the human potential that would thrive under socialism and communism are perhaps most clearly stated in "The Economic and Philosophical Manuscripts," also known as "The Paris Manuscripts," in Fromm, Erich (ed): *Marx's Concept of Man*. New York: Frederick Ungar, 1966. Selections are also included in *The Marx-Engels Reader*.

42. The shortest and possibly the most up-to-date introduction to Marxist economic theory is Ernest Mandel's *An Introduction to Marxist Economic Theory*. New York: Pathfinder Press, 1970. The chapter in Landreth's *History of Economic Theory* on Marx's economics is also quite clear and informative. See the bibliography for other guides to the writings of Marx.

43. Of course, in response to competitive pressures, capitalists find themselves compelled to try to drive the real wage as low as possible—well below the average wage to the barest subsistence wage—in order to increase profit margins.

44. Smith, *Wealth of Nations*, chapter 1.

45. See Braverman, Harry: *Labor and Monopoly Capital*. New York: Monthly Review Press, 1974, and Bowles, Samuel and Richard Edwards: *Understanding Capitalism*. New York: Harper and Row, 1985, chapters 8, 9, and 10.

46. Braverman, *Labor and Monopoly Capital*, pp. 79–82.

47. Braverman, *Labor and Monopoly Capital* and Bowles and Edwards, *Understanding Capitalism*. See also Bluestone, Barry and Bennett Harrison: *The Great U-Turn*. New York: Basic Books, 1988.

48. Although Marxists often seem to be saying that capitalism worsens the *absolute* standard of living of the working class, they generally acknowledge that over time, all incomes tend to rise under capitalism, but worker incomes rise at a slower rate than does their output.

49. See Bowles and Edwards, *Understanding Capitalism*, chapters 7 and 10, and especially, Baran, Paul A. and Paul M. Sweezy: *Monopoly Capital*. New York: Monthly Review Press, 1966.

50. Bowles and Edwards, *Understanding Capitalism*, pp. 203–210.
51. Ibid.
52. This view first attained broad public exposure through the writings of the left-liberal institutionalist economist, John Kenneth Galbraith in *The Affluent Society*. Boston: Houghton Mifflin, 1958, and *The New Industrial State*. Boston: Houghton Mifflin, 1967. See also Baran and Sweezy, *Monopoly Capital*, and Bowles and Edwards, *Understanding Capitalism*. It is worth noting here that the current rise of international competition is, in the Marxist view at least, not a return to a more price-competitive form of capitalism, but a more advanced stage of monopoly capitalism, in which the giants battle for world domination. Indeed, a small number of multinational corporations account for increasing shares of world trade. See, for example, Cavanagh, John and Frederick Clairmonte: *The Transnational Economy*. Washington, D.C.: Institute for Policy Studies, 1982.
53. See Baran and Sweezy, *Monopoly Capital*, chapter 11: "The Irrational System."
54. This does not mean that investing the surplus in plant and equipment, rather than paying it out in wages, is treating workers unjustly. The problem, from the Marxist perspective, is that the surplus does not rightfully belong to the capitalist, but to all who have helped to create it, meaning the workers and the community (society) at large. Hence it is the workers and the community who should decide whether the surplus is invested in plant and equipment or paid out in wages.
55. A radical analysis of the limits of this legitimation strategy is O'Connor, James: *The Fiscal Crisis of the State*. New York: St. Martin's Press, 1973.
56. Davidson and Davidson, *Civilized Society*, p. 152.
57. Mandel, *Marxist Economic Theory*, p. 75 (emphases in original).
58. The failure of socialism in Eastern Europe may appear to undermine the credibility of radical claims that socialism could work because of its ability to draw upon human capacities for compassion and cooperation, and its technically rational organization of the economy through planning. For radical analyses of the problems of socialism in Eastern Europe, see Nove, Alec: *The Economics of Feasible Socialism*. London: George Allen and Unwin, 1983. See also Meurs, Mike and Richard Schauffler: "Not According to Plan: The Collapse of the Soviet Planned Economy," in *Real World Micro*. Third Edition. Somerville, Mass.: Dollars and Sense Economic Affairs Bureau, Inc., 1991.

Bibliography

Intellectual Antecedents of Contemporary Paradigms

Political Foundations

Bonar, James: *Philosophy and Political-Economy*. New York: Augustus M. Kelley, 1968.

The author discusses the economic theories of prominent Western political philosophers, from classical Greece to the nineteenth century.

Hegel, G.W.F.: "Philosophy of Right and Law" (1821) and "The Philosophy of History" (1822). In Carl J. Friedrich (ed): *The Philosophy of Hegel.* New York: Random House, 1954.

The former work sets forth Hegel's philosophy of the modern, liberal state in a capitalist economy; the latter work is his philosophy of social development.

Hobbes, Thomas: *Leviathan.* C. B. Macpherson (ed). New York: Penguin Books, 1980 (1651).

In many ways the first modern political philosopher, Hobbes posed the problem of political legitimacy in a world in which the restraints of religion and custom were giving way to the individual self-interest of early capitalism.

Locke, John: *Two Treatises of Government.* Introduced and edited by Peter Laslett. New York: Cambridge University Press, 1963 (1698).

The second treatise is of most interest and relevance to contemporary issues. It completely rejects the notion that monarchs rule by divine right. Rather, the state is to be thought of as a compact among individuals living in a free market society, for the purpose of protecting the private property that they have appropriated by natural right. Locke's treatise exerted a profound influence on the U.S. Constitution and it remains one of the most important treatises in the philosophy of the democratic capitalist state.

Marx, Karl (See the "Economic Foundations" section of this bibliography, which follows.)

Mill, John Stuart (See the "Economic Foundations" section of this bibliography, which follows.)

Nozick, Robert: *Anarchy, State and Utopia.* New York: Basic Books 1974.

Critique of the contemporary liberal, democratic, capitalist state and a presentation of the libertarian theory of the minimalist state on the basis of Lockean entitlement theory.

Pateman, Carole: *Participation and Democratic Theory.* London: Cambridge University Press, 1970.

An examination of the differences between two traditions in democratic theory, the Benthamite utilitarian tradition and the "classical Greek" tradition of participatory democracy, as expressed in the writings of Rousseau and Mill. Pateman prefers the latter tradition and argues for its extension into the realm of economic decision making.

Rawls, John: *A Theory of Justice.* Cambridge: Harvard University Press, 1971.

A synthesis of the theories of human nature and political structure in the writings of Locke, Rousseau, and Kant, as a basis for the contemporary liberal, democratic, capitalist state.

Rousseau, Jean Jacques: *The Social Contract* (1762) and *A Discourse on the Origin of Inequality* (1755). New York: E.P. Dutton and Company, 1950.

The Social Contract is the more important work. Rousseau describes the ideal form of political decision making as participatory democracy. It succeeds through the exercise of the human capacity for pity and understanding of the needs of others, which leads persons to choose policies that are good for the community as a whole. This work has exerted great influence on the development of both liberal and radical thought.

Strauss, Leo and Joseph Cropsey (eds): *History of Political Philosophy.* Second Edition. Chicago: University of Chicago Press, 1972.

An introduction to the work of 36 of the Western world's most prominent political philosophers, from Plato to Dewey.

Economic Foundations

Bentham, Jeremy: *An Introduction to the Principles of Morals and Legislation.* Wilfrid Harrison (ed). New York: Macmillan Publishing Company, 1948 (1780).

Bentham contributed to the development of modern conservative and liberal political economy through his work on the analytical apparatus of "utility"—a way of classifying and measuring human preference for pleasure and avoidance of pain—which was taken up by marginalist and neoclassical economics in the modeling of consumer behavior. The concept of utility as a common denominator of human preferences provides at least part of the foundation of modern conservative economic theory. It also serves as the foundation for the modern welfare state. Bentham maintained that the interest of the community is simply the *sum* of the interests of each member. Government actions should maximize total social utility, regardless of how they might affect specific individuals. For the most part, however, Bentham advocated that government *not* interfere in the market economy.

Keynes, John Maynard: *The General Theory of Employment, Interest and Money.* New York: Harcourt Brace Jovanovich, 1964 (1936).

In this revolutionary book, Keynes broke with the neoclassical focus on analyzing resource allocation through individual markets, and described how interest rates and profit expectations ultimately determine the level of aggregate investment and the employment level in the entire economy. Like Marx (but quite apart from him), Keynes concluded that the capitalist market economy tends to reach equilibrium (stasis) at less than full employment, and thus to stagnate, as consumer demand becomes satisfied and capitalists perceive no further investment opportunities. Keynes believed that government intervention is necessary to achieve and maintain full employment (as well as to redistribute incomes), but it was his successors who used his theory to develop the practice of national counter-cyclical demand management policy discussed in chapter 1. Economist Joan Robinson termed this use of Keynes's theory "bastard Keynesianism," since, in her view, it ignored Keynes's fundamental critique of capitalism's long-run tendency to stagnate, and turned his concepts into simple technical tools to smooth out the business cycle.

Marshall, Alfred: *Principles of Economics.* Eighth Edition. New York: Macmillan Publishing Company, 1948 (1890).

Marshall is the founder of modern microeconomic analysis. He synthesized the supply focus of the classical economics of Smith, Ricardo, and Mill, with the demand focus of the marginalist economics of William Stanley Jevons, Karl Menger, Leon Walras, and others, in what has come to be known as neoclassical theory. Unlike classical theory, the focus of neoclassical theory is not the nature and causes of economic development or macroeconomic forces, but microeconomic phenomena—the optimal allocation of scarce resources among competing uses. Optimal allocations are those that maximize consumer satisfaction, or "utility." Modern microeconomic analysis consists largely of the attempt to apply the laws of diminishing marginal utility and productivity, via mathematical models, to the study of firms, households (individuals), and markets. Using such mathematical models, microeconomists can, for example, estimate the effects of government intervention in the market on the allocation of resources.

Marx, Karl: *The Marx-Engels Reader.* Robert C. Tucker (ed). New York: W.W. Norton and Company, 1972.

A most comprehensive and useful collection of Marx's writings. Marx's conception of the person and the nature of society is covered in the readings in Part I, especially "Economic and Philosophic Manuscripts of 1844" and "The German Ideology." The interested reader may also wish to consult Fromm, Erich (ed): *Marx's Concept of Man.* New York: Frederick Ungar, 1966. Part II of *The Marx-Engels Reader* includes the most important selections of Marx's writings on the workings of the capitalist economic system. Parts III and V include excerpts from Marx's and Engels's writings on socialism, particularly "Critique of the Gotha Program" and "Socialism: Utopian and Scientific." For those who wish to read the complete version of *Capital*, the Random House edition (1977) includes an excellent introduction by Ernest Mandel. The less ambitious reader should consult Ernest Mandel's *An Introduction to Marxist Economic Theory.* New York: Pathfinder Press, 1970, (see "Radical Views" below).

Mill, John Stuart: *Principles of Political Economy with Some of Their Applications to Social Philosophy.* W.J. Ashley (ed). London: Longmans Green, 1929 (1848).

Mill reinterprets and revises Ricardo's economics, calling for government intervention to redistribute incomes, shorten the working day, and legalize unions, as well as contraception to counteract the Malthusian population growth tendency. See also "On Liberty" and "Representative Government," in *Utilitarianism, On Liberty and Considerations on Representative Government.* H.B. Acton (ed). New York: E.P. Dutton and Company, 1972. In the former work, Mill makes the case for laissez-faire capitalism that is limited by appropriate government intervention. The latter is Mill's theory of government, with thoughts on the nature of the person and social learning through the practice of political decision making.

Ricardo, David: *The Principles of Political Economy and Taxation*. New York: Penguin Publishers, 1971 (1817).

Ricardo built upon the work of his contemporary, Thomas Malthus (see *An Essay on the Principle of Population*. New York: W.W. Norton and Company, 1976 [1798]). Like Malthus, Ricardo believed that human population growth would outstrip the capacity of the land to provide subsistence, thus diverting national wealth to "rents"—payments to the owners of increasingly scarce land and natural resources. The growth in rents would come at the expense of entrepreneurs' profits and workers' wages, thus driving the latter down to and below the level of subsistence. Today, Ricardo is most often cited as the author of the theory of "comparative cost" (advantage), which holds that trade between two countries should take place as long as *each* receives goods that *it* does not produce as cheaply as *it* produces other goods. Ricardo strongly influenced the economics of Mill, Marx, and others. His general theory remains relevant to contemporary economic theory through the work of the "Neo-Ricardians." See Sraffa, Piero: *Production of Commodities by Means of Commodities: Prelude to a Critique of Economic Theory*, Cambridge: Cambridge University Press, 1960, and "Post-Keynesian and Neo-Ricardian Political Economy" in Albelda, Randy, Christopher Gunn, and William Waller, (eds): *Alternatives to Economic Orthodoxy*. Armonk, N.Y.: M.E. Sharpe, Inc., 1987.

Schumpeter, Joseph A.: *Capitalism, Socialism and Democracy*. New York: Harper and Row, 1975 (1942).

Schumpeter's most well-known contribution to political economy is his theory of the capitalist growth process. Unlike the classical economists, who viewed growth as a fairly continuous, incremental process, and unlike the neoclassical school, which paid little attention to growth, Schumpeter believed that capitalism's greatest advantage was the process of "creative destruction" that it fostered. Aggressive entrepreneurs who translate scientific advances into marketable innovations and, in the process, destroy the markets for existing products and the firms and institutions that have grown up around them, are the agents of creative destruction. He believed that the business cycle was a necessary part of this process and advocated a laissez-faire policy for government.

Smith, Adam: *The Wealth of Nations*. R.H. Campbell and A.S. Skinner (eds). Vols. 1 and 2. London: Oxford University Press, 1976 (1776).

This is the foundation of modern political economy. Smith's goal was to discover the nature and causes of economic development. He concluded that free, competitive markets are the primary engines of development, because they foster the division of labor and the specialization of nations, firms, and individuals in the production of goods in which they have particular resources or talents. The beauty of the competitive market is that it relies upon no central direction and only upon the selfish motives of individual participants, yet produces socially beneficial results—namely, increasing wealth and prosperity for everyone. Yet, government has roles to play in the provision of public goods—especially education to mitigate some of the disadvantages of the detail division of labor—and in the administration of justice.

Contemporary Political Economists

Conservative Views

Evans, Michael K.: *The Truth about Supply-Side Economics*. New York: Basic Books, 1983.
    See the annotated bibliography in chapter 3.
Federal Reserve Bank of Atlanta: *Supply-Side Economics in the 1980s: Conference Proceedings*. Westport: Quorum Books, 1982.
    See the annotated bibliography in chapter 3.
Friedman, Milton: *Capitalism and Freedom*. Chicago: University of Chicago Press, 1962, and Friedman, Milton and Rose Friedman: *Free to Choose: A Personal Statement*. New York: Harcourt Brace Jovanovich, 1980.
    Perhaps the clearest explications of the conservative paradigm, these works describe the conservative conception of the person, society, the workings of the market, and the proper role of government in the economy.
Gilder, George: *Wealth and Poverty*. New York: Bantam Books, 1982.
    Like Schumpeter and unlike much of conservative political economy, Gilder explores the roles of what are often considered to be noneconomic factors in the growth and development of the economy, particularly the entrepreneur and the family.
Hayek, Friedrich: *The Road to Serfdom*. Chicago: University of Chicago Press, 1944.
    Hayek criticizes the practice of government intervention in the economy, especially national economic planning, because government can never accumulate the knowledge necessary to plan well. See the discussion of the "knowledge problem" in chapter 4.
Lavoie, Don: *National Economic Planning: What Is Left?* Cambridge, Mass.: Ballinger Publishing Company, 1985.
    See the annotated bibliography in chapter 4.
McKenzie, Richard B.: *The American Job Machine*. New York: Universe Books, 1988.
    See the annotated bibliography in chapter 4.
Niskanen, William A.: *Reaganomics: An Insider's Account of the Policies and the People*. New York: Oxford University Press, 1988.
    See the annotated bibliography in chapter 3.
Roberts, Paul Craig: *The Supply-Side Revolution: An Insider's Account of Policymaking in Washington*. Cambridge, Mass.: Harvard University Press, 1984.
    See the annotated bibliography in chapter 3.

82 *Perspectives on Economic Policy*

Liberal Views

Aronson, J. Richard and Eli Schwartz: *Management Politics in Local Government Finance.* Washington, D.C.: The International City Management Association, 1987.

   A state and local finance text that covers economic, managerial, and philosophical aspects of public revenue raising and budgeting. Both liberal and conservative positions are represented, albeit without these labels.

Davidson, Greg, and Paul Davidson: *Economics for a Civilized Society.* New York: W.W. Norton and Company, 1988.

   A contemporary critique of conservative economic policy as practiced in the 1980s and a clear statement of the liberal view of the role of government in a capitalist market economy, with suggested policy alternatives.

Hansen, Alvin: *The American Economy.* New York: McGraw-Hill, 1957.

   This book extends and applies Keynes's theory of the macroeconomy to national economic policy.

Thurow, Lester C.: *The Zero-Sum Society.* New York: Basic Books, 1980 and *The Zero-Sum Solution.* New York: Simon and Schuster, 1985.

   See the annotated bibliography in chapter 4.

Radical Views

Baran, Paul A. and Paul M. Sweezy: *Monopoly Capital: An Essay on the American Economic and Social Order.* New York: Monthly Review Press, 1966.

   The authors apply Marx's economic analysis to the capitalist system in the twentieth century, focusing on the nature and development of the multinational corporation and its role in transforming the capitalist system itself.

Bluestone, Barry and Bennett Harrison: *The Great U-Turn.* New York: Basic Books, 1988.

   See the annotated bibliography in chapter 4.

Bowles, Samuel and Richard Edwards: *Understanding Capitalism: Competition, Command and Change in the U.S. Economy.* New York: Harper and Row, 1985.

   See the annotated bibliography in chapter 3.

Braverman, Harry: *Labor and Monopoly Capital: The Degradation of Work in the Twentieth Century.* New York: Monthly Review Press, 1974.

   See the annotated bibliography in chapter 4.

Cavanagh, John and Frederick Clairmonte: *The Transnational Economy.* Washington, D.C.: Institute for Policy Studies, 1982.

   See the annotated bibliography in chapter 1.

Cohen, Joshua, and Joel Rogers: *On Democracy: Toward a Transformation of American Society.* New York: Penguin Books, 1983.

   An analysis of the political and economic problems facing the United States in the post–Bretton Woods era that is traced to failures of capitalism. The authors propose democratic control of the economy as a solution.

Mandel, Ernest: *An Introduction to Marxist Economic Theory.* New York: Pathfinder Press, 1970.

This 78-page essay is a very clear exposition and modern application of the major components of Marx's analysis of the capitalist economy.

Nove, Alec: *The Economics of Feasible Socialism.* London: George Allen and Unwin, 1983.

A critical analysis of the failures of socialism in the Soviet Union and the efforts to create socialist alternatives in other countries. In light of these efforts, Nove argues that socialism in the Western capitalist countries should not abolish markets, competition, or democratic politics, but can and should establish a mixed, plan-market system, with substantial decentralization of political and economic power.

O'Connor, James: *The Fiscal Crisis of the State.* New York: St. Martin's Press, 1973.

O'Connor argues that the government's attempt to legitimize the capitalist system through measures such as unemployment insurance and welfare competes with its effort to prop up the system by ensuring, and often subsidizing, private profit rates. The result is public fiscal crisis—a permanent feature of contemporary capitalism, in O'Connor's view.

Analyses and Comparisons of Political-Economic Paradigms

On Paradigms in General

Kuhn, Thomas: *The Structure of Scientific Revolutions.* Second Edition. Chicago: University of Chicago Press, 1970.

Through this book, Kuhn helped to popularize the term paradigm. He describes the sociology of inquiry in the natural sciences, explaining how a community of scientific inquirers works within a paradigm until it can no longer explain reality adequately, at which point, there is a crisis and new theory emerges. For a discussion of the application of Kuhn's ideas to the study of economics, see Blaug, *Economic Theory*, chapter 16, "A Methodological Postscript."

On Political-Economic Paradigms

Albelda, Randy, Christopher Gunn, and William Waller: *Alternatives to Economic Orthodoxy: A Reader in Political Economy.* Armonk, N.Y.: M.E. Sharpe, Inc., 1987.

For those who have mastered the fundamental ideas of the major economic paradigms, this collection of readings provides a useful introduction to the ideas that have arisen in reaction to, or as criticisms of, the major traditions. This includes post-Keynesian, neo-Ricardian, Institutionalist, and Marxian political economy. Marxian theory, of course, is covered in most accounts of major economic traditions, including this book.

Blaug, Marc: *Economic Theory in Retrsopect.* Third Edition. Cambridge: Cambridge University Press, 1978.

A comprehensive and authoritative source on all of the schools of economic thought, beginning with the Physiocrats and Mercantilists of the seventeenth and eighteenth centuries, and proceeding through the classical economists Smith, Malthus, and Ricardo, then Say, Mill, Marx, Marshall, the Austrian School, and Keynes. The book assumes substantial background knowledge of economic theory, however. Those who are just entering the field should consult the sources listed below.

Carson, Robert: *Economic Issues Today: Alternative Approaches.* New York: St. Martin's Press, 1978.

This is a slightly dated, but nevertheless excellent introductory reader on twelve important American economic issues, such as inflation, government regulation, unemployment, fiscal crises, and multinational firms. Each issue is discussed from the liberal, conservative, and radical perspectives.

Gordon, David (ed): *Problems in Political Economy: An Urban Perspective.* Second Edition. Lexington, Mass.: D.C. Heath and Company, 1977.

Like Carson's *Economic Issues Today*, this book is an introductory reader on important urban economic issues, including unemployment, race relations, education, crime, poverty, health, and housing. For each issue, Gordon presents the writings of well-known conservative, liberal, and radical authors.

Heilbroner, Robert: *The Worldly Philosophers.* New York: Simon and Schuster, 1972.

A highly readable introduction to the development of economic thought, beginning with Adam Smith's *Wealth of Nations*. Heilbroner combines useful summaries of the important ideas of the major economic thinkers with interesting background on each thinker's life and personal approach to economic issues.

Landreth, Harry: *History of Economic Theory: Scope, Method and Content.* Boston: Houghton Mifflin Company, 1976.

A survey of economic theory, focusing mostly on thinkers from Adam Smith to John Maynard Keynes. It is easier to grasp than Blaug's *Economic Theory*, which covers most of the same thinkers, but far more analytical than Heilbroner's *Worldly Philosophers*.

CHAPTER 3

The Macroeconomic Framework

The best place to begin a survey of U.S. economic policy choices is at the national, or macro level. Macroeconomics is the analysis of the economy from a bird's eye perspective; its focus is on national supply and demand as a whole, rather than on individual markets. National, or aggregate supply, is gross national product (GNP); aggregate demand can be broken down into several components—consumer spending (C), business investment in new plant and equipment, plus net change in inventories, plus residential construction (I), and exports minus imports (X). (Government is introduced below). This can be stated as an equation:

$$GNP = C + I + X$$

which means aggregate supply equals aggregate demand. Of course, if supply did always equal demand, life would be simpler. In fact, demand outstrips supply during boom times, which we experience as inflation. When supply outstrips demand, we experience falling prices and rising unemployment, or recession.

Since the 1930s and the work of John Maynard Keynes, most economists have believed that government must intervene in the market to smooth out the recessionary and inflationary extremes of the business cycle.[1] For example, when aggregate demand falls below supply because businesses have stopped investing and hiring new workers or because consumers have curtailed their consumption, government can "create" demand by borrowing money to spend in the economy. This expenditure ripples through the economy, creating consumer purchasing power and stimulating business investment. Alternatively, the government can dampen inflationary pressures in the economy by decreasing aggregate demand—either by cutting its own spending or by raising taxes, so as to slow the growth

85

of consumer spending and business investment. Hence the macroeconomic equation can be rewritten as:

$$GNP = C + I + G + X$$

where G equals government spending. Government taxing and spending actions to influence the level of economic activity are known as fiscal policy.

In addition to these tools, government—actually the board of governors of the Federal Reserve System—attempts to steer the macroeconomy on a course between inflation (boom) and widespread unemployment (bust), by lowering or raising the money supply, which affects the interest rate—the price of money. Interest rates influence the levels of business investment, employment, and consumption. For the most part, the Fed coordinates its money supply policy with the president's and Congress's fiscal policies and strategies for the economy. Yet because the Fed is not accountable to either Congress or the president, it can, and sometimes does, pursue monetary policies that differ from the aims of the president and Congress.

With the increasing international trade of the past few decades, and especially in the wake of the demise of the Bretton Woods monetary system, many economists believe that the fiscal and monetary policies of large countries like the United States now exert profound effects on the economies of other countries, and vice versa. This chapter will describe the fiscal and monetary policies practiced by the president and the Federal Reserve Board during the 1980s, the apparent effects of these policies, both national and international, and the resultant debates among conservatives, liberals, and radicals, over appropriate macroeconomic policies for the 1990s.

Domestic Stabilization and Growth Policy Dilemmas

The Supply-Side Revolution

As discussed in chapters 1 and 2, the successful application of demand-side, or "Keynesian" fiscal policy from the 1930s onward, but especially in the 1960s, convinced Americans of the necessity and usefulness of government intervention in the economy to stabilize the inflationary and recessionary cycles of the market. As the postwar expansion progressed and living standards improved, many also came to accept a broader federal stabilization or mitigation role, manifested in Social Security, Medicare, Aid to Families with

Dependent Children, and the community development programs of the War on Poverty. In short, liberal views of economic policy came to be accepted as mainstream, so much so that President Richard M. Nixon, a conservative by the standards of his age, called himself a Keynesian.

The stagflation (persistent inflation *and* unemployment) of the 1970s undermined public confidence in the power of government to stabilize the market or mitigate its ill effects, creating an opening for resurgent conservative views of appropriate national economic policy. The conservatives charged that Keynesian demand-side fiscal policies caused inflation and ultimately undermined economic growth. Liberal administrations and Congresses had proved incapable of cutting government spending. Instead, conservatives alleged, liberals continued to tax and borrow money to stimulate the demand side of the economy and redistribute the earnings of hardworking taxpayers to indolent welfare recipients and overpriced pork barrel projects. This unchecked growth of government spending led to higher inflation, while the continual increases in taxes undermined the incentives of workers to work and businesses to invest, conservatives maintained. Moreover, by shackling businesses in tax and regulatory chains, the U.S. government undermined the economy's international competitiveness.

Conservatives called for a 180-degree reversal in these practices, namely, supply-side fiscal policy and deregulation of businesses. Supply-side fiscal policy would encourage economic growth by stimulating the *supply* side of the national economy—increasing gross national product by encouraging workers to work more hours at the same hourly wage rates and inducing businesses to increase investment in new products and equipment, so as to improve productivity and raise output. The increase in output and employment, without a price increase, would lower inflation and thus cure the problem of stagflation.[2]

Ronald Reagan rode the supply-side wave into the White House in 1980 and quickly pushed a series of reforms through Congress, the most significant of which was the Economic Recovery Tax Act of 1981. The act slashed personal income taxes, accelerated the depreciation rate for new plant and equipment (providing a faster tax write-off for these investments), instituted tax credits for investment in research and development, reduced the corporate income tax, lowered taxes on capital gains (profits made from selling a capital asset, such as land or shares of stock), and created IRAs (individual retirement accounts), in which deposits are sheltered from income tax.

In addition to tax cuts, the supply-side approach called for cuts in government spending on social programs, which many conservatives believe waste taxpayer dollars and promote dependency in the recipients.[3] The Reagan administration also continued the deregulation of industry begun during the Carter administration. The latter had supported deregulation of the airline, trucking, railroad, and financial services industries. President Reagan supported these actions and a few additional ones, notably the deregulation of the savings and loan industry in 1982. Also, the Reagan Justice Department condoned a substantial increase in corporate mergers, in the belief that these mergers would increase company competitiveness.[4]

For some conservatives, even these policies did not go far enough to "get the government off the backs of the people," as President Reagan put it. Economists of the monetarist school, of whom Milton Friedman is the most well-known proponent, argued that the federal government should eschew all fiscal policy manipulations (taxing and spending to stabilize the economy), whether the approach be supply-side or demand-side policy. Instead, the Federal Reserve Board should simply allow the money supply to grow by a predictable 3 to 5 percent each year, so as to provide sufficient funds for continuous economic expansion, without inflation. Freed of its chains, claimed Friedman, the market would perform better than it has during the past half-century of government meddling.[5]

Results of Supply-Side Fiscal Policy and Monetarism

Some conservative economic policies were implemented well before Ronald Reagan took office. As noted above, deregulation of industry began during the Carter administration. Also, faced with double-digit inflation rates in 1979, President Carter stood by while the Federal Reserve under Chairman Paul Volcker adopted the monetarist cure, drastically cutting the growth of the money supply and announcing money supply growth targets, much as Friedman had advocated. President Reagan supported this policy as well.

By cutting the growth rate of the money supply, the Fed increased the cost of money (the interest rate), which dampened business investment and slowed consumer spending, thereby reducing the inflation rate. Yet unfortunate side-effects emerged. The decline of consumer spending plunged the economy into its deepest recession since the Great Depression of the 1930s. At the same time, the rise in U.S. interest rates made the dollar attractive to foreign investors. Their increased demand for dollars escalated the dollar's value on world exchange markets, raising the prices of U.S. goods and services in foreign markets. One result was that American net exports declined from 40.4 billion (1982) dollars in 1982, to a negative 135.2 billion (1982) dollars in 1987, making the U.S. the largest debtor in the world.[6]

Consequently, the Fed relaxed its tight money policy by mid-1982 and stopped setting monetary growth targets. Thus it ended its monetarist experiment and returned to its traditional policy of adjusting money supply and interest rates in pursuit of steady growth with minimal inflation and unemployment. The policy shift came in time to help fuel an economic recovery, but too late to help American firms recapture the markets lost to foreign producers. Moreover, the recession and the loss of export markets significantly weakened many American companies, so that when the dollar's value began to fall after 1985, foreign investors were able to buy American companies cheaply. Between 1980 to 1988, foreign ownership of the American manufacturing base increased from 3 percent to 12 percent.[7]

In the meantime, some of the initial fervor of the supply-side revolution subsided, as it became increasingly apparent that this approach to fiscal policy might not be the panacea it seemed to be in 1980. Two factors appear to be most responsible. First, the supply-side income tax cuts of 1981 failed to induce workers to work more hours (supply more labor). Hence the tax cut simply provided less revenue to the federal treasury.[8] Moreover, the recession of 1980–82 cut further into federal tax receipts, since when incomes decrease, so too do income tax revenues.

Secondly, Congress and the president found it increasingly difficult to agree on how to cut the federal budget to balance revenues and expenditures. President Reagan wanted drastic cuts in domestic spending and increases in defense spending, but Congress became increasingly reluctant to comply. Congress did cut domestic spending, but not enough to offset increases in defense spending. As a result, the budget deficit ballooned, from $59.6 billion in 1980 to $221 billion by 1986, in current dollars.[9] Hence Congress and President Reagan never completely implemented supply-side policy. Supply-side fiscal policy *in theory* entails increasing the supply of goods and services (GNP) without inflation, by slashing both taxes *and* government spending. But, despite the cuts in social welfare programs, government spending overall was never reduced. When the economy moved out of recession in 1983, it was, in large part, due to the *demand* stimulus provided by federal deficit spending—the traditional Keynesian way to rejuvenate the economy.

Yet in one respect at least, the expansion that began in 1983 was unlike others. This one was financed in part by foreign capital, much of it Japanese. Continuing high U.S. interest rates and the resultant high value of the dollar depressed U.S. exports, but also attracted foreign capital—enough to help finance government deficit spending, consumer spending, and business investment.[10] As noted above, however, after the value of the dollar began to fall in 1985, foreign investors continued to finance America's deficit, but now they switched from buying U.S. Treasury bonds to tangible assets—urban real estate and American factories.[11]

From 1983 to 1990, the economy grew at a steady, if modest rate and record numbers of jobs were created. Yet the unemployment rate remained above five percent, income disparities grew dramatically, and the United States found itself groaning under the weight of massive foreign trade and federal budget deficits. Conditions worsened in 1991, as the economy slid into a recession. Policymakers now find themselves in the unenviable position of deciding which problem requires more immediate attention, the budget and trade deficits, or slow growth, unemployment, and poverty. Before considering alternative approaches, let us consider the details of these two problems.

The Budget Deficit

In 1986, the federal budget deficit reached $221 billion, a record and alarming high point. It declined for a few years thereafter, yielding to increased tax revenues from economic growth and federal deficit reduction efforts.[12] Yet by 1990, it had reached $220 billion, it swelled to $282 billion in 1991, and it was projected to approach $350 billion in 1992. One consequence is that the ratio of U.S. government debt (our accumulated deficits) to annual GNP increased rapidly, from less than 29 percent in 1980 to a projected 50 percent in 1992. Hence annual interest payments on the debt have risen to one-fifth of the federal budget for fiscal year 1992.[13] Money that is spent paying for past consumption is not available to pay for new business investment, housing, education, roads, health care, or environmental cleanup, especially since an increasing percentage of this debt service is paid abroad, to the foreigners who have been helping to finance the U.S. budget deficits. The longer the deficit lingers and grows, the greater will be the debt service burden and the longer Americans will have to produce more than we consume, in order to pay down the debt.[14]

To the extent that foreign investors finance our budget deficit, it poses another problem as well—it keeps our trade deficit high.

Because the government cannot easily control the magnitude of consumer borrowing and spending, or the amount of business borrowing and investing, the only certain way to reduce the total amount of funds that the United States borrows from foreigners is to cut government spending. Thus, until we reduce the budget deficit, our foreign trade deficit will not decline by much. Moreover, as the U.S. foreign debt grows, foreign creditors may begin to demand higher interest rates, thus further burdening the economy.[15]

Realizing the gravity of the situation, Congress passed the Gramm-Rudman deficit reduction bill in 1987, which called for a balanced budget by 1993. Yet it soon became obvious that the federal government could not accomplish that goal. Finally, in October 1990, Congress and President Bush signed a Budget Deficit Reduction Compromise that increased some taxes and required all spending increases to be offset by budget cuts.

In 1990, the end of the Cold War between the United States and U.S.S.R. seemed to bring a budgetary "peace dividend" that could be cashed in from reduced defense expenditures. Some analysts predicted that defense reductions of 5 percent per year from 1991 to 1994 would cut the U.S. budget deficit in half by 1995 and produce a budget surplus by 1998.[16]

By mid-1991 however, the peace dividend and the gains of the Budget Deficit Reduction Compromise of 1990 had drowned in the sea of red ink created by the costs of the Persian Gulf War, the lower tax revenues that resulted from the 1990–91 recession, and unanticipated costs of rescuing failed banks. As noted above, the projected budget deficit for fiscal year 1992 is almost $350 billion, and a balanced budget seems impossible until well after 1996.[17]

Even these deficits do not take into account expenses such as the bailout of the savings and loan industry. As noted above, in 1982 the federal government deregulated the industry by relaxing the requirement that federally chartered S & Ls invest depositors' money only in safe, long-term, low-interest home mortgages. Now it allowed them to invest in riskier, high-yield commercial real estate and other ventures, but it continued to insure depositors' money through the Federal Savings and Loan Insurance Corporation (FSLIC). The logic behind the deregulation was that if S & Ls could invest in high-yield ventures, they then could pay higher interest on depositors' accounts and thus compete with banks and money market funds, whose interest rates matched the high rates caused by inflation in the late 1970s and the Fed's monetarism in the early 1980s. By 1989, however, so many S & L ventures had soured that the FSLIC went bankrupt, leaving Congress to devise a plan to pay off depositors and shut down the insolvent S & Ls. The congressional plan, which has been estimated to cost upwards of $300 billion over the next 20 years, will fund the bailout "off budget," from funds raised in the private capital market through bonds. Taxpayers will have to pay whatever interest and principal on the bonds is not covered by the assets (real estate, yachts, and so forth) of the failed S & Ls, which most analysts believe will be a large portion of the estimated $300 billion price tag. Moreover, the bonds will use up scarce capital that could otherwise have funded productive investment in plant and equipment, infrastructure, or other needs.[18]

Growing Disparities of Income and Wealth

Another legacy of the supply-side revolution is an increasing inequality of income and wealth, including a rise in the incidence of poverty. As discussed in chapter 1, income and wealth disparities began to grow after 1969, reversing a previous trend toward greater equality and a reduction in the incidence of poverty. During the 1980s, the trend toward inequality accelerated rapidly.[19] Between 1977 and 1988, the average after-tax income of the poorest fifth of American households fell by 10 percent, and the after-tax income of the middle fifth gained by less than 4 percent, while the after-tax income of the richest fifth increased by 34 percent.[20] In fact, by 1988, the wealthiest one-fifth of the population received as much after-tax income as the rest of the population combined. Put differently, the richest 2.5 million Americans now have nearly as much income as the poorest 100 million Americans.[21] The percentage of Americans with incomes below the poverty line, which had fallen from 22.2 percent in 1960 to 11.1 percent in 1973, rose to 15.2 percent in 1983. Even in 1989, the peak year in the business cycle before the recession of 1990–91 began, the poverty rate remained at 12.8 percent of the population.[22]

A number of factors are responsible for the growth in income disparities. As discussed in chapter 1, the most important factor is the growth in before-tax inequalities caused by the growing polarization of wages and salaries that is partly a result of the global restructuring of production and trade.[23] Yet federal policies have exacerbated the trend toward wage inequality. The government's failure to raise the minimum wage above $3.35 per hour between 1981 and 1989 (in effect, cutting the inflation-adjusted minimum wage from $3.35 to $2.50) is a case in point.[24] Federal tax policies, especially the tax cuts of the Economic Recovery Tax Act of 1981, also fostered income inequality.

> In 1977, the richest one percent of U.S. households paid an average of 35.5 percent of their income in federal taxes. In 1992, [the Congressional Budget Office] estimates they will pay 29.3 percent. During this same period, the percentage of income that middle-income households pay in taxes is expected to tick up from 19.5 percent to 19.7 percent.[25]

Other federal policies compounded the effects of tax rate changes. For example, the sharply rising interest rates discussed above increased the incomes of the holders of Treasury and corporate bonds and those who already owned property (the wealthy), while hurting interest-rate-sensitive industries, such as agriculture and housing, as well as the average consumer.[26]

Meanwhile, government spending on social welfare programs (excluding Social Security and Medicare) declined from 28 percent of federal outlays to 22 percent between 1980 and 1988, reflecting the conservative Reagan administration's belief that these programs are harmful to taxpayers as well as aid recipients. State and local outlays for welfare decreased also, as these governments tried to cut costs to make up for reduced federal aid.[27]

> Especially sharp reductions occurred in the Aid to Families with Dependent Children program, the nation's basic cash assistance program for poor single-parent families. From 1970 to 1991, the maximum AFDC benefit for a family of three with no other income declined 42 percent in the typical state, after adjusting for inflation. In fact, AFDC benefits have eroded so sharply that the average value of AFDC and food stamp benefits *combined* has now fallen to about the same level as the value of AFDC benefits *alone* in 1960, before the food stamp program was created.[28]

Other social welfare and community development spending declined as well. Federal housing assistance funds fell from $27 billion in 1980 to $13 billion in 1982, and remained at or below $11 billion through 1988. Meanwhile, housing costs rose dramatically, making the American dream of home ownership unattainable for many and contributing to a national epidemic of homelessness.[29] In addition, the proportion of unemployed persons receiving unemployment insurance declined during the 1980s, leaving a higher percentage of persons unprotected than at any time since World War II.[30]

Thus the United States now confronts multiple, serious problems. The U.S. budget and trade deficits are growing, but so too are income inequality and poverty and other problems, such as a crumbling infrastructure of roads and bridges (see below). If the United States allows poverty to spread and its infrastructure to deteriorate, it risks a future of unproductive citizens and an inefficient economy overall. If it neglects the budget deficit, it goes deeper into the hole. What is to be done?

Conservative Views

Most conservatives believe that the budget deficit is the most serious problem and that it must be addressed now. In the traditional conservative view, government deficits as well as consumer credit spending drain savings from the economy that would otherwise be available for business investment, and without sufficient investment, neither productivity, nor American competitiveness, nor ultimately, our standard of living, can improve. During the 1980s, the U.S. net savings rate was less than 3 percent of GNP, down from about 7 percent during the 1950s, 1960s, and 1970s.[31] Moreover, federal deficits cause inflation, say conservatives, because they increase aggregate demand and employment and stretch other resources beyond their capacity. As noted above, reducing the budget deficit may be the only way to cut the trade deficit.

Ironically, since the growth of budget deficits under the conservative Reagan administration, this view has been propounded as much or more by centrist-liberal economists as by conservatives.[32] Indeed, Ronald Reagan was elected in 1980 in large part because he promised to mend the spendthrift ways of liberal government and to *balance* the federal budget by 1983. When instead the deficit mushroomed, President Reagan sought to blame congressional Democrats for failing to cut domestic spending, but in the face of a massive military buildup and cuts in many domestic programs, this argument was not completely successful.[33]

A few conservatives, such as Robert Barro of the "rational expectations" school, argue that the deficit is a problem that is not likely to yield to conventional solutions, because consumer spending and saving will thwart the intent of government policy.[34] The more widespread conservative view is close to the supply-side arguments made by conservatives in the early 1980s, namely, that the budget deficit *is* a problem, but its solution lies in reduced government spending, especially on domestic programs, and not increased taxes. The Reagan and Bush administrations have consistently championed this position. Indeed, George Bush adopted a popular "no new taxes" pledge in his successful presidential campaign of 1988, and he has repeatedly sought to win back a tax cut given up to bipartisan compromise in the 1986 Tax Reform Act—the tax on capital gains.[35] Nevertheless, as noted above, even President Bush found it necessary to agree to some tax increases in the 1990 Budget Deficit

Reduction Compromise with Congress, a sign of growing concern about the deficit among conservative policymakers. For the most part, however, the Bush administration is following a conservative course of attempting to hold the line on further tax or spending increases—a position supported by conservative economists, including Michael Boskin of the President's Council of Economic Advisors.[36]

Meanwhile, few conservatives support a return to the monetarist experiment of the early 1980s. Rather, they call for the Fed to steer a course between inflation and unemployment, coordinating its actions with the fiscal policies of the White House.[37]

Given these conservative priorities—deficit reduction and no (or few) new taxes—ambitious federal efforts to reverse trends in income distribution, or new federal outlays for infrastructure, education, or other needs, are out of the question. On the issue of welfare support, particularly Aid to Families with Dependent Children, conservatives maintain that the system fosters in its recipients the unfortunate characteristics of dependency and lack of self-esteem, and that it should be abolished or curtailed.[38] In any case, the federal government should fund at most a part of the AFDC program (as it does now), with the rest to be supplied by the states, which provide varying levels of support.[39] On issues such as public education, conservatives argue that the problem is not money but school curriculum and stifling public school bureaucracies. If states and localities adopt conservative structural and curricular reforms, American primary and secondary education will improve without increases in federal funding.[40] As for roads, bridges, and other infrastructure, conservatives maintain that states and localities should fund these needs, or better yet, we should adopt private ownership and funding (through user fees) of infrastructure.[41]

Liberal Views

Liberals differ in their views of the deficit and appropriate macroeconomic policies. Barry Bosworth, C. Fred Bergsten, and Lawrence Summers take positions similar to conservatives.[42] American consumers and the government are on a "consumption binge," as Bosworth calls it, so we are running a huge government deficit, and we are not saving enough to finance the business investments needed for productivity growth. Foreign investors are financing part of our government deficit, and buying U.S. assets (stocks, factories, and real estate) to finance American investment. In the meantime, our federal deficit is pumping up aggregate demand, leading to inflation.

Cutting the deficit by reducing consumption would dampen inflationary pressures, stem the growth of foreign purchases of American assets, and reduce American imports, thus improving our foreign trade balance as well.[43]

Robert Eisner disputes the contention that the United States has been on a consumption binge. Much of federal spending, such as roads and even military hardware, is investment, not consumption, he maintains.[44] Along with other liberals, such as Paul Davidson and Hyman Minsky, Eisner's position on the deficit lies much closer to the traditional Keynesian view.[45] As long as the economy is *not* at "full employment" of its human and material resources, government deficit spending does not cause inflation. In fact, cutting the deficit when economic resources are not being used to full capacity simply raises the unemployment rate and reduces incomes. As their incomes decline, people pay less income tax, and they also save less. Hence the net result of cutting the deficit is to *reduce* tax receipts and savings, increase unemployment, and reduce investment. Instead, the federal government should maintain spending levels. To stimulate investment, the Federal Reserve should keep interest rates low.

The issue of full employment, especially of human resources, lies at the heart of the conservative-liberal debate over macroeconomic policy. Both camps agree that there is a "natural rate of unemployment." As the unemployment rate approaches and falls below this level, wages (and ultimately prices in general) rise, because lower unemployment increases worker bargaining power. But liberals and conservatives disagree over the natural rate of unemployment. Conservatives set the rate higher, currently 5 to 6 percent, versus 4 to 5 percent in the liberal view.

When unemployment falls below the natural rate, conservatives and some liberals advocate cutting government spending to reduce aggregate demand or urging the Federal Reserve to raise interest rates and thus cut demand by slowing investment, either of which dampens inflationary pressures. Other liberals maintain that the Federal Reserve should keep interest rates low and that Congress and the president should keep inflation in check through government wage and price controls, rather than by allowing unemployment to rise.[46]

Most liberals also take issue with conservatives over the *composition* of the federal budget. Throughout the 1980s, liberals generally opposed the Reagan administration's increased defense outlays and relatively reduced spending on social welfare, education, and infrastructure. This dispute has continued during the Bush administration. Liberals such as Arne Anderson point out that while spending on defense increased from 5.27 percent of GNP in 1981 to 6.08 percent of GNP in 1988, spending on energy, transportation, community development, and education all declined (from very small bases) as a percentage of GNP during this same period.[47] As a result, America now suffers not only from budget and foreign trade deficits, but from a "public investment" deficit as well:

> The Department of Transportation estimates that it will cost $50 billion to repair and replace the nation's 240,000 bridges. Another $315 billion will be required over the next ten years to bring highways back up to their 1983 condition. The cost to modernize the air traffic control system is projected at $25 billion by the year 2000. The Department of Housing and Urban Development estimates a $20 billion price tag on repairing the deteriorating stock of public housing, and no one knows the cost of a serious effort to house the homeless. The annual estimates of total spending needed over the next ten years for infrastructure investment range from $118 billion (1982 dollars) by the Association of General Contractors to a conservative $53 billion (1982 dollars) by the Congressional Budget Office, considerably above the $45 billion currently being spent.... Merely returning federal support for education to 1981 levels (as a percent of GNP) would require $7.8 billion.[48]

Yet how are these public improvements to be financed? As noted previously, the 1990 Budget Deficit Reduction Compromise between Congress and President Bush put spending caps on national defense and domestic programs, and required that any spending increases be offset by reductions elsewhere or by new taxes.

Some liberals, such as Bosworth and Summers, side with conservatives in pushing for deficit reduction *before* enacting new spending programs. Others, such as Eisner, argue that we cannot afford to wait, and that deficit reduction should not be the primary goal of fiscal policy.[49] Anderson, taking a middle position, maintains that deficit reduction and increases in spending on infrastructure, education, and housing can occur only through tax increases. He proposes progressive tax increases that constitute a reversal of supply-side thinking. Anderson would raise income tax rates for middle-to-upper-income persons and for corporations. He would make the Social Security tax progressive, by levying higher taxes on higher earnings, and he would increase estate taxes. Consumption taxes (such as the alcohol, gasoline, and tobacco taxes increased in the October 1990 Budget Deficit Reduction Compromise between President Bush and Congress) are regressive and should therefore be avoided, in Anderson's view.[50]

Similarly, Benjamin Friedman argues that the United States must recognize that, for political reasons, it is unable to cut the budget any further, so its only option is to raise the revenues it needs to buy what it obviously wants. The best way to do this, Friedman argues, would be through a progressive consumption tax, which would raise revenues and promote the savings necessary to finance business investment. If the consumption tax is not politically feasible, Friedman believes that a modest increase in the progressive income tax will raise enough revenue to cure the budget deficit.[51]

As for welfare programs, such as AFDC, liberals call for federal assumption of all welfare payments, or at least the development of national income support standards. They also recommend further experiments with and federal funding of "workfare" programs, in which aid recipients are required to accept training and job placement in return for assistance.[52]

While most liberals hold that tax increases are necessary to achieve their goals for the budget, some also wish to expand the use of a supply-side tax-reduction tool created in 1981 but restricted in 1986—the IRA, or individual retirement account. The IRA is intended to increase savings and thus generate funds for private investment and economic growth, because income deposited in an IRA is tax-exempt. Because of the small amount of money needed to open an IRA, it is generally considered to be a middle-class person's tax cut instrument, analogous to the upper-income person's capital gains tax cut championed by the Bush administration.[53]

Radical Views

To understand radical views of appropriate macroeconomic policy, it is best to begin with the problem of stagflation (stagnation plus inflation) that appeared in the 1970s. Radicals contend that stagnation, the decline of business investment and economic activity, is a fundamental tendency in capitalist systems. Stagnation occurs because supply (production) eventually satisfies demand. With demand sated, consumption slows, and opportunities for further profitable investment cease. This is not to say that human needs are satisfied, as millions of impoverished persons attest, but without purchasing power, these persons are not a source of profit for business. Without the expectation of profits, capitalists do not invest in production.[54]

As Harry Magdoff and Paul Sweezy argue, the dramatic growth of the world economy in the quarter century after World War II occurred because of the fortuitous confluence of five factors:

1. The reconstruction of Europe and Japan required massive amounts of capital, labor, and material resources;
2. The global proliferation of the automobile stimulated supplier industries and investments in road building worldwide, as well as housing and suburban shopping malls in countries like the United States;
3. Technological innovations in space exploration and the military sector created the foundation for new civilian industries, such as jet planes, computers, and other electronic equipment;
4. The new U.S. role as "world policeman" generated demand for military equipment and personnel;
5. The new institutions of world economic cooperation created through the Bretton Woods agreement, as well as unilateral American economic assistance through initiatives like the Marshall Plan, created a basis for worldwide economic expansion.[55]

By the 1970s, these sources had exhausted their power to stimulate the economy, so that worldwide stagnation and rising unemployment set in. Since then, only increasing government spending and explosive growth in the finance industry (and the industries that serve it) have kept the U.S. economy from falling into depression. Even these stimuli have been weak, however. The economic recovery of the mid-1980s left unemployment at record postwar highs and factory capacity utilization at record lows for a postwar recovery. This illustrates just how difficult it is to rejuvenate the capitalist economy in this, its mature stage.[56]

Moreover, the dramatic growth of the finance industry is not a healthy sign for the economy, claim radicals, but a source of inflation.[57] The finance industry grew rapidly in the postwar period, and its advocates pushed Congress to remove the interest rate controls it had established in the aftermath of the Great Depression.[58] The industry had already become a giant by the 1970s when demand for manufacturing investment slackened. Banks responded to the slowdown by finding new customers—making risky loans to Third World countries and inventing new financial instruments that, in effect, enabled banks and money market funds to lend money back and forth to each other, raising interest rates and thus earning profits with each transaction.[59]

Hence, contrary to the views of liberal and conservative economists, radicals assert that government borrowing did not cause high interest rates; instead, deregulation of financial institutions allowed interest rates to rise, and growing concentration in the finance industry undermined the competition that would have kept interest rates low. Indeed, growing industry concentration is the primary cause of inflation in general, since monopolies and oligopolies set prices higher than price-competitive firms. Unionized workers may try to keep up with such cost increases by pressing for wage increases, but they are not, say radicals, the root cause of inflation. Thus, conservative calls for wage cuts and curbs on consumption cannot restrain inflation. Even liberal solutions, like wage-price controls, are unlikely to work because, under capitalist systems, they often amount to only wage controls.[60]

Thus stagflation, in the radical view, did not result from overuse of so-called Keynesian demand-stimulation policies (as conservatives maintain), but neither will it yield to the Keynesian cure. Stagflation arose from the fundamental tendency of the capitalist economy to slide into depression and from the price and interest rate increases imposed by increasingly monopolistic industries, especially finance.

In the radical view, the supply-side policies of the 1980s not only failed to solve the stagflation problem, they seriously harmed the poor and working people:

> With more than ten million people unemployed in 1982, it was impossible for organized labor to maintain wage standards, let alone raise them. Reductions in wages rippled from one industry to the next. The real average weekly wage fell by more than eight percent between 1979 and 1982 and failed to recover at all in the next five years.[61]

Meanwhile, "the 1981 cuts in business taxes were so generous that... 'the value of allowable deductions and actual credits actually exceeded the tax liability on the income that investment in a typical piece of equipment would generate'."[62] The Reagan administration attempted to offset the revenue losses resulting from these tax cuts and increased military expenditures by slashing spending on education and job training, infrastructure, income suppport, and public housing.[63]

Current proposals to cut the trade deficit by cutting the budget deficit also miss the point, in the view of Magdoff and Sweezy. Like some liberals, they maintain that when the economy is not operating at full employment of its human and natural resources, cutting government spending only exacerbates the economy's recessionary tendencies.[64]

The nation must decide that its top priorities are jobs, food, housing, health care, income security, and a healthy environment, argue Magdoff and Sweezy. To finance these aims, it must slash military spending but also borrow money. The latter action should be accompanied by new regulations on interest rates, or better yet, nationalization of banks.[65]

The more pragmatic, progressive economists set forth somewhat less sweeping proposals for reform of the economy. These proposals share many features with liberal reforms, but they are generally distinguishable by their focus on structural, institutional change, particularly their advocacy of "economic democracy."

A good example of progressive macroeconomic policy is the Center for Popular Economics's "Ten Steps to a Democratic Economy," which include some standard liberal measures, such as achieving full employment (albeit at an unemployment rate of 2 to 3 percent, as opposed to the liberals' 4 to 5 percent); raising the minimum wage (to increase aggregate demand, improve the living standards of the poor, and prod employers to seek profits through productivity increases rather than wage cuts); increasing the progressivity of, and yield on, the personal income tax; reducing military spending; and adopting certain liberal international economic stabilization policies (discussed below).[66] Yet their proposals also include a number of reforms unlikely to appear on contemporary liberal lists, such as reform of the unemployment insurance system to discourage layoffs and encourage an equal sharing of work reductions among all employees in a firm; medical and other employee benefits for part-time workers; and a serious commitment to public sector jobs programs in which everyone is guaranteed the right to participate. Taken together, these measures would constitute a "right to a job."

Like many liberals, the Center for Popular Economics analysts call for a strong public commitment to human resources development, and money for basic science research and development. Unlike most liberals, they also advocate free higher education. They argue that labor unions increase productivity and call for a worker's bill of rights as well as punishment of firms that violate labor laws. Most distinctive, however, are their proposals for the following:

1. Conducting a bi-yearly inventory of social needs that "would be a comprehensive accounting and ranking of social needs, as represented by a full cross-section of the population," to identify the extent and magnitude of problems such as homelessness, hunger, and poor transportation. Congress would be required to initiate spending programs in response to the results of the inventory.[67] Some radicals go a bit further, calling for the election of a national planning board that would have the power either to compel firms to invest in and produce necessary minimum levels of essential goods and services as determined by social needs inventories, or to create public enterprises that would take on such tasks.[68]

2. Fighting inflation via price controls through incomes policies—yearly negotiations between business, labor, and government over wages, prices, profits, and interest rates, with government empowered to use tax penalties and rewards to ensure corporate compliance with such agreements.[69]
3. Making the Federal Reserve Board directly accountable to Congress. At present, the Federal Reserve Board's governors are appointed to 14-year terms and are accountable to no one. Hence they tend, in the views of radicals and some liberals, to promote the banking industry's agenda of keeping interest rates high rather than lowering interest rates to stimulate aggregate demand. Congress should appoint Federal Reserve governors to four-year terms. Congress also should select yearly growth, employment, and inflation targets and the Fed should be required to enact policies that attempt to achieve the targets.

Marxists such as Magdoff and Sweezy, however, maintain that the power of the Fed to control the money supply has fallen dramatically since 1960. In fact, the banks create money according to the demands of businesses for credit and their own drive for profits through new financial instruments. The eurodollar market alone exerts more influence on the supply of money than the Fed does, they contend. The most the Fed can do is to accommodate the banks' needs for money, intervene to stave off financial panics when large banks collapse, and smooth out the business cycle. Thus, popular control of the Fed is no panacea. Indeed:

> What stands in the way of full employment, decent housing and adequate medical care, and an improved quality of life for all the people is not the absence of credit. Therefore, tinkering with the money supply or other traditional government mechanisms cannot produce what is needed. Rather, meaningful changes can only be achieved by reforms that challenge the ruling class's property and profit interests, with social goals taking precedence over private gain.[70]

Thus, despite some consensus among the paradigms as to the magnitude of the nation's macroeconomic problems, there is little agreement on the correct approach to solving them.

Toward International Cooperation?

As the foregoing discussion implies, U.S. fiscal and monetary policies affect the economic fortunes of other countries, as their policies affect us. It is likely that this interdependence will continue with the growth of world trade, and we can expect that fiscal, monetary, and trade policies set by one country will have international repercussions, ultimately affecting domestic politics and events. The high U.S. interest rates of the 1980s, for example, attracted foreign capital, leading other countries to raise their interest rates to stem the flow. Also, the high value of the dollar from 1981 to 1986 made American goods more expensive in foreign markets, so our exports declined and our imports increased. Export surplus countries, such as Germany and Japan, sought to avoid inflation by pursuing fiscal policies that dampened domestic demand and demand for imports from the United States. Likewise during the 1980s, Third World countries who were unable to pay the debt service on their massive loans taken out in the 1970s found themselves forced to enact fiscal austerity measures at home that slowed demand for American products, while they focused their energies on producing exports for countries like the United States, as a way to earn hard currency to repay their loans. As a result, world trade declined, hurting all the players.[71]

As explained in chapter 1, the Bretton Woods monetary system had sought to balance and stabilize economic relations to some extent, by fixing currency exchange rates. When that system fell apart in 1971, currency exchange rates began to fluctuate widely, so that the confluence of each country's domestically driven fiscal and monetary policies can now create serious "misalignments" of currencies on world markets that last for a considerable period of time, such as the overvaluation of the dollar from 1981 to 1985. Many economists believe that the dramatic growth of unregulated eurocurrencies and the speculative international financial transactions of multinational corporations undermine domestic policies to control the money supply, thus exacerbating monetary, fiscal, and trade problems.[72]

Some economists believe that if the United States is to resolve its trade deficit problem, the world's major trading countries must achieve greater coordination of their fiscal and monetary policies, either through frequent consultations, through formal agreements, or perhaps through new global monetary institutions. Some economists also believe that if the world economy is to grow at a steady pace, the use of eurocurrencies and indeed, the fast-growing global finance industry in general, must be more tightly regulated. Of course, there is considerable controversy on these issues.

Liberal Views

C. Fred Bergsten places a high priority on reducing the U.S. budget deficit in order to lower the value of the dollar and thus reduce the U.S. trade deficit. If we do not erase the trade deficit, he fears, protectionist sentiments will continue to grow and will come to dominate our policies, leading to a general deterioration in world trade and development. Like Summers, Bosworth, and others, he advocates a reduction in U.S. government spending as well as tax increases to reach this goal.[73]

In addition, Bergsten proposes that the United States coordinate this demand-side contraction with fiscal expansion in the trade surplus countries, especially Germany, Japan, Taiwan, and Korea. These countries must agree to expand consumer spending through tax cuts, or else increase government spending, in order to increase their demand for imports from the United States. The U.S. fiscal contraction will lower the budget deficit and the value of the dollar as well as U.S. demand for imports, thus further helping to erase the U.S. trade deficit. If Germany, Japan, and the other trade surplus countries comply, they will see their surpluses decline to zero, while the U.S. deficit rises to zero. Why should the trade surplus countries agree to this plan? Because, claims Bergsten, if they do not, they will lose their trade advantages and more, as the United States and other deficit countries erect ever-higher protectionist barriers. Moreover, fiscal stimulus will help the trade surplus countries reduce their unemployment rates and solve other domestic problems.[74]

Other liberals, such as Davidson and Minsky, agree that we should induce Germany and Japan to increase their imports of U.S. goods and services, but through "managed trade" policies (discussed in the next chapter), rather than through fiscal policy coordination. As discussed previously, these economists question the wisdom of cutting the budget deficit while unemployment is above 4 percent.[75]

Bergsten also calls for measures to ease the burden of Third World debt and to increase the flow of capital to these countries. Easing the debt burden will allow Third World debtors to export less to countries such as the United States and to stimulate demand within their own countries for domestic products and imports, such as American capital goods.[76]

Yet these measures are only short-term solutions to global problems, in Bergsten's view. Two additional steps are needed to put the world on the path to steady growth—a strategic trade policy (which we will consider in the next chapter) and international monetary reform. Although the world cannot and should not try to return to the fixed exchange rates of the Bretton Woods regime, it should not accept the exchange rate volatility and currency misalignments that have prevailed since the demise of the Bretton Woods system in 1971, says Bergsten.

In fact, many liberal economists believe that the world has been groping toward some form of compromise system since the 1970s, as the finance ministers and leaders of the capitalist world's largest economies have met with increasing frequency to correct currency misalignments and discuss other global economic issues. Through the Plaza Agreement of 1985 and the Louvre Accord of 1987, the central banks of the so-called G-5 countries (the United States, Japan, Germany, France, and the United Kingdom) agreed to intervene in the international capital markets, if necessary, to allow the exchange value of the dollar to fall steadily against other currencies.

These agreements have achieved their aims, claims Bergsten, but they have been ad hoc and thus have created no mechanism to solve the problem of currency misalignments. To do this, Bergsten advocates the adoption of "target zones," under which each of the major trading countries would agree on the exchange value of its currency and would keep it within 10 percent of this value (the target zone), through central bank purchases and sales of its own currency in world markets.[77]

Howard Wachtel's main concern is that central bankers' fiscal and monetary stabilization efforts are dwarfed by the speculative activities of the world's large corporations, which send billions of dollars hurtling back and forth around the globe, 24 hours a day, to earn the highest possible short-term returns. He calls for regulation of the eurocurrency markets, by requiring international banks to hold eurocurrency reserves, just like the reserves that the U.S. Fed requires of domestic banks.[78] In a similar vein, James Tobin advocates the imposition of an international exchange market tax of 1 percent, which, he claims, would not retard the flow of international merchandise trade, but would discourage the frenetic pace of speculative investment flows from one currency to another.[79]

Radical Views

Radical views of international cooperation are divided into two distinct positions, Marxist and progressive. Marxists hold a dim view of the outcomes of international economic cooperation.[80] The crises that characterize the capitalist economy cannot be papered over by international cooperative arrangements, because such arrangements cannot address the root causes of the crises. The current crisis symptoms—exchange rate instability, the dramatic growth of international financial speculation and the proliferation of eurodollars, and intensified international competition with its concomitant capital mobility and community economic dislocation—are caused by stagnation, or, more accurately, overproduction and falling profits—problems inherent in the capitalist market system.[81]

The past two decades have seen essentially conservative public policy responses to the problem—attempts to increase business profits by lowering wages through domestic austerity programs that bring high interest rates and high unemployment levels, fostering the shift of capital to low-wage areas, and providing direct subsidies to business through tax cuts, export subsidies, and the like. These policies have only exacerbated the crisis, say Marxists, as growth has lagged during the entire post-Bretton Woods period and poverty has increased throughout the world.

The liberal prescription for stimulating world growth through international cooperation, though well-intentioned, is naive and unlikely to succeed. As discussed above, the dramatic growth of the world economy in the quarter century after World War II occurred because of the fortuitous confluence of five factors that no longer are present—certainly not to a degree sufficient to stimulate a new world growth spurt—and no new factors are at hand.

In the absence of growth, cooperation among capitalist nations is a zero-sum game, in which some (especially Germany and Japan) must give up some of their trade surpluses for the United States to reduce its deficit. In the current circumstances, there are no points of leverage to induce meaningful and lasting cooperation. Hence the capitalist future promises more of the current public policies of attempting to increase profit rates at the expense of wages and workers' living standards.[82]

Progressives agree with much of the radical analysis just presented, but they propose measures that possibly could be enacted without wholesale change of the capitalist system, which they contend would nevertheless be more humane than the status quo.[83] These proposals are not unlike the liberal proposals described previously. To solve the problem of Third World debt, they advocate a program of debt write-downs that would put the costs of these bad loans where radicals believe they belong—on the banks' shareholders, not on U.S. taxpayers. They also call for more stringent regulation of U.S. banks that lend to Third World countries.[84]

The Center for Popular Economics analysts believe that the proliferation of eurodollars should be checked by an increase in the jurisdiction of the U.S. Federal Reserve Board, in cooperation with the European central banks. They also support Tobin's proposed tax on currency conversion to dampen speculation in the international currency markets.

The Center for Popular Economics also calls for a gradual end to the double role of the dollar as both the U.S. currency and the primary international currency. "National economic policy can be held hostage to the requirements of maintaining an international currency: the declining value of the dollar in late 1979 was the primary factor prompting the Fed's dramatic raising of interest rates," which plunged the U.S. into a deep recession.[85] Rather, the world should move toward creation of a new international currency that would be issued through a world monetary authority. Indeed, Keynes proposed just such an arrangement at the 1944 Bretton Woods Conference, but the United States rejected it.

Conservative Views

There is no single conservative position on the issue of international economic cooperation, but the views espoused by some economists, which are consistent with conservative philosophy generally, are skeptical of the practicality and desirability of formal cooperation on monetary policy and not at all inclined to favor any sort of fiscal policy coordination.

Milton Friedman opposed the fixed exchange rates of the Bretton Woods system as early as 1962, arguing that floating rates more accurately reflect real economic conditions and can respond more easily to changes in those conditions, such as improvements in product quality that might make a country's goods more desirable and thus raise demand for its currency.[86] Stanley Fischer claims that national fiscal and monetary policies do not affect other countries enough to warrant attempting the very difficult task of formal international coordination. The liberals' target zone exchange rate proposal, for instance, would, because of its very flexibility, prove to be unenforceable, yet anything less flexible would not find widespread approval.[87] As for proposals to gradually establish a world monetary authority, Friedman decries the fact that this:

> involves giving great and essentially discretionary powers to an international body independent of any political control by citizens of each member-country short of withdrawal from the agreement.... I regard the independence ... of a national central bank [such as the Federal Reserve] as highly objectionable on political grounds. The objection is vastly stronger to an independent world or tricountry bank.[88]

Similarly, the burgeoning supply of eurodollars and other eurocurrencies has provoked less concern from conservatives than it has from other economists. M. Stefan Mendelsohn argues that concerns about the soundness of the euromarket banks (which are not required to maintain reserve deposits) are overblown. In fact, eurocurrency banks are not free of all forms of supervision in the countries where they are most numerous, he claims. Contrary to those who believe that the eurocurrency market is a source of economic disruption that complicates domestic monetary management and aggravates exchange rate disturbances, Mendelsohn maintains that the euromarket is a channel, not a source, of instability.[89]

This is not to say that conservatives reject all forms of international economic cooperation. As discussed in the next chapter, conservatives strongly support international cooperative efforts to reduce tariffs and other barriers to trade. Martin Feldstein regards this as the appropriate way to solve the Third World debt problem:

> Looking ahead, the key role for official international cooperation in dealing with the debt problem should be maintaining open markets for the exports of the debtor countries. To service their debts while maintaining politically acceptable economic growth, the debtor countries must export. An increase in their exports will require a reorientation of domestic policies by the debtor nations, but it will only be possible if the creditor nations keep their markets open.[90]

In the area of international monetary and fiscal policy, conservatives support the informal coordination that has evolved since the demise of the Bretton Woods system, through the G-5 and G-7 meetings, as well as other international forums. The success of the G-5 countries in engineering the fall of the dollar in 1985, for example, is evidence that present arrangements afford both national flexibility and, when needed, international cooperation.[91]

Conclusion

Macroeconomic stabilization and growth policy, whether practiced at the national or international level, constitutes an important component of the public policy response to the challenges of the new global economy. Yet most economists believe it alone is too blunt an instrument to solve the nation's, let alone the world's, economic problems. Economists of all political persuasions believe that at least some targeted, microeconomic policies are also needed. Some have called for changes in U.S. trade policies; others call for the enactment of industrial policies and reform of the nation's education and training systems. We will consider these proposals, as well as numerous counterproposals, in the chapters that follow.

Notes

1. Although Keynes is credited with inspiring the modern practice of countercyclical demand-side fiscal stabilization policy, economist Joan Robinson claims that this is a misuse of Keynes's work. In any case, Alvin Hansen and Paul Samuelson deserve credit (or blame) for applying Keynes's insights to a theory of macroeconomic stabilization policy. See Hansen, Alvin: *The American Economy*. New York: McGraw-Hill, 1957, in the annotated bibliography in chapter 2.

2. See Roberts, Paul Craig: *The Supply-Side Revolution: An Insider's Account of Policymaking in Washington*. Cambridge, Mass.: Harvard University Press, 1984; Wanniski, Jude: *The Way the World Works*. New York: Simon and Schuster, 1978, chapter 6. See also Phillips, Kevin: *The Politics of Rich and Poor*. New York: Random House, 1990, especially chapter 4, pp. 108–110.

3. See Freeman, Roger A.: *The Wayward Welfare State*. Stanford, Calif.: Hoover Institution Press, 1981; also Brown, Michael K. (ed): *Remaking the Welfare State*. Philadelphia: Temple University Press, 1988, various chapters.

4. Phillips, *Rich and Poor*, chapter 4.

5. Friedman, Milton: *Capitalism and Freedom*. Chicago: University of Chicago Press, 1962, and Friedman, Milton and Rose Friedman: *Free to Choose: A Personal Statement*. New York: Harcourt Brace Jovanovich, 1980.

6. There are several ways to measure net foreign trade balances, each of which takes different factors into account and yields somewhat different results. Nevertheless, by all measures, the U.S. net foreign trade and investment position declined dramatically during the 1980s. See Krugman, Paul: *The Age of Diminished Expectations*. Cambridge, Mass.: MIT Press, 1990, chapters 8–10, and any macroeconomics text, such as Baumol, William J. and Alan S. Blinder: *Economics: Principles and Policy, Macroeconomics*. New York: Harcourt Brace Jovanovich, 1988.

7. See Phillips, *Rich and Poor*, p. 141. Some economists do not find the current level of foreign investment objectionable. Roberts, for example, an architect of the Reagan administration's economic policies, argues that "the charge that America is losing control of its destiny to foreign ownership is farfetched." See Roberts, Paul Craig: "Good News: Foreign Investment Is Not Bad," Scripps Howard News Service, 1989.

8. Supply-siders such as Arthur Laffer (in Wanniski, *Way the World Works*, chapter 6) and Roberts, "Good News," had claimed that the reduction in personal income tax rates would induce workers to work so many more hours that total income tax revenues would actually rise. As other economists pointed out, however, the average worker would have had to increase his or her weekly hours by 43 percent, from 40 to 57 hours, for the federal government to make up the loss in tax revenues from the reduced income tax rate. See Bluestone, Barry and Bennett Harrison: *The Deindustrialization of America*. New York: Basic Books, 1982, p. 199.

9. Mansfield, Edwin: *Economics: Principles, Problems, Decisions.* Sixth Edition. New York: W.W. Norton and Company, 1989, pp. 203–209.

10. For exhaustive discussions of the U.S. reliance upon foreign, especially Japanese capital, see Gilpin, Robert: *The Political Economy of International Relations.* Princeton: Princeton University Press, 1987, chapter 8; also Kuttner, Robert: *The End of Laissez-Faire.* New York: Alfred A. Knopf, 1991, chapter 5.

11. See Phillips, *Rich and Poor*, p. 141.

12. According to Benjamin Friedman, however, most of the budget cuts enacted from 1987 to 1990 were a "farce," *not* "genuine deficit reduction." To cut the 1988 budget, for example, "[a]sset sales were to contribute $5.8 billion, new user fees $1 billion, supposedly increased taxes $9 billion, better IRS enforcement of the current tax laws $1.6 billion, and reduced interest costs $1.2 billion. Supposed cuts in spending, even those that amounted to mere accounting changes, came to just $11.6 billion." See Friedman, Benjamin: *Day of Reckoning.* New York: Random House, 1988, pp. 278–279.

13. See the discussion of this issue in Magdoff, Harry and Paul M. Sweezy: *Stagnation and the Financial Explosion.* New York: Monthly Review Press, 1987, pp. 130–140.

14. Until the dramatic increase in foreign ownership of the debt, economists could say, with some justification, that the debt problem was less than imagined, because we owed the debt to ourselves. Even then, however, the debt constituted a problem from another perspective—the use of taxpayer dollars to pay back the money borrowed from wealthy Treasury bondholders constitutes a wealth transfer from the poor and middle class to the rich. See the discussion in Baumol and Blinder, *Economics.*

15. On this point, see Bergsten, C. Fred: *America in the World Economy: A Strategy for the 1990s.* Washington, D.C.: Institute for International Economics, 1988. Note that the economic development of Eastern Europe, especially the former East Germany, and the rebuilding of Kuwait in the aftermath of the Persian Gulf War, are attracting capital like magnets, pushing up interest rates and making it increasingly expensive for the United States to finance its deficits.

16. "The Peace Economy: How Defense Cuts Will Fuel America's Long-Term Prosperity." *Business Week.* December 11, 1989, p. 53.

17. "Back-to-Back Record Deficits Are Predicted." *Richmond Times Dispatch.* July 15, 1991.

18. By using up scarce capital, the bonds will also put upward pressure on interest rates. For discussion of the savings and loan crisis, see Krugman, *Diminished Expectations*, pp. 135–141; Phillips, *Rich and Poor*, pp. 91–98.

19. Shapiro, Isaac and Robert Greenstein: *Selective Prosperity: Increasing Income Disparities Since 1977.* Washington, D.C.: Center on Budget and Policy Priorities, July 1991. The authors quote the U.S. Census Bureau statement that, from 1979 to 1989, the growth in inequality was "about twice as large as the change between 1969 and 1979," p. x.

20. Ibid., p. vii.

21. Ibid., p. viii.

22. DeParle, Jason: "Urban Poverty Outlasts 'Cures.'" *Richmond Times Dispatch.* January 28, 1991, p. 2. Note that income distribution has been, and continues to be, far more unequal in the United States than in other industrialized nations. See Shapiro and Greenstein, *Selective Prosperity,* p. 22.

23. See the discussions of job and wage polarization in chapters 1 and 4, especially Bluestone, Barry and Bennett Harrison: *The Great U-Turn.* New York: Basic Books, 1988; also Shapiro and Greenstein, op. cit., pp. viii–ix.

24. Land, Phil S.J.: "Minimum Wage: A Global-Local Link." *Center Focus.* Issue 91. Washington, D.C.: Center of Concern, July 1989.

25. Shapiro and Greenstein, *Selective Prosperity,* p. x; see also Phillips, *Rich and Poor,* pp. 74–115.

26. Phillips, *Rich and Poor,* pp. 74–115.

27. Ibid., pp. 86–88. See also note 33, below.

28. Shapiro and Greenstein, *Selective Prosperity,* p. ix. Note that AFDC is funded jointly by federal and state governments.

29. Phillips, *Rich and Poor,* p. 251.

30. Shapiro and Greenstein, *Selective Prosperity,* p. 15.

31. Krugman, *Diminished Expectations,* pp. 66–67. Liberals claim that the decline of savings during the 1980s disproves the supply-siders' predictions that the sharp income tax cuts of the Economic Recovery Tax Act of 1981 would increase savings.

32. See, for example, the arguments of Bergsten, *World Economy,* as well as Barry Bosworth and Lawrence Summers, in Faux, Jeff (ed): *Seminar: Macroeconomic Policy.* Washington, D.C.: Economic Policy Institute, 1990.

33. In *Rich and Poor,* Kevin Phillips, a former advisor to the Republican party, argues that the expansion of the federal deficit did not run counter to the Reagan administration's interests, since it served the administration's conservative financier constituency well. According to Phillips, the Reagan administration's taxing and spending policies consistently benefited conservative Republican constituencies and harmed Democratic ones; thus following a long tradition in American politics of political-economic partisanship. Viewed in this light, one might conclude that supply-side economic policies did not fail because of some lapse in national political decision making, but because they were meant to succeed only in so far as they served important political (electoral) ends.

34. The gist of Barro's theory is that consumers can understand the long-term consequences of government fiscal policy for their own incomes. Hence, for example, if the government were to raise taxes in order to cover spending, taxpaying consumers would realize that the reduced deficit would result in lower taxes *later,* so, looking ahead, they would continue their current consumption levels, borrowing money, if necessary, to make up for the amount they would now have to spend on higher taxes. The overall result would be that national savings would not increase, thus thwarting the government's major reason for lowering the deficit! (See Krugman, *Diminished Expectations,* pp. 72–73.)

112   *The Macroeconomic Framework*

35. Capital gains are the increases in the value of capital—land, buildings, stocks, bonds—between the time an investor buys and sells the asset. The Economic Recovery Tax Act of 1981 lowered the capital gains tax rate below the normal income tax rate, on the rationale that the higher rate inhibited investment and economic growth. The Tax Reform Act of 1986 removed the special treatment for capital gains, partly in an attempt to trim the federal budget deficit. President Bush has continued to press for another reduction, arguing that it will spur private investment and economic growth.

36. Boskin has used the term "flexible freeze" to characterize his approach to the budget deficit. The idea is to freeze inflation-adjusted levels of government spending at current levels, but to allow the composition of the budget to change as needed. If total spending is kept at current levels while the economy grows at 2 to 3 percent per year, tax revenues will rise and gradually erase the deficit. (See Krugman, *Diminished Expectations*, chapter 6.) The Budget Deficit Reduction Compromise adopted by Congress and the Bush administration in October 1990 is similar to Boskin's flexible freeze approach.

37. Krugman, *Diminished Expectations*, chapter 6.

38. See Freeman, *Welfare State*; also Murray, Charles: *Losing Ground*. New York: Basic Books, 1984; Boaz, David: "Saving the Inner City," in Crane, Edward H. and David Boaz: *An American Vision: Policies for the '90s*. Washington, D.C.: The Cato Institute, 1989.

39. See Reischauer, Robert D.: "The Welfare Reform Legislation: Directions for the Future," in Cottingham, Phoebe H. and David T. Ellwood (eds): *Welfare Policy for the 1990s*. Cambridge, Mass.: Harvard University Press, 1989.

40. See the discussion and annotated bibliography in chapter 5, especially Perelman, Lewis J.: "The 'Acanemia' Deception: How the Myth That America 'Lags' in Education Spending Threatens to Undermine National Competitiveness." Hudson Institute Briefing Paper No. 120, May 1990. Indianapolis: Hudson Institute, 1990.

41. User fees are fees charged for the use of a service, such as a toll road. Conservatives generally prefer the expansion of user fees as an alternative to funding public services through taxes on property or income, because, like goods bought in the marketplace, only those who enjoy their use must pay for them. For a detailed discussion of user fees and their advantages and disadvantages, see Aronson, J. Richard and Eli Schwartz: *Management Policies in Local Government Finance*. Washington, D.C.: The International City Management Association, 1987.

42. See Bosworth, Barry and Lawrence Summers, in Faux, *Macroeconomic Policy*; also Bergsten, *America in the World Economy*. It is interesting to note that Lawrence Summers, whose macroeconomic policy views, in some respects, are closer to those of conservatives than liberals, was chief economic advisor to Democrat Michael Dukakis in his unsuccessful presidential bid of 1988. Upon Summers's advice, Dukakis, like the unsuccessful Walter Mondale before him, tried to take a page from the

traditionally conservative strategy book, advocating "fiscal responsibility" through budget cuts and, if necessary, tax increases. George Bush, like his predecessor Ronald Reagan, skirted the deficit issue and pounded home a simple, popular message—"no new taxes."

43. Conservatives and liberals alike tend to revise their recommendations for cutting the deficit or maintaining demand, depending upon the stage of the business cycle. During a recession, for example, few economists strenuously argue that the government should slash the budget deficit, as this would undoubtedly exacerbate the recession and probably the deficit as well. Nevertheless, regardless of the stage of the cycle, compared to each other, economists differ in their penchant for budget trimming or full employment, as discussed further below.

44. Eisner, Robert, in Faux, *Macroeconomic Policy*. Like Thurow and other liberal economists, Eisner advocates a national accounting process that distinguishes between federal spending on consumption (such as welfare and Social Security) and investment in the nation's future productivity through spending on roads, bridges, education, research and development, and so forth. Traditional Keynesian theory makes no such distinction, nor, at present, does the U.S. government. See Thurow, Lester: *The Zero-Sum Solution*. New York: Simon and Schuster, 1985.

45. See Davidson, Paul and Hyman Minsky, in Faux, *Macroeconomic Policy*; also Davidson, Greg and Paul Davidson: *Economics for a Civilized Society*. New York: W.W. Norton and Company, 1988.

46. Davidson and Davidson, *Civilized Society*; also Galbraith, James, in Faux, *Macroeconomic Policy*. Presidents Kennedy and Johnson attempted to implement voluntary inflation-cutting wage and price controls through moral suasion, with mixed results, at best. The Nixon administration instituted nonvoluntary wage-price controls in 1971, which, coupled with a lowering of interest rates by the Federal Reserve Board, stimulated rapid growth with very low inflation. When Nixon lifted the controls in 1973, however, inflation quickly climbed to double-digit levels. (See Davidson and Davidson, *Civilized Society*, chapter 7.)

47. Anderson, Arne: *A Progressive Answer to the Fiscal Deficit*. Washington, D.C.: Economic Policy Institute, 1989, p. 5; see also Phillips, *Rich and Poor*, chapter 4; see also note 44, above.

48. Anderson, *Fiscal Deficit*, pp. 6–7; see also Choate, Pat and Susan Walter: *America in Ruins: Beyond the Public Works Pork Barrel*. Washington, D.C.: The Council of State Planning Agencies, 1981; also Stein, Jay M. (ed): *Public Infrastructure Planning and Management*. Urban Affairs Annual Reviews, Vol. 33. Newbury Park: Sage Publications, 1989.

49. See Bosworth, Summers, and Eisner, in Faux, *Macroeconomic Policy*.

50. Anderson, *Fiscal Deficit*, pp. 13–27. Robert Kuttner (in Faux, *Macroeconomic Policy*, p. 46) believes that liberals can make a case for new programs that have broad popular appeal by targeting current expenditures that favor the rich to be cut in order to fund the new programs. "For

example, in the welfare reform bill [of 1988], Senator Bradley wanted $1 billion a year for day care and training. [To find the money] they proposed that anybody who makes over $200,000 can [no longer] deduct entertainment expenses."

51. Friedman, *Day of Reckoning*, pp. 289-296.

52. See Reischauer, "Welfare Reform"; also Osborne, David: *Laboratories of Democracy*. Boston: Harvard Business School Press, 1988, chapters 6 and 9.

53. In 1991, Senators Bentsen and Roth and Representatives Pickle and Thomas introduced legislation that would restore universal IRA deductibility. See the description and critique of this legislation in Shapiro and Greenstein, *Selective Prosperity*, p. 18.

54. See Magdoff and Sweezy, *Stagnation*, pp. 1-40.

55. Sweezy, Paul and Harry Magdoff: "A New Stage of Capitalism Ahead?" Review of the Month. *Monthly Review*. Vol. 41, No. 1, May 1989, pp. 1-15.

56. Magdoff and Sweezy, *Stagnation*, pp. 79-85. See the discussion in chapter 2 of radical views of the business cycle during different stages of capitalism's development.

57. Magdoff and Sweezy provide the following quote from the September 16, 1985 issue of *Business Week* to indicate that even nonradicals are concerned about the problem: "The volume of transactions has boomed far beyond anything needed to support the economy. Borrowing—politely called leverage—is getting out of hand. And futures enable people to play the market without owning a share of stock. The result: the system is tilting from investment to speculation" (*Stagnation*, pp. 141-142).

58. One obvious result of the deregulation of the finance industry is the savings and loan crisis of the late 1980s. As of 1991, the commercial banking industry is also in crisis.

59. Magdoff and Sweezy, *Stagnation*, p. 147.

60. See Carson, Robert: *Economic Issues Today: Alternative Approaches*. New York: St. Martin's Press, 1978, pp. 112-143; also Mandel, Ernest: *An Introduction to Marxist Economic Theory*. New York: Pathfinder Press, 1970.

61. Bluestone and Harrison: *Great U-Turn*, p. 92.

62. Center on Budget and Policy Priorities, in Bluestone and Harrison, *Great U-Turn*, p. 93.

63. See Piven, Frances Fox and Richard Cloward: *The New Class War: Reagan's Attack on the Welfare State and Its Consequences*. New York: Pantheon Books, 1982; also Phillips, *Rich and Poor*, chapter 4; and Anderson, *Fiscal Deficit*.

64. Magdoff and Sweezy, *Stagnation*, pp. 85-89.

65. Ibid., p. 78.

66. Center for Popular Economics: *Economic Report of the People: An Alternative to the Economic Report of the President*. Boston: South End Press, 1986, pp. 221-243.

67. Ibid., pp. 238-239.

68. See Ackerman, Frank: *Hazardous to Our Wealth: Economic Policies in the 1980s.* Boston: South End Press, 1984, p. 184; see also Bowles, Samuel, David M. Gordon, and Thomas E. Weisskopf: *Beyond the Waste Land: A Democratic Alternative to Economic Decline.* Garden City: Anchor Press/Doubleday, 1983.

69. Liberals such as Davidson and Davidson, *Civilized Society*, and Galbraith, in Faux, *Macroeconomic Policy*, also advocate the use of price controls, albeit without the yearly tripartite negotiation procedure. Such tripartite (business, labor, government) negotiating arrangements are commonplace in several Western European social democracies, including Germany and Sweden. (See Bowles, Samuel and Richard Edwards: *Understanding Capitalism.* New York: Harper and Row, 1985, chapter 6.)

70. Magdoff and Sweezy, *Stagnation*, p. 129; see also Wachtel, Howard M.: *The Money Mandarins: The Making of a Supranational Economic Order.* New York: Pantheon Books, 1986.

71. See the detailed discussion of the global effects of U.S. monetary and fiscal policies in Gilpin, *Political Economy*, chapter 8.

72. See Magdoff and Sweezy, *Stagnation*; also Wachtel, *Money Mandarins*.

73. Bergsten, *America in the World Economy*; Summers, and Bosworth, in Faux, *Macroeconomic Policy*.

74. Benjamin Friedman, *Day of Reckoning*, p. 297, provides a similar argument.

75. Davidson and Minsky in Faux, *Macroeconomic Policy*.

76. Bergsten, *America in the World Economy*. For a more elaborate statement of this idea, see Mead, Walter Russell: "American Economic Policy in the Antemillenial Era." *World Policy Journal.* Vol. 6, No. 3, Summer 1989; also Gilpin, *Political Economy*, chapter 8.

77. Bergsten, *America in the World Economy*. See also Thurow, *Zero-Sum Solution*, chapter 11; and Wachtel, *Money Mandarins*, chapter 9, for discussions of this idea.

78. Wachtel, *Money Mandarins*, chapter 9.

79. Tobin, James: "A Proposal for International Monetary Reform." In *Essays in Economics: Theory and Policy.* Cambridge: MIT Press, 1982, pp. 488–494; see also Gilpin, *Political Economy*, chapter 8.

80. See Magdoff and Sweezy, *Stagnation*; Sweezy and Magdoff, "New Stage of Capitalism"; also Sweezy and Magdoff: "International Cooperation—A Way Out?" Review of the Month. *Monthly Review.* Vol. 39, No. 6, November 1987, pp. 1–19; also Kolko, Joyce: *Restructuring the World Economy.* New York: Pantheon Books, 1988.

81. Magdoff and Sweezy, *Stagnation*; also Gilpin, *Political Economy*, especially chapters 9 and 10.

82. However, Marxists generally advocate economic cooperation among nations that have resolved the fundamental contradictions of capitalism, i.e., among socialist states.

83. Center for Popular Economics, *Economic Report of the People*; also Bluestone and Harrison, *Great U-Turn*.

84. Marxists Magdoff and Sweezy, in *Stagnation*, pp. 186–195, agree with the controls progressives would place upon banks, as well as the Third World debt write-down policy, but they argue that these actions do nothing to solve the larger problem of the exploitation and underdevelopment of the Third World that indirectly caused the debt problem.

85. Center for Popular Economics, *Economic Report of the People*, p. 230.

86. Friedman, *Capitalism and Freedom* and Friedman and Friedman, *Free to Choose*; also Friedman, Milton: "Monetary Policy: Tactics versus Strategy," in Dorn, James A. and Anna J. Schwartz (eds): *The Search for Stable Money*. Chicago: University of Chicago Press and the Cato Institute, 1987.

87. Fischer, Stanley: "International Macroeconomic Policy Coordination," in Feldstein, Martin (ed): *International Economic Cooperation*. Chicago: National Bureau of Economic Research, 1988, pp. 11–43.

88. Friedman, "Monetary Policy," p. 370. Friedman's criticism of the independence of the Federal Reserve Board sounds similar to that leveled by radicals. (See Center for Popular Economics, *Economic Report of the People*, 221–243.) The two propose very different solutions to the problem, however. Whereas Friedman, as a monetarist, would strip the Fed of its decision-making powers, radicals would make the Fed's governors democratically accountable. See also Friedman, *Capitalism and Freedom*.

89. Mendelsohn, M. Stefan: *Money on the Move: The Modern International Capital Market*. New York: McGraw-Hill Book Company, 1980.

90. Feldstein, *International Economic Cooperation*, p. 9.

91. Ibid.; and Fischer, "International Macroeconomic Policy Coordination."

Bibliography

Background

Baumol, William J. and Alan S. Blinder: *Economics: Principles and Policy, Macroeconomics*. New York: Harcourt Brace Jovanovich, 1988.
   A thorough introduction to macroeconomic principles and policies that is frequently updated.

Carson, Robert: *Economic Issues Today: Alternative Approaches*. New York: St. Martin's Press, 1978.
   A slightly dated, but nevertheless informative survey of 12 economic policy issues, including inflation, government regulation, unemployment, fiscal crisis, and multinational corporations. Carson presents liberal, conservative, and radical perspectives on each issue.

Gilpin, Robert: *The Political Economy of International Relations*. Princeton: Princeton University Press, 1987.
   See the annotated bibliography in chapter 1.

Keynes, John Maynard: *The General Theory of Employment, Interest and Money.* New York: Harcourt Brace Jovanovich, 1964 (1935).
See the annotated bibliography in chapter 2.

Krugman, Paul R.: *The Age of Diminished Expectations: U.S. Economic Policy in the 1990s.* Cambridge, Mass.: MIT Press, 1990.

An informative and insightful survey of contemporary economic policy issues, including the trade deficit, inflation, the budget deficit, free trade and protectionism, and Third World debt. While Krugman is clear about his own policy preferences (which, for the most part, fall somewhere on the centrist-liberal part of the spectrum), he presents his views in an evenhanded manner and provides brief, informative background explanations of each issue he tackles. Hence the book serves as a good background piece.

Mansfield, Edwin: *Economics: Principles, Problems, Decisions.* Sixth Edition. New York: W.W. Norton and Company, 1989.
See the annotated bibliography in chapter 1.

Phillips, Kevin: *The Politics of Rich and Poor: Wealth and the American Electorate in the Reagan Aftermath.* New York: Random House, 1990.

This is a detailed description and criticism of the economic policies of the Reagan administration and their impacts on the economy, set within the historical context of previous conservative periods, particularly the Harding-Coolidge-Hoover era of the 1920s.

Reischauer, Robert D.: "The Welfare Reform Legislation: Directions for the Future." In Cottingham, Phoebe H. and David T. Ellwood (eds): *Welfare Policy for the 1990s.* Cambridge, Mass.: Harvard University Press, 1989, pp. 10–40.

An analysis of the welfare reform debate and the consequences of alternative policies.

Spero, Joan Edelman: *The Politics of International Economic Relations,* Fourth Edition. New York: St. Martin's Press, 1990.

A comprehensive overview of international economic relations since World War II. Spero discusses the international monetary system, trade, and the development of the multinational corporation. She devotes special attention to political-economic relations between the developed and developing countries, as well as relations between capitalist and socialist countries.

Spulber, Nicholas: *Managing the American Economy from Roosevelt to Reagan.* Bloomington: Indiana University Press, 1989.

Spulber traces the evolution of macroeconomic policy from the Great Depression to the present. His account shows the interdependent relationship among economic theory, political context, and actual policies.

Conservative Views

Barro, Robert J.: "Reflections on the Current State of Macroeconomic Theory." Papers and proceedings of the ninety-sixth annual meeting of the

American Economic Association, December 1983. *American Economic Review.* Vol. 74, May 1984, p. 417.

Boaz, David: "Saving the Inner City." In Crane, Edward H. and David Boaz: *An American Vision: Policies for the '90s.* Washington, D.C.: The Cato Institute, 1989.

Evans, Michael K.: *The Truth about Supply-Side Economics.* New York: Basic Books, 1983.

    Evans sorts out what he considers to be the unjustifiable claims made for supply-side policies from their long-term benefits.

Federal Reserve Bank of Atlanta: *Supply-Side Economics in the 1980s: Conference Proceedings.* Westport: Quorum Books, 1982.

    Papers and discussions by prominent conservative economists on the tenets of supply-side theory, its relationship to other schools of thought, such as monetarism, and its application as national policy.

Feldstein, Martin (ed): Introduction to *International Economic Cooperation.* Chicago: National Bureau of Economic Research, 1988.

    This is a collection of timely essays and the responses of experts, as presented at a 1987 conference on macroeconomic policy, exchange rate coordination, trade policy, and Third World debt.

Fischer, Stanley: "International Macroeconomic Policy Coordination." In Feldstein, Martin: *International Economic Cooperation.* Chicago: National Bureau of Economic Research, 1988, pp. 11–43.

    Fischer examines the history of international cooperation since World War II and the extent to which various types of cooperation are warranted by the potential gains they might bring. He concludes that such potential gains are rather small and that "the best that each country can do for other countries is to keep its own economy in shape" (p. 39).

Freeman, Roger A.: *The Wayward Welfare State.* Stanford, Calif.: Hoover Institution Press, 1981.

    A critical analysis of the rise of wasteful social welfare expenditures at the state and federal levels, at the expense of defense and economic vitality. Freeman calls for the dismantling of the welfare state and argues that its excesses are bringing about its own demise.

Friedman, Milton: *Capitalism and Freedom.* Chicago: University of Chicago Press, 1962.

    See the annotated bibliography in chapter 2.

⸻: "Monetary Policy: Tactics versus Strategy." In Dorn, James A. and Anna J. Schwartz (eds): *The Search for Stable Money.* Chicago: University of Chicago Press and the Cato Institute, 1987.

    Friedman summarizes his major arguments for requiring the Federal Reserve to adhere to a predictable monetary growth rule and discusses the international monetary implications of such a policy.

Friedman, Milton and Rose Friedman: *Free to Choose: A Personal Statement.* New York: Harcourt Brace Jovanovich, 1980.

    See the annotated bibliography in chapter 2.

Mendelsohn, M. Stefan: *Money on the Move: The Modern International Capital Market.* New York: McGraw-Hill Book Company, 1980.

    This is an informative survey of the genesis, nature, and extent of the eurocurrency and eurobond markets to 1980.

Murray, Charles: *Losing Ground.* New York: Basic Books, 1984.

    Murray argues that the modern American welfare state, particularly the welfare system, perverts the Constitution's guarantee of the right to the pursuit of happiness into a government attempt to guarantee happiness through welfare. That such an attempt cannot succeed is evident in the loss of self-respect and responsibility that, Murray argues, characterizes the recipients of welfare. The system should be abolished or severely curtailed.

Niskanen, William A.: *Reaganomics: An Insider's Account of the Policies and the People.* New York: Oxford University Press, 1988.

    A member of President Reagan's Council of Economic Advisors from 1981 to 1985, Niskanen describes the rationale for the major economic policy decisions during the Reagan presidency and the processes by which they were taken, as well as some of the economic consequences of those decisions.

Roberts, Paul Craig: *The Supply-Side Revolution: An Insider's Account of Policymaking in Washington.* Cambridge, Mass.: Harvard University Press, 1984.

    Like Niskanen (above), Roberts experienced the national economic policymaking process, first as an aide to conservative Congressman Jack Kemp and then as a member of the Reagan administration. His book details both the political events leading to the ascendancy of supply-side economics in Congress and the White House, as well as the underlying economic rationale for the policies.

_____: "Good News: Foreign Investment Is Not Bad." Scripps Howard News Service, 1989.

Wanniski, Jude: *The Way the World Works.* New York: Simon and Schuster, 1978.

    With this book, Wanniski helped to popularize supply-side theory in the early 1980s. He includes an explanation of the now famous Laffer Curve—the theory behind the 1981 cut in personal income taxes.

Liberal Views

Anderson, Arne: *A Progressive Answer to the Fiscal Deficit.* Washington, D.C.: Economic Policy Institute, 1989.

    Anderson claims that the spending policies of the 1980s have created a deficit in public investment in human resource development, public infrastructure, and the environment. Defense cuts alone cannot finance the needed expenditures. Hence he describes, in some detail, changes in various tax rates that would improve progressivity (taxing the rich at a higher rate than the poor) and raise the necessary revenues.

Bergsten, C. Fred: *America in the World Economy: A Strategy for the 1990s.* Washington, D.C.: Institute for International Economics, 1988.

    Bergsten sets forth an action plan for the incoming presidential administration designed to reduce the U.S. trade deficit and inaugurate a new era of international economic growth. His plan includes proposals for ending the U.S. trade and budget deficits, developing an "activist" trade policy, and reducing Third World debt.

Brown, Michael K. (ed): *Remaking the Welfare State: Retrenchment and Social Policy in America and Europe.* Philadelphia: Temple University Press, 1988.

    A collection of 14 essays on the decline and restructuring of the modern welfare state and the political coalitions that supported it in the 1980s. Case material is drawn from the United States, Great Britain, Italy, France, and West Germany.

Davidson, Greg and Paul Davidson: *Economics for a Civilized Society.* New York: W.W. Norton and Company, 1988.

    See the annotated bibliography in chapter 2.

Faux, Jeff (ed), Barry Bosworth, Paul Davidson, Robert Eisner, James Galbraith, Robert Kuttner, Hyman Minsky, Lawrence Summers, and Edward Yardeni (contributors): *Seminar: Macroeconomic Policy.* Washington, D.C.: Economic Policy Institute, 1990.

    The transcript of an extensive roundtable discussion of appropriate macroeconomic policies by some of the nation's foremost liberal economists.

Friedman, Benjamin: *Day of Reckoning: The Consequences of American Economic Policy under Reagan and After.* New York: Random House, 1988.

    Friedman argues that by amassing huge federal budget deficits during the 1980s, we have broken our trust with future generations. We have, in effect, condemned them to pay for our current, profligate spending, argues Friedman. After more than a decade of trying to cut spending to match revenues, we must recognize that we are unable to cut spending further and choose the only responsible course of action—raising revenues, either through a progressive consumption tax or a modest increase in the progressive income tax.

Kuttner, Robert: *The End of Laissez-Faire: National Purpose and the Global Economy after the Cold War.* New York: Alfred A. Knopf, 1991.

    Kuttner traces the development of the global economy since World War II, arguing that the United States's role of global political, military, and economic hegemony is no longer viable. Likewise, the laissez-faire economics promoted by the United States in the international and domestic policy arenas cannot solve current economic problems. The United States must embrace a mixed, government-market system based upon power sharing with other nations.

Land, Phil S.J.: "Minimum Wage: A Global-Local Link." *Center Focus.* Issue 91. Washington, D.C.: Center of Concern, July 1989.

A brief analysis of the national debate over the minimum wage and an argument in favor of raising it.

Mead, Walter Russell: "The United States and the World Economy." *World Policy Journal*. Vol. 6, No. 1, Winter 1988–89.

———: "American Economic Policy in the Antemillenial Era." *World Policy Journal*. Vol. 6, No. 3, Summer 1989.

In these two articles, Mead traces the genesis and history of the Bretton Woods system and the international monetary system in the years since 1971. He calls for a rekindling of the liberal, Keynesian spirit that inspired the Bretton Woods institutions. He recommends the establishment of new, global monetary institutions and policies that would stimulate a new era of world growth and improvements in human welfare.

Osborne, David: *Laboratories of Democracy*. Boston: Harvard Business School Press, 1988.

See the annotated bibliography in chapter 6.

Shapiro, Isaac and Robert Greenstein: *Selective Prosperity: Increasing Income Disparities Since 1977*. Washington, D.C.: Center on Budget and Policy Priorities, July 1991.

An analysis of the "Green Book" report issued by the U.S. House Committee on Ways and Means in May 1991, particularly the report's statistical tables on income distribution prepared by the Congressional Budget Office.

Thurow, Lester: *The Zero-Sum Solution*. New York: Simon and Schuster, 1985.

See the annotated bibliography in chapter 4.

Tobin, James: "A Proposal for International Monetary Reform." In *Essays in Economics: Theory and Policy*. Cambridge, Mass.: MIT Press, 1982, pp. 488–94.

Tobin sets forth his proposal for a 1 percent currency exchange tax to dampen international currency speculation.

Wachtel, Howard M.: *The Money Mandarins: The Making of a Supranational Economic Order*. New York: Pantheon Books, 1986.

See the annotated bibliography in chapter 1.

Radical Views

Ackerman, Frank: *Hazardous to Our Wealth: Economic Policies in the 1980s*. Boston: South End Press, 1984.

Ackerman criticizes the economic policies of the Reagan administration as redistributing wealth and income from the poor to the rich and ultimately undermining the nation's economic welfare. He calls for a democratization of the economy, offering several proposals that bear directly upon macroeconomic policy and others that have broader scope.

Bluestone, Barry and Bennett Harrison: *The Deindustrialization of America: Plant Closings, Community Abandonment and the Dismantling of Basic Industry.* New York: Basic Books, 1982.
> See the annotated bibliography in chapter 4.

———: *The Great U-Turn: Corporate Restructuring and the Polarizing of America.* New York: Basic Books, 1988.
> See the annotated bibliography in chapter 4.

Bowles, Samuel, David M. Gordon, and Thomas E. Weisskopf: *Beyond the Waste Land: A Democratic Alternative to Economic Decline.* Garden City: Anchor Press/Doubleday, 1983.
> See the annotated bibliography in chapter 4.

Bowles, Samuel and Richard Edwards: *Understanding Capitalism: Competition, Command and Change in the U.S. Economy.* New York: Harper and Row, 1985.
> An introductory economics text, written from a left-liberal/radical perspective. The authors compare the Western European tripartite negotiation system for reducing inflation to American policies of economic contraction and unemployment.

Center for Popular Economics: *Economic Report of the People: An Alternative to the Economic Report of the President.* Boston: South End Press, 1986.
> The authors critique the economic policies of the Reagan administration in light of their effects on various segments of the population and argue that the policies undermine the long-term viability of the U.S. economy as a whole. They recommend a number of structural reforms in macroeconomic policy, international trade, and industrial regulation.

Kolko, Joyce: *Restructuring the World Economy.* New York: Pantheon Books, 1988.
> See the annotated bibliography in chapter 4.

Magdoff, Harry and Paul M. Sweezy: *Stagnation and the Financial Explosion.* New York: Monthly Review Press, 1987.
> This is a collection of 16 articles that appeared in the *Monthly Review* from 1982 to 1987. They constitute a compendium of Marxist views on U.S. macroeconomic policy and the Third World debt problem, within the framework of the development of the global economy.

Mandel, Ernest: *An Introduction to Marxist Economic Theory.* New York: Pathfinder Press, 1970.
> See the annotated bibliography in chapter 2.

Piven, Frances Fox and Richard Cloward: *The New Class War: Reagan's Attack on the Welfare State and Its Consequences.* New York: Pantheon Books, 1982.
> A political-economic analysis of the impacts of the first Reagan administration budget on poor people, and the implications for work and welfare.

Sweezy, Paul and Harry Magdoff: "International Cooperation—A Way Out?" Review of the Month. *Monthly Review.* Vol. 39, No. 6, November

1987, pp. 1–19 and "A New Stage of Capitalism Ahead?" Review of the Month. *Monthly Review.* Vol. 41, No. 1, May 1989, pp. 1–15.

The authors critique the liberal notion that new cooperative, international structures alone can create the conditions for a new era of world growth. Indeed, the most fundamental conditions for growth are not at hand. Under these zero-sum conditions, capitalist nations will find it impossible to establish lasting cooperative arrangements.

The "Peace Dividend"

Anderson, Marion, Greg Bischak, and Michael Oden: *Converting the American Economy: The Economic Effects of an Alternative Security Policy.* Lansing, Mich.: Employment Research Associates, 1991.

"The Peace Economy: How Defense Cuts Will Fuel America's Long-Term Prosperity." *Business Week.* December 11, 1989, pp. 50–55.

The U.S. Infrastructure Crisis

Choate, Pat and Susan Walter: *America in Ruins: Beyond the Public Works Pork Barrel.* Washington, D.C.: The Council of State Planning Agencies, 1981.

Stein, Jay M. (ed): *Public Infrastructure Planning and Management.* Urban Affairs Annual Reviews, Vol. 33. Newbury Park: Sage Publications, 1989.

A collection of essays discussing the nature and magnitude of the national infrastructure crisis, and state and local infrastructure planning and finance issues.

CHAPTER 4

Industrial and Trade Policies

Throughout the postwar period, an explicit goal of official U.S. economic policy has been to establish and maintain the conditions that permit the free market system to work, with a minimum of government intervention. In practice, this has meant pursuing domestic economic policies limited, with few exceptions, to macroeconomic stabilization measures.[1] In the international economic realm, the United States has focused on lowering barriers to trade among nations through the General Agreement on Tariffs and Trade (GATT). Both of these practices are now under attack. Advocates for industrial policy seek to involve the federal government in the domestic economy to an unprecedented extent. Proponents of strategic trade policies believe that the United States must abandon the GATT for outcomes-oriented, managed trade policies.

As explained in chapter 1, the establishment of the GATT in 1948 marked a dramatic change in international trade relations. In the 1930s, protective tariffs as high as 50 percent were common. The GATT established a forum in which countries would grant reciprocal concessions to reduce their tariffs.

> In its four decades of operation, the GATT has had many accomplishments. As a result of seven successive rounds of multilateral trade negotiations, average tariffs in industrial countries on industrial products have declined sharply, from over 40 percent in 1947 to about 5 percent today. World trade has expanded markedly, including a twentyfold increase in the volume of trade in manufactured goods. GATT's membership has quadrupled to cover 96 countries that account for over 85 percent of world trade.[2]

Yet by 1990, new developments in the international economy had undermined the ability of GATT to promote free trade. With the rise of postwar trade and foreign competition, first from Japan and Western Europe, and then from the newly industrializing countries (NICs), such as Taiwan, Korea, Brazil, India, Hong Kong, and Singapore, the United States began to experience the painful economic dislocations of plant closings.[3] By 1988, 70 percent of U.S. industrial output was estimated to be directly or indirectly subject to foreign competition.[4]

By and large, the new competitors had achieved their status through export-led growth strategies and protection of their home industries from foreign competition. As competition began to impinge upon the industrial bases of the United States and other developed countries, these nations also began to use, or to intensify, protective measures. But the new strategies are less transparent than tariffs.

While average tariffs on most goods have remained at all-time lows in most countries since the 1970s, nontariff measures (NTMs), which do not violate the letter of GATT agreements, have been used to restrict imports or promote exports. NTMs include discriminatory government procurement requirements, restrictive product licensing standards, and outright import quotas. Also, some nations claim that the internal product distribution system in Japan favors domestic goods over imports and thus constitutes a NTM.[5]

The United States also has been swept up in the protectionist wave. Faced with a ballooning trade deficit, and companies, workers, and communities suffering the ravages of foreign competition, the United States has employed numerous subsidies and restrictions to protect American firms. To assist its steel, auto, and semiconductor industries, for example, the United States imposed "voluntary" export restraints (VERs), under which foreign producers agree to export only a certain number of units to the United States.

In addition to these and a host of other import-restricting measures, virtually all countries have undertaken actions to stimulate exports of their products abroad. These actions range from the relatively benign provision of market information and advice to firms wishing to sell in foreign markets, to export loans, risk insurance, and direct government subsidization of production for export—a practice many consider to be "dumping" and which nations attempt to punish with antidumping duties.[6] The Japanese and European import restrictions and subsidies appear to be part of strategic industrial and trade policies, designed to help high-technology, knowledge-intensive companies capture and maintain dominant shares of world markets. While these policies do not violate GATT rules, they do undermine the purist notion of free trade on which the GATT system is largely based (see chapter 1).

The GATT also has been undermined by the rise of new industries, such as financial services and computer software, for which there are no GATT agreements. Indeed, the GATT now

> has jurisdiction over only 5-7 percent of global economic activity....
> Though it covers 80 percent of merchandise trade flows, the GATT's rules do not extend to agriculture, textiles and apparel, services, direct investment and other capital flows.[7]

The decline of GATT has been accompanied by a rise of other types of international trading agreements—bilateral agreements and regional agreements, such as the U.S.—Canada Free Trade Agreement and the European Common Market, which erase trade barriers among the signatories. More than one-third of world trade now occurs in such regional arrangements.[8] While these arrangements do not explicitly violate GATT rules, they may undermine the overall multilateral spirit of GATT and the free flow of trade throughout the world.

American conservatives deplore the move toward protectionism, both in the United States and abroad. They argue that the United States can solve its trade deficit through appropriate macroeconomic policies (as explained in chapter 3) and a strengthened, expanded GATT system. Liberals believe that the conservative approach is unrealistic, since all nations want to protect and develop certain industries in the interests of national economic security. Rather than attempt to abolish domestic industry subsidies and trade protections, they believe that we should make such policies more rational, explicit, and politically accountable. We also need a national industrial policy, say liberals, to facilitate the smooth transition of the economy from industries that are no longer competitive, to new industries employing high-skill, high-wage workers.

Radicals are split on this issue. Progressives support the notion of industrial policy and strategic trade policy but argue that the liberal versions are not sufficiently democratic. Moreover, liberals underestimate the role of powerful multinational corporations in creating the present global economic crisis. Marxists agree with much of the progressive analysis, but argue that the attempt to rationalize a system dominated by the powerful multinational corporations is ill-fated. Moreover, such efforts divert attention from the struggle of the working class against exploitation at the hands of the multinational corporations.

We now turn to a further explication of these views, beginning with the question of whether the United States should pursue an explicit industrial policy. Next, the debate over U.S. trade policy will be discussed.

Industrial Policy

Liberal Proposals

Since the early 1980s, liberals have maintained that if America is to survive as a first-rate power in the global economy, it must have an industrial policy. "Industrial policies," writes Thurow,

> are to a nation what strategic planning is to a firm. They outline the basic strategy the nation intends to follow in maximizing economic growth and meeting foreign competition.... Industrial policies are both an expression of and a vehicle for bringing about a strategic consensus among government, industry, and labor as to the basic directions in which the economy ought to be moving.[9]

As Chalmers Johnson sees it:

> Industrial policy is the complement, the third side of the economic triangle, to a government's monetary policies (money supply, attitude toward inflation, cost of capital, interest rates, exchange rates) and fiscal policies (government spending, public investment, tax burden).... It involves the specific recognition that all government measures—taxes, licenses, prohibitions, regulations—have a significant impact on the well-being or ill-health of whole sectors, industries, and enterprises in a market economy.[10]

More specifically, liberal industrial policy proposals generally call for most or all of the following: (1) Some form of national economic data gathering, analysis, and public goal-setting discussions (indicative planning); (2) a new public entity that would help to rationalize and restructure mature, noncompetitive industries and provide retraining and relocation assistance to workers; (3) a public investment bank to support new, innovative industries; (4) government matching grants for nonmilitary research and development; (5) public support for productivity-enhancing organizational innovation through labor-management cooperation; (6) procedures and agencies to coordinate and rationalize the plethora of current U.S. industry-related policies and to evaluate the consequences of all government policies and programs for U.S. international competitiveness.

To justify their calls for a national industrial policy and for these measures in particular, liberals point to a number of troubling economic trends. These include the persistent foreign trade deficit and the continuing decline of many of America's traditionally powerful manufacturing industries, including steel, semiconductors, textiles, machine tools, consumer electronics, automobiles, and computers.[11]

Although the trade deficit has several causes, liberals believe that sluggish American productivity growth during the past two decades is a primary cause and a sign of long-term, fundamental economic problems. Productivity, the value of output for every unit of labor input, is, in fact, a most important indicator of a country's wellbeing, since a nation can improve its standard of living only by increasing output with the same or a lesser amount of labor.[12]

"There is little doubt that America's dismal productivity performance during the 1970s and 1980s should be the chief concern of economic policymakers," writes Alan Blinder.

> From 1973 to 1988 output per worker-hour in all U.S. businesses grew at a paltry compound rate of 1.05 percent a year. That is barely more than a third of the growth rate we enjoyed during the halcyon 1947–73 period (2.96 percent a year) and, more important, only about half our long-term historic average. Had U.S. productivity grown at 2 percent since 1973 instead of 1.05 percent, standards of living in the United States would now be about 16 percent higher.[13]

During these years, the productivity of other industrialized countries generally grew by much faster rates. For example, from 1977 to 1982, productivity growth in the United States was 0.2 percent, while in West Germany it was 2.1 percent, in France, 3.0 percent, and in Japan, 3.4 percent.[14]

Productivity problems have many causes, some of which cannot be controlled by national economic policymakers. The entry of the baby boom generation and erstwhile homemakers into the labor force in the 1970s and early 1980s exceeded the increase in business investment in productivity-enhancing plant and equipment to such an extent that the output per labor hour ratio decreased.[15] Other causes of sluggish productivity growth are macroeconomic in nature. Both liberals and conservatives argue that American investment in plant and equipment is inadequate because American savings rates are low. This issue is discussed in chapter 3.[16]

A significant portion of the productivity slowdown, liberals argue, is due to microeconomic problems that an industrial policy could address. The United States invests less in civilian R and D than its major competitors. Indeed, most of the substantial capital invested in R and D is for military uses with little or no direct commercial application. Productivity also depends upon the skills of the workforce, and Americans are now less educated than the citizens of most of our industrial competitors, which indicates a need for greater investment in this area as well. The upshot is that in an increasingly competitive global economy, we are falling behind because we are not investing enough to compete effectively.[17]

Yet it is not simply more investment or higher education levels that liberals want, but investment in and education for high-value, high-wage production. To be successful in the future, American managers must adopt a different philosophy from the one that made them successful in the past. American dominance of the world economy from the 1920s to about 1970 rested upon its perfection of assembly line production processes that produced vast quantities of standardized goods at low prices for mass markets. Production costs were low on a per unit basis, because of the large volume of production and because of the production process itself, in which tasks were broken down and routinized so that low-wage, unskilled workers could perform them. But unionization and other factors increased the wages of American and European workers. As global transportation and communication costs then declined after World War II, American and European firms began to transfer production to countries with substantially lower wages.

In short, the wages of American, European, and now Japanese workers are too high, compared to those of workers in Third World countries, to make low-skill, mass production profitable in industrialized countries. The solution, say liberals, is not to reduce the wages of American workers, as this would reduce living standards and undo the progress of previous generations. Rather, American managers must change their philosophies and methods of production. They must strive to produce innovative, high-quality products at competitive prices by improving cooperation among product design and production units. They must stop resisting unions and seeking to control workers and instead should develop cooperative labor-management relations to improve company performance. Unions, for their part, must help to initiate and support more efficient production and distribution methods.

American companies must also invest in worker education and training and in flexible—as opposed to dedicated, or single-purpose—automation so that they can produce high-value goods and services and respond quickly to changes in market demand. They must learn to work more cooperatively with their parts and materials suppliers, so as to improve product quality and shorten delivery time. They must constantly monitor and learn from the competition as well as from their customers.[18]

In some cases, producing high-value products may require that companies move out of mature product lines where methods are standardized and price competition is stiff, into specialty goods, such as precision castings, specialty steel, and custom-designed office equipment, which require high-skilled labor. But companies in mature industries may also regain a competitive edge by finding market niches where they can compete worldwide.[19]

To date, claim liberals, most American managers have avoided making the tough decisions to reorient production away from the mass markets in which we no longer compete well. They have introduced piecemeal changes, such as the use of quality circles on the shopfloor to monitor and improve minor aspects of production and working conditions, but these systems often break down when management leaves the hierarchical mass-production system intact.[20] Rather than improve production, American corporate management has focused to a large extent on what Reich calls "paper entrepreneurialism"—short-term profit making through financial investments and speculation, at the expense of the long-term, hard work of production restructuring.[21]

The Europeans and Japanese have adopted public policies—industrial policies—to facilitate their transition out of low-wage, low-skill products and production processes, into high-wage, high-skill production. But the United States has adopted no such conscious adjustment policies. On the contrary, the American government's response to the changing global economics of production has been ad hoc, fragmented and inconsistent, and every bit as expensive for taxpayers as the coherent, strategically focused policies of our economic rivals.[22]

In place of a strategic industrial policy, the U.S. government has allowed itself to be pressured into protecting uncompetitive industries from foreign competition. Companies and unions in the steel, electronics, automobile, and other industries have sought and received protection through tariffs, quotas, and voluntary export restraint agreements that limit the amount of a product that foreign countries can export to the United States. Through other measures, such as antidumping provisions, they have imposed sanctions on countries whose companies sell their products at prices lower than the "fair market price" (in order to capture market share and drive U.S. companies out of the market). In addition, companies in industries such as steel, autos, shipbuilding, garment manufacturing, and air travel, suffering from competitive pressures, have sought and received a variety of government subsidies, special tax provisions, and subsidized loans and loan guarantees.

Liberals are more concerned, however, with the fact that these protections have generally escaped public scrutiny and that the federal government has granted them without requiring them to restructure or take other measures to become more competitive. Indeed, steel companies and others have used protection and subsidies as "breathing space" while they disinvested from their industries.[23] Europe and Japan use many of these same subsidies, but unlike U.S. subsidies, theirs are directed strategically to restructure uncompetitive industries and move labor and capital into growing, high-value production. If the United States is to compete effectively in the world economy, it must do likewise. It must, say the liberals, adopt an industrial policy.

> A rational industrial policy must accomplish two interrelated objectives. First, it must strive to integrate the full range of targeted government policies—procurement, research and development, trade, antitrust, tax credits, and subsidies—into a coherent strategy for encouraging the development of internationally competitive businesses. Second, it must seek to facilitate the movement of capital and labor into businesses that permit higher value added per employee. In these ways, industrial policy should complement the strategic decisions of U.S. firms.[24]

To accomplish these ends, liberals advocate a variety of measures, most of which can be grouped under the general headings that follow.

National Indicative Planning. Most liberal industrial policy proposals call for the creation of a federal agency (or new function within an existing agency) that would perform tasks similar to those of the Japanese Ministry of International Trade and Industry (MITI). Such an agency would monitor the changes taking place in technology and human needs that may alter the industrial structure and then attempt to clarify the problems that these changes will generate. Then, through periodic public discussions of these analyses by councils composed of representatives from industries, financial institutions, academia, labor, small business, consumers, and state and local governments, a vision of a desirable industrial structure would emerge. It would then be up to individual corporations to interpret or utilize such visions as they deemed appropriate. Indeed, the primary purpose of such exercises would not be to direct business activity, but to alleviate uncertainties inherent in the market economy, so that private firms could function more effectively.[25]

economy, so that private firms could function more effectively.²⁵ George Lodge's vision calls for an agency such as MITI to coordinate and subsidize the research and development activities of companies within an industry, to help achieve the technological advances and economies of scale necessary to compete on a global basis.²⁶

Restructuring and Adjustment Measures. These address the problems of mature ("sunset") industries that are no longer internationally competitive. The aim of such "triage" measures, as Thurow calls them, "is to rationalize what is, save what can be saved, transfer unneeded resources to the rest of the economy with less pain, and to remake an industry into a viable competitor."²⁷ To rationalize troubled companies, industrial policy advocates like Felix Rohatyn would reestablish the Reconstruction Finance Corporation (RFC), set up by President Hoover in 1931 to infuse capital into troubled companies. Rohatyn's RFC would be a quasi-public investment corporation that could make equity investments in or loans to firms, in exchange for explicit restructuring and austerity measures, including employment and wage cuts, retooling, and retraining of the workforce.²⁸

In addition to such generalized triage policies, Magaziner and Reich advocate that the federal government develop specific policies to address the problems of "key linkage industries," such as steel, autos, machine tools, semiconductors, and others that supply products to, or buy inputs from, and thereby support, the rest of the economy. Public investment is needed in these cases because the return on private investment in say, a steel plant, might not be sufficient to justify the risk. However, if one takes into account the returns to the private investor as well as the "spillover" benefits that accrue to other industries that rely on steel inputs—the "social rate of return"—then the investment is clearly worthwhile. Private investors do not take social returns into account, since they cannot receive them, and so they do not invest in such projects. Hence the government must stimulate private productivity-enhancing investments in these industries by subsidizing them.²⁹

In many cases, restructuring will be less practical than adjusting to new market realities by notifying workers and communities of impending plant shutdowns, retraining workers and helping them find jobs in other, competitive industries. Liberals advocate a variety of training arrangements to help workers make such transitions, including training vouchers that workers could use for on-the-job training provided by companies (see chapter 5). In addition, adjustment policies should help to finance new infrastructure for dis-

novative industries, through federal procurement policies and federal location incentives to firms.[30]

Stimulating Private Investment in Projects with Long-Term Benefits. Many projects in so-called sunrise or infant industries do not attract private investment capital because the returns to investors are too low in the short run or too uncertain. Yet these projects also generate social returns, or spillovers that do not accrue to the private investor but to the economy at large, especially over the long term. Without government involvement, the United States may miss the chance to develop important industries. Thurow's example of the development of the Japanese robot industry makes this point clearly:

> In 1981 Japan had 14,000 programmable robots while America had 4,000. How did the Japanese get such a head start? ... There is a fundamental problem for a firm wishing to produce robots. Initially, it is hard to sell enough robots to get the economies of scale that allow low per-unit costs. Potential buyers do not want to buy very many robots, because they are unsure as to how well they will work and how easily they can be maintained. They want to order a few to experiment, but they do not want to make massive investments. Enter the Japan Development Bank, a government investment bank, and MITI, the Ministry of Industry and Trade. They organized a government-financed leasing company that guaranteed the producers a rapidly growing market and leased the robots on short-term leases to firms that might use them. Since the firms knew that they could return the robots if they did not work as expected and did not have to make major investments with their own money, they were willing to accelerate the initiation of robots into the production process. If the robots had failed, the Japan Development Bank would have taken a loss. What it did was to essentially socialize risk and speed up a market process. As robots did work, the net result was a new industry that has essentially been conquered by the Japanese before we in America ever knew it got started.[31]

The United States should establish a public investment bank that could act as the Japan Development Bank did to develop the robotics industry.

Research and Development Funds. Japan and Germany spend substantially more of their GNPs on civilian research and development projects than does the United States. Thurow recommends that the United States establish an agency that would subsidize private R and D projects through 50 percent matching grants. Grant recipients would be chosen by a panel of peer reviewers of grant proposals, much as the National Science Foundation awards academic research grants currently.[32]

Promoting Organizational Innovation. While it is important that government stimulate the development of new technologies and sunrise industries, many students of industrial development realize that such leaps in technological development rarely happen within established firms and industries. But these firms can improve quality and productivity, lower costs, and sometimes develop new product variations through innovations in production processes and organizational structure.[33]

Government can support and promote such innovation in at least two ways; one is by providing technical assistance to management through "industrial extension agents" working through community colleges.[34] The government also can create a legal environment that is conducive to cooperative, communicative labor-management relations. Productivity-enhancing organizational innovation requires a high degree of trust between labor and management. Yet the legal basis of American labor-management relations, as codified in the National Labor Relations Act of 1935 and the Taft-Hartley Act of 1947 is one of adversarial relations, in which management acts and the union grieves. In order to ensure a legal context conducive to labor-management cooperation, some liberals call for a "national labor policy that encourages continuous innovation and strengthens cooperation in labor-management relations."[35]

Coordination and Accountability. Liberals maintain that current U.S. industrial policies are partially hidden or implicit, contradictory, and ad hoc. The federal government should "tailor and coordinate the broad range of government programs in order to ensure that they facilitate growth in competitive productivity."[36] For example, the federal government should evaluate the effects of its defense procurement programs on the future competitiveness of civilian production, especially the effect of defense production on the supply of skilled engineers for civilian work.[37] Currently, two-thirds of federal R and D spending supports defense work and 30 percent of all American scientists and engineers are employed in defense-related work.[38]

The government should make certain that its loan guarantees, insurance subsidies, tax credits, and other financial programs do not reduce the availability of capital elsewhere in the economy. In the area of trade regulation and antitrust policy, the government should treat businesses that need great economies of scale to compete in the global market differently from firms that only sell domestically.[39] As George Lodge points out, government policy seems to be moving in this general direction, albeit in a limited way.[40]

In addition to program coherence, a rational industrial policy also requires administrative coherence. The federal government must establish a single agency to house and disseminate the substantial data it already collects on industrial trends, but which is now spread among dozens of competing agencies. Most important, no one entity is presently accountable for all of the implicit and hidden industrial policies of the United States. Magaziner and Reich advocate that the president and Congress each establish an agency to evaluate the initial competitive consequences of all government policies and programs.[41]

Radical Proposals

Like liberals, many radicals point to sagging productivity growth as a symptom of economic decline. Yet their primary concern is not with America's international competitiveness, but with plant closings, job loss, and community economic hardship, as firms shift low-wage manufacturing jobs overseas. For radicals, these problems are outcomes of a process of global economic restructuring in which multinational corporations, especially American multinational corporations, have played and continue to play a prominent role. To speak of "foreign competition" when referring to products shipped into the United States by American-owned companies overseas is to miss the point.[42] Thus, by seeking simply to improve U.S. global competitiveness, liberals are addressing the symptoms, rather than the causes, of America's economic problems.

Even radicals, however, dispute the primary causes of economic dislocation. As discussed in chapter 3, Marxists such as Paul Sweezy and Harry Magdoff believe that the root of current problems is a long-term tendency of the capitalist economy to stagnate. Industrial policies are not only doomed to failure; under current conditions of labor weakness, they are likely to require much larger sacrifices from labor than from employers. As discussed below, however, progressives believe that a "radical industrial policy" could improve the economy and the relative power of labor.[43]

For progressives as well as Marxists, an understanding of global restructuring and dislocation begins with an analysis of the production process within the firm, specifically the labor-management relationship. Radicals ascribe sluggish productivity growth not just to lack of investment in plant and equipment, but more importantly, to labor-management conflict and to the costly ways that managers have sought to circumvent that conflict, rather than resolve it, so that they can maintain control over workers.

As noted in chapter 1, labor-management conflict has been a frequent by-product of modern industrial capitalism. To solve their conflicts with increasingly militant workers in the 1930s, managers agreed to a number of compromises with labor. Some of these compromises were codified in law between 1932 and 1947, and others, such as the understanding that wages would tend to rise with profits, were informal. This set of compromises constituted what became known as the "labor accord."

Yet the accord did not stop management from continuing its practices of cheapening labor by dividing production jobs into discrete, low-skill tasks (a process called de-skilling) and creating new supervisory and management positions to control a labor force that was increasingly alienated from this dehumanized production process. By the mid-1960s, many American industrial organizations had become top-heavy, rigid bureaucracies. Radicals point to this bureaucratization of production as a chief cause of the U.S. productivity slowdown.[44] Many liberals agree with this analysis.[45]

Dividing and controlling the labor force is one strategy that American management uses to solve its labor relations problems. Another is to run away from the problems entirely, or to threaten to do so. Long before Americans began to worry about foreign competition, American firms began moving de-skilled jobs to low-wage, nonunion, southern and rural parts of the United States. In recent decades, they have sought even lower wage locations in developing countries. Indeed, these American-owned companies became part of the "foreign competition" that has caused economic dislocation in many American communities.[46]

Hence the way to solve America's productivity problem, say radicals, is through economic policies that resolve the labor-management conflict that has caused the problem. For liberals, industrial policy means minimal government intervention in the economy to help the market work faster and more efficiently, with private businesses firmly in the driver's seat. Even labor-management cooperation and organizational innovation are to be brought about largely through the good sense of enlightened management. For radicals, the crux of the problem is that private businesses and investors are already making too many decisions that powerfully and adversely affect the lives of others. The key to healing the economy, in this view, is to democratize investment decisions and the day-to-day management of the economy. The progressive industrial policy proposals outlined below reflect this view. (Marxists, as noted above, are skeptical of any industrial policy in the absence of fundamental economic changes—particularly public ownership and control of firms in key sectors).[47]

National Planning. Like liberals, progressives believe that the primary purpose of national economic planning is to create a conducive context for economic development, rather than to direct the economy centrally, although they envision a far greater role for state and local governments in guiding economic activity than do liberals. Samuel Bowles, David Gordon, and Thomas Weisskopf suggest a form of national planning, in which a federal Public Planning Administration would use data from an expanded *Current Population Survey*, as well as broad public debate, to develop an annual inventory of unmet basic human needs (say, for certain types of housing, health care, schools, and so on). The Planning Administration would use this inventory to produce an annual "Report on Requirements for Balanced Production," which would

> estimate the annual production targets in goods-producing industries—steel and energy, computers and the like—as well as services—schools and restaurant meals, for example—which would be necessary to realize the major priorities established by the needs inventory. These production targets would be compared to recent trends in production output in the sectors involved. Where current output (or its growth) was falling far below production needs, the Public Planning Administration would provide investment subsidies to private firms, unions, community investment boards, and other democratically controlled investment institutions in order to encourage investment in sectors whose increased output seemed of the highest public priority.[48]

Public Investments. As discussed in chapter 3, some progressives would democratize not just the economic development planning process, but the investment process itself, through publicly controlled banks and insurance companies.[49] Such democratic investment institutions would allocate capital according to criteria that "combine attention to investment return and social need." This could be accomplished through "negotiated planning agreements" in which firms that agree to "stipulated union and community goals such as product development, provision of child-care facilities for employees, or guaranteed production levels over a relatively long planning horizon" would receive investment subsidies.[50]

Other progressives simply recommend public investment criteria similar to those of the liberals: sunrise industries, producing promising new products or using new technologies that need economies of scale to be profitable, should receive public assistance, but with more stringent requirements than liberals propose. Such requirements would include partial public ownership of such firms, as well as "planning agreements," through which private firms receiving subsidies comply with public policies on pricing, location, sourcing of materials, automation, affirmative action, health and safety, workplace democracy, and so on.[51]

Restructuring and Adjustment Measures. Progressives would assist declining sunset industries, but also with more stringent requirements than liberals propose. Before public actions can be taken, government agencies, community organizations, and unions must conduct research to determine why a plant is no longer profitable. If the plant is not profitable because its product or technology is obsolete, then public planning and intervention should determine if the plant can be converted to producing other products profitably. If not, then production should be phased out and the affected workers and communities should be assisted in making the transition to other work.[52]

If the plant is not really part of a sunset industry, but management is abandoning it to set up production elsewhere, public research should determine if this move is really necessary. If management is closing a plant simply to escape its unionized workforce, then restrictions are in order. Alternatively, public agencies should help workers and communities buy out and reestablish such plants. Likewise, worker buyouts should be considered when management is abandoning an economically viable product line for one that brings higher profits.[53]

During the 1980s, progressives called for national legislation to restrict plant closings or at least require that companies give advance notification to workers of plant shutdowns.[54] They won a modest victory with the passage of the national Worker Adjustment and Retraining Notification Act in 1988, which requires businesses with 100 or more employees to provide workers and local governments with written notification 60 days in advance of a plant closing or mass layoff.

What about corporate bailouts, such as the Chrysler and Lockheed cases of the 1980s? These are situations where large companies in competitive industries failed to keep pace with the competition and were about to fold, taking workers and communities with them. Barry Bluestone and Bennett Harrison argue that the public should only grant assistance if a number of stringent conditions are met, including

> public disclosure of company data to enable democratically constituted bodies to decide for themselves whether and to what extent assistance is really needed . . . [,] planning agreements with companies receiving bail-outs, specifying a *quid pro quo* with respect to increased democratic

management of production, restrictions on the subcontracting of components or supplies to non-union or foreign shops, the phasing in (and control over the use) of new technology, new plant location, and product pricing [and] a government equity position in the subsidized corporation to ensure that the public obtains some financial return on its investment in the business.[55]

Workplace Democracy. Like liberal industrial policy advocates, progressives argue that many of the solutions to our economic problems must come from within firms:

> Essentially, the role of workers and unions must be greatly expanded in literally every enterprise within the nation. This is ... a matter of cold, hard-headed economics. Corporate management alone does not hold the secret of how to produce high-quality, competitive products. It must increasingly rely on the entire range of employees within the firm to develop new techniques of production, judge the applicability and usefulness of new technology, assure quality control, and forge new labor-management relations that enhance productivity and equity within the firm.[56]

Unlike liberals, however, who ultimately rely upon management's good sense to develop more flexible, egalitarian workplaces with worker involvement in decision making, radicals believe that the organization of the workplace will not improve as long as management retains an overwhelming share of power. To promote a democratic workplace, progressives advocate several public initiatives, as follows.

A Public Commitment to Democratic Trade Unions. This commitment would be expressed through congressional repeal of the Taft-Hartley Act of 1947 and passage of the Labor Law Reform Act of 1978, which would ease the process of union organizing; the establishment of a Union Organizing Campaign Fund, to which taxpayers could donate up to two dollars of their annual income taxes; and a congressional amendment of the Landrum-Griffin Act to require rank-and-file membership ratification of all union contracts.[57]

A public commitment to workplace democracy would also require a Corporate Disclosure Act mandating full public disclosure of firm information on finances, taxes, stock ownership, employment, environmental impact, and health-and-safety conditions.[58] Most important, such information would be freely available to workers and their union representatives so that they could bargain with management on the basis of shared knowledge. Also,

Congress should amend the National Labor Relations Act to include a 'Bargaining Rights' clause which would sanction and legally protect workers' bargaining over job design, investment, and all other issues concerning the organization of production.[59]

Workers and unions should also seek "cooperative work agreements," say Bowles, Gordon, and Weisskopf, "as separately negotiated contracts with management, to transfer significant portions of decisionmaking and supervisory responsibility from corporate ranks back into the collective bargaining unit."[60] For their part, unions will have to change dramatically the way they do business, say Bluestone and Harrison. They will have to use new methods to organize workers in the service economy, they will have to be willing to negotiate with management over job classifications and work rules, and they will have to contribute in other ways to boosting productivity, while still playing their traditional role of obtaining as high a share of the profits as possible.[61]

Public Support for Worker-and Community-Owned Enterprises. Over the past twenty years, a number of worker-owned businesses have appeared, through worker buyouts of existing firms and as start-ups. Also, community development corporations, such as Mississippi's Delta Foundation and The East Los Angeles Community Union have established community- and worker-owned enterprises. Worker-owned firms are, by and large, more efficient than conventional, investor-owned companies, because of the greater worker commitment they are able to generate and a lack of supervision expenses.[62] Although federal and state legislation gradually has removed some of the legal and financial barriers to worker-owned companies, they remain suspect in the eyes of most financial institutions. Progressives argue that public development agencies and union pension funds should subsidize established community- and worker-owned enterprises through low-interest loans.[63]

Conservative Critiques

Conservative critiques generally focus on the following points: (1) the United States is not deindustrializing, its manufacturing base is not declining or stagnating, and hence, the major problem that industrial policy advocates seek to solve does not exist; (2) the successes of the Japanese economy are not due to its industrial policy; (3) industrial policy proposals fail on technical economic grounds, especially because public bureaucrats cannot accurately predict industrial "winners" and "losers," which is what restructuring and investment policies amount to; and (4) industrial policy would fail in practice because it would be captured by powerful political interests.

Let us begin with the first point. Deindustrialization is, as Schultze puts it, "a non-existent trend." In the 1970s, U.S. employment increased by 24 percent, whereas Japanese employment increased by only 9 percent and West Germany's employment declined. Between 1965 and 1980 the number of U.S. manufacturing jobs remained at about 20 million, while industrial production grew by 24.5 percent from 1975 to 1980, indicating improvements in manufacturing productivity. Of course, the *rate* of growth of U.S. productivity fell in the 1970s, but every country's productivity growth rate fell then, says Schultze. Moreover, that productivity decline was not caused by a shift in production from high productivity manufacturing industries to low productivity service industries.[64]

Although the recent increase in foreign competition is indisputable, its harmful effects are less than commonly believed. U.S. exports exceeded imports in the 1970s, partly because of an undervalued dollar, while the reverse was the case (at least during the early and mid-1980s), because of an overvalued dollar.[65] This is not to deny job losses in certain industries at the hands of foreign competition. But the tremendous growth in total U.S. employment over the past two decades more than offsets these losses.[66] As the conservative economist Joseph Schumpeter observed, any healthy economy experiences both job gains and losses, as new industries are created and old ones are destroyed.[67]

Conservatives also maintain that the much vaunted economies of Western Europe (with the exceptions of Sweden and Switzerland) have not outperformed the U.S. economy.[68] While the Japanese economy has, in many respects, performed better than the U.S. economy, little of this superior performance can be attributed to Japan's industrial policy. Rather, the major causes of the Japanese postwar economic miracle are the following:

> First, over the past two decades, the Japanese saved and invested some 30 to 35 percent of their GNP, compared to 17 to 20 percent in the United States. Second, with an industrial plant technologically far behind those of the United States and Europe, Japanese business firms were able to put the huge savings to work at moderate risk and with good returns by upgrading their capital stock with known technologies. Countries that were much nearer to the technological frontier, like the United States, had to depend more heavily for their economic growth on the gradual advance of technical knowledge. Third, the Japanese appear to have developed a unique set of cooperative labor-management relationships that promote high-quality work and rapid productivity growth.[69]

To be sure, Japanese policy in the postwar period encouraged rapid growth through exports and protectionism, but "the major decisions about where funds would be invested were made by Japanese business leaders, not by MITI."[70] MITI (the Ministry of International Trade and Industry) has successfully influenced industrial restructuring and investment in some cases (such as semiconductors), but such restructuring might have taken place without MITI. Moreover, MITI's attempts to restructure the auto industry and develop a commercial aircraft industry were soundly rejected by the private sector.[71]

Another flaw in the liberal and radical industrial policy proposals and indeed, in all schemes to regulate economic activity through government planning, concerns the "knowledge problem." The gist of the knowledge problem is that it is impossible for government bureaucrats to allocate resources rationally among firms, or to determine which industries to subsidize and which not to subsidize (called "picking winners and losers"), because it is impossible to collect and process all of the information necessary to make such determinations. The beauty of the market is that it transmits such information from one economic agent to another automatically, via the price system. Each individual business person knows her own production capabilities better than anyone else and is better equipped than any government bureaucrat to make decisions about new technology or other investments, as market prices change.

Some economists believe that this problem can be solved with the aid of computer models, which can store and manipulate tremendous amounts of data. Yet, even if it were possible to collect and organize consumption and production data from every individual in the country, the knowledge problem would still remain unsolved, conservatives maintain. This is because some of the most valuable economic knowledge individuals have is tacit, personal, unarticulated, and unarticulatable knowledge. It is embedded in their various skills and specialities, and generated by their contention with one another in the competitive marketplace.[72]

In other words, only when a firm must operate in an environment characterized by shifting resource constraints and competition for profits and economic survival, say conservatives, will the firm be moved to utilize its tacit knowledge to innovate—to create new, better, or less costly products and production processes. In a market economy based on the private ownership of property, every firm is stimulated to generate and utilize its tacit knowledge, and the combined "social intelligence" of these firms is greater and produces a much better result than any political decision-making process could.

To adopt national industrial policies that entail government intervention in the marketplace is to distort the market and thus seriously diminish the creative capacity of firms.[73]

While it may be impossible to pick winners from among the candidates for industrial growth, is it possible to stabilize and reconstruct mature, troubled industries, or at least to ease the transition out of these industries for workers and communities? On the first question, conservatives all seem to agree—no. A Reconstruction Finance Corporation or industrial restructuring board would be prone to the same political pressures that conservatives claim brought disgrace to the original RFC. Even if it somehow managed to avoid corruption, a RFC would, in effect, siphon investment capital away from competitive industries to uncompetitive ones:

> Many of the companies that would seek government aid would be doing so because of the noncompetitive wage demands of their workers. For example, the steel industry, a likely candidate for RFC assistance, saw the relative wages of steel workers rise during most years of the 1970s while their productivity, on average, fell or didn't rise at all. As a consequence, the effect of RFC loans in such cases would often be to redirect investment funds from industries whose wages were competitive and generally lower to industries whose wages were noncompetitive and generally higher. The result would tend to be a reduction in total jobs: employers in high-wage industries would not be able to add as many jobs to their payrolls with RFC subsidies as low-wage industries could have added with the money they had to pay in taxes to finance those subsidies.[74]

Conservatives disagree on policies to help ease workers out of troubled industries. Schultze argues that government should ease transitions for workers suffering economic dislocation, by offering reasonable unemployment compensation, relocation assistance, and generous training opportunities.[75] Richard McKenzie, however, believes that such programs are unnecessary and unfair burdens on other workers. In effect, these programs shift the responsibility and cost for maintaining competitive skills from individuals, where it belongs, to the government, where it does not belong. Without government training subsidies, many workers would train themselves, or their firms would train them. Certainly, the higher wages paid to manufacturing workers are adequate compensation for the risk of job loss and the cost of retraining.[76]

A final point in the conservative critique of industrial policy concerns its political feasibility. Schultze maintains that democracies in general are not very good at making "critical choices among particular firms, muncipalities, or regions, determining cold-bloodedly which shall prosper and which shall not."[77] The American political system, with its tradition of states' rights and regional interests is especially unsuited for making any decisions of this sort on a national level.

> Rather, we can expect a combination of patterns to emerge: Some assistance would be made available, on a formula basis, to all industries that were in trouble; the wheels with the loudest squeaks might get a bit of extra financial grease; and protectionist interests would have a new and highly vulnerable pressure point to exploit. In the process, resources would be misallocated, incentives for industrial efficiency reduced, and competitive forces blunted.[78]

Schultze also criticizes what he regards as the "false allure of coordination" of existing industrial policies, through the rationalization plans offered by industrial policy advocates. Even assuming the correctness of the industrial policy advocates' assertions that U.S. policies are currently contradictory and illogical, "it is curious logic to cite examples of how the American industrial structure has been distorted by political pressures—in support of an argument for entrusting even more economic decisions to the same political system."[79]

Moreover, providing special assistance to failing firms such as Chrysler, Lockheed, and Continental Illinois Bank on an ad hoc basis is precisely the right approach, in Schultze's view. "Should this process of decision by exception be supplanted by an ongoing authority to initiate bailouts, the results would almost surely be a politically vulnerable fund, available to help avoid or delay politically sensitive plant closings."[80] In short, market mechanisms, despite their problems, are far more likely to bring prosperity and growth than political processes that liberal and radical industrial policy advocates would introduce into the economy.[81]

The Policy Record

The United States has not adopted industrial policy in any form similar to those recommended by liberal and progressive advocates. This is due in part, perhaps, to the fact that critics of industrial policy—first Ronald Reagan and now George Bush—have occupied the White House for three straight terms. Various public opinion polls have shown that Americans favor some aspects of industrial policy, such as labor-management cooperation and worker adjustment assistance, but oppose others, such as national indicative planning.[82]

Yet Congress has taken certain initiatives that have features of an industrial policy. For example, congressional passage in 1984 of the National Cooperative Research Act made it possible for companies in the same industry to form research and development consortia, without fear of prosecution under U.S. antitrust laws. The United States took a further step in the direction of industrial policy in 1988, when a group of 14 leading American microelectronics firms created a R and D consortium called Sematech. The stated purpose of this consortium is to develop the manufacturing knowledge required to regain world leadership in semiconductors. Unlike other consortia legalized under the 1984 Act, Sematech is cofunded by the U.S. government and coordinated by the Defense Advanced Research Projects Agency (DARPA). DARPA's role is thus similar to Japan's MITI, which coordinates research and development efforts of large firms in key industries to achieve economies of scale.[83]

Since the late 1980s, industrial policy advocates have pressed their case in different forms. As we will discuss shortly, the managed trade policies advocated by liberals are ultimately dependent upon the existence of some form of industrial policy. Also, proposals for specific sector or industry policies, such as a consumer electronics industry policy, a semiconductor industry policy, or an auto policy, all draw upon the basic liberal industrial policy concept of strategic business-government cooperation to achieve and maintain globally competitive industries.[84]

Another side of industrial policy—company restructuring and worker adjustment assistance—is now appearing in new guise as well, in calls for national economic conversion planning. With the end of the Cold War, the federal government has begun to reduce the defense budget by 5 to 6 percent per year. These cuts are causing base closings and factory shutdowns across the country. Thus far, the federal government has not undertaken any significant effort to smooth the transition from defense employment to the production of civilian goods and services, but states and localities have been forced to do so. As defense cuts continue, pressure for more national adjustment policies is growing as well.[85]

Trade Policy

Liberal and Progressive Views

At present, the main thrust of official U.S. trade policy is to strengthen and expand the multilateral GATT trading rule system and to eschew any form of protectionism. This has been official American trade policy since World War II, and it has been a pillar in the neoclassical (conservative and moderate) economic edifice since the nineteenth century, as it is rooted in the "comparative advantage" trade theory of David Ricardo. Ricardian trade theory holds that total world production is maximized if each nation specializes in producing the goods and services that it can produce most efficiently and trades for everything else it needs. Activist trade policy and industrial policy, indeed government intervention of almost any sort, has no place in such a free trade regime. Free trade logic holds that a government that subsidizes production for export is simply bestowing a gift upon consumers in other countries.

Liberals believe that the goal of completely free world trade is unrealistic, as well as unwise, since even Ricardo did not claim that trade would improve everyone's lot *equally*. American attempts to force other countries, such as Japan, Korea, France, and Germany, to open their markets or stop subsidizing their producers are doomed to failure, since they employ such practices as part of their strategic industrial and trade policies. These policies are designed to help companies headquartered in their countries establish dominant positions in target world markets, as well as to maintain the viability of certain domestic industries and sectors (such as agriculture) that these countries regard as vital to their economic security.[86] Because we do not pursue such strategic policies, say liberals, our industries, our communities, and our economy in general, are captives of the industrial and trade policies of more aggressive nations.

This is not to say that the United States always practices the free trade principles it preaches. But because we remain wedded to the unattainable ideals of free trade on the basis of natural comparative advantages with no government intervention, we fail to address competitiveness problems in key industries until foreign producers have done irreparable damage to American companies' market shares. Then we strike out with unenlightened, highly protectionist policies that expose us as free trade hypocrites.[87]

For example, after years of foreign import penetration in the American auto market, the U.S. government finally caved in to calls for protection by American auto companies and workers, establishing voluntary export restraints (VERs) that limit the number of autos Japan may export to the United States. Because of the strong American demand for Japanese autos, the Japanese were able to shift their exports to high-priced cars, thus increasing their profits at American expense. Likewise in the steel industry, the U.S. government stood by as other countries expanded their production capacity with modern technology and then undersold U.S. producers in the American market with higher quality steel. Hounded by steelmaker claims that foreign producers were dumping in the American market, the Reagan administration finally acted—again by establishing quotas (VERs) on foreign steel.[88] Yet more reasonable U.S. policies, such as the "Super 301" provision of the 1988 Omnibus Trade and Competitiveness Act, are branded by conservative critics as protectionist. Super 301 authorizes the president to initiate actions against countries that maintain large trade surpluses with the United States, the ultimate sanction being closure of the American market to those countries.

In short, U.S. trade policy, claim the liberals, suffers from a self-defeating schizophrenia. In the name of free trade, it eschews strategic trade and industrial policies, but for reasons of pragmatism, it finds itself practicing poorly conceived protectionist policies. The U.S. attitude is all the more remarkable, since neoclassical trade theory itself recently has moved quite a distance from Ricardo's views. Seeking to understand the origins of national comparative advantage, Paul Krugman and others have discovered that national policies and historical accidents can shape a country's comparative trade advantages. Rather than a "natural" trading order based upon relative endowments of land and minerals, climate, and so forth, the international division of labor is essentially arbitrary.[89] Hence liberals conclude that government strategies can shape the international distribution of production advantages and world market domination for generations to come.[90]

This is not to say that specialization and trade, and even global competition, are not beneficial. They are simply inadequate bases for national policy. What is needed is an explicit compromise between the ideal of free trade on the one hand, and the need for national economic security and stability on the other. We can achieve such a compromise through "managed trade" arrangements in which we establish explicit, sector-specific agreements with our major trading partners in the most fiercely contested markets.

A key difference between a managed trade system and the current official system of complete reliance upon the GATT, is that the latter specifies rules for behavior, but is silent on the outcomes of trade. Managed trade specifies the outcomes of trade but is silent on the means that nations and companies use to achieve those outcomes. Liberals claim that a managed trade system would make irrelevant the proliferating nontariff measures (NTMs) that undermine GATT rules, such as product licensing restrictions, antidumping laws, and discriminatory procurement policies.

As an example of a viable managed trade system, Robert Kuttner cites the Multi-Fibre Arrangement (MFA), which regulates trade in natural fibers and apparel by limiting the rate of growth of foreign imports and bargaining among the major trading partners over the shares of that increase. This "flexible protection" arrangement, as Kuttner calls it, was first imposed on the new, low-cost apparel exporters by the United States and other established producers in the 1950s, and it has been extended at regular intervals since then.[91]

The MFA has allowed foreign penetration into the U.S. market to grow by as much as 17 percent annually during the 1980s. At the same time, it has afforded the established textile and apparel producers in the United States and Europe enough stability and predictability of market share that they have invested in state-of-the-art productivity-enhancing machinery. Indeed, Kuttner claims that productivity gains in textiles were the second greatest of any U.S. industry, except for microelectronics:

> Domestic producers responded by automating because the MFA regime struck a good balance between providing a partially protected market (which made it rational to invest) and allowing some import penetration (which maintained competitive pressure to invest).[92]

Laura D'Andrea Tyson argues that managed trade policies, like industrial policies, are particularly important for high-technology industries, since the products and production methods developed there have spillover benefits to other sectors of the economy.[93] Because the high-tech industries are thus organically linked, losing the ability to compete in one industry can result in a domino-effect loss of one high-tech industry after another. Tyson's high-tech managed trade policy has three major components. First, the United States should initiate industry-by-industry negotiations among the world's major high-tech producers to establish international standards for company and government behavior in areas such as antitrust policy.

Second, Tyson reasons that since countries are not about to stop using antidumping laws to protect their domestic industries, the United States should push for more precise and uniform international antidumping procedures and standards to assess dumping penalties. Third, like Kuttner, Tyson advocates the negotiation of agreements that specify numerical goals for imports of American products into foreign markets, such as Japan, where access is now encumbered by various structural barriers.[94]

Progressive writers also advocate managed trade arrangements, albeit within the context of progressive industrial policy proposals seeking to check and monitor corporate power to a greater extent than liberals generally envision.[95]

In addition to the explicit management of international trade in goods and services, liberals and progressives call for the systematic monitoring and regulation of international capital mobility, including foreign direct investment in U.S. plants. During the 1980s, the rise of protectionism in the United States contributed to an increase in foreign direct investment in American firms and the opening of foreign-owned production facilities, such as auto assembly plants.[96]

Norman Glickman and Douglas Woodward contend that U.S. policies toward foreign multinational corporations operating in the United States are as fragmented and incoherent as other aspects of our trade and industry policies. As a result, American communities and domestically owned businesses are vulnerable to foreign company practices that may not be in our best interests. Unlike other industrialized nations, the United States does not monitor foreign investment very carefully, and it applies no systematic set of regulations to foreign investments. Other countries watch foreign companies closely and subject them to "performance requirements," such as minimum numbers of domestic workers hired and minimum notification periods for plant closings. The United States should establish an agency to monitor foreign investments and ensure that they do not undermine critical domestically owned companies, Glickman and Woodward maintain. We should be especially vigilant of proliferating joint ventures between foreign and American-owned companies, both in the United States and abroad, as they may further concentrate economic power among the world's few huge multinational corporations, undermining the security and welfare of communities and nations. We must also establish and enforce performance requirements on foreign-owned businesses, including a 120-day minimum notification period for plant closings. Moreover, the federal government must outlaw the rampant state and local practice of competing for foreign companies by giving extremely generous location subsidies, as these deplete state and local treasuries and, on balance, may not help state and local economies.[97]

Yet in an era of increasingly mobile capital and ever larger multinational corporations, some progressives and liberals believe that national controls on multinational corporations are no longer sufficient to ensure worker and community welfare. Bennett Harrison calls for the development of international labor and environmental standards to regulate multinational corporate practices, and Walter Russell Mead advocates the establishment of an International Trade Organization that would monitor labor laws, environmental sensitivity, the use of export subsidies, and related policies in every country. Nations that violated international standards would be punished through withdrawal of market access, punitive "sin taxes," and other sanctions.[98]

Marxist Views

Marxists have long maintained that the theory of comparative advantage as articulated by Ricardo and subsequent neoclassical economists is fatally flawed. They have argued, as does the new thinking in mainstream economics, that comparative advantage is determined, in part, through accidents of history and conscious government policy. Sweezy and Magdoff, for example, describe the distinctly political roots of Ricardo's own famous comparative advantage example, in which he claims that all are better off if Portugal specializes in the production of wine, and Britain, in textiles.[99] Yet unlike liberals and even progressives, Marxists do not subscribe to managed trade or other schemes to promote economic cooperation among nations and multinational corporations under the current economic system. Their position is that efforts to rationalize the fierce competition among the world's behemoth corporations are doomed to failure.

Early in the century, when revolution seemed close at hand, Marxists greeted the growth of large corporations and their struggle for world domination with some optimism, as they believed the capitalist system would soon crack under the weight of the tremendous crises it generated.[100] Contemporary Marxists are less sanguine that the "irreversible crisis" is about to culminate in a breakdown of the system, but they are nonetheless skeptical of liberal attempts to secure international cooperation under capitalism.[101]

In fact, Marxists maintain that the liberals' focus on international stability misses a crucial point—capitalists wage their struggle for global domination on the backs of the working class. Everywhere, wages, working conditions, and real living standards are falling as capitalists attempt to squeeze profits from workers by constantly shifting or threatening to shift production to lower-wage areas. This is leading governments to deplete their treasuries of funds for education, housing, and health care, so as to bribe firms to locate or remain in their jurisdictions, or simply to enable them to compete with other companies receiving government subsidies.

Under a system of public control of capital, cooperation through managed trade might be an appropriate way to achieve the gains of international trade without harming the participants.[102] Under the present system of private monopoly capital ownership and control, however, managed trade policies at best can temporarily insulate some workers from the ravages of international capital mobility. We would be better advised to focus our energies on the struggle between capital and labor, rather than the struggles between nations in the service of monopoly capital.[103]

Conservative Views

Conservatives criticize both the current drift toward global protectionism and the liberal prescription for managed trade. They assert that protectionism and activist national trade policies cannot solve the problem that most Americans believe is the raison d'etre for trade policies—the huge U.S. foreign trade deficit. This is a macroeconomic policy problem, not a microeconomic trade problem.

As discussed in chapter 3, trade balances are largely the result of countries' relative savings and investment rates. Since U.S. savings are not sufficient to finance the high levels of American consumption, government expenditures and business investment, we borrow funds from foreign investors, such as the Japanese. These investors are attracted by the relatively high U.S. interest rates—a consequence of the Federal Reserve's inflation-fighting policy and the strong demand by the U.S. government and business for capital. In Japan, on the other hand, relatively high levels of saving, and lower government and consumer spending, tend to depress interest rates, driving excess investment capital abroad, to the United States. The result, however, is a high dollar value that depresses foreign demand for U.S. goods. Only a change in U.S. savings and interest rates relative to other countries could change the overall trade balance, say conservatives.[104]

Conservatives and liberals agree, however, that to the extent that U.S. trade policy can induce other countries to increase their demand for American goods and services, it can improve the terms of trade—the amount of U.S. exports needed to buy, say, Japanese imports. Other things being equal, an improvement in America's terms of trade would improve American living standards, since it would enable us to buy more foreign goods with fewer of our own. At issue is the appropriate strategy for improving the terms of trade.

The conservative position is that the pursuit of free trade through the multilateral rules of the GATT system is still the best trade policy.[105] Free trade, argues Anne Krueger, increases the number of competitors in the market, thus lowering prices for everyone—the intermediate users of freely traded production inputs, and the consumers, who are the end-users of goods produced and sold in unprotected markets. Protectionism, on the other hand, is expensive.

It may preserve jobs in protected industries, but it raises costs for other industries and for all consumers. This is unfair and inefficient. Krueger estimates the costs of the Multi-Fibre Arrangement (touted by Kuttner, above) at $11,000 per job in 1984. The voluntary export restraints in steel saved 17,000 jobs, but cost 52,000 jobs in steel-using industries because of higher costs there.[106] Moreover, protectionism is a bellicose action that begets similar actions in others.[107]

Managed trade schemes would not only cost Americans more than free trade, they would also fail, say conservatives, for the same reasons that industrial policies would fail—the knowledge problem and the problem of politics. It is extremely difficult to trace the spillover benefits of specific industries in practice, so we cannot be sure that the benefits of government intervention outweigh the costs. Since we cannot be certain about the nature of the benefits of intervention, the government is likely to find it impossible to resist political pressures to craft managed trade agreements for all industries. This would belie any claims of a "strategic" trade policy.[108]

The United States can and must continue to lead the world toward an ever freer trading system, conservatives maintain. This means working within the GATT framework to establish and enforce multilateral trading rules. During the recent Uruguay Round of the GATT talks, for instance, the United States pushed for rules outlawing the alleged piracy of its companies' software and other intellectual property by newly industrializing countries (NICs). The United States also pressed for reductions in many nations' barriers to imports of U.S. financial services and agricultural products. This policy agenda is appropriate, in the conservative view (although the talks broke off in December 1990 with little progress on these issues). Conservatives also endorse U.S. efforts to strengthen GATT's surveillance activities and dispute resolution procedures.

Rudiger Dornbusch and William Niskanen take a centrist position on U.S. trade policy, calling for "aggressive bilateralism."[109] This view accepts the basic conservative premise that a global, rule-based, multilateral free trade system is a more or less achievable goal, in the long run. To attain the goal and to prosper in the meantime, it may be necessary to pursue policies that violate the norms of global free trade. For example, Dornbusch argues that the United States should deny access to Japanese imports to induce Japan to open its markets more widely to American products. If Japan responds by opening its markets, that is fine. If Japanese companies respond by investing in more American production facilities, that is fine as well, since it creates or maintains U.S. jobs. Either way, the United States has little to lose and much to gain from such a policy in countries where it currently has small market shares.

With its adoption of the Super 301 provision of the 1988 Omnibus Trade and Competitiveness Act, the U.S. Congress enacted a form of aggressive bilateralism. Super 301 authorizes the President to initiate investigations and ultimately to take punitive actions against countries, such as Japan, that maintain high trade surpluses with the United States.[110]

Dornbusch and Niskanen recommend that we take a second departure from the path of free trade as well, by establishing regional trading blocs. Regional trading blocs, such as the European Common Market and the U.S.–Canada Free Trade Agreement, are a burgeoning feature of the international economy. Under the terms of such agreements, companies in member countries typically trade goods and services with few or no restrictions, tariffs, or nontariff barriers.

If the United States sets up trading blocs with Europe, South America, and Mexico, and establishes free trade arrangements with selected countries, argue Dornbusch and Niskanen, it will serve two important purposes. First, it will ensure that the United States is not excluded from the free trade advantages that regional trading blocs can bring to their members. Second, it will motivate those nations that are left out of the arrangements to press the case for multilateral (global) free trade agreements.[111]

At the moment, the merits of a U.S.–Mexico free trade agreement are under considerable debate. Conservative economists estimate that there will be net job gains on both sides of the border from such an agreement. Liberal economists and labor unions predict massive job losses on the American side as American companies accelerate their export of low-skill jobs to Mexico, where workers typically earn less than one-fifth of their American counterparts.

Jagdish Bhagwati presents another centrist variation on the free trade theme, contending that protectionist pressures in the United States can be reduced only if we adopt measures that address the problems that lead to protectionist sentiments. Such measures require compromises with free trade principles. Bhagwati argues that since we cannot end the practice of dumping, or the possibly more pernicious antidumping laws used to discourage this practice, we should establish multilateral panels to investigate dumping complaints and ascertain the magnitude of injury, if any. Likewise, we cannot hope to stop nations from subsidizing and protecting their knowledge-intensive, high-technology industries, but we should set up multilateral procedures that would aim to balance the overall advantages that each government provides to such sensitive industries.[112]

To stave off protectionist policies, Bhagwati also recommends certain domestic adjustment measures. When an industry requests protection from imports, the government should simultaneously consider both the benefits of relief (to companies, workers, and communities) and the costs of protection (to consumers and other workers and companies). Like liberal industrial policy advocates, Bhagwati also suggests that industries receiving protection or direct government assistance (such as the auto industry) be required to pay back the costs of protection after they reestablish their competitiveness. Also, the United States should use temporary tariffs as a way to slow the decline of uncompetitive industries. The tariff revenues could be used to assist and retrain workers who lose their jobs due to foreign competition.[113]

Conclusion

At present, the United States does not appear ready to adopt liberal or progressive versions of industrial policy or trade policy. Yet as discussed previously, the federal government is beginning to take measures inspired by industrial policy concepts. On the trade side of the issue, it seems that neither the liberal nor the conservative visions will prevail in pure form. For the near term at least, aggressive bilateralism and ad hoc protectionism seem likely to dominate U.S. policy, although we can expect the government to continue to promote the GATT, and perhaps enter into managed trade arrangements in a few industries.

Yet even as we debate, and adopt, reject, or compromise on various visions of national industrial and trade policy, the global economy itself continues to change rapidly. As multinational corporations divide and multiply their operations throughout the globe, engaging in joint ventures for research and production with other corporations and governments, they create an increasingly complex web of relationships that supersedes the borders of the nation-state and stretches the bounds of political-economic theory and policy.

It is tempting to assume that these developments will continue inexorably, gradually pushing protectionism aside until the world becomes one big market. But we must avoid such simple assumptions. National nontariff barriers are increasing in significance, as are regional trading blocs. Indeed, the division of the world economy into a yen bloc in the Pacific, a dollar bloc in the Americas, and a mark-dominated bloc in Europe has, to some extent, already occurred. Hence it is important that we make conscious choices among the industry and trade policy options before us, mindful of their consequences not only for world output and income, but for each nation's worker, consumer, and community income and well-being.

Notes

1. There have been notable exceptions to this macroeconomic policy focus. Since the Great Depression, the United States has intervened in the agriculture sector to maintain stable farm prices. Since World War II, its defense procurement policies have largely determined the course of development of the shipbuilding, aerospace, telecommunications, and electronics industries, as well as advanced research and development activity generally. Also, the antipoverty programs initiated during the 1960s constituted a targeted government intervention, mostly in urban labor markets.

2. Kelly, Margaret, Naheed Kirmani, Miranda Xafa, Clemens Boonekamp, and Peter Winglee: *Issues and Developments in International Trade Policy.* Washington, D.C.: International Monetary Fund, December 1988, p. 29. The authors note that trade liberalization has not penetrated the wall of agriculture protection, however. See also Bhagwati, Jagdish: *Protectionism.* Cambridge, Mass.: MIT Press, 1988, chapter 1.

3. The dramatic expansion in world industrial capacity and output would have generated far less painful competitive pressures for the United States and Western Europe had world demand continued to grow at pre-1970s rates. (See the discussions of stagnation in chapters 1 and 3; also Bhagwati *Protectionism,* chapter 4.)

4. Choate, Pat and J.K. Linger: *The High-Flex Society: Shaping America's Economic Future.* New York: Alfred A. Knopf, 1986, p. 7.

5. Kelly, et al., *Issues and Developments,* chapter 2.

6. Economists generally define dumping as selling one's products or services at a lower price in one market than in another. This is a much more restrictive definition than the one used by domestic companies that want protection from imports. They consider dumping to be foreign government subsidy of production for export. As William Niskanen explains in "U.S. Trade Policy," it is easy to assert that all government subsidies support dumping, although the facts suggest that actual dumping is much less prevalent than domestic companies claim. Nevertheless, the U.S. steel industry and others often have accused Japan and Western Europe of dumping products in the American market, and Congress has enacted policies to counter such actions. (See Kelly et al., *Issues and Developments,* chapter 2.)

7. Bergsten, C. Fred: *America in the World Economy: A Strategy for the 1990s.* Washington, D.C.: Institute for International Economics, 1988, p. 72, note 16.

8. Kelly, et al., *Issues and Developments,* p. 4.

9. Thurow, Lester: *The Zero-Sum Solution: Building a World-Class American Economy.* New York: Simon and Schuster, 1985, p. 263.

10. Johnson, Chalmers (ed): *The Industrial Policy Debate.* San Francisco: Institute for Contemporary Studies, 1984, p. 7.

11. On this point, see especially Thurow, *Zero-Sum Solution,* and Dertouzos, Michael L., Richard Lester, Robert Solow, and the MIT Commission on Industrial Productivity: *Made in America: Regaining the Productive Edge.* Cambridge, Mass.: MIT Press, 1989.

12. As most economists acknowledge, it is not correct to equate a country's standard of living with the amount of output it produces, even if one takes into account the amount of work that is necessary to produce that output. For if a country produces many products that are useless, or, more realistically, if it produces output, such as synthetic fiber, in a way that destroys the environment, then it is not clear that, on balance, more output equals a higher standard of living. In short, a country's total output should not be confused with its quality of life, which is an important dimension of the standard of living. Nevertheless, total output is, at least, a rough approximation of a country's living standard.

13. Blinder, Alan S. (ed): *Paying for Productivity: A Look at the Evidence.* Washington, D.C.: The Brookings Institution, 1990, p. 1.

14. Thurow, *Zero-Sum Solution,* p. 49. U.S. manufacturing productivity actually improved substantially between 1979 and 1986, but much of this productivity increase was due to plant shutdowns and the permanent loss of jobs, as well as cyclical productivity improvements as the United States recovered from the recession of 1980-82. In short, the recent productivity gain may well be a temporary one. See Dertouzos, et al., *Made in America,* pp. 30-31. Bergsten, in *America in the World Economy* (p. 56), however, claims that the only outstanding productivity problem the United States faces is in its service sector, which is mostly insulated from foreign competition. Nevertheless, Louise Waldstein shows that American service-sector productivity growth substantially lags that of other industrialized countries. See Waldstein, Louise: *Service Sector Wages, Productivity and Job Creation in the U.S. and Other Countries.* Washington, D.C.: Economic Policy Institute, 1989.

15. The increase in labor supply caused its price to fall relative to that of plant and equipment, so firms hired workers rather than buying labor-saving machines. See Thurow, *Zero-Sum Solution,* p. 87.

16. Another way to look at the investment problem is to ask if investors' profit expectations are high enough to warrant investment at prevailing interest rates. If the economy is slack, and investors do not have confidence that demand will pick up substantially in the forseeable future, they may not invest. Indeed, radicals use this phenomenon to explain the lack of investment in the 1970s and 1980s, rather than the idea that the cost of capital was too high during that period. See Bluestone, Barry and Bennett Harrison: *The Deindustrialization of America.* New York: Basic Books,

1982, and *The Great U-Turn.* New York: Basic Books, 1988. See also the discussion in chapter 3 of this book.

17. Thurow, *Zero-Sum Solution,* pp. 69–89. See also Business Week Team: *The Reindustrialization of America.* New York: McGraw-Hill Book Company, 1982, as well as chapter 5 of this book.

18. See Dertouzos, et al., *Made in America*; also Sabel, Charles: *Work and Politics.* Cambridge: Cambridge University Press, 1981; Walton, Richard: "Establishing and Maintaining High-Commitment Work Systems," in Kimberly, John R. (ed): *Organization Life Cycles.* San Francisco: Jossey-Bass, 1980; Walton, Richard and Paul Lawrence (eds): *Human Resource Management: Trends and Challenges.* Boston: Harvard Business School Press, 1985; Kochan, Thomas A., Harry Katz, and Nancy Mower: *Worker Participation and American Unions: Threat or Opportunity?* Kalamazoo, Mich.: The W.E. Upjohn Institute for Employment Research, 1984; Choate and Linger, *High-Flex Society*; Sanderson, Susan Walsh: *The Consumer Electronics Industry and the Future of American Manufacturing: How the U.S. Lost the Lead and Why We Must Get Back in the Game.* Washington, D.C.: Economic Policy Institute, 1989.

19. Dertouzos, et al., *Made in America.* See also Doeringer, Peter B., David Terkla, and Gregory Topakian: *Invisible Factors in Local Economic Development.* New York: Oxford University Press, 1987.

20. See Kochan, et al., *Worker Participation*; Walton, *Human Resource Management*; Lawler, Edward and Susan Mohrman: "Quality Circles after the Fad." *Harvard Business Review.* January-February 1985; Witte, John: *Democracy, Authority and Alienation in Work.* Chicago: University of Chicago Press, 1980.

21. Reich, Robert B.: *The Next American Frontier.* New York: Times Books, 1983. Many political economists have made this argument. For another liberal account, see Business Week Team, *Reindustrialization*, chapter 4. For a radical version, see Bluestone and Harrison, *Great U-Turn,* or Magdoff, Harry and Paul M. Sweezy: *Stagnation and the Financial Explosion.* New York: Monthly Review Press, 1987, especially Part 2.

22. See Thurow, *Zero-Sum Solution,* pp. 262–264; Reich, *Next American Frontier,* pp. 173–200; Magaziner, Ira C. and Robert B. Reich: *Minding America's Business.* New York: Harcourt Brace Jovanovich, 1982, chapters 5-7; Lodge, George C.: *Perestroika for America.* Boston: Harvard Business School Press, 1990, chapter 1.

23. "Indeed," notes Reich in *Next American Frontier,*

notwithstanding substantial import barriers to protect domestic steel producers, tax incentives, and assorted regulatory rollbacks—all designed to encourage new steel investment—the American steel industry has been enthusiastically diversifying out of steel. In 1979 U.S. Steel walked away from thirteen steelmaking and fabricating facilities while investing in a new shopping center near Pittsburgh and announcing that it would build major chemical facilities near Houston (p. 182). Most firms in the American apparel, textile, footwear, and color television industries have displayed the same

158   *Industrial and Trade Policies*

failure to retool once the government has offered a shield of protection. (p. 180).

Compare Kuttner, Robert: *Managed Trade and Economic Sovereignty*. Washington, D.C.: Economic Policy Institute, 1989.

24. Magaziner and Reich, *Minding America's Business*, p. 343. See also Lodge, *Perestroika*, chapter 2.

25. Thurow, *Zero-Sum Solution*, p. 264.

26. Lodge, *Perestroika*, chapter 2.

27. Thurow, *Zero-Sum Solution*, p. 281.

28. Rohatyn, Felix: "A New RFC Is Proposed for Business." *The New York Times*. December 1, 1974, Section 3, p. 1. See also Reich, *Next American Frontier*, p. 243 and Thurow, *Zero-Sum Solution*, p. 283.

29. Spillovers are also called "positive externalities." Externalities are effects of market transactions that are experienced by those who are not party to the transactions. For example, Midwestern steel mills create pollution that harms residents in the Northeast. The pollution is a negative externality—an effect of the production of steel that is not included in the price of steel. If the costs of eliminating the pollution were included in the market price of steel, the price would be much higher than it is.

Spillovers operate similarly. Research and development of sophisticated production processes and products in one industry helps other industries that can use those products or related processes in their own work. But the industry benefitting from the spillovers does not pay the high costs of generating them. Since the market does not recognize all of the benefits that accrue from the sophisticated production processes and products, private investors tend to under-invest in producing them—they invest only to the extent that they can profit. But since potential gains are, in the liberal view, almost society-wide, liberals believe that society as a whole (acting through government) should invest in the production of such spillovers.

See Luria, Daniel: *Beyond Free Trade and Protectionism: The Public Interest in a U.S. Auto Policy*. Washington, D.C.: Economic Policy Institute, 1989, pp. 2-5; Lodge, *Perestroika*, chapters 1-2; also see Tyson, Laura D'Andrea: "Managed Trade: Making the Best of Second Best," in Lawrence, Robert Z. and Charles L. Schultze (eds): *An American Trade Strategy: Options for the 1990s*. Washington, D.C.: The Brookings Institution, 1990.

30. Magaziner and Reich, *Minding America's Business*, pp. 343-349; also Reich, *Next American Frontier*, pp. 244-245.

31. Thurow, *Zero-Sum Solution*, pp. 278-279. See also Magaziner and Reich, *Minding America's Business*, pp. 335-336; Lodge, *Perestroika*, chapter 2; Tyson, "Managed Trade."

32. Thurow, *Zero-Sum Solution*, pp. 275-277; Magaziner and Reich, *Minding America's Business*, pp. 350-360; Lodge, *Perestroika*, chapter 2.

33. Ettlie, John E.: *Taking Charge of Manufacturing*. San Francisco: Jossey-Bass Publishers, 1988; Schmenner, Roger: "Productivity in the Factory and Industrial Policy," in Goldstein, Harvey A. (ed): *The State and Local Industrial Policy Question*. Chicago: American Planning Association,

1987, pp. 54–59; Walton, Richard: *Innovating to Compete: Lessons for Diffusing and Managing Change in the Workplace.* San Francisco: Jossey-Bass Publishers, 1987.

34. Schmenner, "Productivity in the Factory." See also chapter 5 of this book.

35. Dertouzos, et al., *Made in America* p. 153. See also Walton, "High-Commitment Work Systems"; Reich, *Next American Frontier*, pp. 134–139; Thurow, *Zero-Sum Solution*, pp. 148–182; Luria, *Beyond Free Trade*, pp. 9–16.

36. Magaziner and Reich, *Minding America's Business*, p. 362.

37. See also Dertouzos, et al., *Made in America*, pp. 151–155; Lodge, *Perestroika*, chapter 2; Glickman, Norman J. and Douglas P. Woodward: *The New Competitors.* New York: Basic Books, 1989, chapter 10.

38. From a citation of economist Lloyd J. Dumas, *Business Week*, June 12, 1989. In Professionals' Coalition for Nuclear Arms Control: *Budget for a Strong America*, no date, p. 1. The PCNAC is at 1616 P Street, NW, Suite 320, Washington, D.C., 20036.

39. Magaziner and Reich, *Minding America's Business*, p. 361.

40. Lodge, *Perestroika*. See also Dertouzos, et al., *Made in America*, pp. 151–155.

41. Magaziner and Reich, *Minding America's Business*, p. 373; Reich, *Next American Frontier*, p. 245; Thurow, *Zero-Sum Solution*, p. 268; Dertouzos, et al., *Made in America*, p. 151–155; Lodge, *Perestroika*, chapter 2; Glickman and Woodward, *New Competitors*, chapter 8.

42. Rodberg, Leonard S. and William K. Tabb: "What Can We Learn from the Industrial Policy Debate?" *Social Policy.* Vol. 17, No. 3, Winter 1987, pp. 27–33; Bluestone and Harrison, *Deindustrialization of America*, pp. 113–114; Gilpin, Robert: *The Political Economy of International Relations.* Princeton: Princeton University Press, 1987, chapters 1, 2, and 6.

43. Magdoff and Sweezy, *Stagnation*, Part 1, especially "The Alternative to Stagnation," pp. 79–90.

44. Bowles, Samuel, David M. Gordon, and Thomas E. Weisskopf: *Beyond the Waste Land: A Democratic Alternative to Economic Decline.* Garden City: Anchor Press/Doubleday, 1983, pp. 62–178. See also Braverman, Harry: *Labor and Monopoly Capital: The Degradation of Work in the Twentieth Century.* New York: Monthly Review Press, 1974; Edwards, Richard: *Contested Terrain: The Transformation of Work in the Twentieth Century.* New York: Basic Books, 1979.

45. See for example, Dertouzos, et al., *Made in America*, chapters 3–7.

46. See Bluestone and Harrison, *Deindustrialization of America*, pp. 111–192; Glickman and Woodward, *New Competitors*, passim.

47. Magdoff and Sweezy, *Stagnation*, pp. 79–90; Gilpin, *Political Economy*, chapter 2.

48. Bowles, Gordon, and Weisskopf, *Beyond the Waste Land*, p. 326. See also Alperovitz, Gar and Jeff Faux: *Rebuilding America: A Blueprint for the New Economy.* New York: Pantheon Books, 1984, pp. 262–270;

Ackerman, Frank: *Hazardous to Our Wealth: Economic Policies in the 1980s*. Boston: South End Press, 1984, chapter 11.

49. Bowles, Gordon, and Weisskopf in *Beyond the Waste Land* (pp. 332–335) point out that publicly owned banks and insurance companies in the United States and Europe are as efficient, or more efficient, than private ones. Under their plan for nationalization of the banking system, the federal government would compensate the current, private owners of banks and insurance companies at 100 percent of the full market value of their institutions over a 15 year period. See also Carnoy, Martin and Derek Shearer: *Economic Democracy: The Challenge of the 1980s*. White Plains: M.E. Sharpe, Inc., 1980.

50. Bowles, Gordon, and Weisskopf, *Beyond the Waste Land*, pp. 335–336. The authors argue further that subsidizing investment in production for basic human needs would obviate the need to pick industry winners and losers to receive investment funds. The latter is a shortcoming, in their view, of liberal proposals. Their argument implies, but does not state explicitly, that other measures would ensure that consumers have not only the need (and presumably the desire), but also the ability (income) to purchase the goods produced by such firms. (On this point, see also Rodberg and Tabb, "Industrial Policy Debate.")

51. Bluestone and Harrison, *Deindustrialization of America* pp. 246–247, and *Great U-Turn*, chapter 7. Liberals also support the notion that the public should have an equity share in the businesses that it assists.

52. Bluestone and Harrison, *Deindustrialization of America*, pp. 251–254.

53. Ibid. See also Center for Popular Economics: *Economic Report of the People: An Alternative to the Economic Report of the President*. Boston: South End Press, 1986, chapter 13.

54. For a progressive argument in favor of plant closing legislation, see Bluestone and Harrison, *Deindustrialization of America*, (pp. 235–243). Glickman and Woodward, *New Competitors*, (chapter 10) present a case for a longer notification period. For a conservative argument against plant closing legislation, see O'Connell, Francis A., Jr.: *Plant Closings: Worker Rights, Management Rights and the Law*. New Brunswick: Transaction Books, 1986.

55. Bluestone and Harrison, 1982, *Deindustrialization of America*, p. 256.

56. Bluestone and Harrison, *Great U-Turn*, p. 185.

57. Bowles, Gordon, and Weisskopf, *Beyond the Waste Land*, discuss the research of Richard B. Freeman and James L. Medoff in *What Do Unions Do?* (New York: Basic Books, 1984), which indicates that unionized firms in competitive industries tend to have higher rates of productivity than nonunion firms in the industry, from which they conclude that, in these firms, management, workers, and union representatives all have a stake in boosting the firm's productivity.

58. Bowles, Gordon, and Weisskopf, *Beyond the Waste Land*, p. 312.

59. Ibid., p. 313; Center for Popular Economics, *Economic Report*, chapter 13.
60. Bowles, Gordon, and Weisskopf, *Beyond the Waste Land*, p. 315.
61. Bluestone and Harrison, 1988, *Deindustrialization of America*, p. 187. See also Piore, Michael: "Computer Technologies, Market Structure, and Strategic Union Choices," in Kochan, Thomas (ed): *Challenges and Choices Facing American Labor.* Cambridge, Mass.: MIT Press, 1985, pp. 193–212; Dertouzos, et al., *Made in America*, chapter 11.
62. Rosen, Corey M., Katherine J. Klein, and Karen M. Young: *Employee Ownership in America: The Equity Solution.* Lexington: D.C. Heath and Company, 1986.
63. Bowles, Gordon, and Weisskopf, *Beyond the Waste Land*, pp. 318–320. See also Rosen, Klein, and Young, *Employee Ownership*, and Rothschild, Joyce and J. Allen Whitt: *The Cooperative Workplace: Potentials and Dilemmas of Organizational Democracy and Participation.* Cambridge: Cambridge University Press, 1986. It is important to distinguish the form of worker ownership described here—the worker cooperatives in which workers and sometimes community representatives own company stock and determine company policies on a one-person/one-vote basis—from the employee stock ownership plan, or ESOP. In an ESOP, a company sets up a trust fund to which it contributes stock. The shares of stock are allocated to individual employees based upon their wages. Over time, employees acquire ownership rights to these shares. In almost all cases, however, workers do not acquire majority ownership, and control over policies and day-to-day decisions remains in the hands of management, as in any conventional firm. Bowles, Gordon, and Weisskopf in *Beyond the Waste Land* (pp. 316–317), recommend that where ESOPs are used, worker-owners be given at least a modicum of managerial control through collective profit-sharing agreements. Under this arrangement, which is based on the Swedish Meidner Plan, the workers' stock is voted as a block, rather than individually, so workers have more power to influence company policy.
64. Schultze, Charles: "Industrial Policy: A Dissent." *The Brookings Review*. Vol. 2, No. 1, Fall 1983, pp. 5–6. See also McKenzie, Richard: *Competing Visions: The Political Conflict over America's Economic Future.* Washington, D.C.: The Cato Institute, 1985, pp. 38–39; and Bluestone, Barry, Bennett Harrison, and Lucy Gorham: "Storm Clouds on the Horizon," in Goldstein, Harvey A. (ed): *The State and Local Industrial Policy Question.* Chicago: American Planning Association, 1987, p. 30. In response to the charge that deindustrialization is a nonexistent trend, the authors of the latter book admit that while total manufacturing employment did not, in fact, decline from 1973 to 1980, nevertheless

> the number of jobs for production workers in factories, offices, and stores actually fell by 5 percent. What did grow in the nation's manufacturing firms were jobs for managers, professionals, and supervisors—a growth that many experts . . . have blamed for at least part of the nation's productivity slowdown.

162 *Industrial and Trade Policies*

65. Schultze, "Industrial Policy." See also Robert Z. Lawrence and Charles L. Schultze, "Evaluating the Options," in *An American Trade Strategy: Options for the 1990s.* Washington, D.C.: The Brookings Institution, 1990, pp. 1–68. In response to the argument that most of America's economic problems are due to macroeconomic forces, especially the overvalued dollar in the first half of the 1980s, Ira C. Magaziner and Mark Patinkin argue that from 1985 to 1988, the value of the dollar fell dramatically, making American goods cheaper in other countries, yet the trade deficit fell only slightly.

> Price alone doesn't always make for export success. In many industries, like machine tools, engineering and marketing are more important. In other industries, like microwave ovens, even a drastically lowered dollar won't bridge the price gap with low-wage rivals. To compete, high-wage countries need more complex strategies. Some have mastered those strategies. Despite a soaring yen and a high mark, the Japanese and Germans continue to sell America more in goods than we sell them.

From Magaziner, Ira C. and Mark Patinkin: *The Silent War: Inside the Global Business Battles Shaping America's Future.* New York: Random House, 1989, p. 302.

66. McKenzie, Richard: *The American Job Machine.* New York: Universe Books, 1988, chapter 8.
67. Schumpeter, Joseph: *Capitalism, Socialism and Democracy.* New York: Harper and Row, 1975, chapter 7.
68. McKenzie, *Competing Visions*, p. 21.
69. Schultze, "Industrial Policy," p. 6. See also Tajika, E. and Y. Yiu: "Japan's Public Policies for Investment," in Lee, Chung H. and Ippei Yamazawa (eds): *The Economic Development of Japan and Korea: A Parallel with Lessons.* New York: Praeger Publishers, 1990, pp. 33–52.
70. Schultze, "Industrial Policy," p. 6.
71. Ibid., p. 7. Thurow in *Zero-Sum Solution* (pp. 284–285) responds to Schultze's charges thus:

> Of course, Japanese industrial policies are not the *only* cause of their success.... The Japanese success is due to many high-quality components—high investment; heavy research-and-development spending; a well-educated, well-motivated cooperative labor force; good management; and good macro-economic conditions. At the same time I know of no serious scholar of Japanese economic success who thinks that their industrial policies have had a negative effect.... Similarly, any set of industrial policies will make mistakes.

Thurow goes on to argue that the notorious example of MITI's failure to bring about consolidation of the Japanese auto industry in the 1960s illustrates the fundamental strength of liberal versions of industrial policy—the government plays a largely advisory, facilitative role. The business community ultimately determines what is or is not in its best interests.

72. Lavoie, Don: *National Economic Planning: What Is Left?* Cambridge, Mass.: Ballinger Publishing Company, 1985, p. 6.
73. See also Friedman, Milton and Rose Friedman: *Free to Choose.* New York: Harcourt Brace Jovanovich, 1980, p. 6; Schultze, "Industrial Policy," p. 8; Lawrence and Schultze, "Evaluating the Options," pp. 1–41. Thurow, *Zero-Sum Solution* (pp. 289–290), replies:

> Industrial policies exist not to pick the sunrise industries of the year 2000. That is clearly impossible.... The aim is to strengthen the industries that are now sunrise industries, to restructure old industries so that the parts which remain can exist as world-class competitive entities, to manage decline where decline must occur, and to finance civilian research-and-development projects with long- to medium-term payoffs.

74. McKenzie, *Competing Visions*, p. 91.
75. Schultze, "Industrial Policy," p. 9.
76. McKenzie, *Competing Visions*, pp. 74–75; McKenzie, *American Job Machine*, pp. 178–197. See also O'Connell, *Plant Closings*.
77. Schultze, "Industrial Policy," p. 9.
78. Ibid., p. 10. See also Lawrence and Schultze, "Evaluating the Options," and Shull, Steven A. and Jeffrey E. Cohen (eds): *Economics and Politics of Industrial Policy: The United States and Western Europe.* Boulder: Westview Press, 1986.
79. Schultze, "Industrial Policy," pp. 10–11.
80. Ibid.
81. Liberals agree that the potential for political manipulation of an industrial or trade policy is a problem (Thurow, *Zero-Sum Solution*, pp. 295–296). Nevertheless, Reich asserts:

> to argue that a certain course of public policy is desirable but cannot be implemented is hardly to end the conversation. If other nations are being more strategic about their trade policies than the United States is, to U.S. detriment, then it is entirely reasonable to conclude that the United States must change its ways.

See Reich, Robert B.: "Commentary," in Lawrence and Schultze, *American Trade Strategy*, pp. 215–224.

82. Johnson, *Industrial Policy Debate*, p. 29. See also Bowles, Gordon, and Weisskopf, *Beyond the Waste Land*, p. 386.
83. Lodge, *Perestroika*, chapter 2. See also Dertouzos, et al., *Made in America*.
84. See Magaziner and Patinkin, *Silent War*, pp. 300–307; Luria, *Beyond Free Trade*; Waldstein, *Service Sector Wages*; Sanderson, *Consumer Electronics Industry*; "The Future of Silicon Valley: Does the U.S. Need a High-Tech Industrial Policy to Battle Japan, Inc?" *Business Week.* February 5, 1990, pp. 54–60.
85. See Anderson, Marion, Greg Bischak, and Michael Oden: *Converting the American Economy: The Economic Effects of an Alternative Security Policy.* Lansing, Mich.: Employment Research Associates, 1991;

Gordon, Suzanne and Dave McFadden (eds): *Economic Conversion: Revitalizing America's Economy.* Cambridge, Mass.: Ballinger Publishing Company, 1984; Lynch, John E. (ed): *Economic Adjustment and Conversion of Defense Industries.* Boulder: Westview Press, 1987.

86. In a world of perfectly competitive markets, policies designed to help companies establish dominant positions in target markets would make no sense, since market domination is, by definition, impossible. In fact, there are few or no perfectly competitive markets in the world, but rather, oligopolistic and monopolistically competitive markets. Oligopolistic markets are characterized by barriers to the entry of new firms, such as costly equipment, expensive technology and high-skilled workers, and marketing distribution networks that favor existing firms. The first firms to hit the market with a leading-edge product and technology have a substantial and possibly decisive advantage over latecomers. See Krugman, Paul R. (ed): Introduction to *Strategic Trade Policy and the New International Economics.* Cambridge, Mass.: MIT Press, 1986.

87. Kuttner, Robert: *Managed Trade and Economic Sovereignty.* Washington, D.C.: Economic Policy Institute, 1989, pp. 3–19.

88. See note 6, above.

89. Krugman, *Strategic Trade Policy,* and also *The Age of Diminished Expectations: U.S. Economic Policy in the 1990s.* Cambridge, Mass.: MIT Press, 1990.

90. See Kuttner, *Managed Trade.*

91. Ibid. Compare this with the more conservative account in Kelly, et al., *Issues and Developments,* pp. 72–74.

92. Kuttner, *Managed Trade,* pp. 25–26.

93. See Tyson, "Managed Trade;" Lodge, *Perestroika,* chapter 2. See also note 29.

94. Tyson, "Managed Trade," p. 58. See also Luria's proposal in *Beyond Free Trade,* pp. 16–19, for managed trade in automobiles, combined with a domestic auto industry policy.

95. See Bluestone and Harrison, *Great U-Turn,* pp. 189–193; Ackerman, *Hazardous to Our Wealth,* chapter 11; Center for Popular Economics, *Economic Report,* pp. 231–233.

96. As discussed in chapter 3, other factors contributed to the increase in foreign investment as well. During the first half of the 1980s, the dramatic rise in U.S. interest rates led to an increase in investment by foreigners in the United States, particularly in private stocks and government bonds. With the equally dramatic fall of the dollar after 1985, American assets (real estate, factories, and so forth) became relatively inexpensive, so foreign investors began buying them.

97. Glickman and Woodward, *New Competitors,* chapters 8–10. See also Luria, *Beyond Free Trade,* pp. 19–23 and chapter 6 of this book. Glickman and Woodward, Bluestone and Harrison in *Great U-Turn,* and others worry that foreign investors are mainly buying existing American companies and other assets, rather than investing to create new jobs in America.

98. Harrison, Bennett: "The Return of the Big Firms." *Social Policy.* Vol. 21, No. 1, Summer 1990, pp. 7-19. See also Blackwell, Sir Basil: "The State and the Macro-Industrial Economy—Towards a Coherent Multi-National Policy." *Omega.* Vol. 16, No. 4, July 1988, pp. 265-275; Mead, Walter Russell: "American Economic Policy in the Antemillenial Era." *World Policy Journal.* Vol. 6, No. 3, Summer 1989.

99. Sweezy, Paul and Harry Magdoff: "International Cooperation—A Way Out?" Review of the Month. *Monthly Review.* Vol. 39, No. 6, November 1987, pp. 1-19.

100. See Lenin, V.I.: *Imperialism: The Highest Stage of Capitalism.* New York: International Publishers, 1939 (1917).

101. See Kolko, Joyce: *Restructuring the World Economy.* New York: Pantheon Books, 1988, especially the last chapter.

102. Sweezy and Magdoff, "International Cooperation."

103. Islam, Sadequl: "Free Trade and Protection: The U.S.—Canada Case." *Monthly Review.* Vol. 39, No. 6, November 1987, pp. 20-32.

104. Lawrence and Schultze, "Evaluating the Options," pp. 7-8. Kuttner in *Managed Trade*, pp. 15-16, asserts, however, that

> the cause and effect relationship in the way macroeconomic and trade measures are used to ameliorate the current imbalances can run in either direction. Macroeconomic shifts (smaller public deficit, higher domestic savings, lower interest rates, cheaper dollar) can indeed produce benefits for the trade balance. But an improvement in the competitive position of U.S. industry (whether for structural reasons or as a result of different trade policies) can also produce macroeconomic benefits (more U.S. exports, more jobs, higher growth, higher incomes, more private savings and tax revenue, higher profits and more investment, lower real interest rates, external balance with a stronger currency) at a lower cost to American well-being. The strategy of cheapening the dollar has produced only modest trade benefits, but has put U.S. assets on sale, and has generated inflationary pressures.

105. Note that even Paul Krugman, whose research has helped to discredit Ricardian free trade theory (even in its modern form), maintains that the pursuit of free trade through the GATT rule system remains the best course for U.S. policy. Industrial and managed trade policies are unlikely to succeed, he believes, principally because it is almost impossible to know in advance on technical grounds, which industries to target for subsidy. Hence political pressures would distort and undermine industrial and trade policy. (Krugman, Introduction, *Strategic Trade Policy*, and *Diminished Expectations*, p. 112.)

106. Krueger, Anne O.: "Free Trade Is the Best Policy," in Lawrence and Schultze, *American Trade Strategy*, p. 44.

107. Bhagwati, *Protectionism*, chapter 5.

108. Krugman, Introduction, *Strategic Trade Policy*, pp. 12-20; Lawrence and Schultze, "Evaluating the Options," pp. 1-41. See also Krueger, "Free Trade."

109. Dornbusch, Rudiger W.: "Policy Options for Freer Trade: The Case for Bilateralism," in Lawrence, Robert Z. and Charles L. Schultze (eds): *An American Trade Strategy: Options for the 1990s.* Washington, D.C.: The Brookings Institution, 1990; Niskanen, William A.: "U.S. Trade Policy: Problems and Prospects," in Crane, Edward H. and David Boaz (eds): *An American Vision: Policies for the '90s.* Washington, D.C.: Cato Institute, 1989. See also Bergsten, *America in the World Economy*, and Hufbauer, Gary C.: *The Free Trade Debate: Background Paper.* Twentieth Century Fund, Task Force on the Future of American Trade Policy. New York: Priority Press Publications, 1989.

110. Lawrence finds numerous shortcomings with Dornbusch's proposals for opening the Japanese market through aggressive bilateralism. In particular, Lawrence notes that persistent sectoral negotiations since the mid-1980s have, in fact, led to the substantial growth of American exports to Japan in the affected industries. In short, the United States should continue to push for "sector-specific and more generic rules changes—ideally in a multilateral setting." See Lawrence, Robert Z.: Discussion of Dornbusch's "Policy Options for Freer Trade," in Lawrence and Schultze, *An American Trade Strategy*, pp. 135-136. See also Bhagwati, *Protectionsim*, chapter 5.

111. Dornbusch, "Policy Options," and Niskanen, "U.S. Trade Policy."
112. Bhagwati, *Protectionism*, p. 128.
113. Ibid.

Bibliography

Industrial Policy

Liberal Industrial Policy Proposals

Business Week Team: *The Reindustrialization of America.* New York: McGraw-Hill Book Company, 1982.

This is a centrist-liberal discussion of the problems that have afflicted the U.S. economy since the 1970s, with a focus on the failures of business, labor, and government to adopt behaviors that would lead to solutions. To put the economy back on track, we need an industrial policy that entails macroeconomic measures to increase savings (to lower the cost of investment capital); targeted microeconomic measures to stimulate investment and innovation; a financial institution such as a revived Reconstruction Finance Corporation that would channel capital to, and help to restructure, mature industries; and a national focus on increasing U.S. exports.

"The Future of Silicon Valley: Does the U.S. Need a High-Tech Industrial Policy To Battle Japan Inc?" *Business Week.* February 5, 1990, pp. 54-60.

This issue highlights the views of business leaders and officials in the Bush administration on the question of whether the United States should adopt an industrial policy targeted toward the electronics industry.

Johnson, Chalmers (ed): *The Industrial Policy Debate*. San Francisco: Institute for Contemporary Studies, 1984.

This is an insightful collection of essays written from a perspective that is sympathetic to liberal industrial policies, but which also approaches the subject with a critical eye. The essays cover a broad range of industrial policy issues, including analyses of industrial policy proposals, Japanese industrial policy, technological innovation, protectionism, the defense industry, and tax reform.

Lodge, George C.: *Perestroika for America: Restructuring Business-Government Relations for World Competitiveness*. Boston: Harvard Business School Press, 1990.

Lodge provides a blueprint of the roles business and government must play to achieve competitive excellence. Government must define a national "community need," a vision of an overriding purpose to be served by business and government. Based upon this vision, government must organize collective industry action (for example, to develop new products or production processes) because no individual firm within an industry will generally have either the resources or the authority to organize the others in pursuit of a common aim.

Luria, Daniel: *Beyond Free Trade and Protectionism: The Public Interest in a U.S. Auto Policy*. Washington, D.C.: Economic Policy Institute, 1989.

Luria argues that, for a number of reasons, including its extensive backward linkages to the rest of the U.S. economy (which supply it with parts and materials), the auto industry is a key industry in which the public has a stake in restructuring and supporting to regain international competitiveness. Luria's proposals include labor-management cooperation with government participation to cut costs and improve quality, and managed trade proposals for both imports and foreign direct investment in U.S. auto plants.

Magaziner, Ira C. and Mark Patinkin: *The Silent War: Inside the Global Business Battles Shaping America's Future*. New York: Random House, 1989.

This is a series of nine case studies of businesses in Southeast Asia, Western Europe, and the United States. Most are stories of how companies such as Samsung, Cross, and Corning Glass became, or maintained their status as, industry leaders, some with the help of a national industrial policy. The authors conclude that an industrial policy is essential for U.S. economic prosperity in the future.

Magaziner, Ira C. and Robert B. Reich: *Minding America's Business: The Decline and Rise of the American Economy*. New York: Harcourt Brace Jovanovich, 1982.

One of the most widely read and quoted sources on industrial policy, this book dissects and analyzes several basic components of business behavior that utlimately determine a firm's international competitiveness. It also compares U.S. industrial policies with those of Japan and Western Europe and finds U.S. policies wanting. Finally, Magaziner and Reich set forth their detailed proposal for a U.S. industrial policy.

Reich, Robert B. *The Next American Frontier.* New York: Times Books, 1983.

A companion piece to *Minding America's Business*, this book traces the development of the American economy since the turn of the century, focusing on the rise of scientific management (Taylorism) and mass production. While the global conditions that allowed this type of production system, and thus the American economy, to dominate world trade largely disappeared by 1970, America has still failed to acknowledge this reality. Rather than shift to production of specialty goods and technology-driven products and services through flexible, high-skilled workers, America's business managers and national government have clung to the old ways of mass production. Reich sets forth a series of programmatic alternatives to current U.S. policies commensurate with, but broader than, the recommendations of *Minding America's Business*.

_____: *Tales of a New America.* New York: Times Books-Random House, 1987.

Reich seeks to show that a new government-business relationship is supported by America's fundamental values.

"The Reindustrialization of America." *Business Week* (Special Issue). June 30, 1980.

Rohatyn, Felix. "A New RFC Is Proposed for Business. *New York Times,* December 1, 1974, Section 3, p. 1.

Perhaps Rohatyn's first public statement of his idea of resurrecting the Reconstruction Finance Corporation to solve America's industrial problems.

_____: *The Twenty Year Century: Essays on Economic and Public Finance.* New York: Random House, 1983.

This is a collection of essays previously published in *Business Week, The Wall Street Journal,* and several other publications. Chapter 7 sets forth Rohatyn's ideas on the RFC.

Sanderson, Susan Walsh: *The Consumer Electronics Industry and the Future of American Manufacturing: How the U.S. Lost the Lead and Why We Must Get Back in the Game.* Washington, D.C.: Economic Policy Institute, 1989.

The author traces the decline of the American consumer electronics industry from its position of world leadership in the late 1960s to its second-class-and-fading status today, citing shortsighted management policies and the distorting influences of U.S. defense procurement on product development strategies. If the United States does not take steps to reestablish a competitive position in the industry soon, it risks a permanent diminution in its industrial competitiveness generally. Appropriate steps include government action to create a climate more conducive to private investment in major new technologies, public-private sponsorship of "shared manufacturing" facilities to spread the risks and costs of new investments more widely, and establishment of "teaching factories" to bridge the gap between engineering research and practice.

Starr, Martin K. (ed): *Global Competitiveness: Getting the U.S. Back on Track.* New York: W.W. Norton and Company, 1988.

A collection of ten essays, written from a generally liberal perspective, that argue for specific business management and government policies to enhance U.S. competitiveness.

Thurow, Lester: *The Zero-Sum Solution: Building a World-Class American Economy.* New York: Simon and Schuster, 1985.

An important statement of the liberal perspective on contemporary U.S. economic problems and solutions, including industrial policy, as cited at length in this chapter.

———: *The Zero-Sum Society: Distribution and the Possibilities for Economic Change.* New York: Basic Books, 1980.

Thurow describes the major problems afflicting the U.S. economy and points out that their solutions would require sacrifices from some members of society that would benefit other members (a zero-sum situation). He sets forth a set of policies that would make such trade-offs equitable, but doubts that American political parties can provide the leadership necessary to bring these reforms about.

Waldstein, Louise: *Service Sector Wages, Productivity and Job Creation in the U.S. and Other Countries.* Washington, D.C.: Economic Policy Institute, 1989. Background Paper to Thurow, Lester: *Toward a High-Wage, High-Productivity Service Sector.*

Waldstein delineates the components of the U.S. service sector and compares the sector's performance rather unfavorably to those of France, Japan, and Germany. Two factors contributing to low productivity growth in this sector, especially in retail trade, are public policies that keep wages low and thus encourage firms to use low-wage labor rather than invest in productivity-enhancing equipment and techniques, and a lack of research and development investment in this sector.

Whitford, Vernon (ed): *American Industry.* New York: H.W. Wilson Company, 1984.

A collection of essays previously published in news magazines by prominent spokespersons of liberal views on American economic problems and industrial policy.

Productivity, Innovation, and Labor-Management Relations

Blinder, Alan S. (ed): *Paying for Productivity: A Look at the Evidence.* Washington, D.C.: The Brookings Institution, 1990.

A collection of informative studies on the effects of alternative pay and organizational systems on productivity, including profit sharing, employee stock ownership plans, and worker participation.

Choate, Pat and J.K. Linger: *The High-Flex Society: Shaping America's Economic Future.* New York: Alfred A. Knopf, 1986.

    To survive in the new global economy, the authors argue, America must "become a high-flex society—in which firms can innovate, invest, and quickly take a product or service from development to production to market domination, and then on to the next generation of product or service; in which workers can secure training, find jobs, be productive, advance and shift between jobs and occupations with ease and confidence; and in which government can maintain an environment that facilitates whatever adjustments are needed and do so in a commonsense, socially responsible manner" (p. 9). The book is largely the authors' map for taking America toward those goals.

Committee for Economic Development: *Productivity Policy: Key to the Nation's Economic Future.* Washington, D.C.: Committee for Economic Development, April 1983.

    Analysis of the causes of the U.S. productivity slowdown, and statement of public policies as well as labor and management actions that would promote productivity growth.

Dertouzos, Michael L., Richard Lester, Robert Solow, and the MIT Commission on Industrial Productivity: *Made in America: Regaining the Productive Edge.* Cambridge, Mass.: MIT Press, 1989.

    An analysis of the multiple causes of productivity decline, based in part upon case studies of eight industries, and a set of action recommendations for business, government, labor, and universities.

Doeringer, Peter B., David Terkla, and Gregory Topakian: *Invisible Factors in Local Economic Development.* New York: Oxford University Press, 1987.

    A convincing empirical demonstration of the thesis that mature industries can remain competitive by pursuing a variety of strategies, including production for specialized market niches and labor-management cooperation.

Ettlie, John E.: *Taking Charge of Manufacturing: How Companies Are Combining Technological and Organizational Innovations to Compete Successfully.* San Francisco: Jossey-Bass Publishers, 1988.

    Draws useful lessons for managers from the experiences of several companies that have introduced automation into their production processes.

Kochan, Thomas A., Harry Katz, and Nancy Mower: *Worker Participation and American Unions: Threat or Opportunity?* Kalamazoo, Mich.: The W.E. Upjohn Institute for Employment Research, 1984.

    Useful case studies of worker participation efforts and their strengths and weaknesses in several North American companies.

Lawler, Edward and Susan Mohrman: "Quality Circles after the Fad." *Harvard Business Review.* January–February 1985.

    Based upon their study of numerous firms that introduced quality circles and other worker participation schemes, the authors describe the lifecycle of these workplace innovations. In many cases, they ultimately run out of steam or fail, either because management is not deeply committed to them, or because the underlying, de-skilled job structure remains unchanged.

Levitan, Sar A. and Diane Werneke: *Productivity: Problems, Prospects, and Policies*. Baltimore: The Johns Hopkins University Press, 1984.

    Analysis of U.S. productivity slowdown and presentation of public policy options.

Parker, Mike: *Inside the Circle: A Union Guide to QWL*. Boston: South End Press, 1985.

    As the title implies, this book discusses the theory and practice of quality-of-working-life programs from a union perspective. The author concludes that if unions take an active role in shaping such programs, they can serve both management and worker interests.

Piore, Michael: "Computer Technologies, Market Structure, and Strategic Union Choices." In Kochan, Thomas (ed): *Challenges and Choices Facing American Labor*. Cambridge, Mass.: MIT Press, 1985, pp. 193–212.

    Discussion of the implications of flexible production for labor-management relations.

"A Revolution in Work Rules: New Job Flexibility Boosts Productivity." *Business Week*. May 16, 1983, pp. 100–110.

    A discussion of company efforts to increase worker productivity by restructuring job tasks and changing union worker rules.

Sabel, Charles: *Work and Politics*. Cambridge: Cambridge University Press, 1981.

    Similar to Reich's *The Next American Frontier*, Sabel traces the development of production and work structure in Western capitalist countries, concluding that these countries must now shift to flexible, high-skill production if they are to compete in the contemporary global economy.

Schmenner, Roger: "Productivity in the Factory and Industrial Policy." In Goldstein, Harvey A. (ed): *The State and Local Industrial Policy Question*. Chicago: American Planning Association, 1987, pp. 54–59.

    Schmenner states that the only industrial policy that might work for mature industries would be a "manufacturing extension service" that would provide assistance to management in improving productivity.

Walton, Richard: "Establishing and Maintaining High-Commitment Work Systems." In Kimberly, John R. (ed): *Organization Life Cycles*. San Francisco: Jossey-Bass, 1980.

    Case studies of efforts to introduce automated processing and autonomous work teams in manufacturing.

Walton, Richard and Paul Lawrence (eds): *Human Resource Management: Trends and Challenges*. Boston: Harvard University Press, 1985.

    A collection of essays on the state-of-the-art in organizational and technological innovation, with a focus on achieving a more flexible, productive workforce.

172 *Industrial and Trade Policies*

———: *Innovating to Compete: Lessons for Diffusing and Managing Change in the Workplace*. San Francisco: Jossey-Bass Publishers, 1987.

　　Walton constructs and applies a theory of innovative change, using the maritime shipping industry in eight countries as examples from which he draws implications for action by industries and government.

Witte, John: *Democracy, Authority and Alienation in Work*. Chicago: University of Chicago Press, 1980.

　　Witte presents a detailed case study of an unsuccessful worker participation effort in an American manufacturing company, illustrating the numerous fundamental changes that must precede or accompany successful worker participation efforts.

Progressive and Marxist Views of Industrial Policy

Ackerman, Frank: *Hazardous to Our Wealth: Economic Policies in the 1980s*. Boston: South End Press, 1984.

　　See the annotated bibliography in chapter 3.

Alperovitz, Gar and Jeff Faux: *Rebuilding America: A Blueprint for the New Economy*. New York: Pantheon Books, 1984.

　　Wide-ranging analysis of U.S. economic crisis and reform program, with emphasis on locally based economic democracy.

Alperovitz, Gar and Roger Skurski (eds): *American Economic Policy: Problems and Prospects*. Notre Dame, Ind.: University of Notre Dame Press, 1984.

　　Collection of essays on U.S. economic policies, from left-liberal and radical perspectives, with emphasis on industrial policy, workplace democracy, and monetary policy.

Bluestone, Barry and Bennett Harrison: *The Deindustrialization of America: Plant Closings, Community Abandonment, and the Dismantling of Basic Industry*. New York: Basic Books, 1982.

　　This book traces the development of the U.S. economy since World War II, arguing that America has suffered from deindustrialization since 1971, due to the actions of America's multinational corporations and U.S. government policies. The authors critique liberal industrial policy proposals and outline a "radical industrial policy."

———: *The Great U-Turn: Corporate Restructuring and the Polarizing of America*. New York: Basic Books, 1988.

　　In some ways a sequel to *Deindustrialization*, this book argues that corporate restructuring and federal government policies have promoted a polarization of American incomes. The authors propose a number of strategies to reform the economy, including industrial policy and workplace democracy.

Bluestone, Barry, Bennett Harrison, and Lucy Gorham: "Storm Clouds on the Horizon." In Goldstein, Harvey A. (ed): *The State and Local Industrial Policy Question*. Chicago: American Planning Association, 1987.

The authors respond to the argument that the United States is not deindustrializing.

Bowles, Samuel, David M. Gordon, and Thomas E. Weisskopf: *Beyond the Waste Land: A Democratic Alternative to Economic Decline.* Garden City, N.J.: Anchor Press/Doubleday, 1983.

The authors argue that much of American industry's productivity slowdown can be traced to the bureaucratization of production and other measures that corporate managers have taken since World War II to maintain a position of dominance over labor. Productivity would increase substantially if these and other forms of waste were eliminated through the democratization of the economy.

Carnoy, Martin and Derek Shearer: *Economic Democracy: The Challenge of the 1980s.* White Plains: M.E. Sharpe, Inc., 1980.

This is a blueprint for democratizing the U.S. economy, focusing primarily on measures to democratize firms. The authors cite examples of existing cases of economic democracy in the United States and Western Europe.

Center for Popular Economics: *Economic Report of the People: An Alternative to the Economic Report of the President.* Boston: South End Press, 1986.

See the annotated bibliography in chapter 3.

Goodman, Robert: *The Last Entrepreneurs: America's Regional Wars for Jobs and Dollars.* Boston: South End Press, 1979.

This book focuses on the problems of community economic dislocation caused by hypermobility of capital among regions in the United States and abroad. Chapter 8, "Regional Socialism: An American Alternative," provides one radical view of how economic planning might work in an American political context.

Magdoff, Harry and Paul M. Sweezy: *Stagnation and the Financial Explosion.* New York: Monthly Review Press, 1987.

See the annotated bibliography in chapter 3.

Rodberg, Leonard S. and William K. Tabb: "What Can We Learn From the Industrial Policy Debate?" *Social Policy.* Vol. 17, No. 3, Winter 1987, pp. 27–33.

The authors provide a sober analysis of the barriers to national political consensus on industrial policy and emphasize that radical economic reform would focus on state and locally based democratic planning and production for human needs, with a limited orientation to global competitiveness.

Staudohar, Paul D. and Holly Brown: *Deindustrialization and Plant Closure.* Lexington: D.C. Heath and Company, 1987.

A collection of 26 essays from left-liberal and radical perspectives on the problem and impacts of deindustrialization and plant closures, legislation and public policies to address the problem, and comparisons of the U.S. experience with the experiences of Western Europe and Japan.

Zukin, Sharon (ed): *Industrial Policy: Business and Politics in the United States and France.* New York: Praeger Publishers, 1985.

A series of 21 essays from left-liberal and radical perspectives on industrial policies in the United States and France, as well as strategic planning practices by European businesses and labor unions.

The Organization of Work and Workplace Democracy

Braverman, Harry: *Labor and Monopoly Capital: The Degradation of Work in the Twentieth Century.* New York: Monthly Review Press, 1974.

Braverman provides a modern extension and application, as well as some empirical support, of Marx's proposition that capitalists are driven to continually cheapen and control labor by de-skilling the labor process.

Edwards, Richard: *Contested Terrain: The Transformation of Work in the Twentieth Century.* New York: Basic Books, 1979.

This may be considered a companion piece and extension of Braverman's *Labor and Monopoly Capital,* as it focuses on the same issue of control over the labor process. Yet the focus here is more on the structure of the entire work organization than the individual job. Edwards develops a typology of forms of work control under capitalism.

Rosen, Corey M., Katherine J. Klein, and Karen M. Young: *Employee Ownership in America: The Equity Solution.* Lexington: D.C. Heath and Company, 1986.

The authors analyze over 50 employee-owned companies, both ESOPs (employee stock ownership plans) and worker cooperatives, documenting greater productivity, profitability, and in some cases, growth rates than in conventional, investor-owned firms. This superior performance is traced primarily to the amount of stock that workers receive and to worker participation in management decision making.

Rothschild, Joyce and J. Allen Whitt: *The Cooperative Workplace: Potentials and Dilemmas of Organizational Democracy and Participation.* Cambridge: Cambridge University Press, 1986.

Explains the genesis and rationale for workplace democracy and analyzes the factors that promote stable, successful democratic organizations.

Conservative Views on Industrial Policy

Friedman, Milton and Rose Friedman: *Free to Choose: A Personal Statement.* New York: Harcourt Brace Jovanovich, 1980.

See the annotated bibliography in chapter 2.

Lavoie, Don: *National Economic Planning: What Is Left?* Cambridge, Mass.: Ballinger Publishing Company, 1985.

This is a contemporary and expanded version of the "knowledge problem" argument that Friedrich Hayek developed in the first half of the twentieth century to show the incompatibility of centralized economic planning and freedom. Lavoie brings this argument to bear in his critique of liberal and radical industrial policy proposals.

Lawrence, Robert Z.: *Can America Compete?* Washington, D.C.: The Brookings Institution, 1984.

Lawrence argues that, contrary to the claims of Bluestone and Harrison, America is not deindustrializing. The problems afflicting American manufacturing industries in the 1980s are due, primarily, to macroeconomic factors that the government should address—the 1980–82 recession, the overvalued dollar (which makes American goods too expensive abroad), and the federal budget deficit.

McKenzie, Richard B.: *Competing Visions: The Political Conflict over America's Economic Future.* Washington, D.C.: The Cato Institute, 1985.

———: *The American Job Machine.* New York: Universe Books, 1988.

These books are two of over a dozen published by Richard McKenzie since the late 1970s on the subjects of national economic policy, U.S. industral competitiveness, plant closings, and the role of government in the economy. *Competing Visions* is a detailed analysis and critique of the deindustrialization argument and national industrial policy proposals advanced by liberals and radicals in the 1980s. *The American Job Machine* focuses more on the left-liberal argument that American incomes are becoming polarized with the emergence of the service economy. McKenzie criticizes liberal and radical calls for worker retraining, minimum wages, and plant closing regulations.

O'Connell, Francis A., Jr.: *Plant Closings: Worker Rights, Management Rights and the Law.* New Brunswick: Transaction Books, 1986.

O'Connell argues that attempts to regulate plant closings wrongly presume that workers have property rights in their jobs. Hence the United States should not have plant closing laws. O'Connell's argument was superseded somewhat, with the passage in 1988 of the National Worker Adjustment and Retraining Notification Act, which requires businesses with 100 or more employees to provide written notification 60 days in advance of a plant closing or mass layoff.

Petri, Thomas E., William F. Clinger, Jr., Nancy L. Johnson, and Lynn Martin (eds): *National Industrial Policy: Solution or Illusion.* Boulder: Westview Press, 1984.

This is a collection of essays by prominent critics of industrial policy, including Robert Z. Lawrence, Charles Schultze, and Richard McKenzie, as well as recommendations that to increase U.S. competitiveness, the United States should rely more on market forces and less on government intervention.

Schultze, Charles: "Industrial Policy: A Dissent." *The Brookings Review.* Vol. 2, No. 1, Fall 1983, pp. 3–12.

This is probably the most often-quoted criticism of industrial policy. The criticism consists of four arguments: the United States is not deindustrializing; Japanese economic success is not due to its industrial policy; government bureaucrats are no more competent to pick industrial winners and losers than are private investors; the American political system is not capable of making the tough choices necessary to make industrial policy work.

Schumpeter, Joseph: *Capitalism, Socialism and Democracy.* New York: Harper and Row, 1975 (1942).

See the annotated bibliography in chapter 2.

Shull, Steven A. and Jeffrey E. Cohen (eds): *Economics and Politics of Industrial Policy: The United States and Western Europe.* Boulder: Westview Press, 1986.

This is a collection of seven essays on the politics of industrial policy in America and Western Europe. Overall, the views expressed here are not so much conservative, as the term has been used in this chapter, but skeptical of the feasibility of and prospects for industrial policy.

Tajika, Eiji and Yuji Yiu: "Japan's Public Policies for Investment." In Lee, Chung H. and Ippei Yamazawa (eds): *The Economic Development of Japan and Korea: A Parallel with Lessons.* New York: Praeger Publications, 1990, pp. 33–52.

Based upon their research, the authors conclude that the Japanese government did not practice a coherent industrial policy in the three decades after World War II and that high levels of investment in manufacturing during that period must be attributed to decisions made by the private sector independent of government policy.

Economic Conversion Planning and Adjustment

Anderson, Marion, Greg Bischak, and Michael Oden: *Converting the American Economy: The Economic Effects of an Alternative Security Policy.* Lansing, Mich.: Employment Research Associates, 1991.

See the annotated bibliography in chapter 3.

Center for Economic Conversion: *Positive Alternatives.* Winter 1991.

This quarterly magazine discusses current issues in and approaches to economic conversion. The Center for Economic Conversion is a prominent clearing house of information on economic conversion policies and strategies at the national, state, and local levels.

Gordon, Suzanne and Dave McFadden (eds): *Economic Conversion: Revitalizing America's Economy.* Cambridge, Mass.: Ballinger Publishers, 1984.

A slightly dated but excellent overview of the economics and politics of economic conversion, with useful case studies of conversion planning efforts.

Lynch, John E. (ed): *Economic Adjustment and Conversion of Defense Industries.* Boulder: Westview Press, 1987.

This volume makes the important distinction between conversion of plants from military to civilian production, and adjustment of local economies after a defense plant or base has closed, discussing, through case studies, the appropriate use of conversion and adjustment strategies.

"Who Pays for Peace? Many Companies and Towns Are on a Knife's Edge." *Business Week.* July 2, 1990, pp. 64–70.

This article discusses the impact of defense cuts on companies, workers, and communities, and some state government responses.

Trade Policy

This section includes only those sources not annotated in the "Industrial Policy" section above.

Background

Bhagwati, Jagdish: *Protectionism.* Cambridge, Mass.: MIT Press, 1988.

This is a lucid discussion of the ebb and flow of protectionist pressures in the world trading system since the nineteenth century, with primary emphasis on the postwar period and current U.S. policy alternatives. The author describes how ideas, political-economic interests, and institutional structures all play a role in fashioning and implementing trade policy. He advocates essentially centrist-conservative policies for the United States, as discussed in the chapter.

Gilpin, Robert: *The Political Economy of International Relations.* Princeton: Princeton University Press, 1987.

See the annotated bibliography in chapter 1.

Kelly, Margaret, Naheed Kirmani, Miranda Xafa, Clemens Boonekamp, and Peter Winglee: *Issues and Developments in International Trade Policy.* Washington, D.C.: International Monetary Fund, December 1988.

The authors provide thumbnail sketches of current trade policies and industrial policies of the world's major industrialized and developing countries, with particular emphasis on the relationship of these policies to GATT rules and the Uruguay Round of the GATT talks. The authors express generally conservative views on these issues.

Krugman, Paul R.: *The Age of Diminished Expectations: U.S. Economic Policy in the 1990s.* Cambridge, Mass.: MIT Press, 1990.

See the annotated bibliography in chapter 3.

Krugman, Paul R. (ed): *Strategic Trade Policy and the New International Economics.* Cambridge, Mass.: MIT Press, 1986.

This is a cross section of views on the policy implications of the "new thinking" in international trade—that nations may be able to improve their comparative advantage through activist government policies to promote key industries that have spillover benefits for other sectors of the economy. Krugman himself does not believe that we have the ability to craft an activist trade policy that would work better than the rule-based GATT framework, but some of the volume's contributors do advocate activist policies.

Spero, Joan Edelman: *The Politics of International Economic Relations.* Fourth Edition. New York: St. Martin's Press, 1990.

See the annotated bibliography in chapter 3.

178 *Industrial and Trade Policies*

Liberal and Progressive Views on Trade Policy

Ackerman, Frank: *Hazardous to Our Wealth: Economic Policies in the 1980s.* Boston: South End Press, 1984.
    See the annotated bibliography in chapter 3.

Blackwell, Sir Basil: "The State and the Macro-Industrial Economy—Towards a Coherent Multi-National Policy." *Omega.* Vol. 16, No. 4, July 1988, pp. 265–275.

    The author argues that multinational corporations (MNCs) are uniquely situated to help all nations participate in the "industrial exploitation of technology," if they are properly regulated through cooperative international standards. In fact, when properly regulated, MNCs do a much better job of developing and commercializing technology than the public sector does, in the author's view.

Center for Popular Economics: *Economic Report of the People: An Alternative to the Economic Report of the President.* Boston: South End Press, 1986.
    See the annotated bibliography in chapter 3.

Choate, Pat and J.K. Linger: *The High-Flex Society: Shaping America's Economic Future.* New York: Alfred A. Knopf, 1986.
    See the "Industrial Policy" section of this bibliography.

Glickman, Norman J. and Douglas P. Woodward: *The New Competitors: How Foreign Investors Are Changing the U.S. Economy.* New York: Basic Books, 1989.
    See the annotated bibliography in chapter 6.

Harrison, Bennett: "The Return of the Big Firms." *Social Policy.* Vol. 21, No. 1, Summer 1990, pp. 7–19.

    Contrary to popular myth, argues Harrison, large firms are not giving way to small, innovative firms. Rather, for the past decade, large corporations have been restructuring and diversifying their operations. They are continuing to spread their facilities across the globe, leading to increasing concentration of economic power and decision making. Governments and workers alike must recognize this fact and develop appropriate international policies, so that we can "live with bigness."

Kuttner, Robert: *Managed Trade and Economic Sovereignty.* Washington, D.C.: Economic Policy Institute, 1989.

    Kuttner charges that American adherence to the no-longer-feasible notion of free trade based upon multilateral rules administered through the GATT system puts us at the mercy of other nations, who practice strategic trade and industrial policies. Kuttner traces America's stubborn adherence to the free trade ideal to its postwar role of world "hegemon." But, he points out, we no longer have the economic clout to play this role. If we do not adjust to the new realities with managed trade and industrial policies, the transition to a new world order will be much more difficult for the United States.

Mead, Walter Russell: "American Economic Policy in the Antemillenial Era." *World Policy Journal.* Vol. 6, No. 3, Summer 1989.
    See the annotated bibliography in chapter 3.

Tyson, Laura D'Andrea: "Managed Trade: Making the Best of Second Best." In Lawrence, Robert Z. and Charles L. Schultze (eds): *An American Trade Strategy: Options for the 1990s*. Washington, D.C.: The Brookings Institution, 1990, pp. 142–185.

Untrammeled free trade is not a viable option in today's global economy, especially in high-technology, knowledge-intensive industries, whose spillover benefits for the rest of the economy incline all national governments to subsidize their exports and protect their home markets. The United States needs outcomes-oriented, managed trade arrangements with other countries in these industries, as well as other managed trade policies.

Marxist Views on Trade Policy

Islam, Sadequl: "Free Trade and Protection: The U.S.–Canada Case." *Monthly Review*. Vol. 39, No. 6, November 1987, pp. 20–32.

Sadequl discusses the politics of the U.S.–Canada FTA. He notes that Marx's own views on free trade changed from initial optimism that free trade would develop the social forces of underdeveloped regions more quickly, thus leading to earlier socialist revolution there, to the view that the exploitation of undeveloped regions should be avoided. Sadequl believes the U.S.–Canada pact will not enhance the political power of the working class in either Canada or the United States, and that working conditions, social welfare, and environmental conditions will, if anything, continue to worsen as a result of the agreement.

Kolko, Joyce: *Restructuring the World Economy*. New York: Pantheon Books, 1988.

A rich and detailed account of the restructuring of the world economy since the early 1970s. Kolko argues that the economic stagnation and crisis that have characterized this period, and the actions of capitalists and the state to resolve the crisis and shore up the system, are simply temporary incarnations of the recurrent, systemic problems of capitalism. We should not expect such international economic agreements to last, nor should we expect them to bring improvements in the lives of working people.

Lenin, V.I.: *Imperialism: The Highest Stage of Capitalism*. New York: International Publishers, 1939 (1917).

In this treatise, Lenin sets forth his famous revision to Marx's theory of social development and revolution. Lenin argues that capitalist struggle for world domination is the final stage in the system's development, and that underdeveloped regions, as the weakest link in the capitalist chain, may be the most likely sites for revolution, contrary to Marx's ideas on the matter.

Sweezy, Paul and Harry Magdoff: "International Cooperation—A Way Out?" Review of the Month. *Monthly Review*, Vol. 39, No. 6, November 1987, pp. 1–19.

The authors critique Ricardo's theory of comparative advantage in international trade based upon static endowments of land, minerals, climate, and so on, by tracing the political basis of Ricardo's own famous example of comparative advantage, in which Portugal specializes in wine production and Britain in textiles. Having demonstrated that international trading relationships are fundamentally political ones, they assert that current prospects for international political cooperation in the trade arena do not seem bright, despite the best intentions of liberals. See also the annotated bibliography in chapter 3.

Conservative and Centrist Views on Trade Policy

Bergsten, C. Fred: *America in the World Economy: A Strategy for the 1990s.* Washington, D.C.: Institute for International Economics, 1988.

See the annotated bibliography in chapter 3.

Dornbusch, Rudiger W.: "Policy Options for Freer Trade: The Case for Bilateralism." In Lawrence, Robert Z. and Charles L. Schultze (eds): *An American Trade Strategy: Options for the 1990s.* Washington, D.C.: The Brookings Institution, 1990.

Dornbusch calls for "aggressive bilateralism" and the pursuit of regional trading blocs, not as ends in themselves, but as strategies in the long-term pursuit of a multilateral free trade regime.

Hufbauer, Gary C.: *The Free Trade Debate: Background Paper.* Twentieth Century Fund, Task Force on the Future of American Trade Policy. New York: Priority Press Publications, 1989.

Hufbauer makes the case that the U.S. trade deficit problem is best handled through appropriate macroeconomic policies. The growth of protectionism is a serious problem, however, for the United States and the trading system generally. While a rule-based, multilateral free trade regime is the appropriate goal, it is unrealistic to expect the GATT framework to be sufficient to achieve it. Rather, we should use free trade agreements (such as the U.S.–Canada FTA) as building blocs of a global free trade system. Our next major goal should be the establishment of an OECD-country, free trade and investment area.

Krueger, Anne O.: "Free Trade Is the Best Policy." In Lawrence, Robert Z. and Charles L. Schultze (eds): *An American Trade Strategy: Options for the 1990s.* Washington, D.C.: The Brookings Institution, 1990.

Krueger asserts that increasing specialization of production makes the case for Ricardian free trade even stronger. Protectionism is costly to consumers and to producers in nonprotected industries, and managed trade policies founder on the problem of insufficient knowledge for picking industries to subsidize. Our best strategy is to push for the elimination of all border tariffs within GATT and strengthen the GATT surveillance and investigation (of protectionist practices) capabilities.

Lawrence, Robert Z.: Discussion of Dornbusch's "Policy Options for Freer Trade." In Lawrence, Robert Z. and Charles L. Schultze: *An American*

Trade Strategy: Options for the 1990s. Washington, D.C.: The Brookings Institution, 1990.

Lawrence takes issue with Dornbusch's case for aggressive bilateralism. Dornbusch's "Policy Options" is annotated above.

Lawrence, Robert Z. and Schultze, Charles L. (eds): *An American Trade Strategy: Options for the 1990s*. Washington, D.C.: The Brookings Institution, 1990.

This is a collection of essays and discussions of appropriate U.S. trade policy. The principal contributors are Krueger, Dornbusch, and Tyson, whose papers are annotated elsewhere in this bibliography. The paper by Lawrence and Schultze, "Evaluating the Options," takes a generally conservative approach to the issues, finding flaws in the protectionist, managed trade and aggressive bilateralism approaches. The authors agree in large part with Krueger's view that the only viable course (outside of macroeconomic policies) is to work for greater trade liberalization through the GATT.

Niskanen, William A.: "U.S. Trade Policy: Problems and Prospects." In Crane, Edward H. and David Boaz (eds): *An American Vision: Policies for the '90s*. Washington, D.C.: Cato Institute, 1989.

Niskanen faults the Reagan administration for inconsistency in its trade policies and both Congress and the administration for a drift toward protectionism. The author advocates reducing the trade deficit through macroeconomic policies to encourage saving and reduce the federal deficit, avoiding nontariff measures to restrain imports, and broadening the use of bilateral free trade agreements.

CHAPTER 5

Education and Training Policy

From an economic perspective, the purpose of education is to build "human capital," the knowledge and skills that enable persons to produce goods and services. Economists have long recognized that human capital is at least as significant a factor in a nation's economic growth as are land, physical capital, and management.

During the 1980s, many Americans came to believe that insufficient worker knowledge and skills caused the nation's sagging performance in the global economy. This view led to the conclusion that America's education and training systems were not performing well, sparking an education reform movement that continues to this day. This chapter will present the major criticisms, reform proposals, counterproposals, and policies that emerged during this period of ferment and change in America's public education system.

Education debates differ from controversies over industrial policy, fiscal policy, or other economic issues, in at least one important respect—education serves goals other than economic competitiveness. For this reason, education debates and reforms reflect diverse values, particularly the following:

1. Education should prepare persons for work, by teaching appropriate skills and work attitudes. This value appears under various labels, such as education for business needs; education for economic competitiveness; and education with a focus on achievement, excellence, maintaining high standards, or efficiency.
2. Education should provide persons with the appropriate knowledge, skills, and self-concept to be reflective, active citizens of a democratic society.
3. Education should fulfill a socioeconomic "leveling" function; it should provide everyone with the same base of knowledge

and skills, thus mitigating the unequal socioeconomic circumstances of birth. This value appears under the label of equal opportunity, social mobility, and open access to educational institutions.

Over the course of American history, various reform groups have championed one or another of these values. The successful groups have left their marks on curricula, pedagogy, and especially, the institutional structures of public education and training.

The American system of universal, free, primary and secondary public education is an excellent example of the leveling value. Since its introduction with Horace Mann's Common School reform program in 1837, which made school attendance compulsory for everyone and set standards for curricula and teacher proficiency, the American primary and secondary education system has been the envy of many nations.[1] The value of education for democratic citizenship is perhaps most often associated with the work of John Dewey, the turn-of-the-century philosopher. His views and those of his followers continue to influence curriculum content in primary and secondary schools.[2]

The value of education for business needs is reflected in various education institutions and practices, such as the "tracking" system introduced at the turn of the century to prepare "bright" students for college and the upper levels of corporate hierarchies, and to guide seemingly less gifted or less motivated students toward vocational-technical careers. The value of education for business needs is also apparent in high school course offerings that feature vocational-technical skills, as well as accounting and typing skills.

Thus the current system of universal primary and secondary education, with vocational tracking and a mix of courses in liberal arts, critical thinking, and vocational-technical skills, is a compromise among different and sometimes conflicting values. The array of different education institutions—a situation that is somewhat peculiar to the United States—also reflects these compromises. While most students attend public schools, private schools continue to thrive. Vocational-technical schools serve as a substitute for high school for many students. Beyond the high school level, a vast number of proprietary schools and more than 1,200 community colleges provide individual courses, certificates, and degrees in technical fields. Also, American public and private colleges and universities, whose governance structures and practices vary from state to state and from school to school, reflect different compromises among the three major education values.

While at any given moment, it may appear that these compromises are stable, events external to the education system, particularly changes in the economy, can easily lead to reform movements that upset the status quo. For example, the turn-of-the-century restructuring of the work process from craft to mass production, the growth in firm size, and the rise of new management and planning tasks separate from production, as well as the rapid influx of non-English-speaking immigrants with no industrial skills, created numerous production problems. To secure a labor force with the skills and attitudes necessary to perform increasingly diverse tasks in growing corporations, business leaders and kindred spirits promoted education reforms that would prepare people for increasingly varied jobs in the new workplace. Business leaders pushed for the use of standardized tests and the aforementioned practice of tracking and vocational counseling to divide students into different ability groups.[3]

The Civil Rights Movement (whose roots are in large part economic) promoted the leveling function of education by pressing the government to address the issue of racial discrimination in the education system. The government responded with reform legislation throughout the 1960s and 1970s, seeking to reduce inequities in public school funding, to end racial and gender discrimination in schools, and to assist students with learning disabilities and those from disadvantaged backgrounds.[4] Beginning in 1961, the federal government initiated job training programs for disadvantaged and structurally unemployed workers. It expanded this commitment through numerous acts passed in the next two decades, including the Comprehensive Employment and Training Act of 1973 (CETA); the Targeted Jobs Tax Credit program, established in 1978; and the Job Training Partnership Act (JTPA), established in 1983 as the successor to CETA.[5]

In the 1980s, American education institutions and practices came under attack again, as Americans learned that the average scores of high school students on standardized achievement tests had declined steadily from the mid-1960s to the 1980s, and that American students performed worse than foreign students on achievement tests. Education reformers point to these facts as the symptom and cause of America's economic woes, concluding that America must revitalize its system of public education if it is to regain its competitive edge in the global marketplace.

Yet, educators, economists, and politicians debate the need for change and the forms it should take. How serious are the problems, really? Is a lack of appropriate worker skills to blame for America's economic woes? What skills do Americans really need? What kinds of education or training reform would best address our economic needs in the long run? Which reforms would best serve society in general? These questions not only pit conservatives, liberals, and radicals against each other, they also engender disagreement between educators and political economists, who hold different views about the role and function of education in American society.

Primary and Secondary Education and Workforce Training

Conservative Critiques and Reforms

The most widely known critique of American primary and secondary education is the report of President Ronald Reagan's National Commission on Excellence in Education: *A Nation at Risk*. Because of its importance in, and influence on, the current reform movement, the report will be considered in some detail, beginning with its oft-quoted opening statement:

> If an unfriendly foreign power had attempted to impose on America the mediocre educational performance that exists today, we might well have viewed it as an act of war. As it stands, we have allowed this to happen to ourselves. We have even squandered the gains in student achievement made in the wake of the Sputnik challenge. Moreover, we have dismantled essential support systems which helped make those gains possible. We have, in effect, been committing an act of unthinking, unilateral educational disarmament.[6]

Even as knowledge and skills increasingly determine a nation's competitive advantage in world markets, American education institutions are falling behind those of the rest of the industrialized world. The gravity of the problem, especially at the high school level, is indicated in many of the commission's findings:

- American students consistently score lower than foreign students on internationally standardized tests.
- The average scores of high school students on standardized tests, including the Scholastic Aptitude Test, have declined since 1963.
- There are 23 million functionally illiterate Americans.
- Business and military leaders complain that they must spend millions of dollars on remedial education and training for their workers in reading, writing, spelling, and computation.[7]

The authors of *A Nation at Risk* identified several causes for the perceived declines in high school student achievement since the 1960s:

- Student substitution of "general track" courses for vocational and college preparatory courses.
- Declining standards and expectations, including less time spent on science, mathematics, and foreign languages; less than one hour of homework per night; open admissions by 20 percent of the country's four-year colleges, and lowered admission standards by many other colleges.
- American teachers are drawn from the bottom quarter of high-school and college graduates, their training does not include enough work in their fields of instruction, and they are poorly paid.[8]

In 1987, a *Workforce 2000* study conducted by William Johnston of the conservative and widely respected Hudson Institute showed further cause for concern. Johnston analyzed demographic trends and found (as others have) that U.S. population growth will slow to 1 percent per year in the 1990s, and the average age of the workforce will increase. Nonwhites, women, and immigrants will make up over five-sixths of the net additions to the workforce between 1987 and 2000, yet minorities and immigrants have traditionally been the most disadvantaged and least well educated members of the labor force.

Johnston studied trends in the job market and found that the number of jobs requiring higher level skills will increase by large percentages, while the number of jobs requiring lower level skills will grow at much slower rates. To be sure, the largest number of jobs created in the 1990s will be in the service, administrative support, marketing, and sales occupations (e.g., cooks, nursing aides, waiters, secretaries, clerks, computer operators, and cashiers). Yet even these will require middle-level skills, such as reading directions, adding and subtracting, and thinking and speaking clearly. Growth in jobs requiring low skill levels, such as laborers, hand workers, and transport workers, will be negligible in the 1990s. Juxtaposing the demographic and job requirement trends, Johnston predicted significant skill shortages unless the education and training of disadvantaged persons improves and standards rise dramatically.[9]

Kathleen Miller, a corporate trainer, substantiates Johnston's conclusions, claiming that one-half of all jobs are restructured or replaced every five to eight years.[10] On average, she believes that the new jobs require more skills than the old jobs, and without question, they require *different* skills. Job restructuring in the majority of cases involves the introduction of automation or new computerized equipment:

> Microprocessor technology leads to a shift from physical activity to mental effort. In the airplane industry, riveting, a semiskilled production job, involves fastening together the fuselage and wings of planes. The job used to be done with a hand-held riveting gun, but now a numerically controlled riveting machine has replaced the manual labor. The computer establishes the correct position and procedures for driving the rivets; the operator has no physical contact with the work but observes the process on a television screen, watches for errors, and does some troubleshooting. These changes are not limited to making airplanes. In many modern factories, the production process is computerized so that people are no longer involved in the physical execution of tasks but are responsible for monitoring the automated processes and making judgements pertaining to the entire operation.[11]

Moreover, advanced automated manufacturing sometimes restructures work processes, leaving one worker responsible for several tasks that were previously parts of different jobs. The "new job may not require the same depth of skill in each of the more narrow jobs it absorbs, [but] it does require a wider variety of basic skills than any one of the other jobs."[12]

Miller claims that computerization also tends to push managerial control and decision making responsibility to lower organizational levels.[13] Indeed, there is evidence that some organizational hierarchies have become flatter in recent years, adopting worker problem-solving groups and autonomous teams, often after the introduction of automated process technology.[14] More importantly, the growth of international competition has dramatically increased the speed at which the state of the art changes. The resulting frequency of technological innovations requires workers to "continuously acquire new skills," claims Miller.[15]

So what skills do workers need? In a study prepared for the American Society of Training and Development and the U.S. Department of Labor, Anthony Carnevale, Leila Gainer, and Ann Meltzer claim that employers want workers with more than just basic skills, such as reading, writing, and arithmetic. Employers want workers who can also learn a variety of particular jobs because they know how to learn. They need workers with good listening and oral communication skills, and with problem-solving and creative thinking skills. Employers want workers who have interpersonal and negotiation skills, who can work well in teams and who can motivate and lead co-workers to accomplish the organization's goals. In addition, claim the authors of the study, employers want workers with high self-esteem, the ability to set and achieve goals, and some sense of their personal and career development.[16]

Yet since the number of entry-level workers is decreasing and will continue to do so until the next century, managers must turn to disadvantaged workers and others who lack basic skills in reading, writing, and mathematics. Even more troublesome are business leader complaints that these persons bring to the workplace a lack of appropriate work attitudes and related skills.

To solve these problems, conservatives advocate three types of reforms: changing school curricula, restructuring institutions, and solving the "culture of poverty" problem that undermines labor force quality. *A Nation at Risk* called for several changes to reform school curricula and teacher competence:

- All high school students must take four years of English, three years each of math, science, and social studies, one-half year of computer science, and for the college-bound students, two years of foreign language.
- High schools, colleges, and universities must adopt more rigorous and measurable standards and higher expectations for academic performance and student conduct, including more extensive use of grades and standardized achievement tests.
- Textbooks and other learning tools should be updated and upgraded to assure more rigorous content and current applications of technology.
- The high school day should be increased from six to seven hours, and the school year should be expanded from 180 to 200 or 220 days.
- Student placement, promotion, and graduation should be guided by academic progress, not by student age.
- Teacher quality must be improved through better college preparatory programs with higher standards. Teacher salaries should be "professionally competitive, market-sensitive, and performance-based." Teachers should have 11-month contracts to allow more time for curriculum and professional development, and they should have career ladders that distinguish among beginning instructors, experienced teachers, and master teachers.
- Finally, while state and local governments should continue to fund over 90 percent of primary and secondary school costs, the federal government should provide leadership by defining the national interest in education and by helping to meet the

special needs of the gifted and talented, the socioeconomically disadvantaged, minority and language minority students, and the handicapped.[17]

A Nation at Risk found considerable support among conservative education theorists and policymakers.[18] In the years following its publication, virtually every state enacted some kind of reform of primary and secondary education, including new graduation requirements, textbook improvements, longer school days, longer school years, master teacher programs, higher teacher salaries, teacher career ladders, teacher competence testing, stricter disciplinary policy, and more homework. Most states began to rely on standardized tests to measure student achievement and to assess the quality of education provided by the schools.[19] In 1986, the National Governors' Association adopted education reform as its first priority and commissioned studies on education problems and solutions.

By 1989, reformers began to add structural and institutional changes to the education reform agenda. School districts in Chicago, Rochester, Dade County, and elsewhere have improved school performance by decentralizing decision making to the school level and increasing the power of teachers to make curriculum and textbook decisions.

Yet conservative critics predict failure because these reforms do not free schools from the massive state and local school bureaucracies that, they assert, stifle school initiative.[20] For example, in *Politics, Markets and America's Schools*, John Chubb and Terry Moe study the determinants of student achievement. They conclude that school organizational structure plays a key role in student learning and that students learn better in private schools than in public ones, because the private schools are free to define and pursue their teaching missions without the excessive bureaucracy and politics that characterize public schools. To improve education in America, they argue, we must dismantle the bureaucracy and privatize schooling. In the Chubb and Moe system, the states' only roles would be to certify schools and provide "scholarships" (vouchers) that students would use to pay for education at the schools they choose. Resulting competition among schools would improve productivity and quality.[21] Since only student voucher payments (which could be raised or lowered by the state to compensate for disabilities or disadvantaged backgrounds) would finance operations, schools that did not attract enough students would go out of business.

Chubb and Moe's conclusions and recommendations are not new. Indeed, three decades ago, conservative economist Milton

Friedman articulated a case for the privatization of schooling and the issuance of publicly funded vouchers to all children for tuition payment.[22] Until recently, however, this "voucher movement" or "choice movement," as it is now called, had relatively few adherents and did not exert great influence on the structure of primary and secondary education. But after a decade of sustained criticism of America's performance in education, the choice alternative is attracting new adherents. By 1991, 30 states had enacted or begun to consider legislation to adopt some form of primary and secondary school choice system (although most of them are considerably less sweeping than Chubb and Moe's proposals). In the next few years, it seems likely that other states will follow suit.

An equally ambitious conservative institutional reform is the business-education partnership. With strong encouragement from the Reagan and Bush administrations, businesses and local school districts are initiating joint programs to improve schools in ways suggested by *A Nation at Risk*. By 1988, schools had formed almost 141,000 partnerships with businesses or other private organizations. These arrangements provide support to 40 percent of all public schools. According to Myra Alperson, the nature of these partnerships ranges from "full-fledged programs aimed at producing long-term improvements for students and their families, teachers, and schools," to "public relations ploys that promote a company's name among students and the community without concretely improving education." Business-education partnerships have grown and are likely to last, says Alperson, because "corporations have the money and technology that local governments lack—and the corporations ... need the skilled labor pool that schools should be producing."[23]

One of the most well-known partnerships is the Boston Compact, initiated in 1982. Its 400 corporate members guaranteed jobs for 1,000 city high school graduates by 1985, in exchange for higher reading and math competencies, lower dropout rates, and higher job placement rates. Although the compact fell short of these goals and suffered some stormy times, it has become the prototype for efforts in Atlanta, Cincinnati, Milwaukee, Seattle, and Portland, Oregon.[24]

By 1990, both state and national policymakers had embraced much of the conservative reform agenda. In 1989, President George Bush, the self-styled education president, met with the National Governors' Association in an education summit. The subsequent joint statement called for a nationwide process to develop national education goals to make the nation more internationally competitive; to overhaul federal and state laws and regulations to focus on achieving education results; and to restructure education so that its focus shifts to educational results, decentralized decision making, rigorous instruction, first-rate teachers, and the involvement of parents and the business community in primary and secondary education. Although a 1990 National Governors' Association progress report revealed difficulties in achieving these goals, all signs point to continued emphasis on primary and secondary education reform.

Yet additional efforts are necessary, say conservatives, to cure the culture of poverty problems that afflict city youths and lead to their poor performance on the job and lack of commitment to the labor market generally. David Boaz finds deficiencies in existing programs such as welfare, "second chance" training programs for those without high school degrees or skills, and even workfare programs that require welfare recipients to complete training programs and take jobs. He recommends the abolition of government institutions that foster dependency, such as welfare. He also calls for an end to minimum wages that deter employers from hiring youths with few skills. Such policies will create the kinds of positive role models that youths need to break out of poverty.[25]

Insofar as government-sponsored training and retraining for dislocated or structurally unemployed workers is concerned, some conservatives contend that it is unfair and socially inefficient for the government—other workers really—to shoulder this burden. Each worker should be responsible for providing his or her own training.[26] In short, the thrust of conservative education and training reforms is to refocus curriculum on basic skills and knowledge, and use markets or marketlike incentives to administer education and training services.

Radical Responses to Conservative Reforms

Radicals dispute both the conservative definition of the education and training problem and the solutions conservatives advocate. Education theorists Stanley Aronowitz and Henry Giroux decry a perceived subordination of educational priorities to the corporate order:

> The conservative vision of a school as a small, white-collar factory is mistaken. A school with time boundaries, rules, and productivity norms corresponds not to our collective social needs but to the galloping tendency of our society towards privatization in the conduct of everyday life and in the appropriation of public resources. [Schools should be] places of critical education in the service of creating a public sphere of citizens who are able to exercise power over their own lives and especially over the conditions for knowledge acquisition.[27]

Aronowitz and Giroux also criticize current institutional reforms, such as the growing use of the business-education partnership, which subverts the ability of schools to function as "a critical public sphere dedicated to teaching civic courage and critical literacy. . . . [Such partnerships embrace] business interests that collapse the critical into the instrumental and profitable." Rather than take the money with strings attached, which is offered by the business community, radicals argue that we must restore and increase public funding for schools.[28]

American society faces a crisis, say radical educators, but it is not the crisis identified by conservative reformers. Rather, the problem is a "gradual but relentless growth of antiintellectualism in American life;" a deterioration in American abilities to engage in critical thought, which threatens the very foundations of liberal democracy and renders any sort of radical transformation of society all but impossible.[29] An appropriate pedagogy would encourage critical thought by helping students to analyze the mass culture they experience, moving to successively more sophisticated social, political, and economic issues. For this to succeed, the role of the teacher must change from that of an increasingly de-skilled factory operative to that of an intellectual.

What of the concerns raised by conservatives and some liberals that Americans lack the basic skills, especially the science and math they need to compete internationally? Technical skills are necessary, Aronowitz and Giroux admit, but the current level of emphasis on technical learning is excessive, and the problem of technical illiteracy itself is greatly exaggerated.[30]

Martin Carnoy and Henry Levin worry that the tightened college admission requirements advocated by conservatives, and reduced financial aid for college students as a consequence of federal budget cutbacks, will force more students—especially those from disadvantaged backgrounds—into vocational education alternatives to college.[31] Yet in a world of rapidly changing technology, vocational education certificates and even vocationally oriented college degrees are likely to be in ever less demand in the job market. Contrary to the claims of conservatives that more technical skills are needed, radicals maintain that the long-term trend of the job structure under capitalism is toward de-skilling of the vast majority of jobs, even as a smaller number of higher-skilled jobs are created.

Several factors promote and facilitate de-skilling. As discussed in chapter 2, Adam Smith observed that when production of a good reaches a certain quantity, it is more efficient to have workers specialize in one or a few tasks than to have each worker make the entire product. Some years later, Charles Babbage noted that workers who perform one or a few simplified tasks command much lower wages than workers who perform many complicated tasks.[32] Since lower wages mean higher profits (assuming all else is unchanged), employers in mass markets want to divide the work process into its simplest parts, using cheap, low-skilled labor, instead of high-skilled craft workers. Radical researchers also have found that even where such detailed division of labor into de-skilled jobs is not more efficient, managers may prefer it because it gives them more control over workers.[33] Hence the assumption underlying current education reforms that widespread job *up*-skilling and not de-skilling is occurring, runs counter to the long-term trend of the job structure under capitalism, in the radical view.[34]

Recent findings by the liberal Commission on the Skills of the American Workforce, as reported by Louis Uchitelle of *The New York Times*, support the radical view:

> Many uneducated workers can quickly acquire the necessary skills to man even the most modern and sophisticated factories. If those workers succeed, then the prospect of a drastic shortage of skilled workers may be far less realistic than many had thought.[35]

How does this square with the *Workforce 2000* report discussed previously, which showed an increasing mismatch between job requirements and worker skills? In fact, a close analysis of the data and methods of that study indicates that the mismatch problem may be overstated. Two issues in particular are noteworthy. First, although an estimated 30 percent of the new jobs created between 1985 and 2000 will require college educations, only 23.6 percent of total jobs will require college by then, which is only slightly higher than the 22 percent of all jobs that required college training in 1985. In other words, while the most rapidly growing jobs require college degrees, the absolute number of these jobs is quite small compared to the total number of jobs. If present trends continue, we will need far more janitors than computer programmers.

A second issue is that the *Workforce 2000* study determined job skill requirements by looking at the formal educational *attainments* of persons holding those jobs in 1985. It is quite possible that these jobs did not actually *require* those education levels. Moreover, as radicals argue, jobs can be restructured to require less skill or more skill, depending upon a number of factors, especially management philosophy. Some radicals claim that Americans are overeducated and that employers use degrees more as personality screens than as indicators of knowledge or skills.[36]

The findings of the Commission on the Skills of the American Workforce support this contention:

> While businesses everywhere complain about the quality of their applicants, few refer to the kinds of skills acquired in school. ... The primary concern of more than 80 percent of employers is finding workers with a good work ethic and appropriate social behavior—"reliable," "a good attitude," "a pleasant appearance," "a good personality."[37]

Carol Ray and Roslyn Mickelson argue that the apparent failure of workers to manifest the correct attitudes on the job is less an indication of the workers' shortcomings than it is a rational worker's response to the poor quality of entry level jobs. Indeed, the growth of low-wage, part-time jobs, with no benefits of any kind, shows a lack of commitment on the part of managers to entry-level workers and workers who previously might have had secure positions.[38] Ray and Mickelson also charge that inner-city youths, far from suffering under a culture of poverty and lack of positive role models, accurately perceive the poor quality of jobs to which they have access, even if they have high school educations. Hence they have no rational, job-based motivation to finish high school.[39] Their refusal to willingly participate in their own exploitation is a form of political expression that may erupt into an overt class struggle.

If indeed employers want workers to enhance their skills through training programs, radicals maintain that workers, through their unions, should seek to become the organizers of that training, so as to shift the content of training away from its typically strong pro-management bias and to gain strategic control over the supply of skilled labor. In this way, workers could regain some of the power they have recently lost to management.[40] For example, a number of unions in New York City have initiated innovative workplace literacy programs, in which training ranges from English language instruction for immigrant workers to civil service exam preparation for American-born workers.[41] Increasing numbers of unions also are initiating workforce training programs through joint labor-management arrangements, such as that between the United Auto Workers and Chrysler Motor Company or the Auto Workers and Ford.[42]

But radical educators argue that vocational training should not be the major focus of education. Rather,

> broad, conceptually-oriented curricula where processes of abstraction, the social and historical context of scientific and technological innovation, and preparation in the logical processes underlying all calculations are far more relevant to the changing workplace. In short, what

America needs is a return to the liberal arts if indeed issues of equity as well as labor market penetration are to be successfully addressed.[43]

Liberal Responses to Conservative Reforms

Liberal educators take issue with the conservative approach to education reform. Christopher Hurn contends that the comparison of American and foreign students on standardized achievement tests, critical to the entire reform movement, is inappropriate because both the values and structure of American education differ markedly from those of other countries. Other systems may produce more students who have mastered certain standard subjects, but ours provides education for broader segments of the population, encourages greater local experimentation and attention to students' perceived educational needs, and fosters greater individual autonomy and critical thought.[44]

Harold Howe, the U.S. Commissioner of Education under President Lyndon Johnson, claims that the national alarm over the decline in Scholastic Aptitude Test (SAT) scores is based in part on a misunderstanding of changing school populations. In the 1960s and 1970s public policy opened the schoolhouse door to disadvantaged minority students, who traditionally score lower on the verbal and math portions of the test. Thus, average SAT scores declined. Current improvements in SAT score averages may reflect nothing more than a higher dropout rate that removes potential low scorers from the test pool. In short, test scores alone say little about education or national literacy. In fact, "each successive generation of youth continues to be more literate than the generation before it."[45]

Howe deplores a shift in the national agenda from providing educational opportunity to concern for excellence, a traditional business value:

> [An] economic argument is the engine that is driving the present school reform movement. It demands that schools produce excellence among the children of the poor for the sake of the nation's economic health. It wastes little time with concepts of equity or of our nation's need for independent-minded citizens to make a democracy and a complex society workable. Lip service is paid to these latter concepts, but after appropriate rhetoric has been supplied, school reform is back to the serious business of rescuing our corporations from Japanese competition. Very little has been said, in defining school reform's goals, about developing among youth an interest in international understanding.[46]

Howe accepts the findings of reports such as *Workforce 2000*, which state that job requirements are outstripping worker skills, but he believes that conservatives have proposed incorrect solutions to the problem. Strengthened teacher morale, student motivation, parental interest, and a humane school climate supportive of learning bring excellence, not the legislated standards conservatives demand.[47]

Other liberals attack conservative reforms as reflecting a dangerously narrow concept of curriculum and education goals. Elliott Eisner calls for a curriculum that gives balanced attention to multiple forms of literacy—including discourse, poetry, music, visual arts, math, and dance. Students need to learn how to formulate and solve problems, how to find the resources to deal with the unpredictable and the ambiguous, and how to critically distinguish rhetoric from evidence. Good schools, claims Eisner, develop students' affection for the subject matter—which is not possible through heavy reliance on grades and testing.[48]

Liberal educators also criticize conservative institutional reforms, such as the choice system. They accuse Chubb and Moe, the authors of *Politics, Markets and America's Schools* (discussed above) of faulty statistical analysis in claiming that school structure determines student achievement and that decentralized, private school structures lead to higher student achievement. In fact, claim the critics, the data used by Chubb and Moe support no such conclusion.[49]

Other liberal critics take issue with the underlying values and likely outcomes of a full-fledged choice system. One concern is that if schools become truly free of school board regulations, they will accept only the students they want (as private schools do now), rejecting those with learning disabilities or other problems. The result will be more socioeconomic and racial segregation of America's schools, liberals maintain.[50] Moreover, in a system that shifts all responsibility for ensuring school quality onto parents, children whose parents lack the knowledge and wherewithal to choose, or who lack the resources to transport their children to schools outside their neighborhoods, will fare poorly, exacerbating socioeconomic divisions in our society. Some schools will fare poorly also. For example, those that lose students will soon find themselves on the slippery slope to disaster, claim liberals, as the lost student voucher payments necessitate cuts in programs that make the school even less competitive with other schools.[51]

Most importantly, perhaps, liberals claim that a public school system that focuses solely on parental choice and satisfaction ignores its responsibility to the public at large to educate all children well. Indeed, the very fact that Americans have traditionally supported education with public funds indicates that it is considered a "merit good"—a good that we want everyone to consume because we believe that educated people enhance the prosperity and quality of life of the entire society.[52] Thus while liberal educators support some amount of decentralization of decision making to the school and teacher levels, they oppose competition among schools.

In partial contrast to liberal educators, liberal political economists generally support the conservative call for upgrading education standards and results.[53] Yet they do not accept the conservative view that American firms are, in fact, demanding more highly skilled workers. Rather, they agree with radicals that American managers continue to practice the Tayloristic management principle of deskilling work:

> There seems to be a systematic underevaluation in this country of how much difference it can make when people are well educated and when their skills are continuously developed and challenged. This underestimation of human resources becomes a self-fulfilling prophecy, for it translates into a pattern of training for work that turns out badly educated workers with skills that are narrow and hence vulnerable to rapid obsolescence.[54]

In addition, liberals claim that the American education and training systems are fragmented and hence not effective. In particular, they point to the lack of institutional support to help non-college-bound students make a successful transition from school to work.[55] Once on the job, most workers have few or no opportunities to upgrade their knowledge or skills. According to Paul Osterman:

> Studies of Germany and Japan show that for the same technical set-up productivity is much higher abroad and that the chief difference appears to be the human resource systems, including training, of our competitors.[56]

Indeed, employer-initiated worker training is much less extensive in the United States than is commonly believed. Although training is a $40-billion-per-year industry, only 19 percent of this amount is spent on worker training.[57] A recent study by the Conference Board (a prestigious national business association) found that only 18 percent of manufacturing firms provide training to workers, whereas 33 percent provide such training programs for managers. A Bureau of National Affairs survey found that 60 percent of firms provide courses to managers, 50 percent provide courses to professional and technical workers, but only 18 percent provide them to lower level workers.[58]

For small and midsize firms, the problem is as much financial as it is philosophical. Michael Dertouzos and Osterman find that managers of these firms are reluctant to spend scarce funds on training because they fear that their trained workers might then leave for better paying jobs elsewhere. If sufficient funds were available from the public sector, more firms would provide productivity-enhancing training for their workers.[59]

Federal and state governments do provide some funds for worker training. The federal Job Training Partnership Act (JTPA) provides about $4 billion per year to states, who then distribute the funds to localities. At the local level, private industry councils (PICs) work with local governments to determine how to spend the funds. Typically, JTPA funds support classroom training in basic and occupational skills, on-the-job training, job search assistance, and work experience. In some cases, the JTPA supports job-specific training for local employers who agree to hire the trained workers. The federal Targeted Jobs Tax Credit program provides a tax credit to employers who hire disadvantaged workers; in many cases, this program is used in tandem with other public programs. Other training funds come from the 46 states who provide a variety of customized training packages for companies, particularly those setting up shop within the state.[60]

Nevertheless, the consensus of liberal critics is that public funds are woefully insufficient to induce most employers to invest in the skills and knowledge of their workforces and that the entire education and training system is fragmented and unconnected to the workplace. Some maintain that the United States should restructure its workforce training system, using the German and Japanese systems as models.[61]

Osterman argues for a broad approach to training that would serve firms in all size classes. Training programs that help the disadvantaged, retrain workers with obsolete skills, and provide occupational training for youths should be administered through a single federal agency that has the flexibility to work with local economic development officials to apply its programs to a variety of local situations. This training system should cover all non-college-level-skill occupations, rather than being targeted only to the disadvantaged population, since the effect of such targeting has been to stigmatize the recipients and, ironically, keep them at a disadvantage in landing jobs. Community-based organizations would shoulder the burden for preparing the disadvantaged population for participation in the broader training system.[62]

A proposal by the Commission on the Skills of the American Workforce goes several steps further.[63] It calls for a wholesale transformation of the nation's education and training systems and the marriage of education and training to an industrial policy that fosters the creation of high-skill, high-wage jobs. Inspired by comprehensive systems in Western Europe, this proposal would upgrade both labor supply and demand by establishing new standards and public coordinating bodies.

On the supply side, the major feature of the reform package is a requirement that everyone attain a "certificate of initial mastery." To receive this certificate, each person would have to achieve a national standard of competence in reading, writing, mathematics, and other general school subjects, and demonstrate capacities to learn, think, and work, alone and in groups, solving real-world problems. Students would demonstrate their mastery of these knowledge and skill areas through portfolios, examinations, and projects completed over the course of their middle school and early high school years.

Most people would acquire the certificate of initial mastery by the age of 16. Those who failed to achieve the certificate would not receive work permits. Instead, they would be referred to state-funded and federally funded youth centers that would assist them in studying and mastering the subjects necessary to attain the certificate. These centers also would serve as a high school dropout recovery system.

After attaining the certificate, a student could follow one of several paths. She could complete high school and enter college. Alternatively, she might enter a two-year combined work and study program, in which she would learn broad, transferrable skills within a particular career area. At the end of her training, she would receive, say, a certificate of retail sales, or an electronics technician certificate.

This work-study system, claims the commission, would smooth the transition from school to work that is currently so rocky for high school graduates who do not go directly to college.[64] If they chose to, these persons could then pursue further training and certificates in their fields. The electronics technician, for example, might enter a two-year combined work-study program with college credit, culminating in an electrical engineering certificate. With two more years of college, this person could earn a B.S. in electrical engineering.

The entire system would be coordinated at the local labor market level by state-funded and federally funded employment and training boards. They would manage and oversee the youth centers and ensure a smooth school-to-work transition for young people. They also would manage a "second chance" system for adults seeking the certificate of initial mastery, and they would oversee the system for awarding technical and professional certificates, such as the retail sales and engineering certificates discussed above.

Several features of this system are noteworthy. An independent, national board would establish the standards for each certificate, so that firms throughout the country could be certain of the certificate holders' skills and knowledge. With national standards, decentralized administration of schools, as recommended by conservatives, would be feasible and desirable. Thus the vast array of education and training providers that now characterize the American system could remain in place. Through standardization of basic competencies, persons could acquire certificates at their own pace and enter or reenter the education and training system at different points throughout their lives. The most noteworthy feature, perhaps, is the commission's proposal for federal and state funding of four years of education beyond the certificate of initial mastery. This would finance the last two years of high school and the first two years of college. Alternatively, it would pay for two years of a work-study program leading to a technical certificate, plus two more years of training leading to a professional certificate.

In addition to these labor supply-enhancing efforts, the commission's recommendations include measures to encourage firms to upgrade their job requirements, consistent with the liberal industrial policy proposals discussed in chapter 4. Each firm would be required to spend at least 1 percent of its annual payroll on additional training for its workforce. Those firms that failed to invest in training would pay a 1 percent payroll training tax into a national skills development fund. This fund would finance special training for temporary, part-time, dislocated, and disadvantaged workers.

The commission also calls for the establishment of a national information clearinghouse to provide technical support for companies reorganizing their work processes and upgrading job skill requirements. Best-practice companies would receive national quality awards.

The commission's recommendations for solving the problem of low skills through new government bodies, increased federal and state funding, and new requirements and taxes on firms, clashes with the conservative prescription for turning more to market-based arrangements. It also clashes with radical conceptions of the labor problem and appropriate solutions because it makes a firm's retraining and restructuring efforts largely voluntary, and it fails to recommend other changes, such as a national full employment policy and a shift in labor laws toward worker power. A question worth pondering is whether the commission's recommendations clash with the views of liberal educators. Insofar as the recommendations might further "vocationalize" grade school and high school curricula at the expense of a broader, liberal arts education, they might indeed conflict with the views of liberal educators, as well as radicals and even some conservatives who reject vocational education as too narrow.

Higher Education Policy

Curriculum Content and Achievement Standards

Most of the criticism and reform of American education has focused on primary and secondary schooling and worker training, not on higher education. Yet, higher education policymakers continuously debate issues such as curriculum content, pedagogy, achievement standards, and access for disadvantaged students, and the current reform wave has altered the course of these debates and stimulated policy changes. Other issues, such as the university-business partnership, have emerged since the rise of concern about America's competitiveness in the global economy.

Debates within higher education about these issues reflect the same trio of values that motivates debate in primary and secondary education—economic and business needs, democratic citizenship, and leveling, or equal opportunity. Over the past three decades, higher education policies and institutions have manifested a tenuous balance among these conflicting values. Some universities provide virtually open access, and many give full credit for community college courses, reflecting the value of education as a means of equal opportunity. Colleges and universities address the value of education for democratic citizenship by establishing and continuously debating the appropriate content of a general education core. At the same time, they prepare students to assume more or less specific roles in the economy through major courses of study. Political ideologies play a role in higher education debates and policies, but the differences among camps are somewhat muted. On some of the more important current issues, there is great overlap among the views. The following issues are most relevant to the problem of American competitiveness in the global economy.

Achievement Standards. By the latter half of the 1980s, the conservative call for more testing and quantitative measures of student achievement had spread from the secondary to the post-secondary level. Some states, such as New Jersey, now require that all college students take standardized achievement tests as an indicator of teaching effectiveness. Partly in response to liberal and radical critiques of such policies, other states, such as Virginia, have adopted more liberal versions of student learning assessment, requiring only that colleges and universities find their own ways to assess student learning and use the results of such assessments to improve teaching.[65]

Education Content. Educators have long debated the relative merits of a required core curriculum. The current debates about primary and secondary education have helped to intensify the higher education core curriculum debates. Conservatives such as Allan Bloom and E. D. Hirsch call for a basic, core curriculum built around the study of the great books and events in the history of Western civilization.[66]

Liberals and radicals reject the conservative proposals as culturally biased and narrow. They argue that a core curriculum should help students learn to appreciate diverse cultures and perspectives and to make reasoned value choices to solve problems that are as yet unknown.[67] As a result of these disputes, schools vary in their approaches to the core curriculum issue.

Educators of all political persuasions generally agree on the need to improve student skills in critical thinking, oral communication, and writing. Currently, programs that encourage writing and speaking across the curriculum are spreading throughout higher education. Another relatively uncontroversial issue is the perceived need for more engineers, mathematicians, and scientists, as well as the need for more production management training for business management students. While liberal political economists have been the most vocal proponents of expanding the number of math and science majors, no one has strenuously opposed them.[68]

Higher Education and Economic Development

A development of possibly great significance for American international competitiveness is the university-industry partnership. As the pace of technological change increases, and as human skills and knowledge grow in importance compared to land and physical capital, the potential role of universities in economic development grows apace. Inspired in part by the roles played by MIT and Stanford in stimulating high-tech development in their surrounding regions, colleges and universities have undertaken a number of economic development initiatives. Thomas Chmura lists several types of new roles that universities play in economic development:

1. Human resource development, especially workforce training, targeted to the specific needs of individual firms.
2. Technical assistance in applying existing knowledge and techniques to solve industrial needs, such as helping small or midsize firms learn to use statistical quality control, quality circles, or just-in-time inventory systems. Some universities have organized small business assistance centers or industrial extension services, patterned after the agricultural extension services (as discussed below).
3. Basic and applied research to develop new knowledge, often conducted under the auspices of industry-university cooperative research centers, industrial affiliates, and joint industry-state research programs.
4. Transfer of newly developed technology to industry, through arrangements as simple as faculty consulting or as complex as integrated technology development and transfer programs.
5. Development of new knowledge-based businesses, such as the computer hardware and software companies whose growth was stimulated by Stanford University and MIT. Over time, universities have assumed a variety of roles to help bring ground-breaking research to the commercial stage, including the provision of management training and financial assistance for high-tech entrepreneurs, and the building of office parks or incubator facilities for fledgling high-tech companies.
6. Promotion of international trade by helping firms understand and develop new markets, or by training managers in international business practices, foreign languages, and cultures.
7. Economic analysis and capacity-building assistance for state and local government agencies concerned with economic development.[69]

While the new industry-university relationships raise some of the same issues of academic independence present in high school–business partnerships, and are therefore subject to some of the same criticisms leveled against the latter (as previously discussed) they have not been highly controversial. Liberal industrial policy proposals, for example, generally advocate closer university-industry ties as an important ingredient for U.S. economic competitiveness.[70]

Higher education has played roles in previous national economic development efforts. The Morrill Acts of 1862 and 1890, the Hatch

Act of 1887, and the Smith-Lever Act of 1914 created the highly successful land-grant college system, with its experiment stations and agricultural extension services, to develop the technological base and productivity of the agricultural sector. In recent years, a number of policy analysts have argued that the federal-state, land-grant model should be applied to manufacturing, creating a "nationwide network of engineering research and industrial extension, based in and operated by the [land-grant type institutions] in a manner closely analogous to the agricultural research and extension system."[71] Similarly, James Botkin, Dan Dimancescu, and Ray Stata call for a "High-Technology Morrill Act" that would provide federal matching grants to universities responding to business initiatives and requests for research and development services. Although several states have established inititatives along these lines, the federal government has yet to do so.[72]

Summary

Concerns about American economic competitiveness have stimulated a wave of criticism and reform of American public education, particularly at the primary and secondary levels. Conservatives and some liberals contend that Americans must improve their knowledge and skills to compete in world markets. To increase skills, America must revitalize its public education system. We must raise standards, focus on the basics, test more often using standardized achievement measures, improve the quality of teaching, and, in the view of many conservatives, promote excellence and efficiency in education by requiring schools to compete with each other for students.

Liberal and radical educators object to this vision of public education, claiming that it precludes—by default as much as by design—the value of providing educational opportunities for everyone, especially for the economically disadvantaged. It also tends to preclude the type of curriculum that prepares students to be reflective, critical, active citizens of a democratic society. Introducing competition among schools and sanctioning the spread of business-education partnerships at the primary and secondary levels threatens to distort the curriculum further by giving students an exclusively privatized, business view of the world.

Radicals in particular dispute the extent to which education's failings could have caused America's economic problems. They doubt that the current education reforms, especially those that seek to prepare students with narrow technical skills, will do anything to improve U.S. economic performance. They reason that workers can only use the skills that employers demand, and employers are not demanding more high-skill workers.

Liberal political economists agree that employers are not demanding high-skill workers, but they ascribe this failure not to the inexorable logic of capitalism or to the lack of worker power, but to the absence of public policies that encourage firms to upgrade job skill requirements and to the fragmented education and training systems that fail to link curricula with workplace needs. Like conservatives, they call for a closer link between business and the classroom; unlike conservatives, liberals would structure and mediate the school-business relationship through new public institutions.

In the absence of a strong federal role, states are aggressively pursuing education reform, adopting much of the conservative agenda. Yet conservatives and some liberals argue that we have not gone nearly far enough, while other liberals and radicals protest that we have gone too far in the wrong direction. While the specific policy outcomes are far from certain, it seems clear that the issue of education and training will remain near the top of state and local agendas for the forseeable future.

Notes

1. Carnoy, Martin and Henry Levin: *Schooling and Work in the Democratic State*. Stanford, Calif.: Stanford University Press, 1985, pp. 8–11.

2. See, for example, Dewey, John: *Democracy and Education*. New York: Macmillan Publishing Company, 1916. See also the discussion of education and social philosophy in Moore, T.W.: *Philosophy of Education: An Introduction*. London: Routledge and Kegan Paul, 1982.

3. The restructuring of the work process from craft to mass production entailed a dramatic extension of specialization in the division of labor. In the place of relatively flat organizational hierarchies with mostly skilled craft workers, elaborate hierarchies with many layers of managers, supervisors, semiskilled, and unskilled workers arose. This new, more polarized distribution of tasks required workers with the appropriate distribution of skills. Two factors account for these developments in the division of labor. Dramatic growth of world markets created the potential for new economies of scale in production, and consolidation of smaller firms into a few large corporations created organizations that were equipped to take advantage of these economies of scale.

4. The surge in egalitarian values that influenced the policies of the Roosevelt Administration during the 1930s and 1940s also permeated the institutions of public education. Measures such as the G.I. Bill, which pro-

vided free education for soldiers returning from World War II, and a presidential study commission that championed the expansion of open-door, tuition-free community colleges, promoted the value of education as a leveling tool. In the same spirit, the federal government also established the United States Employment Service, designed to link unemployed workers with training and job opportunities.

5. See Levitan, Sar A. and Frank Gallo: *A Second Chance: Training for Jobs*. Kalamazoo: W.E. Upjohn Institute for Employment Research, 1988, and Kane, Matt and Paula Duggan: *Dislocated Workers: Coping with Competition and Conversion*. Washington, D.C.: Northeast-Midwest Institute, 1991.

6. National Commission on Excellence in Education: *A Nation at Risk: The Imperative for Educational Reform*. Washington, D.C.: U.S. Government Printing Office, 1983, p. 5.

7. Ibid., pp. 8–9.

8. Ibid., pp. 15–24.

9. Johnston, William B.: *Workforce 2000: Work and Workers in the 21st Century*. Indianapolis: Hudson Institute, 1987, pp. xiii–xxvii, 75–104.

10. Miller, Kathleen D.: *Retraining the American Workforce*. Reading, Mass.: Addison-Wesley Publishing Company, 1989, p. 1.

11. Ibid., pp. 22–23.

12. Carnevale, Anthony P., Leila J. Gainer, and Ann S. Meltzer: *Workplace Basics: The Skills Employers Want*. Alexandria, Va.: The American Society for Training and Development, 1988, p. 3.

13. Miller, *Retraining the American Workforce*, pp. 18–20.

14. Ibid., pp. 18–21. See also Walton, Richard: "Establishing and Maintaining High-Commitment Work Systems." In Kimberly, John R. (ed): *Organization Life Cycles*. San Francisco: Jossey-Bass, 1980. See also the bibliography in chapter 4, especially the works listed under "Productivity, Innovation, and Labor-Management Relations."

15. Miller, *Retraining the American Workforce*, p. 24.

16. Carnevale, et al., *Workplace Basics*, p. 8. See also Jacobs, James: "Training the Workforce of the Future." *Technology Review*. Vol. 92, No. 6, August/September 1989.

17. National Commission on Excellence in Education, *Nation at Risk*, pp. 27–33.

18. Finn, Chester E., Jr.: "How Could Anyone Disagree?" *Educational Leadership*. Vol. 41, No. 2, October 1983, pp. 28–29; Glazer, Nathan: "Equity and Excellence in Education: A Comment." *Harvard Educational Review*. Vol. 57, No. 2, May 1987, pp. 196–199; Walberg, Herbert J.: "We Can Raise Standards." *Educational Leadership*. Vol. 41, No. 2, October 1983, pp. 4–7; Kirst, Michael: "The Impact of Postsecondary Admissions Policies on Secondary Education." *Educational Leadership*. Vol. 41, No. 2, October 1983, pp. 16–18.

19. United States Department of Education: *The Nation Responds: Recent Efforts to Improve Education*. Washington, D.C.: U.S. Government Printing Office, 1984, p. 16; Chubb, John E. and Terry M. Moe: *Politics,*

Markets and America's Schools. Washington, D.C.: The Brookings Institution, 1990, p. 10.

20. See Chubb and Moe, *Politics, Markets and America's Schools.* See also DuPont, Pete: "Education in America: The Opportunity to Choose," in Crane, E.H. and D. Boaz (eds): *An American Vision: Policies for the '90s.* Washington, D.C.: The Cato Institute, 1989; Perelman, Lewis J.: "The 'Acanemia' Deception: How the Myth That America 'Lags' in Education Spending Threatens to Undermine National Competitiveness." Hudson Institute Briefing Paper No. 120, May 1990.

21. Johnston, *Workforce 2000*, makes similar arguments.

22. See Friedman, Milton: *Capitalism and Freedom.* Chicago: University of Chicago Press, 1962, chapter 6, "The Role of Government in Education."

23. Alperson, Myra: "Corporate America in the Classroom," in *CEP Research Report.* New York: Council on Economic Priorities, January 1990, pp. 1–2.

24. Alperson, "Corporate America in the Classroom," p. 3. See also Levine, M. and R. Trachtman (eds): *American Business and the Public School: Case Studies of Corporate Involvement in Public Education.* New York: Columbia University, Teachers College, 1988; Frey, Donald N.: "The Economy, Productivity and Training—A CEO's View." *American Education.* December 1982, pp. 15–18; Collins, Sheila: "Workplace Literacy: Corporate Tool or Worker Empowerment?" *Social Policy.* Summer 1989, pp. 26–30.

25. Boaz, David: "Saving the Inner City," in Crane, Edward H. and David Boaz (eds): *An American Vision: Policies for the '90s.* Washington, D.C.: The Cato Institute, 1989, pp. 283–296.

26. See McKenzie, Richard B.: *The American Job Machine.* Washington, D.C.: The Cato Institute, 1988, chapter 8.

27. Aronowitz, Stanley and Henry A. Giroux: *Education under Siege: The Conservative, Liberal and Radical Debate over Schooling.* South Hadley, Mass.: Bergin and Garvey Publishers, 1985, p. xi. See also Roediger, Dave: "Assessment: The Secretary of Education's New Clothes." *Monthly Review.* Vol. 41, No. 1, May 1989, pp. 22–27.

28. Aronowitz and Giroux, *Education under Siege*, p. 197.

29. Ibid., p. 48 and chapter 2, passim.

30. Ibid., pp. 64–66.

31. Ibid. And see Carnoy and Levin, *Schooling and Work.*

32. See Braverman, Harry: *Labor and Monopoly Capital: The Degradation of Work in the Twentieth Century.* New York: Monthly Review Press, 1974.

33. Ibid.

34. See Carnoy and Levin, *Schooling and Work*, pp. 161–176. As discussed in chapter 4, however, many liberal economists (such as Charles Sabel in *Work and Politics*, Robert Reich in *The Next American Frontier*, and Michael Dertouzos and others in *Made in America*) who agree that deskilling has been the long-term trend up to now, argue that the expansion

of world markets and production capabilities presents high-wage countries such as the United States with a challenge and an opportunity—begin producing for the high-value end of markets, or face long-term economic decline. If U.S. companies do begin to produce high-value products, they will have to reverse existing practices and *up*-skill their workforces. See the arguments of liberal political economists in this chapter, especially the report of the Commission on the Skills of the American Workforce: *America's Choice: High Skills or Low Wages*. Rochester, N.Y.: National Center on Education and the Economy, 1990.

35. Uchitelle, Louis: "Surplus of College Graduates Dims Job Outlook for Others." *The New York Times*. Monday, June 18, 1990, section A, p. 1. Uchitelle cites an additional fact to challenge the view that the U.S. population is underskilled:

> The New York Telephone Company contributed greatly to the perception of a nation of unschooled young people by reporting in 1987 that out of 90,000 applicants for jobs there, 84 percent had failed a basic literacy and math test. Unnoticed was that the people were mostly applying for low-wage, temporary jobs. When the American Telephone and Telegraph Company gives a similar test to applicants for full-time clerical or operator jobs, positions that include health and pension benefits, the rate of passing is much higher, said Mary Tenopyr, the company's director of employee testing and selection. "It has been our experience that when you offer a temporary job, you get a lesser quality person," Ms. Tenopyr said. What's more, the pool of applicants is so large that the company intentionally fails 50 percent of the test takers, qualifying only those who can score above average.

36. See Berg, Ivar: *Education and Jobs: The Great Training Robbery*. New York: Praeger Publishers, 1970.

37. Commission on the Skills of the American Workforce: *America's Choice*, p. 24.

38. Ray, Carol Axtell and Roslyn Arlin Mickelson: "Business Leaders and the Politics of School Reform." *Politics of Education Association Yearbook*. 1989, pp. 119–135. Also Ray and Mickelson: "Corporate Leaders, Resistant Youth, and School Reform in Sunbelt City: The Political Economy of Education." *Social Problems*. Vol. 37, No. 2, May 1990, pp. 178–190.

On the development of low-wage, part-time jobs, see the discussions and annotated bibliographies in chapters 1 and 4, particularly Lozano, Beverly: *The Invisible Work Force*. New York: The Free Press, 1989.

39. Ray and Mickelson, "Corporate Leaders." See also Willis, Paul: *Learning to Labor: How Working Class Kids Get Working Class Jobs*. New York: Columbia University Press, 1977.

40. Collins, "Workplace Literacy," pp. 26–30.

41. Collins, Sheila D., Miriam Balmuth, and Priscilla Jean: "So We Can Use Our Own Names, and Write the Laws by Which We Live: Educating the New U.S. Labor Force." *Harvard Educational Review*. Vol. 59, No. 4, November 1989.

42. Carnevale, Anthony P, Leila J. Gainer, Janice Villet, and Shari L. Holland: *Training Partnerships: Linking Employers and Providers.* Alexandria, Va.: The American Society for Training and Development, 1990. See also Jacobs, "Training the Workforce of the Future."

43. Aronowitz and Giroux, *Education under Siege*, pp. 189-190.

44. Hurn, Christopher J.: "The Problem with Comparisons." *Educational Leadership.* Vol. 41, No. 2, October 1983, pp. 7-13.

45. Howe, Harold, II: "Remarks on Equity and Excellence in Education." *Harvard Educational Review.* Vol. 57, No. 2, May 1987, p. 200. *A Nation at Risk* also acknowledges Howe's point that each successive generation of youth is more literate than the generation before it.

46. Ibid., p. 201.

47. Ibid., p. 202.

48. Eisner, Elliott W.: "The Kind of Schools We Need." *Educational Leadership.* Vol. 41, No. 2, October 1983, pp. 48-55. For related arguments, see Tye, Barbara Benham and Kenneth A. Tye: "Naïveté and Snobbery." *Educational Leadership.* Vol. 41, No. 2, October 1983, pp. 29-30.

49. Glass, Gene V. and Dewayne A. Matthews: "Are Data Enough?" Review of *Politics, Markets, and America's Schools. Educational Researcher.* April 1991, pp. 24-27; and Heckman, Paul E.: "Evidence, Values, and the Revitalization of Schools—Response to Raywid." *Educational Leadership.* Vol. 48, No. 4, December 1990/January 1991, pp. 14-15. For an articulate defense of the research supporting choice systems, see Raywid, Mary Anne: "Is There a Case for Choice?" *Educational Leadership.* Vol. 48, No. 4, December 1990/January 1991.

50. See Fege, Arnold: "Target Report: The National PTA Speaks Out on Private School Vouchers." Washington, D.C.: National PTA, 1991. See also Elmore, Richard F.: "No Easy Answers to the Complex Question of Choice: Response to Raywid." *Educational Leadership.* Vol. 48, No. 4, December 1990/January 1991, pp. 17-18.

51. Fege, "Target Report," and Elmore, "No Easy Answers."

52. For further discussion of "merit goods," see any text on public economics or public finance, such as Aronson, J. Richard and Eli Schwartz: *Management Policies in Local Government Finance.* Third Edition. Washington, D.C.: The International City Management Association, 1987, p. 269.

53. See, for example, Thurow, Lester: *The Zero-Sum Solution: Building a World-Class American Economy.* New York: Simon and Schuster, 1985, pp. 183-200; Reich, Robert: *The Next American Frontier.* New York: Times Books, 1983; Dertouzos, Michael L., et al.: *Made in America: Regaining the Productive Edge.* Cambridge, Mass.: MIT Press, 1989.

54. Dertouzos et.al., *Made in America*, p. 82.

55. William T. Grant Foundation Commission on Work, Family, and Citizenship, Harold Howe, II, Chairperson: *The Forgotten Half: Non-College Youth in America: An Interim Report on the School-to-Work Transition.* Washington, D.C.: William T. Grant Foundation Commission on Work, Family, and Citizenship, January 1988; also Commission on the Skills of the American Workforce, *America's Choice.*

56. Osterman, Paul: "Rethinking the American Training System." *Social Policy.* Vol. 19, No. 1, Summer 1988, p. 31.
57. Jacobs, "Training the Workforce of the Future."
58. Osterman, "Rethinking the American Training System," p. 31.
59. Ibid. See also Dertouzos et.al., *Made in America*; Commission on the Skills of the American Workforce, *America's Choice;* William T. Grant Foundation, *The Forgotten Half.*
60. Carnevale et al., *Training Partnerships;* also Levitan and Gallo, *A Second Chance.*
61. See Osterman, "Rethinking the American Training System," and Osterman, Paul: "The Possibilities of Employment Policy," in *Workforce Policies for the 1990s.* Washington, D.C.: Economic Policy Institute, 1989; also Dertouzos et al., *Made in America.*
62. Osterman, "Rethinking the American Training System," pp. 34-35; also Jurmo, Paul, Bill Wiggenhorn, Arnold Packer, and William Zeigler: "Four by Four: How Can Businesses Fight Workplace Illiteracy?" *Training and Development Journal.* Vol. 43, No. 1, January 1989, pp. 18-24; and Jacobs, "Training the Workforce of the Future."
63. Commission on the Skills of the American Workforce, *America's Choice.* For a similar, but less detailed, proposal see O'Toole, James and John Simmons: "Developing the Wealth of the Nation: A Call for a National Human Resources Policy." *Economic Development Quarterly.* Vol. 3, No. 4, November 1989, pp. 275-282.
64. See the William T. Grant Foundation, *The Forgotten Half.*
65. Boyer, C., P. Ewell, J. Finney, and J. Mingle: "Assessment and Outcomes Measurement: A View from the States." *American Association for Higher Education Bulletin.* Vol. 39, No. 7, pp. 8-12; also Roediger, "Assessment."
66. Bloom, Allan: *The Closing of the American Mind: How Higher Education Has Failed Democracy and Impoverished the Souls of Today's Students.* New York: Simon and Schuster, 1987. Hirsch, E.D.: *Cultural Literacy: What Every American Needs to Know.* Boston: Houghton Mifflin, 1987.
67. Edgerton, Russ: "A College Education Up to Beating the Japanese." *AAHE Bulletin.* June 1983, pp. 2-6. See also Aronowitz and Giroux, *Education under Siege*, and Aronowitz, Stanley and Henry A. Giroux: "Schooling, Culture, and Literacy in the Age of Broken Dreams: A Review of Bloom and Hirsch." *Harvard Educational Review.* Vol. 58, No. 2, May 1988.
68. See Thurow, *Zero-Sum Solution*, and Dertouzos et al., *Made in America*, but see also Edgerton, "A College Education," for a cautionary note and Aronowitz and Giroux, *Education under Siege*, for a critique of increasing technical specialization at the expense of liberal arts.
69. Chmura, Thomas J.: "The Higher Education-Economic Development Connection: Emerging Roles for Colleges and Universities." *Commentary.* Vol. 11, No. 3, Fall 1987, pp. 11-17; Osborne, David: *Laboratories of Democracy.* Boston: Harvard University Press, 1988; Powers, D., M. Powers, F. Betz, and C. Aslanian: *Higher Education in Partnership with*

Industry. San Francisco: Jossey-Bass Publishers, 1988; and Lynton, Ernest: *The Missing Connection between Business and the Universities.* New York: Collier Macmillan Publishers, 1984. See also chapter 6 of this book.

70. See, for example, Dertouzos et al., *Made in America.*

71. See Jones, Russel C., Bethany S. Oberst, and Courtland S. Lewis: "The Land-Grant Model." *Change.* Vol. 22, No. 3, May/June 1990, pp. 11–17.

72. Botkin, James, Dan Dimancescu, and Ray Stata: *Global Stakes: The Future of High Technology in America.* Cambridge, Mass.: Ballinger Publishing Company, 1982. See also Osborne, *Laboratories of Democracy.*

Bibliography

Primary and Secondary Education and Training

Conservative Views and Supporting Information— Education Policy*

Alperson, Myra: "Corporate America in the Classroom." In *CEP Research Report.* New York: Council on Economic Priorities, January 1990.

In this brief but valuable report, Alperson describes the state of the art in school-business partnerships and summarizes important, recent research on the topic from conservative and liberal perspectives.

Boaz, David: "Saving the Inner City." In Crane, Edward H. and David Boaz (eds): *An American Vision: Policies for the '90s.* Washington, D.C.: The Cato Institute, 1989.

See the annotated bibliography in chapter 6.

Chubb, John E. and Terry M. Moe: *Politics, Markets and America's Schools.* Washington, D.C.: The Brookings Institution, 1990.

Chubb and Moe seek to demonstrate, via extensive research and statistical analysis, that organizational structure and operations are primary determinants of school quality and student performance. They conclude that the state-local school system bureaucracy effectively impedes the development of quality education. Only a choice system, in which schools would have to compete for students based upon their perceived performance and parental/student choice, could give schools the freedom they need to excel.

DuPont, Pete: "Education in America: The Opportunity to Choose." In Crane, E.H. and D. Boaz (eds): *An American Vision: Policies for the '90s.* Washington, D.C.: The Cato Institute, 1989.

---

*"Supporting Information" refers to sources that have no obvious ideological policy message, but which provide information related to the issues at hand.

Echoing and citing Chubb and Moe, *Politics, Markets, and America's Schools*, DuPont argues that school improvement will come about only when schools must compete for students. Hence we must introduce choice systems into public schooling to explode the "bureaucratic blob" that stifles quality education in our primary and secondary school systems.

Finn, Chester E., Jr.: *Scholars, Dollars and Bureaucrats*. Washington, D.C.: The Brookings Institution, 1978.

A call for reform and streamlining of the federal government's role in higher education. Chester E. Finn, Jr., Assistant Secretary of Education in the Reagan administration, is one of the most widely published and articulate spokespersons for conservative views on education policy. He has been a leader in the back-to-basics movement, the campaign for choice systems in primary and secondary education, and other areas of education reform. This and the following listings are a small sample of his scholarly work on these subjects.

———: "Public Support for Private Education." Parts 1 and 2. *American Education*, May and June, 1982.

Finn advocates government support for private schools through education vouchers.

———: "How Could Anyone Disagree?", *Educational Leadership*. Vol. 41, No. 2, October 1983, pp. 28–29.

The recommendations of *A Nation at Risk* are right on target, argues Finn.

Finn, Chester E., Jr., D. Ravitch, and R. Fancher (eds): *Against Mediocrity: The Humanities in America's High Schools*. New York: Holmes and Meier, 1984.

Humanities education in high schools has deteriorated into a "slough of mediocrity," claim the editors. The 15 contributions to this volume offer appraisals of the current condition of humanities education and proposals for reform.

Friedman, Milton: *Capitalism and Freedom*. Chicago: University of Chicago Press, 1962, chapter 6, "The Role of Government in Education."

See the annotated bibliography in chapter 2.

Glazer, Nathan: "Equity and Excellence in Education: A Comment." *Harvard Educational Review*. Vol. 57, No. 2, May 1987, pp. 196–199.

Glazer argues that equity in education may sometimes have to be sacrificed in the interest of promoting and rewarding excellence, for the good of the whole society—an argument that bolsters the recommendations of *A Nation at Risk* and other conservative policy reforms.

Goldman, Louis: "The Hidden Agenda of the Report on Excellence." *Educational Leadership*. Vol. 41, No. 2, October 1983, pp. 24–27.

Goldman agrees with the conclusions of *A Nation at Risk* but argues that the problems of American education are rooted in a lack of priorities in school objectives, which in turn is traceable to ambivalence among Americans about the purposes of education and reluctance of Americans to pay for improvements.

Johnston, William B.: *Workforce 2000: Work and Workers in the 21st Century.* Indianapolis: Hudson Institute, 1987.

Johnston analyzes the major trends in the U.S. and world economies, and the U.S. job structure and population structure. He concludes that skill shortages will develop in the 1990s unless the education levels of minorities and immigrants rise.

Kirst, Michael: "The Impact of Postsecondary Admissions Policies on Secondary Education." *Educational Leadership.* Vol. 41, No. 2, October 1983, pp. 16–18.

Kirst argues that colleges must increase admissions requirements to force high schools to improve their performance.

Levine, M. and R. Trachtman (eds): *American Business and the Public School: Case Studies of Corporate Involvement in Public Education.* New York: Columbia University, Teachers College, 1988.

A collection of seven case studies of corporate involvement in education, including the famous Boston Compact. The editors draw implications from the case studies for policies and program operations.

National Commission on Excellence in Education: *A Nation at Risk: The Imperative for Educational Reform.* A Report to the Nation and the Secretary of Education, United States Department of Education. Washington, D.C.: U.S. Government Printing Office, 1983.

This is the best-known educational reform report of the 1980s. It accuses the United States of "unilateral educational disarmament" and advocates a number of policies to improve the quality of education, including higher standards, more testing, and focusing on the basics—English, math, science, and social studies.

Perelman, Lewis J.: "The 'Acanemia' Deception: How the Myth That America 'Lags' in Education Spending Threatens to Undermine National Compctitivcncss." Hudson Institute Briefing Paper No. 120, May 1990. Indianapolis: Hudson Institute, 1990.

Perelman argues that the United States spends more per student on prekindergarten through secondary education than any other industrialized country except Switzerland, contrary to the assertions of liberals who argue the spending should be increased. The problem, claims Perelman, is that "American schools are shortchanging the nation by wasting some $100 billion a year through sprawling bureaucracy and outmoded technology."

Raywid, Mary Anne: "Is There a Case for Choice?" *Educational Leadership.* Vol. 48, No. 4, December 1990/January 1991.

Raywid defends the choice concept against criticisms alleging that the research on choice is inadequate and that choice systems undermine education equity.

Walberg, Hebert J.: "We Can Raise Standards." *Educational Leadership.* Vol. 41, No. 2, October 1983, pp. 4–7.

Anticipating Johnston, in *Workforce 2000*, Walberg argues that demographic and economic trends require that America improve its education system and that student achievement standards can be improved without additional public expenditures.

Conservative Views and Supporting Information—Training Policy

Carnevale, Anthony P., Leila J. Gainer, and Ann S. Meltzer: *Workplace Basics: The Skills Employers Want*. Alexandria, Va.: The American Society for Training and Development, 1988.

    The authors describe the skills that employers need to compete in the global marketplace, and recommend an approach to workforce training.

Carnevale, Anthony P., Leila J. Gainer, Janice Villet, and Shari L. Holland: *Training Partnerships: Linking Employers and Providers*. Alexandria, Va.: The American Society for Training and Development, 1990.

    This report describes the types of organizations that provide workforce training and the types of contractual relationships that training providers typically establish with employers.

McKenzie, Richard B.: *The American Job Machine*. New York: The Cato Institute, 1988.

    McKenzie argues, especially in chapters 4 and 8, that public funds should not be used to retrain disadvantaged or displaced workers because that shifts the responsibility for training from the individuals who receive the training, where it belongs, to other individuals (through government), where it does not belong.

Miller, Kathleen D.: *Retraining the American Workforce*. Reading, Mass.: Addison-Wesley Publishing Company, 1989.

    Miller argues that job restructuring in an era of labor shortages requires employers to retrain their existing workforces. The bulk of the book is devoted to a description of typical employer-provider relationships and the nuts and bolts of planning and administering worker retraining programs.

Northeast-Midwest Institute: *Education Incorporated: School-Business Cooperation for Economic Growth*. New York: Quorum Books, 1988.

    This book discusses the need for collaboration between schools and businesses—especially to train and retrain disadvantaged and dislocated workers—and describes examples of successful cooperation. Aside from its advocacy of business-education partnerships, its policy orientation is more liberal than conservative.

Walton, Richard: "Establishing and Maintaining High-Commitment Work Systems." In Kimberly, John R. (ed): *Organization Life Cycles*. San Francisco: Jossey-Bass, 1980.

    See the annotated bibliography in chapter 4.

Radical Views and Supporting Information—Education Policy

Aronowitz, Stanley and Henry A. Giroux: *Education under Siege: The Conservative, Liberal and Radical Debate over Schooling*. South Hadley, Mass.: Bergin and Garvey Publishers, 1985.

This book has two purposes. It seeks to develop a new basis for radical critique of education under capitalism that overcomes the limitations of previous radical views of education—particularly the pessimism, or lack of transformative possibility inherent in radical views of education. Its second purpose is to critique, via this new framework, the conservative reform movement in American education and to offer the basis for an alternative pedagogy.

Braverman, Harry: *Labor and Monopoly Capital: The Degradation of Work in the Twentieth Century.* New York: Monthly Review Press, 1974.

Braverman applies Marxist labor process theory to an analysis of the development of the job structure of American industry in the twentieth century. He argues that the long-run trend is toward de-skilling of the vast majority of jobs, even as jobs requiring high skill levels are created.

Carnoy, Martin and Henry Levin: *Schooling and Work in the Democratic State.* Stanford: Stanford University Press, 1985.

This is a radical analysis of the politics of education reform throughout American history, particularly during the current period of reform. The authors argue that contradictions between the goals of education reform and the changing nature of work—especially the de-skilling process—will undermine the reforms and create increased political conflict. This conflict may be resolved through repressive measures, such as attempts to reduce real wages, or possibly through progressive measures, such as increased worker participation in workplace decision making.

Karabel, Jerome and A.H. Halsey (eds): *Power and Ideology in Education.* New York: Oxford University Press, 1977.

This is a collection of 38 articles covering a wide range of issues in education theory and policy, organized under the following categories: Education and Social Structure; Education and Social Selection; Education, "Human Capital," and the Labor Market; The Politics of Education; Cultural Reproduction and the Transmission of Knowledge; and Social Transformation and Educational Change. While the majority of the articles are written from radical perspectives, conservative and liberal perspectives are also represented.

Lozano, Beverly: *The Invisible Work Force: Transforming American Business with Outside and Home-Based Workers.* New York: The Free Press, 1989.

See the annotated bibliography in chapter 1.

Ray, Carol Axtell and Roslyn Arlin Mickelson: "Business Leaders and the Politics of School Reform." *Politics of Education Association Yearbook*, 1989, pp. 119–135.

The authors contend that the premise of *A Nation at Risk* that America needs a better educated workforce to be competitive is unfounded. Through their case study of business-inspired education reforms in a southern city, they argue that business leaders mainly want a more disciplined labor force, not a more educated one. But discipline and lack of worker commitment to entry-level jobs are only problems because of the poor quality and wages of the jobs offered by businesses.

———: "Corporate Leaders, Resistant Youth, and School Reform in Sunbelt City: The Political Economy of Education." *Social Problems.* Vol. 37, No. 2, May 1990, pp. 178–190.

An elaboration of the publication cited above, this version argues that the current education reforms are not producing hoped for business success because of the reluctance of the business community and public at large to look at the real problem of restructured, de-skilled work.

Roediger, Dave: "Assessment: The Secretary of Education's New Clothes." *Monthly Review.* Vol. 41, No. 1, May 1989, pp. 22–27.

The author criticizes the conservative call for reliance on student achievement test scores as a way of assessing the quality and effectiveness of teaching.

Uchitelle, Louis: "Surplus of College Graduates Dims Job Outlook for Others." *The New York Times.* Monday, June 18, 1990, section A, p. 1.

Uchitelle discusses evidence, collected by the Commission on the Skills of the American Workforce and elsewhere, which indicates that employers are not demanding the large numbers of medium- and high-skill workers predicted by reports such as Johnston's *Workforce 2000*.

Willis, Paul: *Learning to Labor: How Working Class Kids Get Working Class Jobs.* New York: Columbia University Press, 1977.

An ethnographic study of English working-class youths whose interactions with the education system effectively prepare them, despite the best intentions of teachers, for low-skill, low-wage factory jobs.

Radical Views and Supporting Information—Training Policy

Berg, Ivar: *Education and Jobs: The Great Training Robbery.* New York: Praeger Publishers, 1970.

Berg argues that Americans are overeducated for the jobs employers are creating; this leads to employers using degrees as personality screens, rather than as indicators of skills or knowledge.

Collins, Sheila: "Workplace Literacy: Corporate Tool or Worker Empowerment?" *Social Policy.* Summer 1989, pp. 26–30.

Collins argues that since businesses are demanding more skilled workers, trade unions should become the organizers of the required training, so as to influence its content and to gain strategic control of the supply of skilled labor, as a way of redressing the imbalance of power between labor and management.

Collins, Sheila D., Miriam Balmuth, and Priscilla Jean: "So We Can Use Our Own Names, and Write the Laws by Which We Live: Educating the New U.S. Labor Force." *Harvard Educational Review.* Vol. 59, No. 4, November 1989.

The authors describe several innovative workplace literacy programs that were designed and administered by trade unions in New York City.

Liberal Views and Supporting Information—Education Policy

Supporters of Reform through Higher Standards

Commission on the Skills of the American Workforce: *America's Choice: High Skills or Low Wages.* Rochester, N.Y.: National Center on Education and the Economy, 1990.

The commission finds that America's education and training systems are fragmented and not sufficiently linked to the workplace. At the same time, American managers continue to create low-skill, low-wage jobs that will not improve the competitive position of the United States. The solution requires the wholesale transformation of the American education and training system through federal- and state-funded local employment and training boards, as well as financial incentives to help firms restructure and create high-skill, high-wage jobs.

Dertouzos, Michael L. et al.: *Made in America: Regaining the Productive Edge.* Cambridge, Mass.: MIT Press, 1989.

See the annotated bibliography in chapter 4.

Drucker, Peter F.: "The Next American Work Force: Demographics and the U.S. Economy." *Commentary.* Vol. 5, October 1981, pp. 3–10.

Drucker argues that declines in the semiskilled labor force from 1980 to 2000 will diminish the supply of semiskilled manufacturing workers. At the same time, the increasing education levels of American workers make it possible for the United States to specialize in producing the world's high-value goods.

Reich, Robert B.: *The Next American Frontier.* New York: Times Books, 1983.

See the annotated bibliography in chapter 4.

Thurow, Lester: *The Zero-Sum Solution: Building a World-Class American Economy.* New York: Simon and Schuster, 1985.

See the annotated bibliography in chapter 4.

Opponents of Conservative Education Reforms

Aronson, J. Richard and Eli Schwartz: *Management Policies in Local Government Finance.* Third Edition. Washington, D.C.: The International City Management Association, 1987.

See the annotated bibliography in chapter 2.

Eisner, Elliott W.: "The Kind of Schools We Need." *Educational Leadership.* Vol. 41, No. 2, October 1983, pp. 48–55.

A Nation at Risk conveys a dangerously narrow concept of curriculum and of the factors that lead to good schools.

Elmore, Richard F.: "No Easy Answers to the Complex Question of Choice: Response to Raywid." *Educational Leadership.* Vol. 48, No. 4, December 1990/January 1991, pp. 17–18.

Elmore argues that the overall results of the existing education choice system (public vs. private school; magnet schools, and so on)

218 Education and Training Policy

are rather mixed and therefore undermine the case for an expanded choice system.

Fege, Arnold: "Target Report: The National PTA Speaks Out on Private School Vouchers." Washington, D.C.: National PTA, 1991.

A summary of the National PTA's arguments against the use of a choice or voucher system, including issues of equity, practicality, and the public interest.

Glass, Gene V. and Dewayne A. Matthews: "Are Data Enough?" Review of *Politics, Markets, and America's Schools. Educational Researcher.* April 1991, pp. 24–27.

A critique of the data and statistical methodology that underpin the case for choice in Chubb and Moe, *Politics, Markets, and America's Schools..*

Heckman, Paul E.: "Evidence, Values, and the Revitalization of Schools—Response to Raywid." *Educational Leadership.* Vol. 48, No. 4, December 1990/January 1991, pp. 14–15.

A critique of the research supporting the case for choice systems and the values underlying the choice concept.

Howe, Harold, II: "Remarks on Equity and Excellence in Education." *Harvard Educational Review.* Vol. 57, No. 2, May 1987, pp. 199–202.

Howe argues that conservative calls for reform through raised standards place undue emphasis on standardized tests, neglect the goal of achieving equity and equal opportunity through education, and fail to appreciate the factors that create good schools.

Hurn, Christopher J.: "The Problem with Comparisons." *Educational Leadership.* Vol. 41, No. 2, October 1983, pp. 7–13.

Hurn argues that comparing American student test results with those of foreign students is inappropriate, since other systems have different structures, are rooted in different values, and have different strengths and weaknesses from those of the U.S. system.

Tye, Barbara Benham and Kenneth A. Tye: "Naïveté and Snobbery." *Educational Leadership.* Vol. 41, No. 2, October 1983, pp. 29–30.

A Nation at Risk promotes a dangerously narrow conception of the purposes of education. It leaves out the goal of equality of educational opportunity and it neglects the most important factors in improving education—teacher and student communication and participation in improving education.

Liberal Views and Supporting Information—Training Policy

Frey, Donald N.: "The Economy, Productivity and Training—A CEO's View." *American Education.* December 1982, pp. 15–18.

Frey worries that the United States is not doing enough to help experienced, dislocated workers retrain for productive employment and calls for federal training funds and corporate contributions to solve the problem.

Cross, K. Patricia and Anne-Marie McCartan: *Adult Learning: State Policies and Institutional Practices.* Washington, D.C.: Association for the Study of Higher Education, 1984.

This is a descriptive analysis of the institutions and arrangements through which adults can receive continuing education and training. It includes recommendations for state actions to support and improve the conditions of adult education.

Jacobs, James: "Training the Workforce of the Future." *Technology Review.* Vol. 92, No. 6, August/September 1989.

Jacobs calls for a national education and training policy to help make training available to small- and midsize firms, to heal the split between vocational and customized training, and to help community colleges and other training providers focus and specialize on appropriate skill areas.

Jurmo, Paul, Bill Wiggenhorn, Arnold Packer, and William Zeigler: "Four by Four: How Can Businesses Fight Workplace Illiteracy?" *Training and Development Journal.* Vol. 43, No. 1, January 1989, pp. 18–24.

The four authors each assess the state of workforce training in the United States and offer recommendations for national training policy alternatives.

Kane, Matt and Paula Duggan: *Dislocated Workers: Coping with Competition and Conversion.* Washington, D.C.: Northeast-Midwest Institute, 1991.

This is a comprehensive how-to manual for communities facing problems of worker dislocation through plant closings and defense cutbacks. It describes federal programs and local methods for anticipating and responding to dislocations, including worker training and retraining programs.

Levitan, Sar A. and Frank Gallo: *A Second Chance: Training for Jobs.* Kalamazoo: W.E. Upjohn Institute for Employment Research, 1988.

This is a detailed description and analysis of the federal government's largest job training program for disadvantaged and dislocated workers, the Job Training Partnership Act.

Osterman, Paul: "Rethinking the American Training System." *Social Policy.* Vol. 19, No. 1, Summer 1988.

Osterman argues that businesses, especially small- and midsize firms, are underfunding their own workforce training and that a national training policy that provides funding support for locally organized training efforts is required if U.S. firms are to compete effectively with foreign firms. Such a national policy should be broad, covering all non-college-level job skill groups, so that its beneficiaries are not stigmatized in the labor market.

_____: "The Possibilities of Employment Policy." In *Workforce Policies for the 1990s.* Washington, D.C.: Economic Policy Institute, 1989.

An expanded discussion of the issues in his "Rethinking the American Training System," annotated above.

O'Toole, James and John Simmons: "Developing the Wealth of the Nation: A Call for a National Human Resources Policy." *Economic Development Quarterly.* Vol. 3, No. 4, November 1989, pp. 275–282.

The authors call for a national policy that would improve the quality and utilization of human resources through coordination of multiple initiatives, including worker participation in workplace decisions and education, training, and welfare reform.

William T. Grant Foundation Commission on Work, Family, and Citizenship, Harold Howe, II, Chairperson: *The Forgotten Half: Non-College Youth in America: An Interim Report on the School-to-Work Transition.* Washington, D.C.: William T. Grant Foundation Commission on Work, Family, and Citizenship, January 1988.

The report calls for public policies that would help to smooth the transition from school to work for the nation's 20 million high school graduates who do not go on to college. Such policies would provide monitored work experiences for high school students; community and neighborhood service opportunities; career information and counseling; special training for dropouts and disadvantaged students; and measures that encourage equal access to lifelong learning opportunities.

Education Policy Reforms

Education for Economic Security Act. U.S. Public Law 98-377, August 11, 1984 (H.R. 1310).

"To provide assistance to improve elementary, secondary, and postsecondary education in mathematics and science; to provide a national policy for engineering, technical, and scientific personnel...." Congress reauthorized this act in 1988 as the Dwight D. Eisenhower Mathematics and Science Education Act.

National Governor's Association: *Time for Results: The Governors' 1991 Report on Education*, August 1986.

This volume comprises task force reports on the following topics: education technology; college quality; parent involvement in, and choice of, school; readiness; leadership and management; teachers and teaching; and school facilities use.

Headquartered in Washington, D.C., the NGA adopted education reform as a priority issue in 1986. Since then, the NGA has commissioned a number of studies of the problems of primary, secondary, and postsecondary education, and appropriate state responses. These studies include this listing and the ones that follow.

_____: *Results in Education.*

Annual. Follow-up report to *Time for Results* that records state initiatives in education policy and reform.

_____: *A More Productive Workforce: Challenge for Post-Secondary Education and Its Partners.*

Highlights of a conference sponsored by the National Governors' Association and other organizations in Little Rock, Arkansas, in May

1989. The document sets forth numerous proposals for overcoming fragmentation and uncoordinated provision of postsecondary education and training.

———: *America in Transition: The International Frontier.* Report of the Task Force on International Education, 1989.

This report calls for the state to foster the development of primary, secondary, and postsecondary curricula that enhance student knowledge and skills necessary for effective international commerce.

United States Department of Education: *The Nation Responds: Recent Efforts to Improve Education.* Washington, D.C.: U.S. Government Printing Office, May 1984.

This report describes the initiatives of states, local school districts, postsecondary institutions, and private organizations, in responding to the recommendations of *A Nation at Risk* and other calls for education reform.

Higher Education

Curriculum Content and Related Issues

Aronowitz, Stanley and Henry A. Giroux: "Schooling, Culture, and Literacy in the Age of Broken Dreams: A Review of Bloom and Hirsch." *Harvard Educational Review.* Vol. 58, No. 2, May 1988.

The authors provide a radical critique of the controversial works of Bloom, *Closing of the American Mind,* and Hirsch, *Cultural Literacy.*

Bloom, Allan: *The Closing of the American Mind: How Higher Education Has Failed Democracy and Impoverished the Souls of Today's Students.* New York: Simon and Schuster, 1987.

Bloom argues that higher education has succumbed to relativism and anti-intellectualism that is eating away at the foundations of American civilization. As an antidote, we must reintroduce the "Great Books" tradition—"the generally recognized classical texts"—to the general curriculum.

Boyer, C., P. Ewell, J. Finney, and J. Mingle: "Assessment and Outcomes Measurement: A View from the States." *American Association for Higher Education Bulletin.* Vol. 39, No. 7, pp. 8–12.

The authors document the rapid spread of state-mandated outcomes assessment measures at the college and university level, and discuss the variety of approaches to assessment taken by different states.

Edgerton, Russ: "A College Education Up to Beating the Japanese." *AAHE Bulletin.* June 1983, pp. 2–6.

Edgerton argues that the current emphasis on learning more science, math, and languages, and the increasing expectations for performance will not prepare students to compete well in the global economy. Rather, colleges should revive earlier curricular traditions, "especially the development of character and reasoning abilities."

Gaff, Jerry G.: "General Education at Decade's End." *Change.* Vol. 21, No. 4, July/August 1989, pp. 11-19.

Gaff reviews the results of general education reform efforts during the 1980s and argues for a second wave of reform, focused less on content than on creating a college culture that supports, through all activities, the values and purposes of general education.

Hirsch, E.D.: *Cultural Literacy: What Every American Needs to Know.* Boston: Houghton Mifflin, 1987.

Hirsch decries what he sees as a weakening of American civic and public culture, manifested in an increasing lack of common cultural traditions and historical referents. To restore the integrity and cohesiveness of American culture, he recommends that all college students study the great events in Western civilization.

Higher Education and Economic Development

Botkin, James, Dan Dimancescu, and Ray Stata: *Global Stakes: The Future of High Technology in America.* Cambridge, Mass.: Ballinger Publishing Company, 1982.

The authors describe the rise of global competition and recommend policies that the United States should pursue to sustain its role as a world leader, particularly in the area of high technology. Chapter 8 discusses policies for higher education, including the authors' call for a "High-Technology Morrill Act" that would emulate the successful land-grant model to support university-industry cooperation in manufacturing.

Chmura, Thomas J.: "The Higher Education–Economic Development Connection: Emerging Roles for Colleges and Universities." *Commentary.* Vol. 11, No. 3, Fall 1987, pp. 11-17.

Chmura analyzes the importance of universities for contemporary businesses and describes the ways in which universities are working with businesses to develop local and regional economies.

Jones, Russel C., Bethany S. Oberst, and Courtland S. Lewis: "The Land-Grant Model." *Change.* Vol. 22, No. 3, May/June 1990, pp. 11-17.

The authors call for a national policy that would support the application of the land-grant model to manufacturing industries.

Lynton, Ernest: *The Missing Connection between Business and the Universities.* New York: Collier Macmillan Publishers, 1984.

Lynton argues that colleges and universities must expand their roles to become providers of workforce training, for their own survival as well as the good of the economy.

Osborne, David: *Laboratories of Democracy.* Boston: Harvard University Press, 1988.

See the annotated bibliography in chapter 7.

Powers, D., M. Powers, F. Betz, and C. Aslanian: *Higher Education in Partnership with Industry.* San Francisco: Jossey-Bass Publishers, 1988.

The authors describe several examples of successful university-industry cooperation, as well as potential conflicts and the procedures that the parties should use to avoid conflict in successful collaboration.

CHAPTER 6

State and Local Responses to Global Economic Restructuring

Previous chapters have discussed alternative national policy responses to the globalization of production and trade and consequent dislocations in the U.S. economy. The actual impacts of such economic changes are experienced not at some abstract national level, but in the communities where people live and work. While certain features of economic change, such as the shift from manufacturing to services employment, are generalizable across states and localities, there is more to the story.

Different regions, with varied industrial structures and political-economic histories, have experienced economic globalization in different ways. Some workers have benefited while others have suffered. Since the 1930s, the Northeast-Midwest "Rustbelt" has been a net loser of blue-collar manufacturing jobs to the U.S. South, especially in the textile, shoe, and garment industries. Yet the South, too, now faces dislocations as its low-wage plants migrate to lower wage labor markets overseas.[1]

The forces of globalization cut across the North-South shift, as they enrich the coasts at the expense of the country's heartland. The rise of global trade favors transportation nexus points, especially port cities. The growth of producer services (finance, insurance, law, accounting, and advertising) as well as health and education services, and the increasing importance of technological innovation favor the metropolitan areas that have well-developed producer services sectors and research universities, most of which are located in coastal regions. At the same time, the economic mainstays of the nation's interior—manufacturing, agriculture, and mining—face increasingly stiff competition from the newly industrializing countries.

U.S. economic policies in the 1980s compounded the regional impacts of globalization. The dollar's soaring value from 1981 to

1985 closed many export markets to America's manufacturing industries, especially the products of low-skill branch plants in rural areas, whose low wages were not low enough to compete with those of the newly industrializing countries.[2] The dollar's high exchange value also prompted Brazil, India, China, and other buyers of American agricultural products to substitute their own, less efficiently produced foodstuffs for U.S. imports. By the mid-1980s, the combination of high interest rates and low world prices for farm products had wreaked havoc in the agriculture sector, destroying many family farms. From 1975 to 1987, the U.S. farm population dropped from 9 million to less than 5 million persons. The fall in the dollar's value after 1985 sparked a minor resurgence in the industrial region surrounding the Great Lakes, but the agriculture sector continued to struggle.[3]

As noted above, America's massive trade deficits in the 1980s stimulated the economic growth of transportation nodes, especially port cities. These cities continued to benefit, of course, when U.S. exports rebounded in the latter half of the decade. The arms buildup of the 1980s also favored coastal areas, for the most part, as places such as New England, Virginia, and California are home to the nation's naval bases, shipbuilders, and defense R and D contractors.[4]

As examples of the different effects of globalization and economic policy on American regions, consider the fates of two metropolitan areas located less than 300 miles apart—Pittsburgh and Washington, D.C. Overcapacity and structural change in the world steel industry led to a loss of over 100,000 jobs in the Pittsburgh region between 1979 and 1986, thus downgrading the world's largest steel producer to a regional service center and destroying the livelihoods of thousands of people.[5] Washington, D.C., on the other hand, has benefited from the growing role of governments in facilitating international trade linkages, as evidenced by increasing numbers of foreign embassy personnel and a growing international corporate presence in the District.[6]

American border cities also benefit from the globalization of production and trade. The U.S.–Canada Free Trade Agreement is projected to stimulate the sagging economies of Buffalo, Detroit, and other border cities. The economic boom along the U.S.–Mexican border, driven by low-wage, American-owned branch plants on the Mexican side, may expand if the United States signs a free trade agreement with Mexico.[7] The mere prospect of such a pact has stimulated a development boom in San Diego. At the same time, regions of the United States with low-to-moderate-skill manufacturing plants are likely to suffer as these jobs move south of the border.[8]

Within regions as well as among them, global economic restructuring and national policies have fostered uneven development. Since the turn of the century, manufacturing plants have been migrating from inner cities to suburbs, leaving cities with declining economies and revenue bases. Global restructuring has accelerated the flight of manufacturing plants from cities. Cities are attempting to adjust to the new global division of economic functions by creating downtown environments hospitable to producer, consumer, and government services, but this adjustment has a price. As manufacturing firms leave, cities lose the semiskilled, moderate-wage jobs that once supported stable, working-class neighborhoods. At the same time, the office complexes and amenities that producer services require, and the young producer services professionals wishing to live in historic inner-city neighborhoods, displace the few small manufacturing firms that remain in cities, as well as the low- and moderate-income residents. Yet, as discussed in chapter 1, producer and consumer services industries also require relatively low-wage, low-skill workers—a situation that fosters income polarization, as well as needs for low-income housing and services in close proximity to upscale housing and services. These conflicting needs provoke land-use planning dilemmas and social tension in many cities.[9]

Unfortunately, city efforts to adjust to the new global economy by promoting services have not raised sufficient tax revenues to solve the problem of recurrent fiscal crisis. Indeed, for many cities, the forces of globalization have done more harm than good to date. American cities continue to struggle to balance the books, support their growing populations of poor elders and children, and build the foundations of viable economies.

This chapter describes how states and localities are responding to the impacts of global economic restructuring, through economic development programs that seek to replace lost jobs and tax revenues and take advantage of new economic opportunities. Unlike previous chapters, this chapter focuses more on state and local practices than on ideologically based policy debates. As the discussion will show, the need to address problems in a timely fashion forces state and local officials to temper ideology with pragmatism. Yet, ideological values do play a role in the choice and critique of state and local economic development policies, so a brief discussion of the conservative, liberal, and radical paradigms as they appear in state and local policies is in order.

Ideology, Pragmatism, and Policy

As discussed in chapter 2 and throughout this book, conservative political economy holds that a nation maximizes its welfare and the freedom of its citizens by organizing its economic activity through markets, as free as possible from any government intervention. With very few exceptions, government intervention cannot improve upon long-run market outcomes. Moreover, conservatives believe that government efforts to improve upon market outcomes ultimately make matters far worse. Liberals believe that markets are, indeed, powerful and useful tools for organizing economic activity, but government must channel and regulate their energy if they are not ultimately to undermine human welfare, especially the welfare of society's weaker members. Radicals view markets as but one aspect of an entire capitalist system that harms some as it increases the wealth of others, ultimately rendering the entire system unstable. The only way to improve conditions, in the radical view, is to democratize decision making, in each firm and in the economy as a whole. Progressives believe that incremental reforms can accomplish this; Marxists believe that only full-scale revolution can achieve lasting reform.

According to this classification scheme, the state and local economic development policies that have evolved since the Great Depression, and especially those of the 1980s, generally fall within or close to the liberal paradigm. As indicated below, states and localities intervene in the market in numerous ways, through public financing of factories, equipment, and infrastructure, as well as worker training. These and many other state and local practices run counter to the laissez-faire conservative philosophy discussed in previous chapters. Prior to the Great Depression, laissez-faire philosophies were far more common in state houses and city halls than they are today.

From the Depression through the 1970s, state and local economic policies followed more or less liberal precepts, as did federal policies. Thus it is significant that in the realm of economic policy, states and localities did not follow the federal government on the conservative path in the 1980s. In fact, the conservatism of the federal government is at least partly accountable for the increasing liberal interventionism of states and localities in that decade. By the early 1990s, virtually every state and large city had adopted a form of industrial policy.[10]

State and local liberalism survives in a conservative era because state and local officials cannot wait for markets to prove their long-run superiority to government intervention. While federal officials may ignore the impacts of foreign competition on individual states and regions, state and local officials do so at the risk of losing their jobs. Their closeness to the electorate virtually guarantees that they cannot take a laissez-faire approach to the economy.[11]

Yet not all states and localities intervene in all markets to the same extent. All provide business development assistance in the form of below-market-rate financing, infrastructure improvements, worker training, foreign trade leads, and a host of other services. But some discourage unions through right-to-work legislation, while others allow closed-shop unions. Some states levy higher taxes on business than others, and some have more stringent environmental regulations. Some states regulate plant closings, some do not. Some provide higher welfare support payments (in the form of Aid to Families with Dependent Children) than do others.

In short, states and localities choose policies informed by different ideologies. Using the terms employed in previous chapters, the overall policy mixes of states and localities range from moderate to liberal to progressive—to be sure, a narrower spectrum than the one that characterizes national economic policy debates, but one that nevertheless has identifiable differences. Generalizing broadly, the South, the Southwest, and the Rocky Mountain states pursue moderate policy mixes, offering business subsidies, discouraging unions, and avoiding strict environmental regulations. Again generalizing broadly, the overall policy mixes of the Northeast, the Midwest, and the West Coast tend to be liberal. These states offer subsidies and location incentives to business, but many also regulate plant closings or foreign investment, and they allow closed-shop unions.[12] Progressive coalitions have governed or influenced policies in several cities in the Northeast, the Midwest, and California, including Burlington, Boston, Hartford, Cleveland, Chicago, Santa Monica, and Berkeley. Their policies include efforts to stem capital flight through business retention, worker buyouts and cooperative ownership, state-level plant-closing controls, and lawsuits against companies that receive government subsidies but then attempt to leave the community.[13]

No state's or city's policy mix is cast in stone, however. As the remainder of the chapter illustrates, their policies continue to evolve in response to changes in external economic forces, federal policies, and state and local politics.

The Evolution of State and Local Economic Development Policy

Evidence of state and local government intervention in the economy can be traced back to colonial times. Since then, state and local activities have increased in scope and dollar magnitude, not in a gradual way, but in surges of new activity, sparked by economic opportunities and dislocations.

In the nineteenth century, cities and towns scrambled to entice railroad companies to include them on their routes. In the aftermath of the Civil War and into the 1920s, the "New South" boosters sought to reconstruct the South by shedding the region's dependence on agriculture and building a diversified industrial base. They attempted to lure northern firms and finance capital to the South, primarily by marketing the South's low-wage, nonunion workforce and, to some extent, through financial contributions that local residents and boosters made to subsidize plants for companies moving in from the North. Nevertheless, state laws discouraged financial location incentives, and the lack of both a critical mass of factory migrations and an overall economic development strategy retarded the South's economic development.[14]

The Depression sparked another surge in southern industrial recruitment, and this time, the efforts bore more fruit. A number of factors were responsible, including the establishment of state economic development offices with permanent recruitment staffs who aggressively worked the boardrooms of northern companies. The most important attraction continued to be the South's low-wage, nonunion labor. Yet the most widely touted factor, and one that would help to transform the practice of state and local economic development, was the introduction of industrial development bonds to finance the construction of plants, equipment, and infrastructure. Bonds are loan funds raised in the private capital market and paid back at interest. Since the interest on government-issued bonds is exempt from federal income tax, the interest rate charged to the borrower is less than it would be on a conventional loan. By issuing a bond to finance a plant or machinery, a community offers a company a below-market-interest-rate loan.[15]

Prior to the Depression, governments could issue bonds only to finance purely "public" uses, such as schools. As state courts began to interpret the criterion of public use to include job creation, development bonds spread throughout the South. Consequently, industrial migration to the South increased in the 1930s, 1940s, and 1950s, leading northern states first to denounce and then to adopt the use of bonds. By the mid-1960s, 30 states had issued them to finance industrial growth and expansion.[16]

In 1959, North Carolina Governor Luther Hodges expanded the South's business recruitment approach overseas with a trade mission to Europe. During the next decade, 15 states designated international business specialists to recruit foreign companies and capital, and several states opened promotional offices abroad. The OPEC oil crisis of 1973 and the subsequent recession, as well as growing concern about the loss of American jobs to foreign competition, induced a dramatic increase in state efforts to attract foreign investment and to increase American exports, as evidenced by a doubling of economic development personnel and a tripling in expenditures on export promotion from 1976 to 1980.[17]

Changing economic conditions are not the only forces to spark surges in state and local economic development activies. Beginning with the Roosevelt administration's New Deal programs and continuing to the present, federal policies have profoundly influenced state and local policies. For example, with the establishment of the Tennessee Valley Authority in the 1930s, the federal government began targeting economic development assistance to specific regions and later, to urban areas. The National Housing Act of 1949 enabled localities to create urban renewal authorities that could condemn and acquire land for clearance and later sale to developers. This program was intended to remove "urban blight" and revitalize inner cities suffering from disinvestment as firms moved to the suburbs and elsewhere. Although the program itself created more problems than it solved, it helped to develop local government capacity to intervene in the economy, or at least to intervene in the real estate market to promote development.[18]

In the early 1960s, the Kennedy administration established the Appalachian Regional Commission to redevelop that region's economy, whose reliance upon coal mining had been undercut by the rise of oil and gas use. Later in the decade, the liberal Johnson administration established the War on Poverty, which sought to help central cities by providing job training and later, job opportunities, primarily to impoverished black farmworker families who had been displaced decades earlier by the mechanization of agriculture.[19] The conservative Nixon administration consolidated some of the War on Poverty's categorical grant programs (which specify the exact nature and purpose for which money must be spent) into Community Development Block Grants (CDBGs), which states and localities can expend on a variety of projects, including public improvements, neighborhood development, and business equipment and facilities. This effort also shifted administrative power from federal and local governments to state governments.[20]

Through the Urban Development Action Grant (UDAG) program, established in 1977 under the Carter administration, the federal government fostered a growing technical sophistication of local economic development officials. To receive UDAG funds, communities had to secure partial funding of projects from private companies or developers. They could use a UDAG only to make an otherwise infeasible deal (from a market perspective) work. This required that public officials learn the intricacies of company account keeping and real estate finance, and practice effective negotiation tactics, to ensure that the public sector provided only the extra amount of financing necessary to make a project succeed.

A new phrase was coined to describe the closer relationship between the public and private sectors that UDAGs and other financing tools of the 1970s and 1980s, required—the public-private partnership. Together, the two sectors would accomplish development projects that neither could do alone. Although many previous federal, state, and local economic development initiatives also could have been termed partnerships, in the 1970s and 1980s this term resonated with the diminishing belief in the ability of government to solve problems and the growing faith in the ability of the private sector to do so.[21]

By the late 1970s, the federal government had created an infrastructure of agencies and programs—including the Department of Housing and Urban Development, the Small Business Administration, and the Economic Development Administration—that focused on state and local economic development. These agencies encouraged the development of local government capacity to address economic development issues. Most cities established redevelopment authorities engaged in downtown real estate development (a legacy of the urban renewal program) and many also created economic development agencies to recruit and retain businesses and generate jobs. Federal programs of the 1960s and 1970s also helped to create an infrastructure of community-based citizen empowerment and development organizations, some of which have matured into today's sophisticated, nonprofit community development corporations (CDCs) that work with neighborhood residents and businesses to revitalize local economies.

Liberals celebrated and encouraged the expanded federal role in local economic development, but progressives complained that the public-private partnerships through which federal programs were implemented benefited the private sector far more than they did the community as a whole, especially the low-income residents who needed jobs. Conservatives, on the other hand, worried about the growing dependency of local governments on federal funds and spending guidelines, and increasing federal involvement in the economy generally, at the expense of states, and, especially the private sector.

In his 1980 presidential campaign, Ronald Reagan promised to get the federal government off the backs of state and local government. Through his New Federalism initatives, many of which were passed by Congress in the Omnibus Budget Reconciliation Act of 1981, he sought to do just that. He furthered the work begun under the Nixon administration, consolidating 77 federal categorical grant programs into nine block grants. Also, states acquired the power to establish the rules and procedures whereby localities obtain the grants.[22]

The New Federalism, while giving state and local authorities more decision-making power, brought a whole new set of problems. The federal government mandated costly state and local tasks, such as pollution control and wastewater treatment. At the same time, revenue transfers fell dramatically. From 1980 to 1987, federal spending on grants to states and localities declined by 33 percent, with the largest reductions occurring in general-purpose assistance, economic development, employment and training, and social services.[23] The federal government gutted funding for agencies such as the Economic Development Administration and Small Business Administration. It discontinued UDAGs and restricted the use of tax-exempt development bonds. Facing the economic dislocations of the 1980–82 recession and increasing foreign competition, and left to fend for themselves, states and localities dramatically increased their economic development activities. By the early 1990s, virtually every state and major city had established its own version of industrial policy, largely because of the federal government's decision not to enact one (see chapter 4). The rest of this chapter discusses the major features of these policies and examines their implications for the future of the American federal system and the U.S. response to the globalization of production and trade.

Features of State and Local Industrial Policy

Business Recruitment and Its Critics

Until recently, the practice of economic development was virtually synomous with industrial recruitment, or "smokestack chasing." At the time of its initiation in the nineteenth century, this approach consisted mainly of marketing a region's low taxes, low wages, and low-cost financing to companies looking for branch plant

Table 4
State and Local Economic Development Tools and Strategies

Tools	Business Development Strategies			
	Recruit	Retain	Form	Expand
Cost reduction				
Tax abatements, deferrals	Yes	Yes	No	Yes
Development loans and equity	Yes	Yes	Yes	Yes
Grants	Yes	Yes	No	Yes
Export financing	No	No	No	Yes
Market expansion				
Domestic marketing, especially tourism	No	No	No	Yes
Export assistance, including marketing	No	No	No	Yes
Local capacity development				
Strategic planning, targeting	Yes	Yes	Yes	Yes
Worker training	Yes	Yes	No	Yes
Infrastructure improvements	Yes	Yes	No	Yes
Land and site development	Yes	Yes	No	Yes
Building construction	Yes	Yes	Yes	Yes
Information/outreach	Yes	Yes	Yes	Yes

Yes = A particular tool is commonly used to pursue a given strategy.
No = A particular tool is not normally used to pursue that strategy.
Note: This is not a comprehensive listing of all state and local economic development tools. It includes the most commonly used tools.

Sources: Bowman, *Tools and Targets*; NASDA, *State Export Program Database*; Wilson, *State Business Incentives and Economic Growth*.

locations. As the competition for business intensified, however, states and localities added numerous incentives to outbid each other, and numerous ways to market themselves to firms. As Table 4 indicates, states and localities now use two types of tools to recruit businesses—cost reduction tools, such as tax-free bonds, grants, and direct loans, and tools that assist firms while also building local economic capacity, such as infrastructure improvements and site preparation work, worker training, and the construction of buildings suitable for manufacturing. In their search for foreign investment, states and localities have established over 100 permanent trade offices overseas. Scores of state and local executives embark on foreign trade missions every year.

By 1976, the practice of industrial recruitment through subsidies and other incentives became so widespread that *Business Week* magazine dubbed it the "Second War Between the States."[24] In overcoming stiff competition from other suitor states, Pennsylvania's successful courtship of a Volkswagen Rabbit plant in that year used incentives considered extraordinary at the time: $40 million in loans at 1.75 percent interest with payback delayed until 1998, $25 million in highway and rail construction, $3 million in training subsidies, plus five years of local tax abatements. In return, Volkswagen promised 5,000 jobs. Unfortunately, Volkswagen delivered fewer than 3,000 jobs and closed the plant twelve years later, citing declining sales in the American market.[25] Since 1976, the Volkswagen incentive package has proven to be the rule, not the exception, as states now offer millions of dollars annually to attract firms.

Cities also use the business recruitment approach to adjust to global restructuring and redevelop their downtown cores for producer services firms, such as bank headquarters, law offices, accountants, and advertising agencies. They use powers of eminent domain to assemble and write down the costs of land for developers, changing zoning to permit high-rise commercial, office, and residential development, and granting generous property tax breaks.[26] Since 1980, New York City alone has given developers and other businesses over $2 billion in location incentives.[27]

Most cities also try to recruit manufacturing firms into their industrial districts, partly in response to groups concerned with the plight of low-income, central city residents. In the early 1980s a new tool—the enterprise zone—became available to assist in this effort. Enterprise zones are designated low-income areas in which businesses may operate with reduced or no taxes and relaxed government regulations. The supply-side theory underlying this tool is that if the city reduces business costs, businesses will locate in low-income areas. Ronald Reagan made enterprise zones a centerpiece of his urban policy in the 1980 presidential campaign. Although his administration did not pursue the idea, 37 states and the District of Columbia passed enabling legislation for local enterprise zones. Today, there are 400 to 500 active enterprise zones in the United States.[28]

Clearly, states and localities are spending vast sums to recruit businesses. Yet it is difficult to determine an exact amount of expenditures. As Levy explains:

> How much the nation spends on local economic development is not known because the funds come from so many sources and because the government contribution comes from both sides of the budget—direct expenditures and tax expenditures. A very conservative estimate would place the total expenditures at over $10 billion [annually]. The actual total may be several times that.[29]

Levy's uncertainty is borne out by other studies and attempts to ascertain the magnitude of annual federal, state and local expenditures on economic development. Federal direct outlays and tax losses (from tax exempt development bonds) alone amount to well over $100 billion annually. State and local spending on education and infrastructure—two of the most important factors in economic development—cannot easily be included in expenditure analyses because of the difficulty of separating economic development purposes from broader educational or infrastructure goals. Nevertheless, all data and analyses agree that the magnitude of state and local economic development spending has grown dramatically over the past decade, as federal spending has declined. Moreover, while the percentage of total spending on cost reduction assistance to firms has dropped recently in favor of spending for local capacity development and market expansion, the absolute magnitude of spending on cost reduction, primarily for business recruitment, has continued to increase.[30]

The business recruitment approach to development has received a great deal of criticism over the years. Conservative bankers and industrialists of the 1930s equated the South's use of bonds to attract industry with socialism. The selective use of tax incentives and other enticements to attract firms still does not sit well with those conservatives who prefer that the government lower taxes for everyone and stay out of the marketplace, period.[31] Yet most conservatives do not strenuously oppose state and local recruitment subsidies. The criticisms have come from other directions.

Perhaps the most serious shortcoming of business recruitment efforts is that they are expensive and often unproductive. Annual advertising budgets alone can easily exceed $100,000. A permanent overseas recruiting office costs as much as $1 million per year to operate. Yet while only a few hundred firms relocate every year, thousands of state and local development organizations court them.[32]

The most significant costs of the recruitment approach involve the tax abatements, financing, and other cost-reduction measures that states and localities use to outbid each other for firms (see table 4). A tax abatement is a reduction in, or total cancellation of, a firm's taxes. Hence it constitutes an off-budget subsidy, whose value can amount to tens of millions of dollars, but which the public has difficulty tracking. Because property and income taxes are the primary revenue sources from which firms pay for the costs they impose on government for public services, the jurisdiction that abates these taxes puts itself in fiscal jeopardy.[33]

As noted above, location incentives to companies like Chase Manhattan Bank, National Broadcasting Corporation, Shearson-Lehman-Hutton, Drexel-Burnham-Lambert, and others, have cost New York City over $2 billion since 1980. At the same time, the city has raised property taxes on everyone else, businesses and residents alike, and cut services. The Cleveland City Council recently "approved a $122 million tax break for the 60-story Ameritrust Center project, which will include a much-desired Hyatt Regency Hotel. . . . The downside: The hard-up Cleveland school system will lose an estimated $48 million in revenue over the life of the tax break."[34] Thus state and local economic development practices, rather than bolstering tax revenues, may exacerbate the fiscal crises caused by economic dislocation and the New Federalism policies that cut federal funding to cities and states. Politicians and economic development officials claim that the jobs gained through incentive arrangements are worth the expenditures and foregone tax revenues and that, eventually, these businesses will pay taxes. Yet, there is no guarantee that these firms will not simply leave town when the subsidies stop, wooed by another desperate state or city.

Some liberals and progressives argue that state and local economic development based on business recruitment often does not help those who need it most—the poor and working class; or it helps them much less than it helps middle- and upper-income groups.[35] An incoming firm may bring some of its own workers, or it may attract new workers into the area, or it may attract workers from other jobs, thus bidding up wages without necessarily employing the structurally unemployed.

Poor persons living in central cities often find themselves excluded from the benefits of economic development. Lacking transportation to the suburbs where manufacturing jobs often locate, they must either accept the low-wage retail service jobs that serve the new producer service industries or remain unemployed.[36] Moreover, tax reduction tools such as enterprise zones have not proved to be the panacea that many had expected them to be. While some have been quite successful in stimulating local development, most research indicates that success, when it occurs, is due not to the tax breaks and lax regulations, but to management counsulting and other services provided by the locality.[37]

Progressives also argue that current state and local economic development practice generally, but especially the business recruitment approach, is undemocratic. They claim that the process is elitist, in part because public development officials tend to identify with the interests of the businesses and developers they are courting.

Elected and appointed officials underplay the magnitude of the incentives they offer to firms and exaggerate the benefits in jobs and future economic growth that will come from an improved business climate.[38]

The city of Baltimore provides an excellent example of the economic dislocations caused by economic restructuring, as well as some accomplishments and shortcomings of the business recruitment approach to urban economic development. Until recently, Baltimore's economy rested on an export base of steel production and transportation equipment manufacture. Between 1970 and 1985, however, Baltimore lost 40,000 manufacturing jobs—45 percent of its total in this sector. Thus many residents of the city's working-class neighborhoods lost their means of livelihood. At the same time, the postwar flight of the middle class to the suburbs undermined the viability of the city's central business district and harbor area.

In one of the most ambitious and expensive revitalization efforts undertaken by any city, Baltimore converted its downtown and harbor into a comfortable home for producer services, tourism, and conventions. By most measures, the city's efforts have been successful and it has leveraged millions in private investment. Yet the city's low-income persons have largely been excluded from the benefits of revitalization. With the demise of semiskilled blue-collar jobs, they have little choice but to accept the low-wage retail service jobs that support the city's new economic functions. Moreover, as upper-income producer service workers move into their neighborhoods, they face escalating housing costs and the threat of displacement.[39]

Managing the War Between the States

Critics of the competitive business recruitment approach have recommended, and some jurisdictions have adopted, strategies to manage or mitigate the effects of the business subsidy war between the states. These include cost-benefit analysis, subsidy clawbacks, outlawing subsidies, and tax-base sharing.

Cost-benefit analyses are balance sheets that help a government decide if a subsidy is a wise public investment. The costs of development include the dollar value of the subsidies and other incentives that a jurisdiction pays to recruit a firm (such as providing land or buildings at no charge), as well as the indirect costs of development. These include public services (police, fire protection, and road usage) for the firm itself, as well as for the firm's employees (especially if the firm brings in workers from outside the area, as is often the case). Workers require housing and schools for their children, police and fire protection, parks, and cultural amenities. The benefits of development include taxes paid by the firm (if they are not abated), and taxes paid by the firm's employees on real property, sales, and income. If the firm hires previously unemployed workers, the benefits include the reduction in public expenditures to support those workers as well as psychic benefits that workers enjoy when they find jobs. The benefits also may include the jobs gained in retail stores where the newly employed workers spend their earnings.

A skilled cost-benefit analyst can account for the risk that a firm might leave before net benefits become positive and use this to estimate the maximum subsidy that will allow the state or locality to achieve an acceptable return on its investment. Cost-benefit analyses also are relatively easy and inexpensive to conduct, especially with the aid of computer models.[40]

Unfortunately, because economic development officials and politicians equate electoral success with the capture of new businesses and because, as noted above, they may identify more with the needs and interests of businesses than with the community or state as a whole, they tend either to not use thorough cost-benefit analyses, or to build overly optimistic assumptions into the models. Thus while the net community benefits that a given firm will generate (under reasonable assumptions) may not warrant a subsidy package, the mayor's or governor's perceived electoral benefits ultimately lead them to do whatever is necessary to attract the firm.[41]

There are instructive exceptions to this rule. In some economically hard-pressed cities, the failure of heavily subsidized companies to fulfill their job creation promises has provoked the ouster of public officials responsible for the subsidy deals.[42] In others, outraged citizens have organized to oppose tax abatements and to monitor economic development outcomes.[43] It seems that a critical and well-informed public is necessary to ensure the responsible use of cost-benefit analysis.

Clawbacks constitute another solution to the subsidy war between the states. These are provisos written into subsidy agreements that the recipient firm either has to create a certain number of jobs and stay in town a certain number of years, or else pay back the subsidy.[44] Clawbacks are growing in popularity but they suffer from at least one serious shortcoming—competition among states limits their willingness to enforce the agreements, for fear that they will deter new businesses from locating in the state.[45]

Another way to stop the subsidy war might be simply to outlaw the use of subsidies. Norman Glickman and Douglas Woodward, for example, recommend that the National League of Cities or the National Governors' Association negotiate nationwide agreements that would limit the incentives that states or cities may offer to recruit businesses. "The problem of 'cheaters' who continue to give incentives proscribed by the compacts could be addressed by federal legislation cutting aid to cities or states that do not play by the rules, or by taxing state and local subsidies."[46] Despite the possible merits of this proposal, the federal government does not appear ready to adopt such an activist role in state and local economic development policy and practice. Even if it were willing to enforce such agreements, there is a chance that the provisions themselves might simply induce states and localities to search for other means by which to compete for firms. Even efforts to organize regional (interstate) bans on subsidies have foundered upon state reluctance to give up these tools.

Tax base sharing provides yet another possible solution to the subsidy war. Under a tax base sharing system, two or more jurisdictions agree to share a certain portion of the tax revenues from businesses that locate in any one of the jurisdictions. The fact that all jurisdictions benefit directly from the location of a firm in any one of them lessens their motivation to compete for the firm. Tax base sharing has worked on the metropolitan level in Minneapolis–St. Paul and other areas, and it might work on the regional (interstate) level as well. Under a regional system, states would pay each other a percentage of the value of their tax base growth due to business in-migration.

Business Retention

In the meantime, states and localities have adopted additional development strategies that may have more salutary effects on job growth and revenues than does smokestack chasing. In the average developed locality, existing firms, not newcomers, create most of the new jobs each year. Hence business retention and expansion strategies may be more cost-effective than industrial recruitment, as it usually costs less to retain existing plants and jobs than it does to attract new ones.

Retention programs generally help firms in difficulty because of declining demand for their products, increases in energy prices, inability to secure capital to finance improvements in production, increasing taxes, costly or inadequate transportation systems, lack of public services, and costly or inappropriately skilled labor. The public sector may respond by supplying financial subsidies for retooling, worker training, or interest payments on commercial loans. Smaller companies, in particular, may benefit from assistance in developing new markets in the United States or abroad, or from construction of new access roads or sites with better transportation and utilities.

An effective business retention program usually includes a so-called early warning system, which helps a state or locality anticipate plant closings in time for the public sector to take preventive action or at least to help workers make the transition to new jobs through retraining, job search skills enhancement, and home mortgage payment assistance.[47] The U.S. Congress gave a boost to early warning systems in 1988 with the passage of the Worker Adjustment and Retraining Notification Act, which requires companies with 100 or more employees to issue formal, written notification of plant closings or major layoffs 60 days in advance. Some states require an even longer notification period. Even without state plant closing laws, public officials often can anticipate closings several months in advance of the federal notification requirement by maintaining comprehensive data on industry trends and by frequently contacting company managers and workers. As discussed in chapter 4, liberals and progressives favor public efforts to avert plant closings and firm out-migrations. Conservatives, on the other hand, regard government intervention to keep plants open or restructure mature industries as both inefficient and unfair to the taxpayers who must pay for such efforts.

Even if one accepts the business retention approach on ideological grounds, it has several limitations as a development strategy. From the standpoint of both the economic development professional and the politician, it can be riskier than recruitment because it gives them nothing new to show for their efforts, and they may have difficulty explaining how the local economy would have suffered if a firm had left or gone out of business. Officials can mitigate this problem, however, through diligent community education efforts.

Another limitation of the firm retention approach is that it only works in communities that already have viable economic bases. A bedroom community seeking to provide more services without raising residential property taxes has little choice—it must recruit new businesses or merge with other localities. An inner city suffering fiscal crisis because its economic base has deteriorated must certainly practice business retention, but it needs to recruit new businesses also.

A more serious problem is that, increasingly, even retention efforts become part of the interstate bidding game. One state's recruitment agents offer incentives to lure away a company, and soon the state where the company is now located finds that it must, at the very least, meet the bid. New York City has often found itself in this predicament over the past decade. The State of Illinois and one of its localities recently shelled out $178 million to keep a 6,000-worker Sears merchandise group in the state. To counter offers from dozens of cities and states, Illinois provided $20 million in highway improvements, $33 million for on-site infrastructure upgrading, $6 million in tax breaks, $1.1 million for worker training, and a $1 million interest-free loan to establish a child care center. The locality of Hoffman Estates provided Sears with a 786-acre site, worth $86 million.[48]

Business Formation and Expansion

One of the most serious flaws in the business recruitment approach is that, for the most part, it increases the number of jobs in one region by impoverishing others—it simply shifts jobs from one location to another, without increasing the total number of jobs or total national output.[49] In short, it is not economic *development*. Economic development involves the creation of new goods or services, or new processes to make goods and services, through innovation and entrepreneurship. Over the long run, this increases jobs and tax revenues, and improves the standard of living.

Historically, large cities have been the breeding grounds for new businesses, since they offer the great variety of resources necessary for developing new ideas, applying the ideas to commercial ventures, and locating materials suppliers, financing, and skilled workers.[50] Even small towns, however, may have distinctive resources that can support new business formation and expansion. The public sector can enhance these resources to provide an environment that facilitates and encourages business development.

Much of the innovation and job growth in the United States occurs in young firms that have fewer than 100 employees.[51] Yet, because commercial lenders often perceive such firms as greater credit risks than larger, more established firms, and because their capital needs generally differ from those of the larger firms, smaller firms have difficulty obtaining financing to support expansion and development.[52]

The public sector can fill these "capital gaps" by insuring private bank loans (thus lowering the risk for commercial lenders) or by providing public loans. The U.S. Small Business Administration

(SBA) runs programs of this sort, while many states have developed their own programs to complement the SBA, which suffered considerable budget cutbacks during the 1980s. States and localities also can help small and growing firms find new markets or learn to sell their products overseas. New businesses, in particular, may need management assistance or training that state or local agencies can arrange.

In addition, government can help to create an environment conducive to business expansion and development. A popular tool for creating such an environment is the incubator. An incubator is a facility that has space for several fledgling companies, each of which generally begins with fewer than five employees. Rents, utilities, and certain equipment costs may be publicly subsidized, but in any event, costs are low because they are shared by the tenants in the incubator. In the more successful incubators, companies receive assistance in product development, business planning, management, and marketing. Once a company has achieved a certain volume of sales or has been in the incubator for a certain period of time, it must leave to (hopefully) become a successful independent business, making room for another fledgling firm in the incubator. Presently there are over 300 small business incubators nationwide. Because the success rate of their tenants (80 percent) is so much higher than that of the average start-up business (20 to 40 percent), their popularity is likely to increase in the future.[53]

The public sector can facilitate growth and expansion of small and midsize businesses by fostering the development of local linkages and networks among firms. Like the research and development consortia among large firms, discussed in chapter 4, linkages among smaller firms in related or interdependent industries can help each firm to utilize its full capacity, as it helps to generate economies of scale in production that improve the profitability of each firm. Yet, by remaining independent from the others or from larger firms, each firm retains its ability to respond to other market opportunities and to innovate continually. In this way, a community of producers exhibits the advantages of both small and large firms.[54]

Institutions of higher learning constitute another feature of the environment that can foster business formation and expansion. As the pace of technological change and the intensity of global competition increase, collaborations between business and academe become essential for healthy economic development. The commercial application of university research created the well-known high-technology economies of California's Silicon Valley, Massachusetts's Route 128, and North Carolina's Research Triangle. The successes of these regions have inspired other states and localities to support the application of university research to commercial ventures. Pennsylvania's Ben Franklin Partnership, for example, provides state matching grants to university-based research projects that develop new products or production processes.[55]

Of course, the resources of academia can be deployed in a variety of ways that serve the goal of economic development. The Virginia Center for Innovative Technology (CIT), for instance, coordinates the resources of higher education institutions throughout the state to provide a variety of services that facilitate development. CIT promotes new product and process development by underwriting, in partnership with the business community, "technology development centers," at major state universities, in areas such as fiber optics, semicustom integrated circuits, and bioprocess products. CIT promotes the introduction of new products, processes, and services into the marketplace through its support of entrepreneurship centers at five universities in the state. It also supports four separate small business incubators in cooperation with universities. CIT facilitates the application of new technology to practical business problems through its sponsorship of "technology transfer agents" housed at eight community colleges. These agents link business managers with universities throughout Virginia to solve business problems ranging from locating reliable, low-cost suppliers, to solving accounting problems, to managing complex organizational change processes.[56]

Export Promotion

A growing form of business expansion strategy that treats the globalization of production and trade as an opportunity, is export promotion. State export promotion efforts consist primarily of information services and financing assistance to help companies sell their goods in foreign markets. For example, 36 states produce export-import directories that list companies by county and product classification, and send them to U.S. embassies, foreign banks, importers' associations, and similar groups abroad. Virtually every state provides training and counseling services to businesses, which include advice on how to export, where to find legal advice, how to determine price quotations, and other issues related to doing business abroad.[57] Many states conduct mentor programs, which match experienced exporters and technical assistance providers (such as universities and certain federal agencies) with new-to-export companies.[58] Most states also provide market studies and trade leads for domestic firms, and arrange for American companies to act as hosts to foreign buyers visiting the United States.[59]

Export financing programs are growing rapidly in both scope and magnitude. In 1988, 22 states allocated over $32 million to export financing. Generally, export financing assistance is limited to pre- and postexport guarantees that take some of the risk and uncertainty out of foreign trade. Several states have established shared foreign sales corporations (SFSCs), through which exporters receive tax deductions on export-related income for offshore-based operations.[60] Some states also have established export trading companies (ETCs). Through ETCs, firms can join together to share services such as market research, transportation, insurance, documentation, trade lead development, and financing assistance, without violating federal antitrust laws.[61] In addition to these export promotion activities, tourism promotion is an increasingly significant state activity. In 1989 state and local spending for tourism promotion reached $300 million.[62]

Cities also engage in export promotion efforts. In a survey conducted in 1987, more than 80 percent of all cities with populations over 150,000 claimed to be engaged in economic development programs that include an international activity. Of these, most focus on export promotion, especially training and counseling on issues such as patents, licensing, export regulation, and international trade data. In most cities, the chamber of commerce, the port authority, and local universities play significant roles in organizing or delivering export promotion services.[63]

Many cities now use foreign trade zones (FTZs) as an inducement to trade. Foreign trade zones, like enterprise zones, seek to attract economic activity by lowering taxes. FTZs are areas into which a company may import goods without paying a duty. The company may use the goods as inputs in a production process and reexport them, still with no duty. The company must only pay import duties if it ships the goods out of the zone into other parts of the United States.[64] Another local export promotion innovation is the world trade center, of which there were 186 worldwide as of January 1989. (Seventy-two were operational; others were coming on line.) Sixteen U.S. cities have operating world trade centers, and more are in the planning stages. A world trade center

> complements and supports existing services and governmental agencies related to the promotion of world trade. . . . Each WTC must have [its] own office space and space available for tenants which may be international financial institutions, trading companies, custom brokers,

freight forwarders, legal and insurance services, or government trade promotion services.[65]

Some observers claim that the creation of new, innovative businesses and the expansion of existing ones through local networks and export promotion are becoming significant components of state and local development strategies.[66] There is no denying that these efforts have increased in scope and magnitude during the past decade. Yet others point out that, to date, the absolute amount of state and local expenditures for innovation and business formation still does not equal direct and indirect expenditures for business recruitment.[67] Others note that the impacts of efforts focused on small firms are likely, in any case, to be small.[68]

The "Third Wave" in Economic Development

In an effort to increase the scale and impact of business formation and expansion and export promotion programs, states and localities are finding new ways to deliver these services without increasing their costs. In a word, states and localities are "privatizing" the delivery of business development services. They are cosponsoring, along with private donors or investors, private organizations (both for-profits and not-for-profits) to provide business development services. Some observers call this a "third wave" in economic development, as it follows the first wave of business recruitment and the second wave of business formation and expansion through direct state and local government services. The third wave is simply a decentralized, market-based way to implement second-wave strategies. Some call this approach wholesaling, since the government creates or cosponsors the product but then passes it off to others who provide it to the end user.[69]

One example of a third-wave initiative is the aforementioned Virginia Center for Innovative Technology, which brokers productive associations between universities and businesses. Another example is Pennsylvania's Manufacturing Technology Resources Center (MANTEC). MANTEC is a consortium of 3,200 manufacturers in south-central Pennsylvania that assists firms in developing new production techniques and markets, coordinates company labor requirements with vocational school programs, and provides other services as requested by companies. Its goal is to improve company efficiency and global competitiveness. The state provided $30 million over three years, and private sources are contributing at least that much through in-kind services. Those who use MANTEC's services must pay a fee as well.[70]

Still another type of third-wave arrangement involves the community development corporation (CDC). Many CDCs were created under the federal Economic Opportunity Act of 1964 in an effort to stimulate economic development in low-income areas and to empower the poor. Many began as neighborhood advocacy groups that fought against insensitive redevelopment or government neglect of their neighborhoods and later evolved into proactive improvement organizations. Their boards of directors typically include a large percentage of neighborhood representatives as well as representatives of business and government. CDCs engage in a variety of development activities, including commercial revitalization and development, housing rehabilitation and construction, and industrial development. As CDCs have become more sophisticated, and as state and local governments have sought to lower the costs and improve the effectiveness of their services to low-income communities, CDCs and governments have crafted third-wave agreements in which the CDC organizes and manages economic development efforts with government subsidies.[71]

Table 4 depicts the various development strategies that states and localities pursue and the tools associated with them. Note that most strategies can be pursued through various cost reduction, local capacity development, and market expansion tools. Critics of existing development practices argue that states and localities should try to confine themselves to using tools that develop local capacity, whether they are recruiting, retaining, or facilitating the expansion of a firm. In this way, the state or locality is sure to gain something from its efforts, even if the firms that it assists leave before the community has reaped the tax and employment benefits they promise.[72]

The Rise of Strategic Planning

As economic development becomes a more important, complex, and costly undertaking, whose success is determined by many variables in the global economy, states and localities find it necessary to conduct more analytical and deliberate decision-making processes. At least 31 states now have comprehensive economic development plans and an estimated 50 percent of all cities larger than 50,000 population do as well.[73] This emphasis on analysis and planning, coupled with growing citizen concern about both the fiscal and economic health of their communities and elitism in economic development, has led to more open, participatory economic planning and decision-making processes.

One type of comprehensive economic development planning process that is increasingly used and that is potentially open and participatory, is strategic planning. Strategic planning is a way of systematically analyzing the most important features of an economy and determining which of these are strengths that should serve as the foundation for future development and which are weaknesses in need of improvement. Strategic economic development planning compares the local or state economy to other competing economies in the region, nation, and world to capitalize on the distinctive strengths of the home economy. A brief description of a typical strategic planning process will help to elucidate the nature of state and local industrial policy and its ideological variations.[74]

To initiate a strategic planning effort, public officials organize interest groups, such as bankers, labor leaders, industrialists, neighborhood and civic groups, and public officials, into a steering committee to oversee the planning process. The committee reviews detailed information about the state of the economy, and identifies strengths and weaknesses based upon trends in industries and employment; labor force skills and the presence of universities; community location and infrastructure; business financing availability; taxes and regulations; and overall quality of life.

Using its analyses of strengths, weaknesses, and trends, the steering committee identifies opportunities and threats that can be addressed by taking advantage of existing strengths or by changing weaknesses to strengths. An example of a threat would be an economy that is overly dependent upon one industry, particularly one facing stiff foreign competition, such as the basic steel industry. On the other hand, the presence of fine research universities in the area might present an opportunity for new product development.

After the committee has developed a prioritized list of opportunities and threats, it chooses specific goals and objectives to address each issue. To address the decline of the basic steel industry, for example, a committee with a liberal philosophy might decide to preserve as many jobs as possible by subsidizing the restructuring and modernization of the competitive parts of the industry. For those whose jobs cannot be saved, the committee might set up a special fund to ease their transition to new careers. A committee with a more conservative philosophy might regard an attempt to intervene in the operations of the steel industry as an unwarranted intrusion into the market. It might also reject a worker adjustment fund as an unfair burden on taxpayers. Such a committee might focus its energies and resources on marketing the existing plants to new buyers and seeking to attract new businesses to the jurisdiction.

Finally, the steering committee molds its goals and objectives into an action plan, which it submits to the appropriate legislative body for approval and implementation. After about five years, the entire planning process may be repeated, since economic conditions change continuously.[75]

Of course, cities and states may tackle specific economic issues through less comprehensive forms of planning. Chicago's Task Force on Steel, its Apparel and Fashion Task Force, and Massachusetts's Mature Industries Commission, are examples of government efforts to bring business, labor, and other parties together to restructure and revitalize declining industries, much as industrial policy advocates have suggested the national government should do.[76] Also, as the federal government reduces defense spending in the aftermath of the Cold War, states and localities are planning the conversion of defense plants to civilian production and planning to replace military bases with civilian firms.[77]

Thus, states and localities have responded to the dislocations of global restructuring and the federal economic policies of the 1980s by developing their own forms of industrial policy.[78] The final section of this chapter discusses the implications of this decentralized industrial policy for the future of American federalism, as well as America's ability to compete in the world economy and foster the economic welfare of its citizens.

Global Restructuring and American Federalism

As noted in previous chapters, American economic policies in the Bretton Woods era can be characterized as "Keynes at home and Smith abroad," since the United States promoted free markets with no government intervention in the international economy, and economic stability and social welfare at home through extensive government intervention in the marketplace. The demise of the Bretton Woods system undermined the national consensus supporting this policy mix. In the 1980s the federal government attempted to construct a new set of policies that one might call "Smith at the federal level and Smith abroad." As discussed in this chapter, states and localities responded by pursuing more interventionist, albeit not quite Keynesian, policies.[79]

It is too soon to tell if these trends in federal, state, and local policy will continue, much less to evaluate their results. But we can note their apparent advantages and disadvantages and the issues they raise for the future of federalism.

Many observers believe that the growth of state and local competence and responsibility improves the United States's ability to respond to the globalization of production and trade. Because of their close proximity to firms and their intimate knowledge of the business environment, states and localities can devise and implement programs tailored to the needs of firms and workers within their jurisdictions.[80] State governments are ideally suited to the economic development role, because they are small enough to understand firms' needs, yet large enough to organize the resources necessary to conduct state-of-the-art economic development programs.[81]

The globalization of production and trade has increased the economic importance of cities as well. They are the critical linkage points in global finance, production, transportation, and communications. They house the headquarters of multinational corporations, intergovernmental organizations, and the seats of national and state governments. Richard Knight claims that cities are the primary sources of wealth and economic growth and therefore deserve support from state and federal governments. Yet it is up to the cities themselves to define their roles in the global economy and then to secure the resources they need to play those roles from state and federal governments.[82]

The growth of state and local initiatives in the global economy poses certain problems for the federal system, however. One problem is the confusion about who has the authority to take action in the international arena. Although the U.S. Constitution reserves for the federal government, the right to conduct foreign policy, state and local actions increasingly encroach upon this turf. For example, agreements between border states and Mexican or Canadian subnational governments to solve regional problems, or state and local policies to divest in South Africa until the country dismantles its racial apartheid system, undermine the federal government's foreign policy authority.[83]

More serious are the problems arising from the clash of the current U.S. policies of 'Smith' at the federal level and 'Keynes' at the state level. For example, while the federal government adheres to GATT agreements on government procurement policies, many states ignore, and thus undermine, these agreements.[84] Also, in the recent Uruguay Round of GATT negotiations, the United States sought multilateral accords to proscribe government interventions in the market—interventions such as foreign and domestic investment incentives and "performance requirements" that stipulate how much of a firm's product must be produced locally, how much notice it must give before closing its plant, and so forth. If the federal government's efforts succeed, states and localities will lose important tools in their economic development arsenals.[85] Similarly, while some states restrict foreign investment and require foreign firms to disclose detailed information on their operations, the federal government currently opposes such restrictions.[86] These are thorny policy problems, particularly because they involve conflicting ideological beliefs about the role of government in the marketplace.

Decentralized economic development policy also raises issues of public resource waste and underutilization of economies of scale in program implementation. In the field of export promotion, these problems are slowly yielding to cooperative efforts among different levels in the federal system. Since the mid-1980s, for example, states have been working with the U.S. Export-Import Bank and the Commerce Department's U.S. and Foreign Commercial Service to enhance state export promotion efforts.[87] Although cooperation between localities and higher levels of government has developed more slowly, a number of such efforts now are under way.[88] Also, cooperation among states on a regional basis is on the rise. Groups such as the six-state, Mid-South Trade Council share costs and personnel on overseas trade missions to promote tourism as well as exports of goods and services.[89]

The practice of business investment attraction, however, remains a competitive, zero-sum game. Progressive and liberal critics assert that as states and localities outbid each other's incentive packages to attract investment, they unwittingly engage in a massive wealth transfer from the taxpaying public to multinational corporations. They argue that the federal government should outlaw business location incentives and control the movement of capital across state lines.[90]

Conservatives view state and local competition for investment with less concern. While most conservatives do not advocate the selective use of tax incentives, they hold that tax cuts are generally good for economic growth. Most conservatives also believe that the smaller the role played by the federal government, the better, since it is important to maximize individual and business choices among different packages of state and local services and taxes.[91] Hence, the New Federalism is a dramatic improvement over the interventionism of previous arrangements. Moreover, the aggressive responses of states and localities to the challenges of the global economy prove the soundness of the New Federalism's basic logic of decentralizing responsibility to states and localities.[92]

The decentralization of economic development policy also raises questions of equity and income distribution. Liberals and progressives charge that the Reagan administration's New Federalism and supply-side economic policies are responsible for the rising incidence of poverty and the growing concentration of dependent populations in decaying inner cities and rural areas. They claim that state and local industrial policies have done little or nothing to stem the growth of poverty and the maldistribution of income and opportunity. While this failure stems in part from the elitist, pro-business bias of most economic development programs, the New Federalism policies also must share a large part of the blame for the rise of poverty and the exacerbation of fiscal disparities.[93] Those communities and states most in need of more jobs and tax revenues cannot afford to conduct expensive economic development efforts; they certainly cannot outbid wealthier jurisdictions for footloose firms.[94] Moreover, the low education levels and relatively low wages that characterize the poorest communities no longer draw investors as they did in the 1930s. With the rise of global production and trade, the lowest American wages cannot begin to compete with the lower wages that prevail in Third World countries.

Hence liberals and progressives call for increased federal assistance for community development and welfare/workfare programs. David Osborne, for example, suggests a restructuring of the federal system that he believes would combine the advantages of decentralization and the power of the federal government to redistribute incomes:

> When the appropriate model [for addressing an economic problem or opportunity] differs from one region to another, programs should be run by the states. The federal role should be to provide funds, particularly for poorer states; to create financial incentives for states to act; to evaluate state efforts; and, above all, to provide the leadership necessary to create nationwide support for reform. When problems transcend the capacities of individual states, on the other hand, or when they are rooted in national realities that do not vary from region to region, the federal government should administer the programs.[95]

States could retain planning and administrative control, says Osborne, over initiatives in the areas of education and training, over programs to stimulate entrepreneurship, university-industry cooperation, and economic development of poverty-stricken areas, and over programs to finance formation and expansion of businesses, since these conditions tend to vary from one region to another. The federal government, however, "can play a critical role in providing funds and in creating incentives for states to act," through such vehicles as "challenge grants" that reward states and localities for their own efforts and for achieving results.[96]

The federal government, says Osborne, should take the initiative on issues such as the negotiation of agreements to regulate the terms of trade among nations; the creation of institutions to facilitate increased exports by American firms; the creation of a national labor-management relations framework that encourages flexibility and innovation in American firms; the creation of industry-wide research consortia (in industries such as superconductors and high-definition television); the restructuring of mature and uncompetitive industries, such as shoes, textiles, steel, and automobiles; social adjustment—taxing, welfare, employment, and training policies; and finally, strategic analysis and the collection of data on the U.S. economy and the performance of our competitor nations.[97]

Progressive reform proposals, while similar to liberal reforms, call for stronger federal and local government roles in economic development. Progressives believe that the federal government should establish a national framework in which state and local economic democracy can flourish. This includes encouraging regional cooperation to stop the interstate war for jobs; supporting and encouraging state and regional long-range economic planning and incorporating such plans into national policies; and helping localities build economic development capacity and expertise.[98]

As discussed in chapter 4, some progressives believe that the federal government should establish a national social needs assessment process that would inform national development policy. Social needs assessments would draw, in part, upon the work of local government planning boards and community-based organizations. These latter entities would have major responsibility for implementing national policies in ways appropriate to local conditions.[99] Most progressive economic development proposals also include a national development bank that would channel capital to depressed regions and inner cities, to be administered at the regional or state level. Also, progressives call for greater labor-management cooperation and worker-owned businesses, to promote economic democracy and productivity. This requires a supportive national legal context, but also state and local government capacity to support and facilitate the process of democratizing firms.

These proposals for more federal government involvement in the economy and in state and local affairs run counter to conservative thinking. Conservatives acknowledge rising poverty in central cities and rural areas but, as discussed in chapter 3, many believe that government intervention is the primary cause of this problem, not its solution. They call for an end to the welfare system for able-bodied, working-age people, so as to break their dependence on handouts.[100] Some conservatives urge the legalization of drugs, so as to break juvenile dependence on this source of a fast buck. They argue against raising the minimum wage, because they believe that a higher minimum wage would deter inner-city employers from hiring persons with low skills.[101]

Some conservatives support federal income maintenance and fiscal equalization payments to states and localities, but they believe that the proper vehicle for such transfers is a simple cash grant from the federal government to the states. Such a grant system would obviate the need for the massive federal welfare and grant program bureaucracy that now burdens the economy. Moreover, giving states the power to choose how to spend federal funds would empower citizens to shape their destinies. This, in turn, would induce them to handle their tax dollars with more care and responsibility. While the New Federalism of the 1980s did not succeed in giving this much power to states, it was, in the conservative view, a step in the right direction.[102]

Summary

States and localities have experienced the effects of global economic restructuring in very different ways—some as economic and social disasters, others as mere disruptions, and others as opportunities for new growth and expansion. In response, they have established increasingly sophisticated economic development programs to replace lost jobs and tax bases and take advantage of new opportunities in the global economy. Due in part to the retreat of the federal government from their affairs, they have focused energies on competing with each other for jobs through business recruitment programs. Yet as they see the shortcomings of this approach, states and localities are adding other approaches to their repertoires, including business retention, formation, and expansion. They also are using more deliberate analysis and planning procedures to establish appropriate development goals and strategies.

Despite the successes of these policies, however, states and localities have yet to solve the problems of structural unemployment and poverty in their inner cities and rural areas. Some think that an expansion in the federal role is necessary to solve such problems, but others believe that the present system affords the right balance of power between the levels of government. In any case, a change in the federal government's current approach to states and localities would seem to require both a resolution of its budget deficit problems and a shift in ideological perspective.

With or without a change in federal priorities, several trends seem irreversible. States and localities are rapidly acquiring the expertise to understand regional and global economic forces, and they are developing increasingly sophisticated tools to promote their own economic prosperity. They are building partnerships with the private sector, with their counterparts in their respective regions, and with subnational jurisdictions abroad. These new capacities and linkages are making states and localities more adaptable and powerful.

Yet the ultimate success or failure of state and local economic development efforts will also depend upon the development of global economic forces and the policies of the United States and other national governments. The task ahead for states and localities, as well as for the federal government, is to develop mutually reinforcing policies that promote human welfare.

Notes

1. See Rosenfeld, Stuart A., Edward M. Bergman, and Sarah Rubin: *After the Factories: Changing Employment Patterns in the Rural South.* Research Triangle Park, N.C.: Southern Growth Policies Board, 1985. As discussed in chapters 1 and 4, the location of a firm depends, in part, upon the structure of its costs, which depends upon the firm's stage in the product-process cycle. In the first stage, the product design is still changing, and firms need a relatively large proportion of design engineers who can work out the bugs in the product and production process. Profits tend to be high because the firm has an edge in the technology and may enjoy patent protection as well. Competition is based on the newness of the product itself. Firms need to be near sources of technical expertise, supplies, and communication links. Hence cities in the Northeast or West Coast are likely locations.

By the second stage, one or a few workable product designs and production processes have been developed. Fewer high-salaried engineers are needed, since the product can now be mass-produced using standardized production processes and lower skill workers. More firms have entered the market, so price competition and production costs are now salient determinants of profitability. The firm may seek a lower wage location, such as a rural area in the North, South, or abroad. The third stage is one of decline. The market is saturated and price competition is keen. Firms seek even lower cost locations, some sell their businesses, and some try to restructure.

2. Gaventa, John, Barbara Ellen Smith, Alex Willingham (eds): *Communities in Economic Crisis: Appalachia and the South.* Philadelphia: Temple University Press, 1990.

3. Phillips, Kevin: *The Politics of Rich and Poor: Wealth and the American Electorate in the Reagan Aftermath.* New York: Random House, 1990, chapter 6.

4. Although the coastal and southern border states have the vast majority of U.S. defense contracts and military bases, a few interior states, such as Ohio, have communities with high concentrations of defense-related employment.

5. Clark, Gordon L.: "Pittsburgh in Transition: Consolidation of Prosperity in an Era of Economic Restructuring." In Beauregard, Robert A. (ed): *Economic Restructuring and Political Response.* Urban Affairs Reviews. Vol. 34. Newbury Park: Sage Publications, 1989.

6. Fuller, Stephen S.: "The Internationalization of the Washington, D.C. Area Economy." In Knight, Richard and Gary Gappert (eds): *Cities in a Global Society.* Urban Affairs Annual Reviews. Vol. 35. Newbury Park: Sage Publications, 1989.

7. The development of these "maquiladora" assembly plants, as they are called, has received attention as a possible model for industrial development, as well as criticism from those who believe the plants steal American workers' jobs. See, for example, Perlo Cohen, Manuel: "Exploring the Spatial Effects of the Internationalization of the Mexican Economy." In Henderson, Jeffrey and Manuel Castells (eds): *Global Restructuring and Territorial Development.* Newbury Park: Sage Publications, 1987.

8. See Gaventa et.al., *Communities in Economic Crisis*, and the discussion in chapter 4 on the controversy over a possible U.S.–Mexico Free Trade Agreement.

9. Sassen, Saskia: "New Trends in the Sociospatial Organization of the New York City Economy," and Giloth, Robert P. and Robert Mier: "Spatial Change and Social Justice: Alternative Economic Development in Chicago." In Beauregard, *Economic Restructuring.*

10. See Goldstein, Harvey A. (ed): *The State and Local Industrial Policy Question.* Chicago: American Planning Association, 1987.

11. For insights on this point, see Osborne, David: *Laboratories of Democracy.* Boston: Harvard Business School Press, 1988. Note that some conservatives who oppose federal government intervention in the economy are more willing to tolerate state and local intervention.

12. Markusen, Ann Roell: "Industrial Restructuring and Regional Politics." In Beauregard, *Economic Restructuring.*

13. See Clavel, Pierre: *The Progressive City: Planning and Participation, 1969–1984.* New Brunswick, N.J.: Rutgers University Press, 1986; also Giloth and Mier, "Spatial Change and Social Justice."

14. The South's lack of early success is reflected in President Roosevelt's 1938 statement that the South was "the nation's number one economic problem." See Cobb, James C.: *The Selling of the South: The Southern Crusade for Industrial Development, 1936–1980.* Baton Rouge: Louisiana State University Press, 1982.

15. According to Cobb, in *Selling of the South*, states initially used general obligation bonds, which pledge the full faith and credit of the issuing jurisdiction, backed by its tax base. Later, they began using revenue bonds, which pledge only the assets of the project that is constructed with the bond. Revenue bonds are the most widely used form for economic development

purposes today. For a thorough introduction to bond financing, see Aronson, J. Richard and Eli Schwartz: *Management Policies in Local Government Finance*. Third Edition. Washington, D.C.: International City Management Association, 1987.

16. Virtually all states use tax-exempt revenue bond financing now, although Congress restricted the use of bonds in the 1980s.

17. Kline, John M.: "The States and International Affairs." Draft prepared for the Advisory Commission on Intergovernmental Relations, September 5, 1989, pp. 32–33.

18. Under the urban renewal program, local authorities could virtually confiscate private land, as long as they adhered to national guidelines for classifying an area as blighted and as long as they paid the owner the "fair market value" of the property.

19. See Fusfeld, Daniel R.: *The Basic Economics of the Urban Racial Crisis*. New York: Holt, Rinehart and Winston, 1973, chapter 2.

20. Presidents traditionally use the federal system to shift power and resources to their electoral base. For most of this century, Democrats have controlled the cities, and national policies under Democrats have favored cities at the expense of states. The Republican base is in state houses, so Republican presidents enact national policies that enhance state power at the expense of cities.

21. See the discussion of Urban Development Action Grants in Luke, Jeffrey S., Curtis Ventriss, B.J. Reed, and C.M. Reed: *Managing Economic Development: A Guide to State and Local Leadership Strategies*. San Francisco: Jossey-Bass Publishers, 1988, chapter 11. See also Squires, Gregory D. (ed): *Unequal Partnerships: The Political Economy of Urban Redevelopment in Postwar America*. New Brunswick, N.J.: Rutgers University Press, 1989.

22. Cole, Richard L., Delbert A. Taebel, and Rodney V. Hissong: *America's Cities and the 1980s. The Legacy of the Reagan Years*. Arlington: Institute of Urban Studies, The University of Texas at Arlington, March 1990. See also note 20.

23. Ibid., pp. 4–5. Many states chose to make up the difference between their expenditure needs and federal revenues by raising taxes on middle- and lower-income persons. Few raised taxes on upper-income persons by equal or greater amounts. See McIntyre, Robert S., Douglas P. Kelly, Michael P. Ettlinger, Elizabeth A. Fray: *A Far Cry from Fair: CTJ's Guide to State Tax Reform*. Washington, D.C.: Citizens for Tax Justice, April 1991.

24. "The Second War Between the States: A Bitter Struggle for Jobs, Capital and People." *Business Week*. May 17, 1976, pp. 92–114.

25. Osborne, *Laboratories of Democracy*, p. 46; also Hansen, Susan B.: "Comparing Enterprise Zones to Other Economic Development Techniques." In Green, Roy E. (ed): *Enterprise Zones: New Directions in Economic Development*. Newbury Park: Sage Publications, 1991.

26. For background on the history of postwar urban development from moderate, liberal, and radical perspectives, see Dahl, Robert A.: *Who Governs? Democracy and Power in an American City*. New Haven: Yale Uni-

versity Press, 1961; Domhoff, G. William: *Who Really Rules New Haven?* New Brunswick, N.J.: Transaction Books, 1977; Tabb, William K. and Larry Sawers (eds): *Marxism and the Metropolis: New Perspectives in Urban Political Economy.* New York: Oxford University Press, 1978.

27. Guskind, Robert: "The Giveaway Game Continues." *Planning.* Vol. 56, No. 2, February 1990, pp. 4–8.

28. See Beaumont, Enid: "Enterprise Zones and Federalism." In Green, Roy E. (ed): *Enterprise Zones: New Directions in Economic Development.* Newbury Park: Sage Publications, 1991.

29. Levy, John M.: *Economic Development Programs for Cities, Counties and Towns.* Second Edition. New York: Praeger Publishers, 1990, pp. 1–2.

30. Chi, Keon S.: *The States and Business Incentives: An Inventory of Tax and Financial Incentive Programs.* Washington, D.C.: The Council of State Governments, 1989; Fisher, Peter S.: "The National Consequences of Decentralized Industrial Policy in the United States." Unpublished paper presented at the Annual Meeting of the Association of Collegiate Schools of Planning, October 1990, in Austin, Texas; Glickman, Norman J. and Douglas P. Woodward: *The New Competitors: How Foreign Investors Are Changing the U.S. Economy.* New York: Basic Books, 1989; National Association of State Development Agencies: *State Export Program Database.* Washington, D.C.: NASDA, July 1988; Wilson, Roger: *State Business Incentives and Economic Growth: Are They Effective?* Washington, D.C.: The Council of State Governments, 1989.

31. See Levy, *Economic Development Programs*, especially chapter 13; Boaz, David: "Saving the Inner City." In Crane, Edward H. and David Boaz (eds): *An American Vision: Policies for the '90s.* Washington, D.C.: The Cato Institute, 1989; McKenzie, Richard B.: *Competing Visions: The Political Conflict over America's Economic Future.* Washington, D.C.: The Cato Institute, 1985.

32. Levy, *Economic Development Programs*, pp. 47 and 72–73; Glickman and Woodward, *The New Competitors*, p. 234.

33. Blair, John P.: *Urban and Regional Economics.* Homewood, Ill.: Richard D. Irwin, Inc., 1991, p. 527.

34. Guskind, "The Giveaway Game," p. 6.

35. See Ladd, Helen F. and John Yinger: *America's Ailing Cities: Fiscal Health and the Design of Urban Policy.* Baltimore: The Johns Hopkins University Press, 1989, chapters 10, 11, and 12; Squires, *Unequal Partnerships.*

36. Kasarda, John D.: "Urban Industrial Transition and the Underclass." In *The Annals of the American Academy of Political and Social Sciences.* Vol. 501. Newbury Park: Sage Publications, January 1989.

37. Green, *Enterprise Zones*; Weiss, Julian: "Enterprise Zones Are Just Part of the Answer for Reviving an Urban Economy." *Governing.* August 1988; Wilder, Margaret G. and Barry M. Rubin: "Targeted Redevelopment through Urban Enterprise Zones." *Journal of Urban Affairs.* Vol. 10, No. 1, 1988, pp. 1–17.

38. Rubin, Herbert J.: "Shoot Anything That Flies; Claim Anything That Falls: Conversations with Economic Development Practitioners." *Economic Development Quarterly*. Vol. 2, No. 3, August 1988, pp. 236–251; Sharp, Elaine B. and David R. Elkins: "The Politics of Economic Development Policy." *Economic Development Quarterly*. Vol. 5, No. 2, May 1991, pp. 126–139; Squires, *Unequal Partnerships*.

39. Levine, Mark V.: "Urban Redevelopment in a Global Economy: The Cases of Montreal and Baltimore." In Knight and Gappert, *Cities in a Global Society*.

40. See, for example, the basic models in Levy, *Economic Development Programs*; and Howland, Marie: "Measuring Capital Subsidy Costs and Job Creation: The Case of Rural UDAG Grants." *Journal of the American Planning Association*. Vol. 56, No. 1, Winter 1990, pp. 54–63.

41. Rubin, "Shoot Anything That Flies."

42. Guskind, "Giveaway Game."

43. Sharp and Elkins, "Politics of Economic Development Policy."

44. Ledebur, Larry C. and Douglas P. Woodward: "Adding a Stick to the Carrot: Location Incentives with Clawbacks, Recissions and Recalibrations." *Economic Development Quarterly*. Vol. 4, No. 3, August 1990, pp. 221–237. Such tools have precedents in the South's Depression-era programs, according to Cobb in *Selling of the South*.

45. Peters, Alan: "Controlling the War Between the States with Clawbacks." Unpublished paper presented at the Association of Collegiate Schools of Planning Conference, November 1990, in Austin, Texas.

46. Glickman and Woodward, *New Competitors*, p. 251.

47. See Kane, Matt and Paula Duggan: *Dislocated Workers: Coping with Competition and Conversion*. Washington, D.C.: Northeast-Midwest Institute, 1991.

48. Guskind, "Giveaway Game," p. 4.

49. In fact, the interstate bidding process is not just a zero-sum game, but, as Arthur Sullivan explains:

> The bidding process is often a negative-sum game. In other words, the gain of the winner is less than the loss of the loser, so the bidding process decreases national welfare. Consider a computer firm that initially locates in city E instead of city S because transport costs are $10 lower in E. Suppose that city S offers the firm a subsidy of $11, causing the firm to move to the city. From the national perspective, the move to S is inefficient: although the firm may produce the same number of computers, it spends more on transportation, using up resources (e.g., labor, capital, fuel) in the process. In general, local subsidies cause firms to choose inefficient locations, generating net losses to the national economy.

Sullivan, Arthur M.: *Urban Economics*. Homewood, Ill.: Richard D. Irwin, Inc., 1990.

50. Jacobs, Jane: *Cities and the Wealth of Nations*. New York: Random House, 1984.

51. See Birch, David: *The Job Generation Process*. Program on Neighborhood and Regional Change. Cambridge, Mass.: Massachusetts Institute of Technology, 1979; Case, John: "The Disciples of David Birch." *INC.* January 1989, pp. 39–45. Harrison, however, claims that small firms generate few jobs per firm and that they have a high mortality rate. See Harrison, Bennett: "The Return of the Big Firms." *Social Policy.* Vol. 21, No. 1, Summer 1990, pp. 7–19.

52. Bingham, Richard D., Edward W. Hill, and Sammis B. White (eds): *Financing Economic Development: An Institutional Response.* Newbury Park: Sage Publications, 1990; Richards, Judith W.: *Fundamentals of Development Finance.* New York: Praeger Publishers, 1983; Morrison, Edward F.: "Small Business, A Strategic Perspective." *Commentary.* Vol. 9, No. 2, Spring 1985.

53. Osborn, Maria: "Entrepreneurs Find Happy City Home." *Richmond Times Dispatch.* Sunday July 3, 1988, section D, pp. 1–5; also Campbell, Candace: *Change Agents in the New Economy: Business Incubators and Economic Development.* Minneapolis: Hubert H. Humphrey Institute of Public Affairs, University of Minnesota, 1988; and Luke, Ventriss, Reed, and Reed, *Managing Economic Development.*

54. Doeringer, Peter B., D. Terkla, and G. Topakian: *Invisible Factors in Local Economic Development.* New York: Oxford University Press, 1987; Miller, Roger and Marcel Cote: *Growing the Next Silicon Valley: A Guide for Successful Regional Planning.* Lexington, Mass.: D.C. Heath and Company, 1987; Sabel, Charles: *Work and Politics.* Cambridge: Cambridge University Press, 1981.

55. Osborne, *Laboratories of Democrary*, pp. 48–51; Chmura, Thomas J.: "The Higher Education–Economic Development Connection: Emerging Roles for Colleges and Universities." *Commentary.* Vol. 11, No. 3, Fall 1987, pp. 11–17. See also chapter 5 of this book.

56. Accordino, John and Morton Gulak: "Collaboration for Economic Development: Virginia's Universities and Local Public Officials." *Virginia Review.* Vol. 67, No. 3, May/June 1989; also Schmenner, Roger W.: "Productivity in the Factory and Industrial Policy." In Goldstein, Harvey A. (ed): *The State and Local Industrial Policy Question.* Chicago: American Planning Association, 1987; also chapter 4 of this book.

57. National Association of State Development Agencies, *State Export Program Database*, pp. 8–11.

58. Kline, John M.: "The States and International Affairs," pp. 34–35.

59. National Association of State Development Agencies, *State Export Program Database*, p. 11.

60. Ibid., p. 15; Wilson, *State Business Incentives*, p. 9.

61. Kline, "The States and International Affairs," p. 39; but see the critique of export trading companies in Egan, Mary Lou: "The Export Trading Company Act of 1982: Japanese-Style Exporting for America?" *Economic Development Quarterly.* Vol. 3, No. 3, August 1989, pp. 243–254.

62. Maffin, Robert W.: "Local Government in the International Arena: The Federal System in a Global Economy." Draft prepared for the Advisory Commission on Intergovernmental Relations, October 2, 1989.

63. Ibid., pp. 23–24; also National League of Cities: "International Trade: Cities Make Their Move: A Survey of Local Government Activities in International Trade." Draft publication by the National League of Cities, Washington, D.C., 1987.

64. Douress, J.: "Multinationals Attracted to New Jersey's FTZ." *Global Trade Executive.* Vol. 105, September 1986, p. 35.

65. White, Sammis B.: "Increasing Exports through World Trade Centers." In Bingham, Hill, and White, *Financing Economic Development*, pp. 216–217.

66. Eisinger, Peter K.: *The Rise of the Entrepreneurial State: State and Local Economic Development Policy in the United States.* Madison: University of Wisconsin Press, 1988; Osborne, *Laboratories of Democracy;* Hansen, "Comparing Enterprise Zones."

67. Fisher, "National Consequences of Decentralized Industrial Policy."

68. Harrison, "Return of the Big Firms."

69. Herbers, John: "A Third Wave of Economic Development." *Governing.* June 1990, pp. 43–50; Ross, Doug and William Schweke: "The Emerging Third Wave: New Economic Development Strategies in the 1990s." *News and Views.* Economic Development Division, American Planning Association, February 1991, pp. 1–6.

70. Herbers, "Third Wave."

71. Ibid.; also Task Force on Community-Based Development: *Community-Based Development: Investing in Renewal.* Washington, D.C.: National Congress for Community Economic Development, September 1987.

72. Glickman and Woodward, *New Competitors;* also Rosenfeld, Stuart A.: "Education, Training, and Industrial Policy," and Peterson, George E.: "Infrastructure Support for Industrial Policy," in Goldstein, *State and Local Industrial Policy.* See also chapter 5 of this book.

73. Wilson, *State Business Incentives;* Bowman, Ann O'M.: *Tools and Targets: The Mechanics of City Economic Development.* Washington, D.C.: National League of Cities, October 1987.

74. The stages described here are suggested in Luke, Ventriss, Reed, and Reed, *Managing Economic Development*, chapter 3. There are numerous variations of strategic planning processes, however.

75. While any planning process can be conducted in either a participatory or nonparticipatory way, some critics claim that strategic planning tends to be undemocratic. See, for example, Swanstrom, Todd: "The Limits of Strategic Planning for Cities." *Journal of Urban Affairs.* Vol. 9, No. 2, pp. 139–157.

76. For descriptions of progressive economic development planning, see Giloth and Mier, "Spatial Change and Social Justice"; also Mier, Robert, Kari J. Moe, and Irene Sherr: "Strategic Planning and the Pursuit of Reform, Economic Development, and Equity," in Goldstein, *State and Local Industrial Policy.*

77. States that are actively engaged in coping with defense cuts through some form of planning and economic conversion activity include Arizona,

Colorado, Connecticut, Florida, Kentucky, Louisiana, Maine, Maryland, Minnesota, Missouri, New York, Ohio, Rhode Island, and Washington. One source of news on economic conversion planning and related issues is *Positive Alternatives*, a publication of the Center for Economic Conversion, Mountain View, Calif.

78. See Goldstein, *State and Local Industrial Policy*.

79. It is important not to stretch the Keynes analogy too far. Keynesian stabilization policy concerns macroeconomic policy, which, by definition, is beyond the power of any individual state. If one is defining Keynesian in contrast to Smithian, to mean substantial government intervention in the marketplace to ease economic adjustments or stimulate private investment, then it is possible to say that states pursued Keynesian-like policies.

80. Kline, "States and International Affairs," p. 45; also Maffin, "Local Government in the International Arena," p. 4.

81. Kline, "States and International Affairs."

82. Knight, Richard V.: "City Building in a Global Society," in Knight and Gappert, *Cities in a Global Society;* see also Jacobs, *Cities and the Wealth of Nations*.

83. Kline, "States and International Affairs," pp. 60-73.

84. The GATT (General Agreement on Tariffs and Trade) is discussed in chapter 4. Procurement is the term used to denote government purchase of goods and services.

85. The GATT's nondiscrimination standard requires that a country treat foreign and domestic firms equally. See Kline, "States and International Affairs," p. 67; also Glickman and Woodward, *New Competitors*, pp. 250-251.

86. Kline, "States and International Affairs," p. 67; Glickman and Woodward, *New Competitors*, pp. 250-251.

87. Miller, Marcine L.: "The Feds Can Help: Programs, Publications, and People." *Public Management*. Vol. 68, April 1986, p. 13.

88. Maffin, "Local Government in the International Arena," p. 37.

89. Kline, "States and International Affairs," pp. 94-95; Maffin, "Local Government in the International Arena," p. 13.

90. See, for example, Squires, *Unequal Partnerships;* Guskind, "Giveaway Game"; Glickman and Woodward, *New Competitors;* also Goodman, Robert: *The Last Entrepreneurs: America's Regional Wars for Jobs and Dollars*. Boston: South End Press, 1979.

91. See Friedman, Milton: *Capitalism and Freedom*. Chicago: University of Chicago Press, 1962. For a theoretical discussion of this point, see Tiebout, Charles: "A Pure Theory of Local Expenditures." *Journal of Political Economy*. Vol. 64, October 1956, pp. 416-24.

92. Tiebout, "Pure Theory," pp. 416-24; also Reischauer, Robert D.: "The Welfare Reform Legislation: Directions for the Future," in Cottingham, Phoebe H. and David T. Ellwood (eds): *Welfare Policy for the 1990s*. Cambridge, Harvard University Press, 1989; Boaz, "Saving the Inner

City"; Freeman, Roger A.: *The Wayward Welfare State.* Stanford, Calif.: Hoover Institution Press, 1981.

93. See Judd, Dennis R. and David Brian Robertson: "Urban Revitalization in the United States: Prisoner of the Federal System." in Parkinson, Michael, Bernard Foley, and Dennis R. Judd (eds): *Regenerating the Cities: The UK Crisis and the US Experience.* Glenview: Scott, Foresman and Company, 1989; also Squires, *Unequal Partnerships.*

94. Ladd and Yinger, *America's Ailing Cities*; Hansen, "Comparing Enterprise Zones."

95. Osborne, *Laboratories of Democracy*, p. 285.

96. Ibid., pp. 285, 315–316; also Maffin, "Local Government in the International Arena," pp. 40–45.

97. Osborne, *Laboratories of Democracy*, pp. 285–287; also Glickman and Woodward, *New Competitors;* and see the discussion of strategic trade policy in chapter 4 of this book.

98. Faux, Jeff: "Industrial Policy and Democratic Institutions," in Goldstein, *State and Local Industrial Policy.*

99. See, for example, Judd and Robertson, "Urban Revitalization"; also Alperovitz, Gar and Jeff Faux: *Rebuilding America.* New York: Pantheon Books, 1984; Bowles, Samuel, David Gordon, and Thomas Weisskopf: *Beyond the Waste Land.* Garden City, N.J.: Anchor Press, 1983; and see the discussion of industrial policy in chapter 4 of this book.

100. Boaz, "Saving the Inner City"; Murray, Charles: *Losing Ground.* New York: Basic Books, 1984; Reischauer, "Welfare Reform Legislation."

101. Reischauer, "Welfare Reform Legislation."

102. Freeman, *Wayward Welfare State*, chapter 4; Reischauer, "Welfare Reform Legislation."

Bibliography

State and Local Impacts of Global Restructuring and National Policies

Beauregard, Robert A. (ed): *Economic Restructuring and Political Response.* Urban Affairs Annual Reviews, Vol. 34. Newbury Park: Sage Publications, 1989.

This is a collection of seven essays written from radical perspectives. They discuss the nature of global economic restructuring; its impact on Pittsburgh, New York, Philadelphia, and Chicago; and the responses of interest groups and local governments.

Blakely, Edward J.: *Planning Local Economic Development: Theory and Practice.* Newbury Park: Sage Publications, 1989.

See the next section of this bibliography.

Clark, Gordon L.: "Pittsburgh in Transition: Consolidation of Prosperity in an Era of Economic Restructuring." In Beauregard, Robert A. (ed):

Economic Restructuring and Political Response. Urban Affairs Annual Reviews. Vol. 34. Newbury Park: Sage Publications, 1989.

    Clark discusses the impacts of economic restructuring on the Pittsburgh regional economy and muses about the region's future economic role.

Cobb, James C.: *The Selling of the South: The Southern Crusade for Industrial Development, 1936–1980.* Baton Rouge: Louisiana State University Press, 1982.

    A detailed history of the politics of the "New South's" drive for industrial development and its impacts on the practice of state and local economic development nationwide.

Cole, Richard L., Delbert A. Taebel, and Rodney V. Hissong: *America's Cities and the 1980s: The Legacy of the Reagan Years.* Arlington: Institute of Urban Studies, The University of Texas at Arlington, March 1990.

Douress, J.: "Multinationals Attracted to New Jersey's FTZ." *Global Trade Executive.* Vol. 105, September 1986, p. 35.

    A brief description of the foreign trade zone concept and its apparent success in New Jersey.

Fuller, Stephen S.: "The Internationalization of the Washington, D.C., Area Economy." In Knight, Richard V. and Gary Gappert (eds): *Cities in a Global Society.* Urban Affairs Annual Reviews. Vol. 35. Newbury Park: Sage Publications, 1989.

    Fuller describes the growth of the international economic role of Washington and the limits to further development.

Fusfeld, Daniel R.: *The Basic Economics of the Urban Racial Crisis.* New York: Holt, Rinehart and Winston, 1973.

    Despite its age and brevity, this is a useful account of black farmworker migrations to northern cities and an economic analysis of the formation of black ghettos in those cities, from a liberal perspective.

Gaventa, John, Barbara Ellen Smith, Alex Willingham (eds): *Communities in Economic Crisis: Appalachia and the South.* Philadelphia: Temple University Press, 1990.

    Thirteen case studies from Central Appalachia, the Piedmont, and the Deep South describe the adverse impacts of economic change in these regions, from a progressive perspective. Several chapters discuss progressive policy alternatives.

Henderson, Jeffrey and Manuel Castells (eds): *Global Restructuring and Territorial Development.* Newbury Park: Sage Publications, 1987.

    Ten essays on the spatial and industry-specific impacts of global restructuring, including the automobile and electronics industries, labor force issues, and changes in the economies of Mexico, Malaysia, and the United States.

Judd, Dennis R. and David Brian Robertson: "Urban Revitalization in the United States: Prisoner of the Federal System." In Parkinson, Michael, Bernard Foley, and Dennis R. Judd (eds): *Regenerating the Cities: The*

UK Crisis and the US Experience. Glenview: Scott, Foresman and Company, 1989.

Kasarda, John D.: "Urban Industrial Transition and the Underclass." In *The Annals of the American Academy of Political and Social Sciences.* Vol. 501. Newbury Park: Sage Publications, January 1989.

    Kasarda analyzes the shift in blue-collar jobs to the suburbs, the lack of public transportation to the new jobs, and the growing concentration of poor minorities in central cities.

Knight, Richard V.: "City Building in a Global Society." In Knight, Richard V. and Gary Gappert (eds): *Cities in a Global Society.* Urban Affairs Annual Reviews. Vol. 35. Newbury Park: Sage Publications, 1989.

    Knight discusses the roles of cities in the emerging global order and suggests strategies for appropriate city development.

Knight, Richard V. and Gary Gappert (eds): *Cities in a Global Society.* Urban Affairs Annual Reviews. Vol. 35. Newbury Park: Sage Publications, 1989.

    This collection of 23 essays describes the impacts of the globalization of society on the nature and functions of cities, including Washington, D.C.; New York; Boston; Baltimore; and Tokyo. Several essays discuss new spatial and social organization requirements of cities in a global society, and several discuss government and policy implications from a liberal, urban planning perspective.

Ladd, Helen F. and John Yinger: *America's Ailing Cities: Fiscal Health and the Design of Urban Policy.* Baltimore: The Johns Hopkins University Press, 1989.

    The authors establish uniform measures for assessing the fiscal health of cities. Applying this measure to the 1972–1982 period, they conclude that city fiscal health has generally worsened and that cities would have fared even worse but for the federal aid they received during that period. Since 1982, federal aid has decreased. The authors argue that both states and the federal government should provide more aid to cities that are in poor fiscal health because of economic and social trends—but not to those that simply refuse to collect revenues from relatively healthy bases.

Perlo Cohen, Manuel: "Exploring the Spatial Effects of the Internationalization of the Mexican Economy." In Henderson, Jeffrey and Manuel Castells (eds): *Global Restructuring and Territorial Development.* Newbury Park: Sage Publications, 1987.

    An analysis of the effects of global restructuring on the Mexican economy, with particular attention to the industrialization of the northern border region.

Phillips, Kevin: *The Politics of Rich and Poor: Wealth and the American Electorate in the Reagan Aftermath.* New York: Random House, 1990.

    See the annotated bibliography in chapter 3.

Rosenfeld, Stuart A., Edward M. Bergman, and Sarah Rubin: *After the Factories: Changing Employment Patterns in the Rural South.* Research Triangle Park, N.C.: Southern Growth Policies Board, 1985.

This monograph provides a quantitative description and analysis of the major changes in the economy of the South from 1977 to 1982, changes in the location of industry, and implications for public policy.

Sassen, Saskia: "New Trends in the Sociospatial Organization of the New York City Economy." In Beauregard, Robert A. (ed): *Economic Restructuring and Political Response.* Urban Affairs Annual Reviews. Vol. 34. Newbury Park: Sage Publications, 1989.

The author discusses the transformation of the Manhattan economic base, the competition for space engendered thereby, and the possibility that the outcome of this competition may undermine the very viability of the new economy.

Sawers, Larry and William K. Tabb (eds): *Sunbelt/Snowbelt: Urban Development and Regional Restructuring.* New York: Oxford University Press, 1984.

This is a collection of 16 essays written from progressive perspectives. Some describe the regional and local impacts of economic restructuring in places such as New England, Houston, and Silicon Valley; others critique federal and local policies, such as enterprise zones; and a few articles offer progressive policy alternatives.

State and Local Economic Development Policy and Planning—Texts

Bingham, Richard D., Edward W. Hill, and Sammis B. White (eds): *Financing Economic Development: An Institutional Response.* Newbury Park: Sage Publications, 1990.

This collection of 18 timely essays describes the nature and use of various public sector economic development financing tools, such as industrial revenue bonds; tax increment financing; public finance-and-development organizations, such as product development corporations, enterprise zones, community development corporations, and revolving loan funds; and private financing sources, such as venture capital.

Blair, John P.: *Urban and Regional Economics.* Homewood, Ill.: Richard D. Irwin, Inc., 1991.

This is a basic urban and regional economics text, suitable for upperclass undergraduates and graduate students, with a focus on applications to urban and regional economic development planning issues.

Blakely, Edward J.: *Planning Local Economic Development: Theory and Practice.* Sage Library of Social Research. Vol. 168. Newbury Park: Sage Publications, 1989.

A useful primer for planners and local economic development practitioners, the book covers all aspects of the economy relevant to development planning, useful tools, and case studies.

Levy, John M.: *Economic Development Programs for Cities, Counties and Towns.* Second Edition. New York: Praeger Publishers, 1990.

A useful primer, written mostly from the perspective of the practitioner rather than the planner. It includes detailed discussions of some planning tools, however, such as benefit-cost analysis.

Luke, Jeffrey S., Curtis Ventriss, B.J. Reed, and C.M. Reed: *Managing Economic Development: A Guide to State and Local Leadership Strategies.* San Francisco: Jossey-Bass Publishers, 1988.

    This text is written for development planning organizers and practitioners. It includes useful discussions of strategic planning, business recruitment, retention, and formation strategies.

Miller, Roger and Marcel Cote: *Growing the Next Silicon Valley: A Guide for Successful Regional Planning.* Lexington, Mass.: D.C. Heath and Company, 1987.

    An analysis of the economics and institutional infrastructure necessary for the creation and development of high-technology industry clusters of independent, but mutually supportive firms, with implications for economic development strategy.

Richards, Judith W.: *Fundamentals of Development Finance.* New York: Praeger Publishers, 1983.

    This volume describes the type of financing needed at each stage of the business growth and development process, the gaps between business financing needs and available financing, and the types of financing roles the public sector can play. The description of public financing programs is somewhat dated, however.

Sullivan, Arthur M.: *Urban Economics.* Homewood, Ill.: Richard D. Irwin, Inc., 1990.

    An introductory urban economics text for upperclass undergraduates and graduate students.

State and Local Policy and Planning—Other Works

Accordino, John and Morton Gulak: "Collaboration for Economic Development: Virginia's Universities and Local Public Officials." *Virginia Review.* Vol. 67, No. 3, May/June 1989.

Alperovitz, Gar and Jeff Faux: *Rebuilding America: A Blueprint for the New Economy.* New York: Pantheon Books, 1984.

    See the annotated bibliography in chapter 4.

Beaumont, Enid: "Enterprise Zones and Federalism." In Green, Roy E. (ed): *Enterprise Zones: New Directions in Economic Development.* Newbury Park: Sage Publications, 1991.

    The author discusses the development of enterprise zones under minimal federal involvement and speculates about the contributions and possible problems that an enhanced federal role would bring.

Birch, David: *The Job Generation Process.* Program on Neighborhood and Regional Change. Cambridge, Mass.: Massachusetts Institute of Technology, 1979.

    This book reported Birch's research on business growth and decline, using Dun and Bradstreet files. Its conclusion that innovation and job growth tend to take place in smaller firms spawned a generation of small business development programs at the state and local levels.

Boaz, David: "Saving the Inner City." In Crane, Edward H. and David Boaz (eds): *An American Vision: Policies for the '90s*. Washington, D.C.: The Cato Institute, 1989.

    To help the growing urban underclass escape its plight, we must remove the institutions that foster its dependency. We must abolish welfare for working-age adults, minimum wages, and business licenses.

Bowles, Samuel, David M. Gordon, and Thomas E. Weisskopf: *Beyond the Waste Land: A Democratic Alternative to Economic Decline*. Garden City, N.J.: Anchor Press/Doubleday, 1983.

    See the annotated bibliography in chapter 4.

Bowman, Ann O'M.: *Tools and Targets: The Mechanics of City Economic Development*. Washington, D.C.: National League of Cities, October 1987.

    This volume reports the findings of a national survey of the economic development strategies and tools used by cities.

Campbell, Candace: *Change Agents in the New Economy: Business Incubators and Economic Development*. Minneapolis: Hubert H. Humphrey Institute of Public Affairs, University of Minnesota, 1988. An overview of the concept and genesis of business incubators, followed by several in-depth case studies of incubators in the United States, Canada, and Europe.

Case, John: "The Disciples of David Birch." *INC*. January 1989, pp. 39–45.

    A brief review of the research and arguments of David Birch and others, which supports the view that innovation and job growth are more likely to take place in smaller firms.

Crane, Edward H. and David Boaz (eds): *An American Vision: Policies for the '90s*. Washington, D.C.: The Cato Institute, 1989.

    This is a collection of 21 essays on U.S. economic policy, foreign and defense policy, domestic policy (including urban policy, privatization, and education), and the Constitution, written from a conservative perspective.

Chi, Keon S.: *The States and Business Incentives: An Inventory of Tax and Financial Incentive Programs*. Washington, D.C.: The Council of State Governments, 1989.

    An exhaustive review and listing of state financial incentives to promote business development.

Chmura, Thomas J.: "The Higher Education–Economic Development Connection: Emerging Roles for Colleges and Universities." *Commentary*. Vol. 11, No. 3, Fall 1987, pp. 11–17.

    See the annotated bibliography in chapter 5.

Clavel, Pierre: *The Progressive City: Planning and Participation, 1969–1984*. New Brunswick, N.J.: Rutgers University Press, 1986.

    The author traces and explains the rise of progressive governing coalitions in the politics of Hartford, Cleveland, Berkeley, Santa Monica, and Burlington in the 1970s and early 1980s. Causes of stress and strain are explored as well.

Doeringer, Peter B., D. Terkla, and G. Topakian: *Invisible Factors in Local Economic Development.* New York: Oxford University Press, 1987.

Basing their work upon a longitudinal analysis of the economy of the Montachusett region of Massachusetts, the authors identify several invisible factors that play important roles in economic development, including labor-management relations and tight supplier-customer linkages among local firms.

Egan, Mary Lou: "The Export Trading Company Act of 1982: Japanese-Style Exporting for America?" *Economic Development Quarterly.* Vol. 3, No. 3, August 1989, pp. 243–254.

The export trading companies created by the act cannot accomplish their mission of increasing U.S. exports because other policies are needed first, to stimulate the overall growth of exports.

Eisinger, Peter K.: *The Rise of the Entrepreneurial State: State and Local Economic Development Policy in the United States.* Madison: University of Wisconsin Press, 1988.

Eisinger surveys the evolution of state economic development policy and concludes that a major shift is occurring, from business recruitment strategies (which he calls "supply-side") to public entrepreneurship strategies, such as business formation and expansion through public venture capital (which he calls "demand-side").

Faux, Jeff: "Industrial Policy and Democratic Institutions." In Goldstein, Harvey A. (ed): *The State and Local Industrial Policy Question.* Chicago: American Planning Association, 1987.

Faux sets forth the major institutional features of a national, state, and local democratic industrial policy in action.

Fisher, Peter S.: "The National Consequences of Decentralized Industrial Policy in the United States." Unpublished paper presented at the Annual Meeting of the Association of Collegiate Schools of Planning, October 1990, Austin, Tex.

Fisher analyzes state economic development expenditure data and concludes that, contrary to the assertions of Eisinger in *Rise of the Entrepreneurial State*, states have not made a major shift in policy away from business recruitment.

Freeman, Roger A.: *The Wayward Welfare State.* Stanford, Calif: Hoover Institution Press, 1981.

See the annotated bibliography in chapter 3.

Friedman, Milton: *Capitalism and Freedom.* Chicago: University of Chicago Press, 1962.

See the annotated bibliography in chapter 2.

Giloth, Robert P. and Robert Mier: "Spatial Change and Social Justice: Alternative Economic Development in Chicago." In Beauregard, Robert A. (ed): *Economic Restructuring and Political Response.* Urban Affairs Annual Reviews. Vol. 34. Newbury Park: Sage Publications, 1989.

The authors describe various economic development initiatives undertaken during the Harold Washington administration with broad popular participation.

Glickman, Norman J. and Douglas P. Woodward: *The New Competitors: How Foreign Investors Are Changing the U.S. Economy.* New York: Basic Books, 1989.

The authors describe the nature and extent of foreign direct investment in the United States in recent years, the attempts of states to capture that investment, and the state and national policy dilemmas that this creates.

Goldstein, Harvey A. (ed): *The State and Local Industrial Policy Question.* Chicago: American Planning Association, 1987.

This collection of 15 articles, written from liberal and progressive perspectives, covers the major issues in the industrial policy debate, with particular emphasis on state and local initiatives and impacts, including productivity enhancement, new technology, service industries, education and training, infrastructure, and the institutional structures for planning and implementation.

Goodman, Robert: *The Last Entrepreneurs: America's Regional Wars for Jobs and Dollars.* Boston: South End Press, 1979.

This is a radical analysis and critique of the negative impacts of capital mobility on communities and state efforts to recapture investment through subsidies and low-wage labor. In response, Goodman proposes a system of "regional socialism" that would promote economic democracy and regional economic self-sufficiency.

Grady, Dennis O.: "State Economic Development Incentives: Why Do States Compete?" *State and Local Government Review.* Vol. 19, No. 3, Fall 1987, pp. 86–94.

Despite considerable evidence that tax subsidies and other location incentives are not of major importance to firms, states continue the incentive bidding game because each fears that if it does not, the others will do so and will catch the elusive firms.

Green, Roy E. (ed): *Enterprise Zones: New Directions in Economic Development.* Newbury Park: Sage Publications, 1991.

This is a collection of 15 essays that assess the development of the enterprise zone concept and the status of current practice in the United States, from mostly liberal perspectives.

Guskind, Robert: "The Giveaway Game Continues." *Planning.* Vol. 56, No. 2, February 1990, pp. 4–8.

The author describes numerous recent cases which show that states and localities continue to offer large subsidies to lure and keep firms within their borders.

Hansen, Susan B.: "Comparing Enterprise Zones to Other Economic Development Techniques." In Green, Roy E. (ed): *Enterprise Zones: New Directions in Economic Development.* Newbury Park: Sage Publications, 1991.

A survey of state development policies in the 1980s, from a liberal perspective.

Harrison, Bennett: "The Return of the Big Firms." *Social Policy.* Vol. 21, No. 1, Summer 1990, pp. 7–19.

See the annotated bibliography in chapter 4.

Herbers, John: "A Third Wave of Economic Development." *Governing.* June 1990, pp. 43–50.

    The author describes three cases in which this wholesaling approach to providing economic development services is being tried with some success.

Howland, Marie: "Measuring Capital Subsidy Costs and Job Creation: The Case of Rural UDAG Grants." *Journal of the American Planning Association.* Vol. 56, No. 1, Winter 1990, pp. 54–63.

    Howland provides a methodology for measuring the public costs and benefits of low-interest loan programs to retain businesses in rural areas.

Jacobs, Jane: *Cities and the Wealth of Nations.* New York: Random House, 1984.

    Jacobs asserts that cities are the primary sources of wealth generation and that national and local policies ought to reflect that fact.

Kane, Matt and Paula Duggan: *Dislocated Workers: Coping with Competition and Conversion.* Washington, D.C.: Northeast-Midwest Institute, 1991.

    This is a comprehensive how-to manual for communities facing problems of worker dislocation through plant closings and defense cutbacks. It describes federal programs and local methods for anticipating and responding to dislocations, including worker training and retraining programs.

Kaplan, Marshall and Franklin James (eds): *The Future of National Urban Policy.* Durham: Duke University Press, 1990.

    A collection of 20 articles that describe the current status of urban problems and set forth proposals for national policies, from liberal perspectives. Issues include housing, infrastructure, fiscal stress, neighborhood policy, and downtown development.

Kline, John M.: "The States and International Affairs." Draft prepared for the Advisory Commission on Intergovernmental Relations, September 5, 1989.

    The author provides a comprehensive survey of state economic development efforts in the global market, including foreign direct investment attraction, export promotion, interstate and state-federal cooperation for export promotion, and the ways in which these actions undermine the traditional power of the federal government in international affairs.

Ledebur, Larry C. and Douglas P. Woodward: "Adding a Stick to the Carrot: Location Incentives with Clawbacks, Recissions and Recalibrations." *Economic Development Quarterly.* Vol. 4, No. 3, August 1990, pp. 221–237.

    The authors describe techniques for recapturing subsidies paid to firms that do not fulfill promises to provide jobs and to remain in communities that provide subsidies.

Levine, Mark V.: "Urban Redevelopment in a Global Economy: The Cases of Montreal and Baltimore." In Knight, Richard V. and Gary Gappert (eds): *Cities in a Global Society*. Urban Affairs Annual Reviews. Vol. 35. Newbury Park: Sage Publications, 1989.

    The author chronicles the economic dislocations suffered by these two cities since 1970, their efforts to revitalize their economies, and the limitations of those efforts as effective strategies.

Maffin, Robert W.: "Local Government in the International Arena: The Federal System in a Global Economy." Draft prepared for the Advisory Commission on Intergovernmental Relations, October 2, 1989.

    This is a comprehensive discussion of local government economic development efforts in the global economy, based upon interviews with local officials. The author considers stresses on the federal system and provides recommendations for appropriate policies to address these issues.

Markusen, Ann Roell: "Industrial Restructuring and Regional Politics." In Beauregard, Robert A. (ed): *Economic Restructuring and Political Response*. Urban Affairs Annual Reviews. Vol. 34. Newbury Park: Sage Publications, 1989.

    The author discusses the different responses of various regions to economic restructuring.

McIntyre, Robert S., Douglas P. Kelly, Michael P. Ettlinger, Elizabeth A. Fray: *A Far Cry from Fair: CTJ's Guide to State Tax Reform*. Washington, D.C.: Citizens for Tax Justice, April 1991.

    The authors present data on, and critique the distribution of, the tax burden in each of the 50 states.

McKenzie, Richard B.: *Competing Visions: The Political Conflict over America's Economic Future*. Washington, D.C.: The Cato Institute, 1985.

    See the annotated bibliography in chapter 4.

———: *The American Job Machine*. Washington, D.C.: The Cato Institute, 1988.

    See the annotated bibliography in chapter 4.

Mier, Robert, Kari J. Moe, and Irene Sherr: "Strategic Planning and the Pursuit of Reform, Economic Development, and Equity." In Goldstein, Harvey A. (ed): *The State and Local Industrial Policy Question*. Chicago: American Planning Association, 1987.

    The authors describe the efforts of Chicago under Mayor Harold Washington to pursue local industrial policy in a participatory fashion.

Miller, Marcine L.: "The Feds Can Help: Programs, Publications, and People." *Public Management*. Vol. 68, April 1986, p. 13.

    A brief discussion of the federal government's export promotion services.

Morrison, Edward F.: "Small Business: A Strategic Perspective." *Commentary*. Vol. 9, No. 2, Spring 1985.

    The author discusses the government role in facilitating the growth of small businesses.

Murray, Charles: *Losing Ground*. New York: Basic Books, 1984.

See the annotated bibliography in chapter 3.
National Association of State Development Agencies (NASDA): *State Export Program Database*. Washington, D.C.: NASDA, July 1988.

This volume provides the results of a biannual survey of the nature and cost of each state's export promotion efforts.

———: "Survey of States on FDI Efforts." *The NASDA Letter*. Washington, D.C.: NASDA, 1989.

A brief report on the current status of state efforts to attract foreign investment.

National League of Cities: "International Trade: Cities Make Their Move: A Survey of Local Government Activities in International Trade." Draft publication by the National League of Cities, Washington, D.C., 1987.

Results of a survey of major city initiatives in the global economy, with policy recommendations.

Osborn, Maria: "Entrepreneurs Find Happy City Home." *Richmond Times Dispatch*. Sunday July 3, 1988, section D, pp. 1–5.

A brief report on the origins and functions of Richmond, Virginia's small business incubator.

Osborne, David: *Laboratories of Democracy*. Boston: Harvard Business School Press, 1988.

The author provides a description and analysis of the efforts of several states—Pennsylvania, Arkansas, Arizona, Michigan, Massachusetts, and New York—to approach economic development from a strategic planning perspective, and to overcome the traditional reliance on business recruitment approaches. Osborne draws implications for other states and for national policies to facilitate state development.

Peters, Alan: "Controlling the War Between the States with Clawbacks." Unpublished paper presented at the Association of Collegiate Schools of Planning Conference, Austin, Tex., November 1990.

The author describes the efforts of European and American states to control capital mobility through clawbacks, concluding that such efforts are unlikely to control the war between the states.

Peterson, George E.: "Infrastructure Support for Industrial Policy." In Goldstein, Harvey A. (ed): *The State and Local Industrial Policy Question*. Chicago: American Planning Association, 1987.

The author argues that infrastructure planning should be undertaken in conjunction with, and should reinforce, economic development planning, as opposed to the current, narrow focus on engineering concerns.

Reischauer, Robert D.: "The Welfare Reform Legislation: Directions for the Future." In Cottingham, Phoebe H. and David T. Ellwood (eds): *Welfare Policy for the 1990s*. Cambridge, Mass.: Harvard University Press, 1989.

See the annotated bibliography in chapter 3.

Rosenfeld, Stuart A.: "Education, Training, and Industrial Policy." In Goldstein, Harvey A. (ed): *The State and Local Industrial Policy Question*. Chicago: American Planning Association, 1987.

The author argues that education, training, and retraining should be core features of industrial policy. He suggests state and local policy options.

Ross, Doug and William Schweke: "The Emerging Third Wave: New Economic Development Strategies in the 1990s." *News and Views.* Economic Development Division, American Planning Association, February 1991, pp. 1–6.

A brief description of the new, wholesaling technique in state and local economic development.

Rubin, Herbert J.: "Shoot Anything That Flies; Claim Anything That Falls: Conversations with Economic Development Practitioners." *Economic Development Quarterly.* Vol. 2, No. 3, August, 1988, pp. 236–251.

The author finds that economic development professionals perceive that they have little control over the ultimate decisions of businesses and that their efforts are not well understood by the public. Hence they tend to identify with the interests of the business community and to take credit for positive economic development outcomes, whether or not their actions caused the outcomes.

Sabel, Charles: *Work and Politics.* Cambridge: Cambridge University Press, 1981.

See the annotated bibliography in chapter 4.

Schmenner, Roger W.: "Productivity in the Factory and Industrial Policy." In Goldstein, Harvey A. (ed): *The State and Local Industrial Policy Question.* Chicago: American Planning Association, 1987.

The author is skeptical of the efforts to improve productivity at existing plants through government restructuring or tax incentive programs. However, as new management ideas may improve productivity, he advocates a "management extension service" that might disseminate information and advice to existing firms.

"The Second War Between the States: A Bitter Struggle for Jobs, Capital and People." *Business Week.* May 17, 1976, pp. 92–114.

This is the first well-known popular report to describe the fierce interstate competition for firms.

Sharp, Elaine B. and David R. Elkins: "The Politics of Economic Development Policy." *Economic Development Quarterly.* May 1991, Vol. 5, No. 2, pp. 126–139.

The authors examine the political determinants of local tax subsidies for economic development. They note that well-organized citizen groups can, on occasion, bring about changes in tax subsidy policies.

Squires, Gregory D. (ed): *Unequal Partnerships: The Political Economy of Urban Redevelopment in Postwar America.* New Brunswick, N.J.: Rutgers University Press, 1989.

Fifteen essays on the political economy of urban redevelopment in cities including Boston, New York, Philadelphia, Pittsburgh, Cleveland, Detroit, Chicago, Milwaukee, Louisville, New Orleans, Houston, and Sacramento. The authors write from a progressive perspective.

Storper, Michael and Richard Walker: "The Spatial Division of Labor: Labor and the Location of Industries." In Sawers, Larry and William K. Tabb (eds): *Sunbelt/Snowbelt: Urban Development and Regional Restructuring.* New York: Oxford University Press, 1984.

The authors contend that labor is the only factor of production that remains highly differentiated across regions and nations. Hence firms seek the "right" labor force culture, work attitudes, and skills when choosing a location. The authors provide a useful typology that matches labor force characteristics with industrial job features.

Swanstrom, Todd: "The Limits of Strategic Planning for Cities." *Journal of Urban Affairs.* Vol. 9, No. 2, 1987, pp. 139–157.

Swanstrom argues that strategic planning, through its claims to rationality and the importance of the external environment, undermines democratic decision making and biases the results of planning toward business interests at the expense of the rest of the community.

Task Force on Community-Based Development: *Community-Based Development: Investing in Renewal.* Washington, D.C.: National Congress for Community Economic Development, September 1987.

This report chronicles the histories of community development corporations (CDCs) in five localities, illustrating how a mix of federal funding, local public and private funding, and self-help initiative has improved these communities. The report calls on corporations to help underwrite the efforts of CDCs.

Tiebout, Charles: "A Pure Theory of Local Expenditures." *Journal of Political Economy.* Vol. 64, October 1956, pp. 416–424.

This model treats residence from a consumer choice perspective, in which persons choose their communities based largely upon the prices (taxes) of public services there. Since the model reflects reality to some degree, it has been used, primarily by conservatives, to support arguments against state and federal intervention in local policies.

Weiss, Julian: "Enterprise Zones Are Just Part of the Answer for Reviving an Urban Economy." *Governing.* August 1988.

Weiss interviews economic development practitioners and scholars and concludes that enterprise zones can be effective local development tools, but only if other, more important conditions are met—a solid infrastructure, a healthy regional economy, and job training.

White, Sammis B.: "Increasing Exports through World Trade Centers." In Bingham, Richard D., Edward W. Hill, and Sammis B. White: *Financing Economic Development: An Institutional Response.* Newbury Park: Sage Publications, 1990.

White discusses the nature, extent, and usefulness of world trade centers as a tool to stimulate export activity.

Wilder, Margaret G. and Barry M. Rubin: "Targeted Redevelopment through Urban Enterprise Zones." *Journal of Urban Affairs.* Vol. 10, No. 1, 1988, pp. 1–17.

Based upon their study of the Evansville, Indiana enterprise zone, the authors conclude that zones can be effective development tools, but that such success is not the result of the tax and regulatory incentives themselves but of the effectiveness of a local coordinating organization and knowledgeable executive director to provide appropriate assistance to the firms in the zone.

Wilson, Roger: *State Business Incentives and Economic Growth: Are They Effective?* Washington, D.C.: The Council of State Governments, 1989.

A thorough review of the literature on state economic development programs, with particular emphasis on business incentives and critiques of these tools.

Young, Peter: "Privatization: Better Services at Less Cost." In Crane, Edward H. and David Boaz (eds): *An American Vision: Policies for the '90s.* Washington, D.C.: Cato Institute, 1989.

The author contends that citizens will be better served if states and localities turn over the provision of certain services—including public housing, wastewater treatment facilities, and highway, bridge, and tunnel construction and maintenance—to the private sector.

CHAPTER 7

Conclusion

History moves forward. Never again will the United States enjoy unquestioned economic supremacy as it did in 1945. The Japanese and Europeans have rebuilt their economies—in many respects surpassing the United States. As the revolutions in transportation, communication, and corporate organization spread (unevenly) around the globe, the United States and other industrialized nations experience increasing competitive pressures from the newly industrializing countries—Brazil, India, Hong Kong, Singapore, Taiwan, and South Korea. Within the next decade, China and some of the Eastern European countries may join this group as well.

The rise of foreign competition is a mixed blessing. On the one hand, it indicates that, at least to some extent, the postwar international economic arrangements rejuvenated the world economy. Many nations enjoy more prosperity today than five decades ago. Certainly, American consumers and many businesses benefit from having a wider variety of (often lower-cost) goods to purchase from abroad. On the other hand, foreign competition and the development of excess production capacity in many industries have created a dilemma for the United States. Now it either must find new roles to play in the global production and trading system or limit its relations with the global economy. Deciding which goods and services the United States will provide to the world and which it will purchase, and determining the processes by which such decisions will be made, are the subjects of intense debate. Should the United States pursue strategic trade and industry policies, concluding managed trade agreements with other countries? Should it apply tariffs or quotas to imports? Or should it allow market forces to determine comparative advantages and allocate capital among industries and sectors?

What kinds of domestic policies would be most compatible with different roles in the global economy? Should the federal government lower interest rates to reduce unemployment and stimulate growth, or should it focus on fighting inflation and reducing the budget deficit? How fast should we divert spending from defense to infrastructure, housing, and health care? Should we devote more resources to education and training policies, and should the focus of such policies be on enhanced technical training, or a recommitment to liberal arts? The breakdown of the dollar-based international monetary framework that facilitated the growth of world trade in the first three decades after World War II complicates the American policy dilemma. Since the demise of the Bretton Woods monetary system, all countries labor under the cloud of international monetary instability. Thus the United States not only must reconstitute its role in the global economy and enact domestic policies to support that role, it must reconstruct the international framework within which it will play that role.

When last faced with this task, in 1944, the United States was so powerful that it could follow its own inclinations, largely ignoring the objections of others, such as Great Britain's Bretton Woods representative, John Maynard Keynes. Now it must work in cooperation with other powers, specifically Japan and Western Europe, to build and maintain a stable international monetary and trading system. Yet these powers do not share all of America's official views of the most desirable international arrangements. Moreover, history records no examples of stable and harmonious relations based upon a sharing of economic power among nations. When the Pax Britannica, or pound-sterling-based international trade and finance regime, broke down in 1914, the world trading system degenerated into rival trading blocs, which prefigured the belligerents in World War II.

In the 1990s the specter of a world divided into European, American, and Pacific trading blocs looms ominously. While some economists believe that the direct economic losses of such a fragmentation of trade would be minor, others disagree.[1] Robert Gilpin, for instance, worries that the economies of scale necessary to produce modern, high-tech products and achieve global economic potential cannot be reached in the absence of an integrated world trading system. Moreover, a world divided into hostile trading blocs is a world that may be prone to ignore the poorer regions that belong to no bloc—such as sub-Saharan Africa and the southern part of

Latin America.² It also may be a world prone to serious political and military confrontations, as the Second World War would indicate. Hence it seems imperative that the United States and its major trading partners attempt to defy historical precedent and reestablish a stable international monetary and trading system that promotes the prosperity of all. This book has sought to clarify alternative domestic and international policies the United States might adopt in pursuit of that goal.

The policies that guided the postwar economic system have been characterized as "Keynes at home and Smith abroad"—demand-side fiscal stabilization policy at home and free trade based upon comparative advantage abroad. Conservative visions of the new global economic order call for Smith at home and Smith abroad. American foreign economic policy should push for renewed trade liberalization through the GATT system and a continuation of floating exchange rates, modified by occasional G-7 agreements as necessary.³ On the domestic front, the federal government must seek to reduce the budget deficit and prevent inflation, even at the expense of rising unemployment. Markets should be allowed to determine the proper allocations of capital and labor among industries, states, and localities. States and localities must promote educational excellence by encouraging school-business partnerships and fostering competition among schools through choice systems.

If liberal visions prevail, the new order might be characterized as Keynes at home and Keynes abroad. In the global economy, the United States will seek managed trade agreements; formal coordination of monetary and fiscal policies among the G-7 nations, or at least with Japan and Germany; and tight regulation of the eurocurrency markets. At home, the federal government will seek to reduce unemployment, even at the risk of rising inflation, and shift military spending into outlays for infrastructure, education and training, health care, and housing. The government will enact industrial policies to manage the decline of mature industries and foster the growth of promising new ones. It will redistribute wealth from rich to poor states and cities, and possibly seek to regulate the interstate war for jobs and capital. It will play an active role in restructuring the public education and training systems, implementing national education standards and enhancing work-study programs.

Radical visions also call for aggressive public management of the international economy along Keynesian lines as well as Keynesian demand-management policies at home. Yet radical Keynesianism also would feature initiatives to democratize economic decision making, including Congressional appointment and oversight of the Federal Reserve Board of Governors; aggressive enforcement of labor laws and new laws that support workplace democracy and worker-managed cooperatives; economic planning at the national, state, and local levels; socialization of the finance sector, or at least much tighter banking regulations and the establishment of public development banks; and public regulation of capital movement into, out of, and within, the United States.

Many political economists discussed in this book have articulated views on both domestic and international economic policies, and they see a natural coherence and congruence between the two. They would argue—despite the success for almost three decades of the "Smith abroad, Keynes at home" policy mix—that it is self-defeating to pick and choose positions from various paradigms. They also would claim that their recipes for reform in each issue area must be followed closely if the desired results are to materialize. These arguments make sense, since paradigms are world views that attempt to explain and encompass, in one intellectual system, all relevant economic phenomena and to draw the logical implications for public policy. But policymakers do not always behave accordingly. Real economic policies often reflect a compromise of ideologies and interests.

For some issues discussed in this volume, the outlines of such compromises now may be visible. On the industrial policy issue, for example, the emergent consensus position seems to be that if the United States is to remain competitive, the government should support and facilitate collaboration among firms within an industry for complex and expensive research and development. Likewise, economic adjustment assistance for workers and communities dependent upon declining industries, as called for by industrial policy advocates, may come to pass through policies designed to help communities convert from military to civilian production, now that the Cold War has ended. On the other hand, it seems unlikely that the federal government will adopt proposals for national economic planning or a formalized triage system of restructuring mature industries. Thus, a moderate-liberal compromise on industrial policy seems to be forming, although only time will tell if this is actually the case.

In education policy as well, some of the outlines of a compromise are discernible. While outright privatization of public education is improbable, and even pure choice systems seem unlikely, limited or modified choice arrangements and efforts to decentralize decision making to the school level are taking root across the country. The role of business in education now seems well established, and the back-to-basics curriculum has touched virtually every school system in the country. Yet other conservative reforms, such as merit pay and teacher testing, have made little headway. Although the situation is still quite fluid, a centrist-conservative consensus on education policy seems to be taking shape.

As such compromises form, it is important to ask two questions: First, do they constitute real improvements over the current state of affairs? Second, do they fit well with emerging compromises on other issues? For example, are the emergent compromise positions on education policy and industrial policy mutually supportive, or at least compatible? If one can answer both questions in the affirmative, then perhaps we are making progress.

Progress notwithstanding, we still have a long way to go. On no contemporary issue does the degree of shared vision and sense of common purpose come close to matching that which prevailed over a broad range of fundamental economic issues during the 1950s and much of the 1960s. Like other nations, the United States is struggling to find its way in the new and complex world of heightened foreign competition, global production and trade, and financial and monetary uncertainty. If America and its global neighbors are to create new domestic and international economic arrangements that bring prosperity and relative stability and harmony to the world, we cannot afford to ignore or discard any ideas or reform proposals. Nor can we afford to reject out of hand compromises among ideologically opposed positions. What we can and must do is promote and engage in the healthy exchange of ideas from across the political spectrum.

Notes

1. Krugman, Paul: *The Age of Diminished Expectations: U.S. Economic Policy in the 1990s.* Cambridge: MIT Press, 1990, p. 103. See the annotated bibliography in chapter 3.

2. Gilpin, Robert: *The Political Economy of International Relations.* Princeton: Princeton University Press, 1987, chapter 10. See the annotated bibliography in chapter 1.

3. "G-7" stands for "Group of Seven," the seven largest capitalist economies—Japan, the United States, Canada, Germany, France, Italy, and Great Britain. Through their annual summits, the G-7 nations discuss, and occasionally agree to coordinate, macroeconomic policies. See the discussion in chapter 3.

APPENDIX

A Guide to Resources
by Claire Hoffman

The constant flow of books and articles on the subjects covered in this book provides a wealth of information for those interested in changes in the U.S. economy. This appendix offers a guide to reference sources and periodicals that the reader can consult to maintain current knowledge about the issues. Many of the sources mentioned can be found in the average academic library as well as in larger public libraries.

Periodicals (magazines and journals) appear at regular intervals in the following listings. They provide more current information than books. Persons seeking a general treatment of a topic will consult magazines (for example, *Time* and *Newsweek*), while those needing more scholarly discussion will use journals (for example, *Journal of Economic History* and *Journal of Urban Economics*). Depending upon the researcher's need, articles from either type may be appropriate. Usually the articles in these periodicals are covered by one or more indexing service.

Reference sources offer two kinds of information: (1) access to the published works on a topic and (2) factual information. The sources that provide access to published works are: library catalogs—listings of works, usually books, by author, title, and subject in a particular library; bibliographies—listings of materials on a particular subject, usually by author and subject; and indexes—lists of sources of materials such as journal articles. Reference sources that provide factual information include encyclopedias, handbooks, dictionaries, and directories.

In the first stages of research on a topic, it is good to think of associated general terms and concepts. These terms will be helpful in searching in library catalogs and indexes. Some of the key words and concepts used in this book are: public policy, economic policy, and economic conditions. Most reference tools will have cross references to the appropriate term to be used in their particular index.

Library Catalogs

Many libraries now have automated catalogs that permit author, title, subject, and in some cases, keyword searching. In addition to the more traditional single-term searching, some catalogs permit combinations of multiple types of searches and allow for limiting by such factors as dates and the format of materials.

In most cases, the use of library card catalogs and online catalogs is straightforward. Libraries sometimes will have separate card catalogs for author, title, and subject, or the cards might all be interfiled. Online computer catalogs will require that you enter codes for the type of search that you are interested in performing. Each online catalog system will be different and should have documentation and/or help screens available for assistance.

Author Searching. To find a book by an author, search by the author's last name, followed by the first name and middle initial. For example, when looking for a book by Howard M. Wachtel, the search term will be "Wachtel, Howard M." If the library owns multiple books by this author, there will be multiple cards in the catalog, or a list will appear on the terminal from which you can make your selection(s).

Title Searching. If you were looking for the specific book by Howard Wachtel entitled *The Money Mandarins: The Making of a Supranational Economic Order*, you would do a title search for "Money Mandarins. . . ." Remember to drop any article that is the first word of a title.

Subject Searching. Most academic libraries assign Library of Congress subject headings to the materials in their catalogs. These are standardized terms established by the Library of Congress and published in *Library of Congress Subject Headings (LCSH)* for use by library staff and patrons. Library staff members review titles for subject content and use *LCSH* to assign subject headings. Patrons can use *LCSH* to identify search terms that will lead them to books on the topic. Library of Congress subject headings also are used by the Government Printing Office for cataloging materials in the *Monthly Catalog of United States Government Publications*. Most titles have multiple subject headings assigned.

When you use the publication *Library of Congress Subject Headings,* you may not find the search terms you have in mind. For example, if you are looking for material on public policy related to the activities of multinational corporations, you might expect that two subject headings to use would be "public policy" and "multinational corporation." Note that *LCSH* uses neither but will indicate the appropriate term to use. For example, under the term "public policy," you will find the following information:

Public policy
USE subdivision Government policy under subjects; and headings of the type [Topic] and state and [Topic] policy, e.g., Science and state; Economic policy.

Likewise, to find a book about multinational corporations, LCSH directs the user as follows:

Multinational corporation
USE International business enterprises

Thus to find a book that deals with public policy on multinational corporations the correct subject heading search requires:

International business enterprises—Government policy

Some of the terms listed in the publication *Library of Congress Subject Headings* that will be helpful in searching for material on the U.S. economy include:

- Economic policy
- International economic relations
- United States—Economic policy
- United States—Economic conditions
- United States—Foreign economic relations

Keyword Searching. Using keyword searching is one of the true pleasures of the new automated library catalogs, because you do not have to search for a specific author, title, or subject. It is possible to put in any term, and the automated system will search in a variety of indexes. The other advantage to keyword searching is that you do not have to know the exact order of the terms. While keyword searching can uncover titles missed when using the prescribed subject headings, keyword searching can miss titles that do not contain the specific term in them. Once a book has been found through keyword searching, you can expand your list of search terms by including the subject headings assigned to the book. This is especially useful if you do not have the *Library of Congress Subject Headings* publication at your fingertips.

Classification

Location on the shelves is determined by the call number prescribed by the classification system. If you know the call number(s), you can go to the shelves and browse the collection. Many times researchers have uncovered pertinent materials when browsing the shelves. The three major classification systems used in academic and public libraries today are: (1) the Library of Congress (LC) classification system, (2) the Dewey Decimal classification system, and (3) the Superintendent of Documents (SuDoc) classification system. Most academic libraries shelve materials by the Library of Congress classification system, with many having their government documents collections separate and organized by the SuDoc classification system. Many public libraries and some academic libraries use the Dewey Decimal system.

Guides to Bibliographic Reference Works

Bibliographies can be selective or comprehensive. The former often reflect the expertise of the compiler who draws upon his or her knowledge of a subject and its literature to develop a list of titles useful for research on the subject. Sometimes bibliographic information will be presented in a bibliographic essay devoted to a discussion of the topic. The most comprehensive bibliographies are often merely lists of all the books published during the year, which are then grouped under subject headings. An example of this type is *Books in Print*. Bibliographies range from the very broad to the very specific. They cover the most general popular literature and the most highly specialized scholarly treatises. They can include both published and unpublished works.

At the most general level of bibliography we find bibliographies of bibliographies. These sources list bibliographies in a wide range of disciplines. At the next lowest level are guides to the works in a given discipline, such as economics, political science, history, and so on. Bibliographies are also available at the subject level, for example, multinational corporations, industrial policy, and so on. With perserverance, a researcher should be able to find a bibliography on virtually any subject. One way to do this is to use the subdivision "bibliographies" along with the Library of Congress subject heading. Thus to find a bibliography on multinational corporations, you could search the term "International business enterprises—Bibliographies."

Lists

This section is devoted to very general reference works that are not limited to a special subject area. These are lists rather than true bibliographies.

Books in Print. New York: R. R. Bowker, 1948– .
  An annual index to the publishers' trade list. Indexed by author, title, and series.
Subject Guide to Books in Print. New York: R. R. Bowker, 1957– .
  A companion to *Books in Print*, listed by Library of Congress subject headings.
Dissertation Abstracts International. Ann Arbor: University Microfilms International (UMI), 1938– .
  A monthly compilation of abstracts of doctoral dissertations, arranged alphabetically by subject and university. A subject index and author index are included. Beginning with volume 27, the title is separated into two sections: (1) the humanities and social sciences, appropriate for this subject, and (2) the sciences and engineering. The dissertations are available on microfilm from UMI.

Resources for Popular Literature

This section lists resources oriented toward the popular press. These materials are helpful for establishing a chronology and for finding current discussions on a topic.

Newsbank. New Canaan, Conn.: Newsbank, Inc., 1970– .
  News reports about events and developments selected from 200 U.S. newspapers. Available as a monthly printed index and/or a CD-ROM index. All articles listed are available as part of a microfiche collection.
The National Newspaper Index. Los Altos, Calif.: Information Access, 1979– .
  Indexes the *New York Times, Wall Street Journal, Christian Science Monitor, Washington Post,* and *Los Angeles Times.* Available in a microfilm format or online (Dialog-File 111).
The New York Times Index. New York: New York Times Company, 1851– .
The Official Washington Post Index. Woodbridge, Conn.: Research Publications, 1979– .
  Print index also available online (Dialog-File 184).
VuText
  An online index to newspapers.

Bibliographies of Bibliographies

Research often follows a process that guides one from the very general to the highly specific. A good place to start is with bibliographies of bibliographies. A useful first step is to identify bibliographies pertinent to the topic.

Besterman, Theodore: *World Bibliography of Bibliographies.* Fourth Edition. Geneva, Switzerland: Societies Bibliographica, 1965.
    A useful resource tool for the international literature.

Bibliographic Index. New York: Wilson, 1937/42– .
    An index of published bibliographies arranged alphabetically by subject.

Scull, Roberta A.: *Bibliography of U.S. Government Bibliographies.* 2vols. Ann Arbor: Pierian, 1975–79.
    An annotated listing of bibliographies published by the federal government between 1968 and 1976.

Sheehy, Eugene P.: *Guide to Reference Books.* Tenth Edition. Chicago: American Library Association, 1986.
    An annotated guide to basic reference sources and to sources in specific subject areas. Arranged by subject—with subject, author, and title indexing.

Information Sources by Discipline: Guides, Handbooks, Etc.

This section examines reference materials, mostly guides and bibliographies, in the specific subject areas of the social sciences, which include economics, political science, and public administration.

Brock, Clifton: *The Literature of Political Science: A Guide for Students, Librarians, and Teachers.* New York: R. R. Bowker, 1969. 232 pp.
    Intended primarily for undergraduate majors, divided into two parts: (1) information sources and how to use them, and (2) bibliographies and other reference sources.

Englefield, Dermot and Gavin Drewry (eds): *Information Sources in Politics and Political Science: A Survey Worldwide.* London: Butterworths, 1984. 509 pp.
    Includes monographs and periodical titles as well as reference sources.

Fletcher, John (ed): *Information Sources in Economics.* Second Edition. London, Butterworths, 1984. 339 pp.
    Has a British emphasis but provides a comprehensive current survey of economic literature.

Holler, Frederick L.: *Information Sources of Political Science.* Third Edition. Santa Barbara: ABC-Clio, 1980. 278pp.
    A guide to over 1,750 works in political science with subject, author, and title indexes.

Hutchinson, William Kenneth: *American Economic History: A Guide to Information Sources.* Economic Information Guide Series, Vol. 16. Detroit: Gale, 1980. 296pp.

This guide covers economic history from the colonial period to around 1960.

Rouse, John E., Jr.: *Public Administration in American Society: A Guide to Information Sources.* Gale Information Guide Library, American Government and History Information Guide Series. Vol. 11. Detroit: Gale, 1980. 553pp.

Over 1,700 citations from the fields of political science, history, psychology, business, management, sociology, social work, and economics which provide an overview of American public administration.

Webb, William H.: *Sources of Information in the Social Sciences: A Guide to the Literature.* Third Edition. Chicago: American Library Association, 1986. 777pp.

A guide to the literature in the social sciences divided into eight fields: history, geography, economics and business administration, sociology, anthropology, psychology, education, and political science. This is a revised edition of *Sources of Information in the Social Sciences* by Carl M. White and others, Second Edition, 1973.

Wynar, Lubomyr Roman: *Guide to Reference Materials in Political Science: A Selective Bibliography.* 2vols. Denver: Bibliographic Institute, 1966–68.

Volume 1 covers general reference sources in the social and political sciences, political theory, and ideology. Volume 2 covers international relations; public administration; political behavior, public opinion, and political parties; government publications; and law.

York, Henry E.: *Political Science: A Guide to Reference and Information Sources.* Englewood, Colorado: Libraries Unlimited, Inc., 1990. 249 pp.

Over 800 entries in six sections: general social science reference sources, social science disciplines, general political science reference sources, political science geographic fields, political science topical fields, and public policy. Has an author-title and a subject index.

Bibliographies by Discipline

This section looks at an important group of sources on the discipline level. The advantage to consulting bibliographies is that you can rely on someone else's expertise. Compilers of bibliographies usually have a knowledge of both the structure of the subject covered (its subdivisions and the topics) and the literature.

Economics Working Papers Bibliography. Dobbs Ferry, N.Y.: Trans-Media Publishing Group, 1980– .

A semiannual index to a collection of working papers in the University of Warwick library. There are author, series, and subject indexes.

Harmon, Robert B.: *Political Science Bibliographies.* Vol. 1. Metuchen, N.J.: Scarecrow Press, Inc., 1973, 181pp.; Vol. 2, 1976, 233pp.

A series of bibliographies attempting to list as many bibliographies in the field of political science as possible. The entries are arranged by subject heading, and in addition there are author and title indexes.

International Bibliography of Economics. London: Tavistock; New York: Methuen, 1952– .

Annual bibliography providing international coverage of economics material published in all major languages. Includes books, journal articles, and research reports. Arranged in a classification scheme with 15 main categories including economic policy. Access to specific citations is provided by author and subject indexes.

Public Administration Series: Bibliography. Monticello, Ill.: Vance Bibliographies, 1978– .

Series of bibliographies on public administration topics including titles on public policy. Periodic indexes prepared as part of the series.

Recent Publications on Governmental Problems. Chicago: Joint Reference Library, 1932– .

Weekly unannotated bibliography of books and articles dealing with external problems of public administration.

University Research in Business and Economics, a Bibliography of Publications. Morgantown, W.V.: Bureau of Business Research, 1956– .

Also known as the AUBER Bibliography. An annual compilation of university-sponsored research published by the Association for University Business and Economic Research (AUBER) and the American Assembly of Collegiate Schools of Business (AACSB) in the area of business and economics.

Indexes and Abstracts

Indexes provide access to articles within the selected list of journal titles and, in some cases, include monographic (book) titles in a subject area. Indexes vary, with some including abstracts (summaries) of the material covered and some consisting of tables of contents of journals.

The basic indexing of the material will also make a difference in the usage. The most common types of indexes are author, title, and subject indexes, with some indexes having special sections for entries by report numbers. The author indexes are alphabetical by the author's last name. Title indexes are usually alphabetical by the title and sometimes by keyword. Subject indexes sometimes use standardized, predetermined subject headings, such as the LCSH mentioned earlier; some use their own indexing vocabularies, which might or might not result in a print thesaurus that accompanies the index. When searching an index without a thesaurus, it is important to think of possible synonyms and consider any cross-references that may be indicated.

Many indexes are available in multiple formats (in print, on CD-ROM, and through online database vendors) with different degrees of currency for the different types of products.

ABC Pol Sci: A Bibliography of Contents: Political Science and Government. Santa Barbara: ABC-Clio, 1969– .
    A listing of tables of contents of about 300 international journals in the original language in the field of political science and government as well as the related disciplines of law, sociology, and economics. It is published five times per year with an annual index. There are five-year cumulative indexes for volumes 1–5 (1969–1973), volumes 6–10 (1974–1978), and volumes 11–16 (1979–1983).

Business Periodicals Index. New York: H.W. Wilson Company, 1958/59– .
    A cumulative index to English language business periodical articles. Published monthly (except August) with an annual cumulative index.

Current Index to Journals in Education (CIJE). Phoenix: Oryx, 1969– .
    A monthly index with abstracts and semiannual cumulations to about 800 education periodicals, *CIJE* is a product of the U.S. Department of Education's Educational Research Information Clearinghouse (ERIC) and is published by a private firm.

Education Index. New York: H.W. Wilson, 1929– .
    A monthly index, with an annual cumulation, covering about 350 education periodicals using a combined subject-and-author approach.

Index of Economic Articles in Journals and Collective Volumes. Homewood, Ill.: Richard D. Irwin, 1886– .
    Annual index to articles published in English or with English summaries from over 300 journals. Part 1 includes the subject index, and part 2 consists of an alphabetical author index.

Index to International Statistics (IIS). Washington, D.C.: Congressional Information Service, 1983– .
    Lists statistical publications of major intergovernmental organizations. There is a multiple-year, cumulative index for 1983–1987.

International Political Science Abstracts. Oxford, England: Basil Blackwell, 1951– .
    A bimonthly index with abstracts covering about 650 periodicals in English and French. The final issue of the year has a cumulative subject and author index.

Journal of Economic Literature. Nashville, Tenn.: American Economic Association, 1969– .
    Quarterly periodical which contains articles, book reviews, and a periodical index with selected abstracts. Includes a table of contents of current economic periodicals, a subject index, and an author index.

PAIS International in Print. New York: Public Affairs Information Service, 1991– .

    A selective list of the latest books, pamphlets, government documents, reports of public and private agencies, and periodical articles relating to business, economic and social conditions, public policy and administration, and international relations. This title continues the PAIS Bulletin, incorporating the PAIS Foreign Language Index. Issued monthly with an annual cumulative index.

Social Sciences Index. New York: H.W. Wilson Company, 1974– .

    Indexes over 300 international English language periodicals in the social sciences by author and subject.

Social Sciences Citation Index (SSCI). Philadelphia: Institute for Scientific Information, 1969– .

    A quarterly citation index covering books, journals, and proceedings in the social and behavioral sciences in three parts, called the Citation Index, the Corporate and Source Index, and the Permuterm Subject Index. The index has annual cumulations and five-year cumulations for the years 1966–70, 1971–75, 1976–80, and 1981–85.

Statistical Reference Index (SRI). Washington, D.C.: Congressional Information Service, 1980– .

    Indexes statistical publications from trade, professional, and nonprofit associations; business organizations; commercial publishers; independent research organizations; state government agencies; and universities and affiliated research centers. There are multiple-year, cumulative indexes for 1980–85 and 1986–89.

United States Political Science Documents (USPSD). Pittsburgh: University of Pittsburgh, NASA Industrial Applications Center (NIAC), 1975– .

    This is an annual index with abstracts of core journals in the fields of history, economics, public administration, foreign policy, international affairs, and all related areas in the political, behavioral, and social sciences.

Journals

Journals are an important source of information because of their currency and because an article will usually look at a more narrowly defined topic than a book. Some of the journals listed are selected from *Magazines for Libraries* by Bill Katz and Linda Sternberg Katz from the subject sections on economics, political science, and urban studies. Other journals can be identified by looking at the list of titles covered by an indexing service of interest. For example, a review of *Social Sciences Index* will provide a useful list of journal titles.

AAHE Bulletin. Washington, D.C.: American Association for Higher Education, 1978– .
   Issued ten times per year, the bulletin covers topical issues in higher education. This is the reporting mechanism for the association and includes information on conferences and meetings.
American Economic Review. Nashville: American Economics Association, 1911– .
   Quarterly general economics journal with articles that reflect progress in economic thought and events of fundamental importance.
The Brookings Review. Washington, D.C.: The Brookings Institution, 1962– .
   A quarterly, interdisciplinary journal covering economics, government, and social and foreign policy.
Business Week. New York: McGraw-Hill Publications Company, 1929– .
   A popular weekly business and economics magazine.
The Cato Journal: An Interdisciplinary Journal of Public Policy Analysis. Washington, D.C.: The Cato Institute, 1981– .
   A triennial, interdisciplinary journal of public policy.
Change: The Magazine of Higher Learning. Washington, D.C.: Heldref Publications, 1968– .
   A bimonthly magazine with a broad coverage of higher education in the United States.
Commentary: Journal of Significant Thought and Opinion on Contemporary Issues. New York: American Jewish Committee, 1945– .
   A monthly that covers cultural and political topics from a conservative point of view.
The Economist. London: Economist Newspaper, Ltd., 1843– .
   A weekly publication reporting world news and current events.
Economic Development Quarterly: The Journal of American Economic Revitalization. Newbury Park: Sage Periodicals, 1987– .
   A quarterly journal designed for practitioners, academics, and informed citizens in the field of economic development.
Economic History Review. Cambridge: Economic History Society, 1927– .
   A quarterly journal of importance to both the economist and the historian, dealing with the theory, development, and impact of social decisions.
Educational Leadership. Alexandria, Va.: Association for Supervision and Curriculum Development, 1943– .
   A magazine that focuses on practical problems of K–12 schools, seen from an administrator's point of view.
Fortune. New York: Time, Inc., 1930– .
   A well-known popular, semimonthly business magazine.
Governing; The States and Localities. Washington, D.C.: Congressional Quarterly, Inc., 1987– .
   A monthly magazine for executive and legislative decision makers.
Harvard Business Review. Boston, Mass.: Harvard University, 1922– .

A bimonthly, scholarly journal publishing in the areas of business and management.

Harvard Educational Review. Cambridge, Mass.: Harvard University, 1931– .

A quarterly journal on education specializing in the relationship between American education and social and cultural development.

Journal of Economic History. New York: Cambridge University Press, 1941– .

A monthly journal devoted strictly to economic history, specializing in topics related to the United States.

Journal of Economics and Business. Philadelphia: Temple University, 1949– .

A journal containing highly theoretical scholarly articles in all fields of economics and business.

Journal of Political Economy. Chicago: University of Chicago Press, 1892– .

A bimonthly scholarly journal with broad subject coverage, focusing on development of new analytical methods, economic theory, and measurement of the impact of economic forces. The journal has a somewhat more micro- than macroeconomic orientation.

Journal of Public Economics. Lausanne, Switzerland: Elsevier, 1972– .

A journal, issued nine times per year, that encourages contributions to the problems of public-sector economics.

Journal of the American Planning Association. Chicago: American Planning Association, 1978– .

A quarterly, professional, interdisciplinary journal intended for planners, planning educators, and those in related fields such as economists, urban affairs specialists, and public policy officials.

Journal of Urban Affairs: The Journal of the Urban Affairs Association. Greenwich, Conn.: JAI Press, Inc., 1979– .

A quarterly journal focusing on urban research and policy analysis.

Journal of Urban Economics. New York: Academic Press, Inc., 1974– .

A bimonthly scholarly journal emphasizing research on U.S. housing problems and covering a wide range of topics related to urban economics.

Monthly Review: An Independent Socialist Magazine. New York: Monthly Review Press, 1949– .

A monthly publication (except July/August) that offers a Marxist analysis of world events.

The New Republic. Washington, D.C.: New Republic, Inc., 1914– .

A liberal weekly that gives conservative as well as liberal viewpoints on political and economic issues.

Omega, the International Journal of Management Science. New York: Pergamon Press, 1973– .

A bimonthly journal for reporting developments in the field of management services.

Quarterly Review of Economics and Business. Champaign, Ill.: University of Illinois at Urbana-Champaign, 1960– .

    A quarterly interdisciplinary journal discussing relationships among business, economics, and society.

Social Policy. New York: Social Policy Corporation, 1970– .

    A quarterly journal publishing research-based articles, theoretical articles, or opinion pieces on public policy, social welfare, and politics, generally from a progressive standpoint.

State and Local Government Review. Athens, Ga.: Carl Vinson Institute of Government, University of Athens, Georgia, 1968–

    A triennial publication for practitioners and academics on the study and practice of public management.

Technology Review. Cambridge, Mass.: Massachusetts Institute of Technoloby, Alumni Association, 1899– .

    Issued eight times per year, the review extensively covers new technology developments with an emphasis on practical and industrial applications.

Training and Development Journal. Alexandria, Va.: American Association for Training and Development (ASTD), 1966– .

    A monthly association publication designed for individuals in human resource devleopment. It provides quality articles of interest to training practitioners, managers, administrators, consultants, academicians, and theorists.

World Policy Journal. New York: World Policy Institute, 1983– .

    A quarterly on world affairs and international politics analyzing existing U.S. economic and social policies, and recommending new policy directions.

Government Publications

The United States government produces many materials of interest to economists and researchers in related fields. Government information is available in a variety of formats that include print, microfiche, CD-ROM, and online databases. Some government information has been privatized and is sold by commercial publishers. The first section that follows is a listing of indexes, and the second section is a listing of agencies with titles of interest that they publish.

General Indexes

Monthly Catalog of United States Government Publications. Washington, D.C.: Government Printing Office, 1895– .

    The index issued by the Superintendent of Documents listing publications on the government. Issued monthly with a semiannual and an annual cumulative index.

Index to U. S. Government Periodicals. Chicago: Infordata International Inc., 1970- .

An index of over 170 major periodical titles published by more than 100 agencies of the U.S. government. The indexing is based on a thesaurus created specifically for this title. It is published quarterly, with the fourth quarter being the annual cumulative index.

American Statistics Index (ASI). Washington, D.C.: Congressional Information Services, 1973- .

This is a monthly index, which is cumulated quarterly and annually, listing statistical publications of the U.S. government. The abstract section is arranged by issuing agency and includes reference to the SuDoc classification number. The indexing is by subject, title, category, and series/report number. There are multiple-year cumulative indexes for 1974-79, 1980-84, and 1985-88.

Congressional Information Service (CIS). Washington, D.C.: Congressional Information Service, 1970- .

Comprehensive index and abstracts of congressional documents, reports, committee prints, hearings, and special publications. There are multiple-year cumulative indexes for 1970-74, 1975-78, 1979-82, 1983-86, and 1987-90.

Statistical Masterfile. Bethesda: Congressional Information Service, 1983.

A CD-ROM index to statistical publications covered in the print counterparts: ASI, IIS, and SRI.

Congressional Masterfile. Bethesda: Congressional Information Service.

A CD-ROM index to congressional publications. Masterfile 1 covers the print counterpart indexes: CIS U.S. Serial Set Index (1789-1969), CIS US Congressional Committee Hearings Index (1833-1969), CIS Index to Unpublished U.S. Senate Committee Hearings (1823-1964), and CIS U.S. Congressional Committee Prints Index (1830-1969). Masterfile 2 covers the CIS/Index (1970-).

Agencies of Interest

Numerous agencies publish economic information. This section will give a brief summary of the offices of different agencies and a listing of titles, especially periodicals, that are of interest. Classification numbers are listed for specific titles included in this section. The numbers are in the Superintendent of Documents (SuDoc) classification system used by many larger documents collections.

Department of Commerce, Bureau of the Census

The Bureau was established in 1902 as a general purpose statistical agency that collects, tabulates, and publishes a wide variety of statistical data about the people and the economy of the nation.

Statistical Abstract of the United States. 1878- . C 3.134.

An annual compendium of statistics that is an indispensable reference source. Summary statistics on political, social, and economic conditions in the United States. An effective way to use this title is to locate the more general tables and obtain the SOURCE publication title, which will in most cases contain more detailed tables.

County Business Patterns. C 3.204.

Annual volumes with data on economic activity at the county level for the 50 states, the District of Columbia, and a U.S. summary volume. Data are available by SIC (the standard industrial classification code) excluding government employees, self-employed persons, farm workers, and domestic workers. The SIC is a statistical classification standard used to define industries in accordance with the composition and structure of the economy.

Department of Commerce, Bureau of Economic Analysis

The Bureau was established in 1953, and its goal is to provide a clear picture of the U.S. economy.

Business Conditions Digest. 1961–1990. C 59.9.

A monthly periodical that presented cyclical indicators useful to business analysts and forecasters. This title was discontinued in March 1990, with the indicators being incorporated into the *Survey of Current Business.*

Business Statistics. 1951– . C 59.11/3.

A biennial publication of data for approximately 2,000 statistical series. A compendium of historical statistics that are updated monthly by the *Survey of Current Business.*

Survey of Current Business. 1921– . C 59.11.

A monthly statistical guide to the U.S. economy that includes reviews and articles.

Department of Commerce, Economic Development Administration

The administration was established under the Public Works and Economic Development Act of 1965 (42 U.S.C. 3121) to generate new jobs, to help protect existing jobs, and to stimulate commercial and industrial growth in the economically distressed areas of the United States.

Department of Commerce, International Trade Administration

The International Trade Administration was established in 1980 by the Secretary of Commerce to promote world trade and strengthen the international trade and investment position of the United States.

Foreign Economic Trends and Their Implications for the United States. 1980– . C 61.11.

An individual country report which includes key economic indicators, a brief summary of the state of the economy, economic trends, the foreign trade situation, and living costs, an industrial report, and an agricultural report.

Department of Education

American Education. 1965–1985. ED 1.10.

Issued ten times per year, this publication contains articles on federal programs in the field of education. It is aimed at educators, government officials, and the general public.

A Nation at Risk: The Imperative for Educational Reform. April 1983. ED 1.2:N 21.

The report of the National Commission on Excellence in Education on the quality of education in America. The report looks at the strengths and weaknesses of the current system and makes recommendations for improvement.

Federal Reserve System, Board of Governors

The Federal Reserve System was established by the Federal Reserve Act (12 U.S.C. 221) approved in 1913. It serves as the nation's central bank.

Federal Reserve Bulletin. 1915– . FR 1.3.

This publication contains announcements and articles regarding the actions of the board of governors.

Department of Labor, Bureau of Labor Statistics

The Bureau of Labor Statistics is one of the principal data-gathering agencies of the federal government. It has no enforcement or regulatory functions. The bureau collects, processes, analyzes, and disseminates data relating to employment, unemployment, and other characteristics of the labor force; prices and family expenditures; wages, other worker compensation, and industrial relations; productivity and technological change; and occupational safety and health.

CPI Detailed Report. 1952– . L 2.38/3.

A report on monthly price movements for consumer goods.

Monthly Labor Review (MLR). 1915– . L 2.6.

This publication reports labor conditions, with statistics, regular features, and articles.

Executive Office of the President

Economic Report of the President. 1950– . Pr.

The annual report transmitted to Congress that reviews the state of the economy and the president's economic initiatives. Contains the *Annual Report* of the Council of Economic Advisors.

Executive Office of the President, Council of Economic Advisers

Established by the Employment Act of 1946 (15 U.S.C. 1023), the council consists of three members. They are appointed by the president to analyze the national economy and its various segments; advise the president on economic developments; appraise the economic programs and policies of the federal government; recommend policies for economic growth and stability; assist in the preparation of the *Economic Report of the President* to Congress; and prepare the *Annual Report* of the Council of Economic Advisors.

Executive Office of the President, Office of Policy Development
The Executive Office was designated in 1981 to replace the Domestic Policy Staff. The office advises the president in the formulation, evaluation, and coordination of long-range domestic and economic policy.

Department of State, Bureau of Economic and Business Affairs
The bureau has overall responsibility for formulating and implementing policy regarding foreign economic matters.

Congress, Joint Economic Committee

Economic Indicators 1948– . Y 4.Ec7:Ec7/.
This publication contains charts and tables on current economic conditions.

Other Periodic Sources

Sources issued on a recurring basis that are useful in doing beginning research include directories and handbooks. Handbooks often provide brief topical summaries, bibliographies, and names and addresses.

Encyclopedia of Associations. Detroit: Gale Research, Inc. 1956– .
An annual directory to national and international associations giving pertinent information on their organization and their publications.

Fildes, Robert and Thana Chrissanthaki (eds): *World Index of Economic Forecasts, Including Industrial Tendency Surveys and Development Plans.* Third Edition. Aldershot, England: Gower, 1988.
This publication profiles 329 organizations that provide forecasts, plans, and surveys of countries. This edition features a new section dealing with surveys.

Research Centers Directory. Detroit: Gale Research, Inc. 1960– .
A biennial directory to university and other nonprofit research organizations.

World Development Report. Oxford: Oxford University Press. 1978– .
An annual published for the World Bank covering financial topics relating to economic development and statistics on world development.

Associations, Institutes, and Research Centers

Associations, institutes, and research centers issue numerous reports and other publications. These publications are often difficult to find. Following is a list of some groups that produce publications related to public policy. They are arranged according to their dominant ideological orientation.

Conservative/Moderate

American Conservative Union, 38 Ivy Street, S.E., Washington, D.C. 20003. (202) 546-6555
    A lobbying organization founded in 1964 to further the cause of conservatism. Publication: *Capital Review*, periodic.

American Enterprise Institute for Public Policy Research, 1150 17th St., N.W., Washington, D.C. 20036. (202) 862-5800
    One of the largest of the nonprofit research centers, founded in 1943. An influential publisher of studies on public policy. Publications: *AEI Economist*, monthly; *Public Opinion*, bimonthly; *Regulation: AEI Journal on Government and Society*, bimonthly.

Brookings Institution, 1775 Massachusetts Ave., N.W., Washington, D.C. 20036. (202) 797-6000
    An independent, nonprofit organization founded in 1927 and supported by endowment income, foundation gifts, and contracts. The institution conducts research on economics, government regulations, social policy, and foreign and defense policy. Publications: *Brookings Papers on Economic Activity*, semiannual; *Brookings Review*, quarterly.

Cato Institute, 224 Second St., S.E., Washington, D.C. 20003. (202) 546-0200
    A nonprofit research organization, founded in 1977, that studies all matters related to public policy, domestic and international, and is dedicated to increasing policy debate. Publications: *The Cato Journal: An Interdisciplinary Journal of Public Policy Analysis*, triennial; *Cato Policy Report*, bimonthly; *Regulation*, triennial.

Conservative Alliance, 1315 Duke Street, Alexandria, Va. 22314. (703) 683-4329
    An organization founded in 1977, interested in promoting a strong national defense, private enterprise, and less government intervention, regulation, and spending. Publications: *Call for Action*, monthly; *Congressional Scorecard*, annual.

Heritage Foundation, 214 Massachusetts Avenue, N.E., Washington, D.C. 20002. (202) 546-4400
    A nonprofit organization, founded in 1973, that has become a leader of conservative thinking on current policy issues. Publication: *Policy Review*, quarterly.

Hoover Institute on War, Revolution and Peace, Stanford University, Stanford, Calif. 94305. (415) 723-1754

A nonprofit organization doing research in political, economic, and social change; founded in 1919. Publications: *Yearbook of International Communist Affairs,* annual; *Hoover Institution Annual Report.*

Hudson Institute, Herman Kahn Center, 5395 Emerson Way, P.O. Box 26-919, Indianapolis, In. 46226. (317) 545-1000

An independent nonprofit research center founded in 1961. It conducts research on public policy issues. Publications: *Hudson Institute Briefing; Hudson Institute Opinion; Hudson Institute Report.*

National Chamber Foundation, 1615 H St., N.W., Washington, D.C. 20062. (202) 463-5552

An organization concerned with issues vital to the health of the economic system; founded in 1967. Publication: *Journal of Economic Growth,* quarterly.

Reason Foundation, 2718 Ocean Park Blvd., Suite 1062, Santa Monica, Calif. 90405. (213) 392-0443

An organization founded in 1978 that seeks to provide a better understanding of the intellectual basis of a free society, and develops new ideas in public policy. It promotes an individualistic philosophy and free market principles. Publication: *Privatization Watch,* monthly.

Twentieth Century Fund, 41 E. 70th St., New York, N.Y. 10021. (212) 535-4441

A research foundation founded in 1919 that undertakes studies of major economic, political, and social issues. Publication: *Twentieth Century Fund Newsletter,* three or four times per year.

Liberal and Progressive

Academy for State and Local Government, 444 N. Capitol St., N.W., Suite 349, Washington, D.C. 20001. (202) 638-1445

A nonprofit public policy center, founded in 1971 and operated by the Council of State Governments, International City Management Association, National Association of Counties, National Conference of State Legislatures, National Governors' Association, National League of Cities, and U.S. Conference of Mayors. Publications: *Court Report,* monthly; *Election Center Reports,* monthly; *Public Innovation Abroad,* monthly.

Center for Policy Alternatives, 2000 Florida Ave. N.W., 4th Fl., Washington, D.C. 20009. (202) 387-6030

Founded in 1975, the center acts as a clearinghouse and forum for ideas on progressive public policy affecting state and local governments. Publication: *Ways and Means,* quarterly.

Center for Policy Research, c/o Dr. Amitai Etzioni, 3 Hubbard Park Road, Cambridge, Mass. 02138. (617) 495-6991

300 *Appendix*

The center was founded in 1968 to serve public and private policymaking bodies by providing the environment and facilities to conduct social research dealing with public policy issues.

Center on Budget and Policy Priorities, 236 Massachusetts Avenue, N.E., Suite 305, Washington, D.C. 20002. (202) 544-0591
  Founded in 1981, the center provides research in national budget and policy issues. Publication: *Women, Infants, and Children Newsletter,* monthly.

Economic Policy Institute, 1730 Rhode Island Ave., N.W., Suite 812, Washington, D.C. 20036. (202) 775-8810
  The institute was founded in 1984 to conduct research and to provide a forum for the exchange of information on economic policy.

Institute for Policy Studies, 1601 Connecticut Ave., N.W., Washington, D.C. 20009. (202) 234-9382
  A nonprofit research and educational institute founded in 1963, which studies domestic policy, foreign policy, national security, and human rights.

Northeast-Midwest Institute, 218 D Street, S.E., Washington, D.C. 20003. (202) 544-5200
  The institute was founded in 1977 as an independent source of economic information to an 18-state region of the Northeast-Midwest. Publications: *The Budget and the Region,* annual; *Guide to Government Resources for Economic Development,* biennial; *Guide to State and Federal Resources for Economic Development,* triennial.

Urban Institute, 2100 M Street, N.W., Washington, D.C. 20037. (202) 833-7200
  A research organization founded in 1968 that conducts studies and proposes solutions to social and economic problems. Publication: *Policy and Research Report,* triennial.

Marxist and Other Radical

Alternative Education Project, c/o Radical America Journal, 1 Summer Street, Somerville, Mass. 02143. (617) 628-6585
  A nonprofit publisher founded in 1967, concerned with grassroots organization and social and economic issues. Publication: *Radical America,* bimonthly.

Democratic Socialists of America, 15 Dutch Street, Suite 500, New York, N.Y. 10038. (212) 962-0390
  An organization that works to promote civil liberties and distribute wealth more equitably; founded in 1982. Publications: *Democratic Left,* bimonthly; *Socialist Forum,* triennial; *Women Organizing,* semiannual.

Foundation for National Progress, 1663 Mission St., San Francisco, Calif. 94103. (415) 558-8881

The foundation researches problems related to political and economic progress; founded in 1975. Publication: *Mother Jones*, nine times per year.

Nonpartisan

American Assembly, 412 Altschul Hall, Barnard College, Columbia University, New York, N.Y. 10027. (212) 854–3456

Founded in 1950, the organization holds nonpartisan national assemblies on issues of public interest. Publication: *Annual Report*.

Bureau of National Affairs, 1231 25th St., N.W., Washington, D.C. 20037. (202) 452–4200

A for-profit publishing company, specializing in looseleaf services in law, labor, and economics.

Policy Studies Organization, University of Illinois, 361 Lincoln Hall, 702 S. Wright Street, Urbana, Ill. 61801. (217) 359–8541

An organization founded in 1971 that promotes interdisciplinary thought on policy problems. Publications: *Policy Studies Journal*, quarterly; *Policy Studies Review*, quarterly.

Author-Title Index

AAHE Bulletin, 210, 221, 291
ABC Pol Sci: A Bibliography of Contents: Political Science and Government, 289
Abernathy, W., 35, 40
Academy for State and Local Government, 299
"The 'Acanemia' Deception: How the Myth That America 'Lags' in Education Spending Threatens to Undermine National Competitiveness," 112, 207, 213
Accordino, John, 258, 265
Ackerman, Frank, 115, 121, 160, 164, 172, 178
"Adding a Stick to the Carrot: Location Incentives with Clawbacks, Recissions and Recalibrations," 257, 269
Adult Learning: State Policies and Institutional Practices, 219
AEI Economist, 298
The Affluent Society, 76
After the Factories: Changing Employment Patterns in the Rural South, 253, 263
Against Mediocrity: The Humanities in America's High Schools, 212
The Age of Diminished Expectations: U.S. Economic Policy in the 1990s, 109, 117, 164, 177, 279
Agnew, John, 34, 39
Albelda, Randy, 71, 80, 83
Alperovitz, Gar, 159, 172, 261, 265
Alperson, Myra, 190, 207, 211
Alternative Education Project, 300
"The Alternative to Stagnation," 159

Alternatives to Economic Orthodoxy: A Reader in Political Economy, 71, 80, 83
America in Ruins: Beyond the Public Works Pork Barrel, 113, 123
America in the World Economy: A Strategy for the 1990s, 110, 111, 112, 115, 120, 155, 156, 166, 180
America in Transition: The International Frontier, 221
American Assembly, 301
American Assembly of Collegiate Schools of Business (AACSB), 288
American Association for Higher Education Bulletin, 210, 221
American Business and the Public School: Case Studies of Corporate Involvement in Public Education, 207, 213
American Conservative Union, 298
American Economic History: A Guide to Information Sources, 287
"American Economic Policy in the Antemillenial Era," 115, 121, 165, 178
American Economic Policy: Problems and Prospects, 172
American Economic Review, 291
The American Economy, 74, 82, 109
American Education, 207, 212, 218, 296
American Enterprise Institute, 298
American Industry, 169
The American Job Machine, 37, 41, 73, 81, 162, 163, 175, 207, 214, 270
American Society of Training and Development, 187
American Statistics Index (ASI), 294

An American Trade Strategy: Options for the 1990s, 158, 162, 163, 165, 166, 179, 180, 181
An American Vision: Policies for the '90s, 112, 118, 166, 181, 207, 211, 256, 266, 265, 274
America's Ailing Cities: Fiscal Health and the Design of Urban Policy, 256, 261, 263
America's Choice: High Skills or Low Wages, 208, 209, 210, 217
America's Cities and the 1980s: The Legacy of the Reagan Years, 255, 262
Anarchy, State and Utopia, 72, 77
Anderson, Arne, 97, 113, 114, 119
Anderson, Marion, 123, 163, 176
The Annals of the American Academy of Political and Social Sciences, 256, 263
Annual Report of the Council of Economic Advisors, 297
"Are Data Enough?" 209, 218
Aristotle, 73
Aronowitz, Stanley, 191, 192, 207, 209, 210, 214, 221
Aronson, J. Richard, 74, 82, 112, 209, 217, 255
"As the World Turns," 35, 40
Aslanian, C., 210, 222
"Assessment and Outcomes Measurement: A View from the States," 210, 221
"Assessment: The Secretary of Education's New Clothes," 207, 216
Association for University Business and Economic Research (AUBER), 288

Babbage, Charles, 62
"Back-to-Back Record Deficits Are Predicted," 110
Balmuth, Miriam, 208, 216
Baran, Paul A., 75, 76, 82
Barro, Robert J., 94, 111, 117
The Basic Economics of the Urban Racial Crisis, 33, 34, 255, 262
Baumol, William J., 36, 38, 109, 110, 116
Beaumont, Enid, 256, 265
Beauregard, Robert A., 254, 261, 264, 267, 270
Bentham, Jeremy, 72, 78
Berg, Ivar, 208, 216
Bergman, Edward M., 253, 263
Bergsten, C. Fred, 95, 103, 104, 105, 110, 111, 112, 115, 120, 155, 156, 166, 180

Besterman, Theodore, 286
Betz, F., 210, 222
Beyond Free Trade and Protectionism: The Public Interest in a U.S. Auto Policy, 158, 159, 163, 164, 167
Beyond the Waste Land: A Democratic Alternative to Economic Decline, 115, 122, 159, 160, 161, 163, 173, 261, 266
Bhagwati, Jagdish, 153, 154, 155, 165, 166, 177
Bibliographic Index, 286
Bibliography of U.S. Government Bibliographies, 286
Bingham, Richard D., 258, 259, 264, 273
Birch, David, 258, 265, 266
Bischak, Greg, 123, 163, 176
Blackwell, Sir Basil, 164, 178
Blair, John P., 256, 264
Blakely, Edward J., 261, 264
Blaug, Marc, 71, 83, 84
Blinder, Alan S., 36, 38, 109, 110, 116, 128, 156, 169
Bloom, Allan, 202, 210, 221
Bluestone, Barry, 34, 35, 37, 40, 75, 82, 109, 111, 114, 115, 122, 138, 140, 156, 157, 159, 160, 161, 164, 172, 175
Boaz, David, 112, 118, 166, 181, 191, 207, 211, 256, 260, 261, 265, 266, 274
Bonar, James, 76
Books in Print, 284, 285
Boonekamp, Clemens, 31, 39, 177
Bosworth, Barry, 95, 97, 104, 111, 112, 113, 115, 120
Botkin, James, 204, 211, 222
Bowles, Samuel, 32, 33, 38, 75, 76, 82, 115, 122, 137, 140, 159, 160, 161, 163, 173, 261, 266
Bowman, Ann O'M., 259, 266
Boyer, C., 210, 221
Braverman, Harry, 75, 82, 159, 174, 207, 215
Brenner, Harvey, 37
Brock, Clifton, 286
Brookings Institution, 298
Brookings Papers on Economic Activity, 298
The Brookings Review, 161, 175, 291, 298
Brown, Holly, 173
Brown, Michael K., 36, 40, 109, 120
The Budget and the Region, 300
Bureau of National Affairs, 197, 301
Business Conditions Digest, 295

"Business Leaders and the Politics of School Reform," 208, 215
Business Periodicals Index, 289
Business Statistics, 295
Business Week, 37, 39, 41, 110, 114, 123, 159, 163, 166, 168, 171, 176, 232, 255, 272, 291
Business Week Team, 157, 166

Call for Action, 298
Campbell, Candace, 258, 266
Can America Compete? 175
Capital, 79
Capital Review, 298
Capitalism and Freedom, 72, 73, 81, 109, 116, 118, 207, 212, 260, 267
Capitalism, Socialism and Democracy, 72, 80, 162, 176
Carnevale, Anthony P., 187, 206, 209, 210, 214
Carnoy, Martin, 160, 173, 192, 205, 207, 215
Carson, Robert, 84, 114, 116
Case, John, 258, 266
Castells, Manuel, 254, 262
Cato Institute, 298
The Cato Journal: An Interdisciplinary Journal of Public Policy Analysis, 291, 298
Cato Policy Report, 298
Cavanagh, John, 35, 39, 76, 82
Center Focus, 111, 120
Center for Economic Conversion, 176, 260
Center for Policy Alternatives, 299
Center for Policy Research, 299
Center for Popular Economics, 33, 34, 37, 40, 101, 106, 107, 114, 115, 116, 122, 160, 161, 164, 173, 178
Center on Budget and Policy Priorities, 114, 300
Challenges and Choices Facing American Labor, 161, 171
Change Agents in the New Economy: Business Incubators and Economic Development, 258, 266
Change: The Magazine of Higher Learning, 211, 222, 291
Chi, Keon S., 256, 266
Chmura, Thomas J., 203, 210, 222, 258, 266
Choate, Pat, 113, 123, 155, 157, 169, 178
Chrissanthaki, Thana, 297
Chubb, John E., 189, 190, 196, 206, 207, 211, 212, 218

Cities and the Wealth of Nations, 257, 260, 269
Cities in a Global Society, 254, 257, 260, 263, 269
"City Building in a Global Society," 260, 263
Clairmonte, Frederick, 35, 39, 76, 82
Clark, Gordon L., 254, 261
Clavel, Pierre, 254, 266
Clinger, William F., Jr., 175
The Closing of the American Mind: How Higher Education Has Failed Democracy and Impoverished the Souls of Today's Students, 210, 221
Cloward, Richard, 114, 122
Cobb, James C., 254, 257, 262
Cohen, Jeffrey E., 163, 176
Cohen, Joshua, 5, 32, 33, 34, 35, 40, 82
Cole, Richard L., 255, 262
"Collaboration for Economic Development: Virginia's Universities and Local Public Officials," 258, 265
"A College Education Up to Beating the Japanese," 210, 221
Collins, Sheila D., 207, 208, 216
"Commentary," 163
Commentary, 210, 217, 222, 258, 266, 270
Commentary: Journal of Significant Thought and Opinion on Contemporary Issues, 291
Commerce, U.S. Department of, Bureau of Economic Analysis, 32, 36, 42, 295
Commerce, U.S. Department of, Bureau of the Census, 294
Commerce, U.S. Department of, Economic Development Administration, 295
Commerce, U.S. Department of, International Trade Administration, 295
Commission on the Skills of the American Workforce, 194, 199, 208, 208, 209, 210, 216, 217
Committee for Economic Development, 170
Communities in Economic Crisis: Appalachia and the South, 253, 254, 262
Community-Based Development: Investing in Renewal, 259, 273
"Comparing Enterprise Zones to Other Economic Development Techniques," 255, 259, 261, 268
Competing Visions: The Political Conflict over America's Economic

306 Author-Title Index

Future, 73, 161, 162, 163, 175, 256, 270
Computer Technologies, Market Structure, and Strategic Union Choices, 161, 171
Conference Board, 197
Congress, Joint Economic Committee, 297
Congressional Information Service (CIS), 294
Congressional Masterfile, 294
Congressional Scorecard, 298
Conservative Alliance, 298
The Consumer Electronics Industry and the Future of American Manufacturing: How the U.S. Lost the Lead and Why We Must Get Back in the Game, 157, 163, 168
Contested Terrain: The Transformation of Work in the Twentieth Century, 159, 174
"Contribution to the Critique of Hegel's Philosophy of Right," 74
"Controlling the War Between the States with Clawbacks," 257, 271
Converting the American Economy: The Economic Effects of an Alternative Security Policy, 123, 163, 176
The Cooperative Workplace: Potentials and Dilemmas of Organizational Democracy and Participation, 161, 174
"Corporate America in the Classroom," 207, 211
"Corporate Leaders, Resistant Youth, and School Reform in Sunbelt City: The Political Economy of Education," 208, 216
Cote, Marcel, 258, 265
Cottingham, Phoebe H., 112, 117, 260, 271
County Business Patterns, 37, 295
Court Report, 299
CPI Detailed Report, 296
Crane, Edward H., 112, 118, 166, 181, 207, 211, 256, 265, 274
"Critique of the Gotha Program," 75, 79
Cropsey, Joseph, 78
Cross, K. Patricia, 219
Cultural Literacy: What Every American Needs to Know, 210, 221, 222
Current Index to Journals in Education (CIJE), 289
Current Population Survey, 137

Dahl, Robert A., 255
Davidson, Greg, 54, 56, 73, 74, 76, 82, 113, 115, 120
Davidson, Paul, 54, 56, 73, 74, 76, 82, 96, 104, 113, 115, 120
Day of Reckoning: The Consequences of American Economic Policy Under Reagan and After, 110, 114, 115, 120
"The Decline of U.S. Power," 31, 39
The Deindustrialization of America: Plant Closings, Community Abandonment, and the Dismantling of Basic Industry, 34, 35, 37, 40, 109, 122, 156, 159, 160, 161, 172, 173
Democracy and Education, 205
Democracy, Authority and Alienation in Work, 157, 172
Democratic Left, 300
Democratic Socialists of America, 300
DeParle, Jason, 111
Dertouzos, Michael L., 156, 157, 159, 161, 163, 170, 198, 207, 209, 210, 211, 217
"Developing the Wealth of the Nation: A Call for a National Human Resources Policy," 210, 220
Dewey, John, 205
Dialogue on Debt: Alternative Analyses and Solutions, 32
Dicken, Peter, 34, 39
Dimancescu, Dan, 204, 211, 222
Diminished Expectations, 110, 111, 112, 165
"The Disciples of David Birch," 258, 266
A Discourse on the Origin of Inequality, 77
Discussion of Dornbusch's "Policy Options for Freer Trade," 166, 180
Dislocated Workers: Coping with Competition and Conversion, 206, 219, 257, 269
Dissertation Abstracts International, 285
"Distribution of Full-Time Equivalent Employment by Sector and Industry, 1947–1983," 33
Doeringer, Peter B., 157, 170, 258, 267
Dollars and Dreams: The Changing American Income Distribution, 15, 33, 34, 36, 37, 41
Domhoff, G. William, 256
Dorn, James A., 118, 116
Dornbusch, Rudiger W., 152, 153, 166, 180, 181
Douress, J., 259, 262
Drewry, Gavin, 286

Drucker, Peter F., 217
Duggan, Paula, 206, 219, 257
Dumas, Lloyd J., 159
DuPont, Pete, 207, 211, 212
"A Dynamic Model of Process and Product Innovation," 35, 40

Economic Adjustment and Conversion of Defense Industries, 164, 176
"Economic and Philosophic Manuscripts of 1844," 75, 79
Economic Conversion: Revitalizing America's Economy, 164, 176
Economic Democracy: The Challenge of the 1980s, 160, 173
The Economic Development of Japan and Korea: A Parallel with Lessons, 162, 176
Economic Development Programs for Cities, Counties and Towns, 256, 257, 264
Economic Development Quarterly: The Journal of American Economic Revitalization, 210, 220, 257, 258, 267, 269, 272, 291
Economic History Review, 291
Economic Indicators, 297
Economic Issues Today: Alternative Approaches, 84, 114, 116
Economic Policy Institute, 300
Economic Report of the People: An Alternative to the Economic Report of the President, 114, 115, 116, 122, 160, 161, 173, 178
Economic Report of the President, 32, 33, 34, 36, 42, 296
Economic Restructuring and Political Response, 254, 261, 262, 264, 267, 270
Economic Theory in Retrospect, 71, 83, 84
Economics: Principles and Policy, Macroeconomics, 36, 38, 109, 110, 116
Economics: Principles, Problems, Decisions, 36, 38, 110, 117
Economics and Politics of Industrial Policy: The United States and Western Europe, 163, 176
Economics for a Civilized Society, 73, 74, 76, 82, 113, 115, 120
The Economics of Feasible Socialism, 76, 83
Economics Working Papers Bibliography, 287
The Economist, 291

"The Economy, Productivity and Training—A CEO's View," 207, 218
Edgerton, Russ, 210, 221
Education and Jobs: The Great Training Robbery, 208, 216
Education for Economic Security Act, 220
"Education in America: The Opportunity to Choose," 207, 211
Education Incorporated: School-Business Cooperation for Economic Growth, 214
Education Index, 289
Education under Siege: The Conservative, Liberal and Radical Debate over Schooling, 207, 209, 210, 214
"Education, Training, and Industrial Policy," 259, 271
Education, U.S. Department of, 296
Educational Leadership, 206, 209, 212, 213, 217, 218, 291
Educational Research Information Clearinghouse (ERIC), 289
Educational Researcher, 209, 218
Edwards, Richard, 32, 33, 75, 76, 82, 115, 122, 159, 174
Egan, Mary Lou, 258, 267
Eggert, Jim, 38
Ehrenreich, Barbara, 34, 39
Eisinger, Peter K., 259, 267
Eisner, Elliott W., 196, 209, 217
Eisner, Robert, 96, 97, 113, 120
Election Center Reports, 299
Elkins, David R., 257, 272
Ellwood, David T., 112, 117, 260, 271
Elmore, Richard F., 209, 217
"The Emerging Third Wave: New Economic Development Strategies in the 1990s," 259, 272
Employee Ownership in America: The Equity Solution, 161, 174
Encyclopedia of Associations, 297
The End of Laissez-Faire: National Purpose and the Global Economy after the Cold War, 110, 120
Engels, Friedrich, 67, 74, 75
Englefield, Dermot, 286
"Enterprise Zones and Federalism," 256, 265
"Enterprise Zones Are Just Part of the Answer for Reviving an Urban Economy," 256, 273
Enterprise Zones: New Directions in Economic Development, 255, 256, 265, 268

"Entrepreneurs Find Happy City Home," 258, 271
"Equality and Efficiency: The Big Trade-Off," 74
"Equity and Excellence in Education: A Comment," 206, 212
An Essay on the Principle of Population, 80
Essays in Economics: Theory and Policy, 115, 121
"Establishing and Maintaining High-Commitment Work Systems," 157, 159, 171, 206, 214
"Estimating the Social Costs of National Economic Policy: Implications for Mental and Physical Health and Clinical Aggression," 37
Ettlie, John E., 158, 170
Ettlinger, Michael P., 255, 270
Evaluating the Options, 162, 163, 165, 181
Evans, Michael K., 73, 81, 118
"Evidence, Values, and the Revitalization of Schools—Response to Raywid," 209, 218
Ewell, P., 210, 221
Executive Office of the President, 296
Executive Office of the President, Council of Economic Advisers, 296
Executive Office of the President, Office of Policy Development, 297
"Exploring the Spatial Effects of the Internationalization of the Mexican Economy," 254, 262
"The Export Trading Company Act of 1982: Japanese-Style Exporting for America?" 258, 267

Fancher, R., 212
A Far Cry from Fair: CTJ's Guide to State Tax Reform, 255, 270
Faux, Jeff, 111, 115, 120, 159, 172, 261, 265, 267
Federal Reserve Bank of Atlanta, 73, 81, 118
Federal Reserve Bulletin, 296
Federal Reserve System, Board of Governors, 296
Federal Tax Policy for Economic Growth and Stability, 74
"The Feds Can Help: Programs, Publications, and People," 260, 270
Fege, Arnold, 209, 218
Feldstein, Martin, 108, 116, 118
A Field Guide to the U.S. Economy, 33, 34, 37, 40
Fildes, Robert, 297

Financing Economic Development: An Institutional Response, 258, 264, 273
Finn, Chester E., Jr., 206, 212
Finney, J., 210, 221
The First Treatise of Government, 72
The Fiscal Crisis of the State, 76, 83
Fischer, Stanley, 107, 116, 118
Fisher, Peter S., 256, 259, 267
Fletcher, John, 286
Foley, Bernard, 261, 262
Foreign Economic Trends and Their Implications for the United States, 295
The Forgotten Half: Non-College Youth in America: An Interim Report on the School-to-Work Transition, 209, 210, 220
Fortune, 37, 291
Foundation for National Progress, 300
"Four by Four: How Can Businesses Fight Workplace Illiteracy?" 210, 219
Fray, Elizabeth A., 255, 270
Free to Choose: A Personal Statement, 33, 40, 72, 73, 81, 109, 116, 118, 163, 174
Free Trade and Protection: The U.S.–Canada Case, 165, 179
The Free Trade Debate: Background Paper, 166, 180
"Free Trade Is the Best Policy," 165, 180
Freeman, Richard B., 160
Freeman, Roger A., 36, 40, 109, 112, 118, 261, 267
Frey, Donald N., 207, 218
Friedman, Benjamin, 98, 110, 114, 115, 120
Friedman, Milton, 33, 40, 45, 46, 49, 51, 72, 73, 81, 88, 107, 109, 116, 118, 163, 174, 207, 212, 260, 267
Friedman, Rose, 40, 72, 81, 109, 116, 118, 163, 174
Fromm, Erich, 75, 79
Fuentes, Annette, 34, 39
Fuller, Stephen S., 254, 262
Fundamentals of Development Finance, 258, 265
Fusfeld, Daniel R., 33, 34, 40, 255, 262
The Future of National Urban Policy, 269
The Future of Silicon Valley: Does the U.S. Need a High-Tech Industrial Policy to Battle Japan, Inc? 163, 166

Gaff, Jerry G., 222
Gainer, Leila J., 187, 206, 209, 214
Galbraith, James, 113, 115, 120

Author-Title Index 309

Galbraith, John Kenneth, 71, 76
Gallo, Frank, 206, 210, 219
Gappert, Gary, 254, 257, 260, 262, 263, 269
Gaventa, John, 253, 254, 262
"General Education at Decade's End," 222
The General Theory of Employment, Interest and Money, 73, 78, 117
The Geography of the World Economy, 34, 39
"The German Ideology," 74, 79
Gilder, George, 72, 73, 81
Giloth, Robert P., 254, 259, 267
Gilpin, Robert, 16, 34, 38, 110, 115, 116, 159, 177, 276, 279
Giroux, Henry A., 191, 192, 207, 209, 210, 214, 221
"The Giveaway Game Continues," 256, 257, 260, 268
Glass, Gene V., 209, 218
Glazer, Nathan, 206, 212
Glickman, Norman J., 149, 159, 160, 164, 178, 238, 256, 259, 260, 261, 267
Global Competitiveness: Getting the U.S. Back on Track, 169
Global Restructuring and Territorial Development, 254, 262
Global Shift: Industrial Change in a Turbulent World, 34, 39
Global Stakes: The Future of High Technology in America, 211, 222
Global Trade Executive, 259, 262
Goldman, Louis, 212
Goldstein, Harvey A., 158, 161, 171, 172, 254, 258, 259, 260, 261, 267, 268, 270, 271
"Good News: Foreign Investment Is Not Bad," 109, 119
Goodman, Robert, 173, 260, 268
Gordon, David, 71, 74, 84, 115, 122, 137, 140, 159, 160, 161, 163, 173, 261, 266
Gordon, Suzanne, 163, 176
Gorham, Lucy, 161, 172
Governing: The States and Localities, 256, 259, 268, 273, 291
Grady, Dennis O., 268
The Great Transformation: The Political and Economic Origins of Our Times, 34, 38
The Great U-Turn: Corporate Restructuring and the Polarizing of America, 40, 75, 82, 111, 114, 115, 122, 157, 160, 164, 172
Green, Roy E., 255, 256, 265, 268

Greenstein, Robert, 110, 111, 114, 121
Growing the Next Silicon Valley: A Guide for Successful Regional Planning, 258, 265
Guide to Government Resources for Economic Development, 300
Guide to Reference Books, 286
Guide to Reference Materials in Political Science: A Selective Bibliography, 287
Guide to State and Federal Resources for Economic Development, 300
Gulak, Morton, 258, 265
Gunn, Christopher, 71, 80, 83
Guskind, Robert, 256, 257, 260, 268

Halsey, A. H., 32, 215
Hansen, Alvin, 56, 74, 82, 109
Hansen, Susan B., 255, 259, 261, 268
Harmon, Robert B., 288
Harrison, Bennett, 34, 35, 37, 40, 41, 75, 82, 109, 111, 114, 115, 122, 138, 140, 149, 156, 157, 159, 160, 161, 164, 172, 175, 178, 259
Harvard Business Review, 157, 170, 291
Harvard Educational Review, 206, 208, 209, 210, 212, 216, 218, 221, 292
Hayek, Friedrich, 45, 46, 72, 81, 174
Hazardous to Our Wealth: Economic Policies in the 1980s, 115, 121, 160, 164, 172, 178
Heckman, Paul E., 209, 218
Hegel, G. F. W., 52, 58, 77
Heilbroner, Robert, 71, 84
Heilbrun, James, 34, 41
Henderson, Jeffrey, 254, 262
Herbers, John, 259, 268
Heritage Foundation, 298
"The Hidden Agenda of the Report on Excellence," 212
Higher Education in Partnership with Industry, 211, 222
"The Higher Education–Economic Development Connection: Emerging Roles for Colleges and Universities," 210, 222, 258, 266
The High-Flex Society: Shaping America's Economic Future, 155, 157, 170, 178
Hill, Edward W., 258, 259, 264, 273
Hirsch, E. D., 202, 210, 221, 222
Hissong, Rodney V., 255, 262
History of Economic Theory: Scope, Method and Content, 71, 75, 84
History of Political Philosophy, 78
Hobbes, Thomas, 73, 77

Holland, Shari L., 209, 214
Holler, Frederick L., 286
Hoover Institute on War, Revolution and Peace, 298
Hoover Institution Annual Report, 299
"How Could Anyone Disagree?" 206, 212
Howe, Harold, II, 195, 209, 218
Howland, Marie, 257, 269
Hudson Institute, Herman Kahn Center, 299
Hudson Institute Briefing, 299
Hudson Institute Opinion, 299
Hudson Institute Report, 299
Hufbauer, Gary C., 166, 180
Human Resource Management: Trends and Challenges, 37, 41, 157, 171
Hurn, Christopher J., 195, 209, 218
Hutchinson, William Kenneth, 287

"The Impact of Postsecondary Admissions Policies on Secondary Education," 206, 213
Imperialism: The Highest Stage of Capitalism, 165, 179
"Increasing Exports through World Trade Centers," 259, 273
Index of Economic Articles in Journals and Collective Volumes, 289
Index to International Statistics (IIS), 289
Index to U. S. Government Periodicals, 294
"Industrial Policy and Democratic Institutions," 261, 267
The Industrial Policy Debate, 156, 163, 167
"Industrial Policy: A Dissent," 161, 162, 163, 175
Industrial Policy: Business and Politics in the United States and France, 174
"Industrial Restructuring and Regional Politics," 254, 270
Information Sources in Economics, 286
Information Sources in Politics and Political Science: A Survey Worldwide, 286
Information Sources of Political Science, 286
"Infrastructure Support for Industrial Policy," 259, 271
Innovating to Compete: Lessons for Diffusing and Managing Change in the Workplace, 159, 172
Inside the Circle: A Union Guide to QWL, 37, 41, 171
Institute for Policy Studies, 300

International Bibliography of Economics, 288
"International Cooperation—A Way Out?" 115, 122, 165, 179
International Economic Cooperation, 116, 118
"International Macroeconomic Policy Coordination," 116, 118
International Political Science Abstracts, 289
"International Trade: Cities Make Their Move: A Survey of Local Government Activities in International Trade," 259, 271
"The Internationalization of the Washington, D.C., Area Economy," 254, 262
An Introduction to Marxist Economic Theory, 75, 76, 79, 83, 114, 122
An Introduction to the Principles of Morals and Legislation, 72, 78
Invisible Factors in Local Economic Development, 157, 170, 258, 266
The Invisible Work Force: Transforming American Business with Outside and Home-Based Workers, 37, 41, 208, 215
"Is There a Case for Choice?" 209, 213
Islam, Sadequl, 165, 179
Issues and Developments in International Trade Policy, 32, 39, 155, 156, 164, 177

Jacobs, James, 206, 209, 210, 219
Jacobs, Jane, 257, 260, 269
James, Franklin, 269
Japan's Public Policies for Investment, 162, 176
Jean, Priscilla, 208, 216
The Job Generation Process, 258, 265
Johnson, Chalmers, 127, 156, 163, 167
Johnson, Nancy L., 175
Johnston, William B., 186, 206, 207, 213, 216
Jones, Russel C., 211, 222
Journal of Economic Growth, 299
Journal of Economic History, 292
Journal of Economic Literature, 289
Journal of Economics and Business, 292
Journal of Political Economy, 260, 273, 292
Journal of Public Economics, 292
Journal of the American Planning Association, 257, 269, 292
Journal of Urban Affairs: The Journal of the Urban Affairs Association, 256, 259, 273, 292

Journal of Urban Economics, 292
Judd, Dennis R., 261, 262
Jurmo, Paul, 210, 219

Kane, Matt, 206, 219, 257
Kant, Immanuel, 52, 58, 77
Kaplan, Justin D., 73
Kaplan, Marshall, 269
Karabel, Jerome, 32, 215
Kasarda, John D., 256, 263
Katz, Bill, 290
Katz, Harry, 157, 170
Katz, Linda Sternberg, 290
Kelly, Douglas P., 255, 270
Kelly, Margaret, 31, 39, 155, 156, 164, 177
Keynes, John Maynard, 51, 52, 53, 73, 78, 84, 107, 109, 117
Kimberly, John R., 157, 171, 206, 214
"The Kind of Schools We Need," 209, 217
Kirmani, Naheed, 31, 39, 155, 177
Kirst, Michael, 206, 213
Klein, Katherine J., 161, 174
Kline, John M., 255, 258, 260
Knight, Richard V., 248, 254, 257, 260, 262, 263, 269
Knox, Paul, 34, 39
Kochan, Thomas A., 157, 161, 170, 171
Kolko, Joyce, 115, 122, 165, 179
Krueger, Anne O., 151, 152, 165, 180, 181
Krugman, Paul R., 109, 110, 111, 112, 117, 147, 164, 165, 177, 279
Kuhn, Thomas, 71, 83
Kuttner, Robert, 110, 113, 120, 148, 152, 158, 164, 165, 178

Labor and Monopoly Capital: The Degradation of Work in the Twentieth Century, 75, 82, 159, 174, 207, 215
Labor, U.S. Department of, 32, 42, 187
Labor, U.S. Department of, Bureau of Labor Statistics, 296
Laboratories of Democracy, 114, 121, 210, 211, 222, 254, 255, 258, 259, 261, 271
Ladd, Helen F., 256, 261, 263
Laffer, Arthur, 109
Land, Phil S. J., 111, 120
"The Land-Grant Model," 211, 222
Landreth, Harry, 71, 75, 84
The Last Entrepreneurs: America's Regional Wars for Jobs and Dollars, 173, 260, 268

Lavoie, Don, 46, 72, 81, 163, 174–75
Lawler, Edward, 157, 170
Lawrence, Paul R., 37, 41, 157, 171
Lawrence, Robert Z., 158, 162, 163, 166, 175, 179, 180, 181
Learning to Labor: How Working Class Kids Get Working Class Jobs, 208, 216
Ledebur, Larry C., 257, 269
Lee, Chung H., 162, 176
Lenin, V. I., 67, 165, 179
Lester, Richard, 156, 170
Leviathan, 73, 77
Levin, Henry, 192, 205, 207, 215
Levine, M., 207, 213
Levine, Mark V., 257, 269
Levitan, Sar A., 171, 206, 210, 219
Levy, Frank, 15, 33, 34, 36, 37, 41
Levy, John M., 233, 234, 256, 257, 264
Lewis, Courtland S., 211, 222
Library of Congress Subject Headings (LCSH), 282, 283, 284
"The Limits of Strategic Planning for Cities," 259, 273
Linger, J. K., 155, 157, 170, 178
The Literature of Political Science: A Guide for Students, Librarians, and Teachers, 286
"Local Government in the International Arena: The Federal System in a Global Economy," 258, 260, 261, 270
Locke, John, 45, 46, 51, 52, 71, 72, 77
Lodge, George C., 132, 134, 157, 158, 159, 163, 164, 167
Losing Ground, 112, 119, 261, 270
Lozano, Beverly, 37, 41, 208, 215
Luke, Jeffrey S., 255, 259, 265
Luria, Daniel, 158, 159, 163, 164, 167
Lynch, John E., 164, 176
Lynton, Ernest, 211, 222

Made in America: Regaining the Productive Edge, 156, 157, 159, 161, 163, 170, 207, 209, 210, 211, 217
Maffin, Robert W., 258, 260, 261, 270
Magaziner, Ira C., 35, 39, 132, 135, 157, 158, 159, 162, 163, 167, 168
Magazines for Libraries, 290
Magdoff, Harry, 67, 94, 100, 102, 110, 114, 115, 116, 122, 135, 150, 157, 159, 165, 173, 179
Malthus, Thomas, 80
Managed Trade and Economic Sovereignty, 158, 164, 165, 178
"Managed Trade: Making the Best of Second Best," 158, 179

Management Policies in Local Government Finance, 74, 82, 112, 209, 217, 255
Managing Economic Development: A Guide to State and Local Leadership Strategies, 255, 258, 259, 265
Managing the American Economy from Roosevelt to Reagan, 117
Mandel, Ernest, 67, 75, 76, 79, 83, 114, 122
Mansfield, Edwin, 36, 38, 110, 117
Mao, 67
Markusen, Ann Roell, 270
Marshall, Alfred, 45, 51, 79, 84
Martin, Lynn, 175
Marx, Karl, 57, 58, 59, 62, 67, 74, 75, 77, 78, 79, 80, 82, 84, 174, 179
The Marx-Engels Reader, 74, 75, 79
Marxism and the Metropolis: New Perspectives in Urban Political Economy, 256
Marx's Concept of Man, 75, 79
"The Mass Market Is Splitting Apart," 37
Matthews, Dewayne A., 209, 218
McCartan, Anne-Marie, 219
McFadden, Dave, 163, 176
McIntyre, Robert S., 255, 270
McKenzie, Richard B., 37, 41, 73, 81, 143, 161, 162, 163, 175, 207, 214, 256, 270
Mead, Walter Russell, 115, 121, 149, 165, 178
"Measuring Capital Subsidy Costs and Job Creation: The Case of Rural UDAG Grants," 257, 269
Medoff, James L., 160
Meltzer, Ann S., 187, 206, 214
Mendelsohn, M. Stefan, 107, 108, 119, 116
Meurs, Mike, 76
Mickelson, Roslyn Arlin, 194, 208, 215
Mier, Robert, 254, 259, 267, 270
Mill, John Sturt, 51, 52, 53, 74, 77, 79, 80, 84
Miller, Kathleen D., 186, 187, 206, 214
Miller, Marcine L., 260, 270
Miller, Roger, 258, 265
Minding America's Business: The Decline and Rise of the American Economy, 157, 158, 159, 167, 168
Mingle, J., 210, 221
"Minimum Wage: A Global-Local Link," 111, 120
Minsky, Hyman, 96, 104, 113, 115, 120
The Missing Connection between Business and the Universities, 211, 222

MIT Commission on Industrial Productivity, 156, 170
Moe, Kari J., 259, 270
Moe, Terry M., 189, 190, 196, 206, 207, 211, 212, 218
Mohrman, Susan, 157, 170
"Monetary Policy: Tactics versus Strategy," 116, 118
The Money Mandarins: The Making of a Supranational Economic Order, 31, 32, 34, 35, 38, 115, 116, 119, 121
Monopoly Capital: An Essay on the American Economic and Social Order, 75, 76, 82
Monthly Catalog of United States Government Publications, 282, 293
Monthly Labor Review, 32, 42, 296
Monthly Review: An Independent Socialist Magazine, 114, 115, 122, 123, 165, 179, 207, 216, 292
Moore, T. W., 205
A More Productive Workforce: Challenge for Post-Secondary Education and Its Partners, 220
Morrison, Edward F., 258, 270
Mother Jones, 301
Mower, Nancy, 157, 170
"Multinationals Attracted to New Jersey's FTZ," 259, 262
Murray, Charles, 112, 119, 261, 270

"Naïveté and Snobbery," 209, 218
A Nation at Risk: The Imperative for Educational Reform, 185, 186, 188, 189, 190, 206, 209, 212, 213, 215, 217, 218, 221, 296
The Nation Responds: Recent Efforts to Improve Education, 206, 221
National Association of State Development Agencies (NASDA), 256, 258, 270
National Chamber Foundation, 299
National Commission on Excellence in Education, 206, 213, 296
"The National Consequences of Decentralized Industrial Policy in the United States," 256, 259, 267
National Economic Planning: What Is Left? 72, 81, 163, 174
National Governors' Association, 220
National Industrial Policy: Solution or Illusion, 175
National League of Cities, 259, 271
The National Newspaper Index, 285
The New Class War: Reagan's Attack on the Welfare State and Its Consequences, 114, 122

The New Competitors: How Foreign Investors Are Changing the U.S. Economy, 159, 160, 164, 178, 256–61, 267
The New Industrial State, 76
"The New Look in Tax and Fiscal Policy," 74
The New Republic, 35, 40, 292
"A New RFC Is Proposed for Business," 158, 168
"A New Stage of Capitalism Ahead?" 114, 115, 123
"New Trends in the Sociospatial Organization of the New York City Economy," 254, 264
New York Times, 158, 168, 208, 216
New York Times Index, 285
News and Views, 259, 272
Newsbank, 285
The Next American Frontier, 157, 158, 159, 168, 171, 207, 209, 217
"The Next American Work Force: Demographics and the U.S. Economy," 217
Niskanen, William A., 73, 81, 119, 152, 153, 155, 166, 181
"No Easy Answers to the Complex Question of Choice: Response to Raywid," 209, 217
Northeast-Midwest Institute, 214, 300
"Not According to Plan: The Collapse of the Soviet Planned Economy," 76
Nove, Alec, 76, 83
Nozick, Robert, 72, 77

Oberst, Bethany S., 211, 222
O'Connell, Francis A., Jr., 160, 163, 175
O'Connor, James, 76, 83
Oden, Michael, 123, 163, 176
The Official Washington Post Index, 285
Okun, Arthur M., 54, 74
Omega, 35, 40, 165, 178, 292
On Democracy: Toward a Transformation of American Society, 32, 33, 34, 35, 40, 82
"On Liberty," 79
Organization Life Cycles, 157, 171, 206, 214
Osborn, Maria, 258, 271
Osborne, David, 114, 121, 210, 211, 222, 250, 254, 255, 258, 259, 261, 271
Osterman, Paul, 197, 198, 210, 219
O'Toole, James, 210, 220

Packer, Arnold, 210, 219
PAIS International in Print, 290
Parker, Mike, 37, 41, 171
Parkinson, Michael, 261, 262
Participation and Democratic Theory, 74, 77
Pateman, Carole, 74, 77
Patinkin, Mark, 35, 39, 162, 163, 167
Paying for Productivity: A Look at the Evidence, 156, 169
"The Peace Economy: How Defense Cuts Will Fuel America's Long-Term Prosperity," 110, 123
Perelman, Lewis J., 112, 207, 213
Perestroika for America: Restructuring Business-Government Relations for World Competitiveness, 157, 158, 159, 163, 164, 167
Perlo Cohen, Manuel, 254, 262
Peters, Alan, 257, 271
Peterson, George E., 259, 271
Petri, Thomas E., 175
Phillips, Kevin, 26, 36, 37, 41, 109, 110, 111, 113, 114, 117, 253, 263
Philosophy and Political-Economy, 76
Philosophy of Education: An Introduction, 205
The Philosophy of Hegel, 77
"The Philosophy of History," 77
"Philosophy of Right and Law," 77
Piore, Michael, 161, 171
"Pittsburgh in Transition: Consolidation of Prosperity in an Era of Economic Restructuring," 254, 261
Piven, Frances Fox, 114, 122
Planning Local Economic Development: Theory and Practice, 261, 264
Plant Closings: Worker Rights, Management Rights and the Law, 160, 163, 175
Polanyi, Karl, 34, 38
Policy Options for Freer Trade: The Case for Bilateralism, 166, 180
Policy and Research Report, 300
Policy Studies Journal, 301
Policy Studies Organization, 301
Policy Studies Review, 301
The Political Economy of International Relations, 34, 38, 110, 115, 116, 159, 177, 279
Political Science: A Guide to Reference and Information Sources, 287
Political Science Bibliographies, 288
"The Politics of Economic Development Policy," 257, 271

Author-Title Index

Politics, Markets and America's Schools, 189, 196, 207, 209, 211, 212, 218
Politics of Education Association Yearbook, 208, 215
The Politics of International Economic Relations, 117, 177
The Politics of Rich and Poor: Wealth and the American Electorate in the Reagan Aftermath, 26, 36, 37, 41, 109, 110, 111, 113, 114, 117, 253, 263
Positive Alternatives, 176, 260
"The Possibilities of Employment Policy," 210, 219
"Post-Keynesian and Neo-Ricardian Political Economy," 80
Potter, George Ann, 32
Power and Ideology in Education, 32, 215
Powers, D., 210, 222
Powers, M., 210, 222
Principles of Economics, 79
The Principles of Political Economy and Taxation, 31, 38, 80
Principles of Political Economy with Some of Their Applications to Social Philosophy, 51, 79
Privatization Watch, 299
"Privatization: Better Services at Less Cost," 274
"The Problem with Comparisons," 209, 218
Problems in Political Economy: An Urban Perspective, 71, 74, 84
Production of Commodities by Means of Commodities: Prelude to a Critique of Economic Theory, 80
"Productivity in the Factory and Industrial Policy," 158, 159, 171, 258, 272
Productivity Policy: Key to the Nation's Economic Future, 170
Productivity: Problems, Prospects, and Policies, 171
Professionals' Coalition for Nuclear Arms Control, 159
A Progressive Answer to the Fiscal Deficit, 113, 114, 119
The Progressive City: Planning and Participation, 1969-1984, 254, 266
"A Proposal for International Monetary Reform," 115, 121
Protectionism, 155, 165, 166, 177
Public Administration in American Society: A Guide to Information Sources, 287

Public Administration Series: Bibliography, 288
Public Infrastructure Planning and Management, 113, 123
Public Innovation Abroad, 299
Public Management, 260, 270
Public Opinion, 298
"Public Support for Private Education," 212
"A Pure Theory of Local Expenditures," 260, 273

"Quality Circles after the Fad," 157, 170
Quarterly Review of Economics and Business, 293

Radical America Journal, 300
Ravitch, D., 212
Rawls, John, 73, 74, 77
Ray, Carol Axtell, 194, 208, 215
Raywid, Mary Anne, 209, 213
Reaganomics: An Insider's Account of the Policies and the People, 73, 81, 119
Real World Micro, 76
Reason Foundation, 299
Rebuilding America: A Blueprint for the New Economy, 159, 172, 261, 265
Recent Publications on Governmental Problems, 288
Reed, B. J., 255, 258, 259, 265
Reed, C. M., 255, 258, 259, 265
"Reflections on the Current State of Macroeconomic Theory," 117
Regenerating the Cities: The UK Crisis and the US Experience, 261, 262
Regulation: AEI Journal on Government and Society, 298
Reich, Robert B., 35, 40, 130, 132, 135, 157, 158, 159, 163, 167, 168, 171, 207, 209, 217
The Reindustrialization of America, 157, 166, 168
Reischauer, Robert D., 112, 114, 117, 260, 261, 271
Remaking the Welfare State: Retrenchment and Social Policy in America and Europe, 36, 40, 109, 120
"Remarks on Equity and Excellence in Education," 209, 218
Report of the Task Force on International Education, 1989, 221
"Representative Government," 74, 79
Research Centers Directory, 297

Restructuring the World Economy, 115, 122, 165, 179
Results in Education, 220
"Rethinking the American Training System," 210, 219
Retraining the American Workforce, 206, 214
"The Return of the Big Firms," 37, 41, 165, 178, 258, 259, 268
"A Revolution in Work Rules: New Job Flexibility Boosts Productivity," 37, 41, 171
Ricardo, David, 3, 31, 38, 45, 51, 58, 79, 80, 84, 146, 147, 150, 165, 180
Richards, Judith W., 258, 265
Richmond Times Dispatch, 110, 111, 258, 271
The Rise of the Entrepreneurial State: State and Local Economic Development Policy in the United States, 259, 267
The Road to Serfdom, 72, 81
Roberts, Paul Craig, 73, 81, 109, 119
Robertson, David Brian, 261, 262
Rodberg, Leonard S., 159, 160, 173
Roediger, Dave, 207, 210, 216
Rogers, Joel, 5, 32, 33, 34, 35, 40, 82
Rohatyn, Felix, 132, 158, 168
"The Role of Government in Education," 207, 212
Rosen, Corey M., 161, 174
Rosenfeld, Stuart A., 253, 259, 263, 271
Ross, Doug, 259, 271
Rothschild, Joyce, 161, 174
Rouse, John E., Jr., 287
Rousseau, Jean Jacques, 52, 58, 74, 77, 78
Rubin, Barry M., 256, 273
Rubin, Herbert J., 257, 271
Rubin, Sarah, 253, 263

Sabel, Charles F., 35, 40, 157, 171, 207, 258, 272
Samuelson, Paul A., 57, 74, 109
Sanderson, Susan Walsh, 157, 163, 168
Sassen, Saskia, 254, 264
"Saving the Inner City," 112, 118, 207, 211, 256, 261, 265
Sawers, Larry, 256, 264, 273
Schauffler, Richard, 76
Schmenner, Roger W., 158, 159, 171, 258, 272
Scholars, Dollars and Bureaucrats, 212
Schooling and Work in the Democratic State, 205, 207, 215

"Schooling, Culture, and Literacy in the Age of Broken Dreams: A Review of Bloom and Hirsch," 210, 221
Schultze, Charles L., 141, 143, 144, 158, 161, 162, 163, 166, 175, 179, 180, 181
Schumpeter, Joseph A., 45, 72, 141, 162, 176
Schwartz, Anna J., 116, 118
Schwartz, Eli, 74, 112, 209, 217, 255
Schweke, William, 259, 272
Scull, Roberta A., 286
The Search for Stable Money, 116, 118
A Second Chance: Training for Jobs, 206, 210, 219
The Second Treatise of Government, 72
"The Second War Between the States: A Bitter Struggle for Jobs, Capital and People," 232, 272
Selective Prosperity: Increasing Income Disparities Since 1977, 110, 111, 114, 121
The Selling of the South: The Southern Crusade for Industrial Development, 1936–1980, 254, 257, 262
Seminar: Macroeconomic Policy, 111, 112, 113, 120
Service Sector Wages, Productivity and Job Creation in the U.S. and Other Countries, 156, 163, 169
Shapiro, Isaac, 110, 111, 114, 121
Sharp, Elaine B., 257, 272
Shearer, Derek, 160, 173
Sheehy, Eugene P., 286
Sherr, Irene, 259, 270
"Shoot Anything That Flies; Claim Anything That Falls: Conversations with Economic Development Practitioners," 257, 272
Shull, Steven A., 163, 176
The Silent War: Inside the Global Business Battles Shaping America's Future, 35, 39, 162, 163, 167
Simmons, John, 210, 220
Skurski, Roger, 172
"Small Business, A Strategic Perspective," 258, 270
Smith, Adam, 3, 31, 38, 45, 46, 47, 51, 58, 61, 62, 71, 72, 73, 75, 79, 80, 84, 192
Smith, Barbara Ellen, 253, 262
"So We Can Use Our Own Names, and Write the Laws by Which We Live: Educating the New U.S. Labor Force," 208, 216
The Social Contract, 74, 77, 78

Social Policy, 37, 41, 159, 165, 173, 178, 207, 210, 216, 219, 258, 268, 293
Social Problems, 208, 216
Social Sciences Citation Index (SSCI), 290
Social Sciences Index, 290
"Socialism: Utopian and Scientific," 74, 79
Solow, Robert, 156, 170
Sources of Information in the Social Sciences: A Guide to the Literature, 287
"Spatial Change and Social Justice: Alternative Economic Development in Chicago," 254, 259, 267
"The Spatial Division of Labor: Labor and the Location of Industries," 273
Spero, Joan Edelman, 117, 177
Spulber, Nicholas, 117
Squires, Gregory D., 255, 256, 257, 260, 261, 272
Sraffa, Piero, 80
Stagnation and the Financial Explosion, 110, 114, 115, 116, 122, 129, 157, 159, 173
Starr, Martin K., 169
Stata, Ray, 204, 211, 222
State and Local Government Review, 268, 293
The State and Local Industrial Policy Question, 158, 161, 171, 172, 254, 258–61, 267, 270, 271
The State and the Macro-Industrial Economy—Towards a Coherent Multi-National Policy, 165, 178
State Business Incentives and Economic Growth: Are They Effective? 256, 258, 259, 274
"State Economic Development Incentives: Why Do States Compete?" 268
State Export Program Database, 256, 258, 270, 274
State, U.S. Department of, Bureau of Economic and Business Affairs, 297
The States and Business Incentives: An Inventory of Tax and Financial Incentive Programs, 256, 266
"The States and International Affairs," 255, 258, 260, 269
Statistical Abstract of the United States, 294
Statistical Masterfile, 294
Statistical Reference Index (SRI), 290
Staudohar, Paul D., 173
Stein, Jay M., 113, 123

Steinberg, Bruce, 37
Storm Clouds on the Horizon, 161, 172
Storper, Michael, 271
"Strategic Planning and the Pursuit of Reform, Economic Development, and Equity," 259, 270
Strategic Trade Policy and the New International Economics, 164, 165, 177
Strauss, Leo, 78
The Structure of Scientific Revolutions, 71, 83
Subject Guide to Books in Print, 285
Sullivan, Arthur M., 257, 265
Summers, Lawrence, 95, 97, 111, 112, 113, 115, 120
Sunbelt/Snowbelt: Urban Development and Regional Restructuring, 264, 273
Supply-Side Economics in the 1980s: Conference Proceedings, 118
The Supply-Side Revolution: An Insider's Account of Policymaking in Washington, 73, 81, 109, 119
"Surplus of College Graduates Dims Job Outlook for Others," 208, 216
Survey of Current Business, 32, 36, 42, 295
"Survey of States on FDI Efforts," 271
Swanstrom, Todd, 259, 273
Sweezy, Paul M., 67, 75, 76, 82, 98, 100, 102, 110, 114, 115, 116, 122, 135, 150, 157, 159, 165, 173, 179

Tabb, William K., 159, 160, 173, 256, 264, 273
Taebel, Delbert A., 255, 262
Tajika, Eiji, 162, 176
Taking Charge of Manufacturing: How Companies Are Combining Technological and Organizational Innovations to Compete Successfully, 158, 170
Tales of a New America, 168
"Target Report: The National PTA Speaks Out on Private School Vouchers," 209, 218
"Targeted Redevelopment through Urban Enterprise Zones," 256, 273
Task Force on Community-Based Development, 259, 273
Technology Review, 206, 219, 293
Terkla, David, 157, 170, 258, 267
A Theory of Justice, 73, 74, 77
The Theory of Moral Sentiments, 71
"A Third Wave of Economic Development," 259, 268

Author-Title Index

Thurow, Lester C., 54, 74, 82, 113, 115, 121, 127, 132, 133, 156, 157, 158, 159, 162, 163, 169, 209, 210, 217
Tiebout, Charles, 260, 273
Time for Results: The Governors' 1991 Report on Education, 220
Tobin, James, 105, 106, 115, 121
Tools and Targets: The Mechanics of City Economic Development, 259, 266, 274
Topakian, Gregory, 157, 170, 258, 267
Toward a High-Wage, High-Productivity Service Sector, 169
Trachtman, R., 207, 213
Training and Development Journal, 210, 219, 293
Training Partnerships: Linking Employers and Providers, 209, 210, 214
"Training the Workforce of the Future," 206, 209, 210, 219
The Transnational Economy: Transnational Corporations and Global Markets, 35, 39, 76, 82
Transportation, U.S. Department of, 34
The Truth about Supply-Side Economics, 73, 81, 118
Tucker, Robert C., 74, 75
Twentieth Century Fund, 299
The Twenty Year Century: Essays on Economic and Public Finance, 168
Two Treatises of Government, 45, 72, 77
Tye, Barbara Benham, 209, 218
Tye, Kenneth A., 209, 218
Tyson, Laura D'Andrea, 148, 158, 164, 179, 181

Uchitelle, Louis, 208, 216
Understanding Capitalism: Competition, Command, and Change in the U.S. Economy, 32, 33, 38, 75, 76, 82, 115, 122
Unequal Partnerships: The Political Economy of Urban Redevelopment in Postwar America, 255, 256, 257, 260, 261, 272
Union Government and Organization in the United States, 33, 41
"The United States and the World Economy," 121
United States Department of Education, 206, 221
United States Political Science Documents (USPSD), 290
University Research in Business and Economics, a Bibliography of Publications, 288
Urban and Regional Economics, 256, 264
Urban Economics, 257, 265
Urban Economics and Public Policy, 34, 41
"Urban Industrial Transition and the Underclass," 256, 263
Urban Institute, 300
"Urban Poverty Outlasts 'Cures'," 111
"Urban Redevelopment in a Global Economy: The Cases of Montreal and Baltimore," 257, 269
"Urban Revitalization in the United States: Prisoner of the Federal System," 261, 262
U.S. Census Bureau, 37
U.S. Council of Economic Advisors, 32, 34, 42
"U.S. Trade Policy: Problems and Prospects," 155, 166, 181
Utilitarianism, On Liberty and Considerations on Representative Government, 74, 79
Utterback, J., 35, 40

Ventriss, Curtis, 255, 258, 259, 265
Villet, Janice, 209, 214
Virginia Review, 258, 265
VuText, 285

Wachtel, Howard M., 31, 32, 34, 35, 38, 39, 105, 115, 121
Walberg, Hebert J., 206, 213
Waldstein, Louise, 156, 163, 169
Walker, Richard, 273
Wall Street Journal, 168
Waller, William, 71, 80, 83
Wallihan, James, 33, 41
Walter, Susan, 113, 123
Walton, Richard E., 37, 41, 157, 159, 171, 172, 206, 214
Wanniski, Jude, 35, 41, 109, 119
The Way the World Works, 35, 41, 109, 119
Ways and Means, 299
The Wayward Welfare State, 36, 40, 109, 112, 118, 261, 267
"We Can Raise Standards," 206, 213
Wealth and Poverty, 72, 73, 81
The Wealth of Nations, 31, 38, 45, 71, 72, 73, 75, 80, 84
Webb, William H., 287
Weiss, Julian, 256, 273

Weisskopf, Thomas E., 115, 122, 137, 140, 159, 160, 161, 163, 173, 261, 266
Welfare Policy for the 1990s, 112, 117, 260, 271
"The Welfare Reform Legislation: Directions for the Future," 112, 114, 117, 260, 261, 271
Werneke, Diane, 171
"What Can We Learn from the Industrial Policy Debate?" 159, 160, 173
What Do Unions Do? 160
What Is Economics? 38
White, Sammis B., 258, 259, 264, 273
Whitford, Vernon, 169
Whitt, J. Allen, 161, 174
Who Governs? Democracy and Power in an American City, 255
"Who Pays for Peace? Many Companies and Towns Are on a Knife's Edge," 177
Who Really Rules New Haven? 256
Wiggenhorn, Bill, 210, 219
Wilder, Margaret G., 256, 273
William T. Grant Foundation Commission on Work, Family, and Citizenship, 209, 210, 220
Willingham, Alex, 252, 253, 262
Willis, Paul, 208, 216
Wilson, Roger, 256, 259, 274
Winglee, Peter, 31, 39, 155, 177
Witte, John, 157, 172
Women in the Global Factory, 34, 39
Women, Infants, and Children Newsletter, 300
Women Organizing, 300
Woodward, Douglas P., 149, 159, 160, 164, 178, 238, 256–61, 267, 269
Work and Politics, 35, 40, 157, 171, 207, 258, 272
Worker Participation and American Unions: Threat or Opportunity? 157, 170

Workforce Policies for the 1990s, 210, 219
Workforce 2000: Work and Workers in the 21st Century, 186, 193, 195, 206, 207, 213, 216
Workplace Basics: The Skills Employers Want, 206, 214
"Workplace Literacy: Corporate Tool or Worker Empowerment?" 207, 208, 216
World Bibliography of Bibliographies, 286
World Development Report, 297
World Index of Economic Forecasts, Including Industrial Tendency Surveys and Development Plans, 297
World Policy Journal, 115, 121, 165, 178, 293
The Worldly Philosophers, 71, 84
Wynar, Lubomyr Roman, 287

Xafa, Miranda, 31, 39, 155, 177

Yamazawa, Ippei, 162, 176
Yardeni, Edward, 120
Yearbook of International Communist Affairs, 299
Yinger, John, 256, 261, 263
Yiu, Yuji, 162, 176
York, Henry E., 287
Young, Karen M., 161, 174
Young, Peter, 274

Zeigler, William, 210, 219
The Zero-Sum Society: Distribution and the Possibilities for Economic Change, 74, 82, 113, 115, 121, 156, 157, 158, 159, 162, 163, 169, 209, 210, 217
The Zero-Sum Solution: Building a World-Class American Economy, 74, 82, 113, 115, 121, 156, 157, 158, 159, 162, 163, 169, 209, 210, 217
Zukin, Sharon, 174

Subject Index

aggressive bilateralism, as trade policy, 152–54, 166, 180–81
agricultural extension service, 203, 204, 224; *see also* industrial extension; manufacturing extension service
agricultural production, U.S. self-sufficiency in, 5
agriculture sector
  effects of U.S. tax policy on, 93
  employment in, 14, 15
  mechanization of production in, 14, 33, 229
agriculture, trade and tariffs, 126, 146, 152, 155, 223, 224
Aid to Families with Dependent Children (AFDC), 15, 24, 25, 87, 93, 95, 98, 111, 227
American corporate investment in postwar reconstruction abroad, 17, 20, 34
American job machine, 25
Appalachia, effects of economic restructuring on, 262
Appalachian Regional Commission, 229
Arizona
  economic conversion planning in, 259
  economic development policies of, 271
Arkansas, economic development policies of, 271
Atlanta, business-education partnership in, 190
Austrian School, of political economy, 84
automation, 13, 14, 33, 129, 138, 148, 170, 171, 187

autonomous teams, 187

Babbage, Charles, management principle of, 62, 193
Baltimore, response to economic restructuring, 236, 263
Ben Franklin Partnership, 242
benefit-cost analysis, *see* cost-benefit analysis
Bentsen, Lloyd, U.S. Senator, 114
Berkeley, economic development policies of, 227, 266
board of governors, see Federal Reserve
bond financing, of state and local development, 234, 255
Boskin, Michael, flexible freeze advocacy, 95, 112
Boston
  economic development policies of, 227, 263, 272
  Route 128 high-tech, 241
Boston Compact, business-education partnership, 190, 213
Bradley, Bill, U.S. Senator, 114
Brazil
  agricultural production in, 224
  as U.S. competitor, 1, 19, 20, 125
Bretton Woods Agreement, provisions and workings of, 4, 6, 16, 32, 39, 99
Bretton Woods monetary system
  in contemporary monetary policy debates, 57, 86, 103, 104, 107, 108, 121
  demise of, 20, 21, 23, 35
budget deficit, U.S.
  causes and magnitude of, xvi, 25, 89, 90

efforts to reduce, 91
implications for macroeconomic policy, 93–100, 103, 104, 111, 112, 117, 120, 175, 181, 276, 277
Budget Deficit Reduction Compromise of 1990, 91, 95, 97, 112
Buffalo, effect of U.S.–Canada Free Trade Act on, 224
Burlington, economic development policies of, 227, 266
Bush, President George, 25, 57, 91, 94, 97, 98, 112, 113, 144, 167, 190
business cycle, 6–10, 53, 63, 66, 79, 80, 85, 92, 102, 113, 114
business-education partnership, 190, 192, 203–205, 211, 214, 277
business formation and expansion, as state and local economic development approach, 240–44, 252, 265, 267
business incentives, for economic development, 274
business investment, and economic growth, 7, 9, 36, 85, 86, 88, 90, 94, 95, 98, 128, 151
business investment attraction, as economic development approach, 249
business location and investment subsidies, *see* subsidies, of business investment
business recruitment, as state and local economic development approach, 228–40, 244, 252, 265, 267, 271, 274
business retention, as state and local economic development approach, 227, 230, 238, 239, 252, 265, 269, 274

California
 defense expenditures in, 224
 economic policies of, 227
capital gains
 defined, 112
 tax cut, 87, 94, 98, 112
Carter, President Jimmy, 88, 229
Chase Manhattan Bank, 235
Chicago
 Apparel and Fashion Task Force, 247
 economic policies of, 227, 261, 270
 school system, 189
 Task Force on Steel, 247
China, agricultural production in, 224

choice system, in primary and secondary education, 190, 196, 209, 211–13, 217, 218, 220, 277, 288
Chrysler Motor Company, 138, 144, 194
Cincinnati, business-education partnership in, 190
civic values, in liberal philosophy, 52–54, 56, 59, 68, 69, 73
Civil Aeronautics Board, 10
Civil Rights Movement, 184
class, in Marxist economic theory, 60
clawbacks, as economic development tool, 236, 237, 271
Cleveland, economic policies of, 227, 235, 266, 271
closed-shop union
 defined, 11, 32
 states that allow, 227
Cold War
 stimulative economic effects of, 8
 impact on U.S. economic policy, 32
 end of, and conversion planning, 91, 145, 247, 278
 see also peace dividend; economic conversion
collective action, in liberal philosophy, 48, 49, 53
Colorado, economic conversion planning in, 260
community college, 10, 11, 134, 183, 201, 206, 219
Community Development Block Grant (CDBG), 229
community development corporation (CDC), 230, 245, 264, 273
comparative advantage
 as basis of trade policy, 146, 147, 150, 276, 277
 cited in the literature, 177, 180
 defined, 3
competitive capitalism, 64; *see also* monopoly capitalism
Comprehensive Employment and Training Act of 1973 (CETA), 11, 184
Congress
 industrial development bonds, 255
 industrial policy, 135, 137, 144
 labor legislation, 139, 140
 New Federalism, 231
 role in macroeconomic policy formulation, 9, 37, 42, 86, 87, 89, 91, 95, 97, 99, 101, 102, 112, 119
 trade policy, 32, 155, 181

Congressional Budget Office, 121
Connecticut, economic conversion
 planning in, 260
consumption tax, 120
Continental Illinois Bank, 144
core
 industries, 13, 33, 64; see also
  periphery
 countries, 39; see also periphery
corporate restructuring, 20, 28, 145,
 172, 178, 216; see also global
 restructuring
cost-benefit analysis, 236, 237, 264
creative destruction, 80
crisis of overproduction, 63; see also
 business cycle
culture of poverty, 191, 194

Dade County, school system, 189
Davis-Bacon Act of 1931, 9
declining industries, 247; see also
 mature industries
Deep South, economic conditions, 262
defense expenditures
 and the budget deficit, 89
 and industrial policy, 134, 155, 167,
  168
 as a public good, 47, 55
 and regional employment, 254
 stimulative economic effect of, 5
 versus social spending, 96, 97, 118,
  276
defense reductions
 after the Cold War, 91, 119, 145; see
  also peace dividend; economic
  conversion
 state and local responses, 219, 247,
  259, 269
Defense Advanced Research Projects
 Agency (DARPA), 145
deindustrialization, 140, 141, 161, 172,
 173, 175,
demand-side fiscal policy, see fiscal
 policy, demand side
democratic decision making
 liberal views, 48, 54, 74
 radical views, 69, 83, 173, 226, 273,
  277
Democratic party, 94, 111, 255
depression, in the business cycle, 6, 7,
 53, 63, 99, 100
Depression, the Great, xvi, 6, 7, 52, 53,
 99, 117, 155, 226, 228
deregulation
 under Carter administration, 88, 91,
  99
 conservative calls for, 70, 87

of financial institutions, 88, 91, 99
de-skilling
 defined, 19, 62
 and education and training policy,
  192, 193, 197, 207, 215, 216
 and labor market segmentation, 13
 as management policy, 29, 136, 171,
  174
Detroit
 economic development policies of,
  272
 effect of U.S.-Canada Free Trade
  Agreement on, 224
developing countries, wage rates in, 19
Drexel-Burnham-Lambert, location
 subsidies paid to, 235
Dukakis, Michael, 112
dumping, 125, 147, 148, 153, 155
Dwight D. Eisenhower Mathematics
 and Science Education Act, 220

East Germany, 110
The East Los Angeles Community
 Union, 140
Eastern Europe, 76, 110, 275
economic conversion, from defense to
 civilian production, 145, 176, 247,
 259, 260, 278
economic cooperation, among nations,
 see international economic
 cooperation
economic democracy, 101, 172, 173,
 268; see also democratic decision
 making, radical views
economic development, in states and
 localities, 222, 225, 240, 271
Economic Opportunity Act of 1964, 15,
 245
economic planning, radical views, 67,
 173; see also national economic
 planning
Economic Recovery Tax Act of 1981,
 87, 92, 111, 112
economic warfare, as trade policy, 3, 4
education
 for business needs and economic
  competitiveness, 182, 183, 201
 for democratic citizenship, 30, 182,
  183, 201
 as a socioeconomic leveling tool,
  182–84, 206
employee stock ownership plan
 (ESOP), 161, 169, 174
Employment Act of 1946, 9
England, 2, 6; see also Great Britain;
 United Kingdom

322   Subject Index

enterprise zone, 233, 235, 243, 264, 265, 268, 273
equal opportunity, in education, 30, 183, 195, 201, 204, 218; *see also* education, as socioeconomic leveling tool
eurobond markets, 119
eurocurrencies, 103, 107, 108, 119, 277
eurocurrency banks, 105, 108
eurodollars, 22, 39, 102, 105–7
Europe
  competition with U.S., 18, 20, 125
  education and training in, 199
  industrial policy, 130, 131, 141, 160, 167, 168, 174, 266, 271–72, 276
  managed trade with, 148
  postwar economic reconstruction of, 16, 17, 24, 32, 99, 275
  social democracies of, 115, 122, 125, 173
  as trading bloc, 153–55, 276
  wages, 129
  welfare policy, 36
European Common Market, 126, 153
Evansville, Indiana, enterprise zone, 273
exchange rate, of currencies, 4, 21, 22, 31, 103–8, 118, 127
export promotion, as state and local development approach, 69, 229, 242, 244, 269, 270
export subsidies, as trade policy, 106, 150; *see also* dumping
export trading companies (ETCs), 243, 258, 267
exports
  balance of trade, 5, 13, 17, 28
  effects of macroeconomic policy on, 22, 85, 89, 90, 103, 104, 108
  industrial and trade policy implications, 3, 18, 125, 130, 142, 146, 151, 153, 155, 162, 166, 179
  state and local impacts, 224, 229, 249, 251, 267
externalities, 47, 52, 158

Fair Labor Standards Act of 1938, 9
Federal Aviation Administration, 10
Federal Deposit Insurance Corpration, 10
Federal Reserve Act of 1913, 9
Federal Reserve
  Board of Governors, 9, 22, 25, 86–89, 95, 102, 105, 107, 113, 116, 118, 151, 278
  system, 86, 107

Federal Savings and Loan Insurance Corporation (FSLIC), 91
federalism and federal system, xvii, 30, 231, 247, 248, 250, 270
First World War, 2
fiscal crisis, 27, 83, 84, 116, 225, 235, 239
fiscal policy
  demand-side, 1, 6, 8, 9, 13, 23, 52, 64, 69, 70, 78, 86–88, 109, 277
  global effects of, 103, 115
  rational expectations theory, 111
  supply-side, 51, 55, 57, 68–70, 74, 86–89, 94, 97–100, 109, 111, 118, 119, 233, 249
flexible freeze, 112
Florida, economic conversion planning in, 260
food stamps, 15
forces of production, 75
Ford Motor Company
  global production process, 18
  worker training, 194
foreign competition, 16, 20, 23, 25, 28, 36, 39, 57, 125, 127, 130, 135, 136, 141, 156, 229, 231, 275, 279
foreign investment and investors, xvi, 16, 88, 89, 90, 95, 103, 109, 126, 149, 151, 164, 167, 227, 232, 248, 268, 271
foreign investment attraction, as state and local policy, 269
foreign ownership, of U.S. national debt, 110
foreign trade deficit, *see* trade deficit
foreign trade zone (FTZ), 243, 262
France
  G-5 membership, 105
  industrial and trade policy of, 146
  productivity growth in, 128
  service sector, 169, 174
  Versailles Treaty, 2
  welfare policy of, 120
full employment, 9, 15, 16, 23, 56, 57, 66, 69, 78, 96, 100, 101, 201

G-5 (Group of Five) countries, 105, 108
G-7 (Group of Seven) countries, 108, 277, 279
GATT (General Agreement on Tariffs and Trade), 4, 24, 124–26, 145, 147, 151–54, 165, 177–81, 248, 260, 277
General Foods, 64
General Motors, 19
general obligation bonds, 254

Subject Index 323

Germany
  education and training policy of, 198
  industrial policy of, 128, 133, 141, 162, 197
  international economic cooperation, 104
  postwar economic growth, 17
  service sector, 169
  social democracy, 67, 115
  Versailles Treaty, 2
  wages in, 19
  welfare policy of, 120
G.I. Bill, 10, 205
global monetary institutions, 121
global production, 18, 19, 22–25, 28, 30, 39, 40, 250
global restructuring, xv, xvi, xvii, 18, 20, 27, 30, 92, 135, 179, 223, 225, 233, 247, 252, 261–63; *see also* corporate restructuring
globalization, xv, 18, 39, 57, 223, 224, 231, 242, 247, 248, 263
GNP, *see* gross national product
government regulation
  of business, 9, 127
  of currency markets, 22, 52, 103–6
  views of, 24, 27, 47, 48, 50, 52, 65, 84, 87, 116, 142, 149, 157
Gramm-Rudman deficit reduction bill, 91
Great Britain
  Bretton Woods representative, 276
  economic hegemony, 4
  welfare policy, 36, 120; *see also* England; United Kingdom
Great Depression, *see* Depression, the Great
Greece, postwar aid, 5
gross domestic product, 17
gross national product (GNP), 14, 17, 85, 87, 89, 90, 94, 97, 133

Hartford, economic development policies of, 227, 266
High-Technology Morrill Act, 222
high-value products, and production, 129–31, 208, 217
historical materialism, 58, 65, 75
Hodges, Luther, 228
Hoffman Estates, Illinois, business location subsidy, 240
Hong Kong
  as U.S. competitor, 1, 20, 125
  wages in, 19
Horace Mann Common School, 183
Houston
  corporate investment in, 157, 264

  economic policies of, 272
human capital, 10, 182, 215

Illinois, business location subsidy, 240
imports, U.S.
  balance of trade, xvi, 13
  effect of macroeconomic policy on, 22, 85, 96, 103, 104
  effects on state and local economies, 224
  industrial and trade policy implications, 3, 104, 125, 146, 148, 154–57, 167, 181, 275
income
  distribution, 30, 52, 95
  inequality, 25, 26, 37, 51, 90–93, 250
  polarization, 27, 225
  tax, 55, 96–98, 101, 109–12, 120, 228, 234
incomes policy, 66, 102
incubator, 203, 241, 242, 266, 271
India
  agricultural production in, 224
  as U.S. competitor, 125
individual retirement account (IRA), 87, 98, 114
industrial extension, 134, 203, 204, 272; *see also* agricultural extension service
industrial recruitment, state and local development approach, 228, 231, 232, 238
industrial revenue bonds, *see* revenue bonds
inflation, defined, 6, 7
institutionalist paradigm, 71, 76, 83
interest rates
  effects on balance of trade, 89, 90, 103, 151, 164, 165, 224
  effects of financial deregulation on, 91
  effects on industries and incomes, 93
  effects of monetary policy on, 9, 22, 86, 88, 96, 106, 110, 113, 127, 156, 276
  on government bonds, 228
  Keynesian view of, 78
  regulation of, 99, 100, 102
International Bank for Reconstruction and Development, *see* World Bank
international economic cooperation, and coordination, xvii, 2, 68–70, 103–8, 118, 123
international exchange market tax, 105
International Monetary Fund (IMF), 4, 31, 32

international monetary system, 1, 4, 39, 117, 121, 276, 277
interstate competition, *see* war between the states
investment bank, 133
investment subsidies, by government, 137
Italy, welfare policy of, 120

Japan
  competition with U.S., 18, 24, 195
  economic cooperation with U.S., 103–6, 146, 276, 277
  education and training system, 198
  industrial policy, 130–33, 140–42, 162, 167, 168, 173–76
  postwar reconstruction of, xv, 1, 5, 16, 17, 20, 99, 125, 275
  productivity growth of, 128, 197
  service sector, 169
  trade policy of, 146, 148, 151–55, 166
  U.S. borrowing from, xvi, 90, 110, 151
  wages in, 19, 129
Japan Development Bank, 133
Japanese Ministry of International Trade and Industry (MITI), 131–33, 142, 145, 162; *see also* Japan, industrial policy
Jevons, William Stanley, 79
job and wage polarization, 28, 62, 92, 111, 172; *see also* income, polarization
job restructuring, 187, 214; *see also* corporate restructuring
Job Training Partnership Act (JTPA), 11, 184, 198, 219
Johnson, President Lyndon, 15, 113, 229

Kemp, Jack, U.S. Congressman, 119
Kennedy, President John F., 113, 229
Kentucky, economic conversion planning in, 260
Keynes at home and Keynes abroad, 277
Keynes at home and Smith abroad, 16, 247, 277
Keynesian demand management, 8, 16, 30, 50, 71, 82, 86–89, 96, 100, 113, 121, 260, 277; *see also* fiscal policy, demand-side
knowledge problem, 81, 142, 152, 174
Korea, *see* South Korea
Korean War, 5, 8, 20

Labor Law Reform Act of 1978, 139
labor-management
  accord, 11, 12, 16, 23, 28, 29
  conflict, 10, 11, 135, 136
  cooperation, 127, 129, 134, 136, 139, 141, 144, 167, 170, 194, 251, 267
labor market segments, defined, 13
Laffer Curve, 119
laissez-faire, 38, 48, 72, 79, 80, 120, 226–27
land-grant, college system, 204, 222
Landrum-Griffin Act, 139
Latin America, in the global economy, 277
liberal arts, in education, 183, 195, 201, 210, 276
libertarian philosophy, 68, 77
linkage industries, and industrial policy, 132; *see also* spillovers
location incentives, for business, 227, 228, 233, 235, 249, 268; *see also* business recruitment
Lockheed company, 138, 144
Louisiana, economic conversion planning in, 260
Louisville, economic development policy of, 272
Louvre Accord of 1987, 105

macroeconomic equation, 86
Maine, economic conversion planning in, 260
Malaysia, global production restructuring, 263
managed trade, 104, 124, 145–48, 150–54, 164–67, 178–81, 275, 277
Manhattan, economic restructuring, 264
manufacturing
  automation, 14, 33, 171
  effects of macroeconomy on, 99, 175, 224
  employment in, 15, 27, 28, 33, 140, 161
  extension service, 171, 204; *see also* industrial extension
  foreign investment and competition in, 17, 89, 128, 135, 176, 223
  labor-management relations in, 29, 171, 172
  labor supply in, 217
  movement from cities to suburbs, 34, 223, 225, 235
  productivity in, 141, 156
  research and development consortia, 145

Subject Index 325

state and local development policy, 232
university-business cooperation, 222
worker training in, 143, 197
Manufacturing Technology Resources Center (MANTEC), 244
maquiladora, 254; *see also* Mexico
Marshall Plan, 5, 32, 34, 99
Maryland, economic conversion planning in, 260
Massachusetts
  economic development policies in, 267, 271
  Mature Industries Commission of, 247
  Revenue Enforcement and Protection Program (REAP), 56
mature industries, 130, 132, 143, 166, 170, 171, 239, 277
means of production, 58, 60
Medicaid, 15, 24
Medicare, 15, 24, 86, 93
Meidner Plan, 161
mercantilism, 3, 84
merit good, 197, 209
Mexico
  agreements with U.S. states, 248
  free trade agreement negotiations with U.S., 153
  global production in, 20, 153, 224, 262, 263
Michigan, economic development policies of, 271
Mid-South Trade Council, 249
migration, of black farmworkers to cities, 14, 33, 41, 262
military
  conversion to civilian use, 247
  location in U.S., 254
  research and development, 99, 129
  spending, 16, 24, 25, 34, 35, 94, 96, 99–101, 277; *see also* defense
  U.S. postwar leadership, xv, 1, 2, 5, 32, 120
Miller Beer, 64
Milwaukee
  business-education partnership in, 190
  economic development policies of, 272
minimum wage, xvi, 9, 24, 25, 27, 50, 92, 101, 121, 175, 191, 252, 266
Minneapolis–St. Paul, tax base sharing, 238
Minnesota, economic conversion planning in, 260

Missouri, economic conversion planning in, 260
MIT (Massachusetts Institute of Technology), 202, 203
MITI, *see* Japanese Ministry of International Trade and Industry
mode of production, 58, 60, 65, 67, 75
Mondale, Walter, 112
monetarism, 51, 68, 70, 88, 116, 118
monetarist experiment, by Federal Reserve Board, 88–91, 95
monetary policy, 8, 9, 16, 30, 38, 48, 69, 86, 102–7, 115, 127, 172
money supply, 9, 22, 31, 35, 51, 52, 68–70, 86–89, 102, 103, 127
monopolies, 100
monopoly capitalism, 64, 65, 76, 150, 151; *see also* competitive capitalism
Morrill Acts of 1862 and 1890, 203
Multi-Fibre Arrangement (MFA), 148, 152
multinational corporation (MNC), 20, 22, 38, 64–66, 76, 84, 103, 116, 117, 126, 135, 149, 150, 154, 172, 178, 248, 249

National Broadcasting Corporation, 235
National Cooperative Research Act, 145
national economic planning, 137, 278
National Governors' Association, 189–91, 238
National Housing Act of 1949, 229
national indicative planning, 127, 131, 144
National Labor Relations Act of 1935, 134, 140
National Labor Relations Board, 11
National League of Cities, 238
National Science Foundation awards, 133
National Worker Adjustment and Retraining Notification Act of 1988, 37, 138, 175, 239
natural rate of unemployment, 96
neighborhood effects, 47, 48
neo-Ricardian paradigm, 71, 80, 83
New Deal, 8, 229
New England
  economic conditions in, 264
  military spending in, 224
New Federalism, under President Reagan, 231, 235, 249, 250, 252
New Jersey
  education achievement standards, 202

foreign trade zone in, 262
New Orleans, economic development policies of, 272
New South, *see* South, the
New York
  economic conversion planning in, 260
  economic development policy of, 271
New York City
  global restructuring and economic policies in, 194, 233, 235, 240, 261, 263, 271
  worker education programs, 216
newly industrializing countries (NICs), xv, 1, 20, 39, 125, 152, 223, 224
Nixon, President Richard, 21, 87, 113, 229, 231
nontariff measures (NTMs), 125, 147, 153, 154, 181

OECD (Organization of Economic Cooperation and Development), 180
Ohio
  defense employment in, 254
  economic conversion planning in, 260
Omnibus Budget Reconciliation Act of 1981, 231
Omnibus Trade and Competitiveness Act of 1988, 147, 153
OPEC (Organization of Petroleum Exporting Countries), xvi, 23, 25, 35, 36, 229
open access to education, 183; *see also* equal opportunity
open-shop union, 11, 32; *see also* closed-shop union
Oregon, business-education partnership in, 190

Pacific trading bloc, 276
paper entrepreneurialism, 130
paradigm
  political-economic, 43–45, 83
  natural science, 71
participatory democracy, 77, 78; *see also* democratic decision making
participatory economic planning, 245, 270
Pax Britannica, 276
peace dividend, 91, 123
Pennsylvania, economic development policies, 232, 244, 271
performance requirements, on companies, 248
periphery
  countries, 39
  industries, 13, 33, 64; *see also* core
Persian Gulf War, 91, 110
Philadelphia, economic development policies of, 261, 272
Philip Morris company, 64
Piedmont, economic conditions in, 262
Pittsburgh
  economic decline of, 157, 224, 262
  economic policies of, 261, 272
plant closings
  causes, 28
  impacts, 26, 125, 173, 219, 269
  and industrial policy, 132, 135, 144, 156
  regulation, 37, 138, 149, 160, 175, 227, 239
Plaza Agreement of 1985, 105
Point Four Aid, to Greece and Turkey, 5
Portland, business-education partnership in, 190
Portugal, comparative trade advantage example, 150, 180
poverty
  alternative solutions, 50, 53, 54, 66, 84, 90, 106, 250–52
  trends, 16, 92, 93
President's Council of Economic Advisers, 9, 95, 119
price controls, 102, 113
private industry councils (PICs), 198
privatization
  of education, 189–91, 278
  other areas, 266
problem-solving groups, in the workplace, 187
product-process cycle, 34, 253
productivity, U.S.
  policies to improve, 3, 87, 94, 95, 101, 113, 127, 132, 134, 139, 140, 143, 148, 160, 171, 174, 198, 204, 268, 272
  reasons for decline of, 28, 36, 129, 135, 136, 161, 169–73, 197
  trends, 17, 24, 41, 128, 141, 156
profits
  and investment, 6, 7, 19, 49, 61, 66, 75, 78, 80, 83, 98, 106, 136, 142, 158, 253
  public policies, 102, 138, 140, 146, 158, 165, 241
  trends, 12, 17, 25, 99
  and work organization, 174, 193
property tax, 27, 233, 235, 239
proprietary schools, 183

protection/protectionism, 30, 104, 117, 124–26, 130–31, 142–58, 167, 177, 180–81
public goods, 47, 52, 55, 81
public investment bank, 127, 133
public investment deficit, 97
public-private partnership, 230

quality circles, in the workplace, 130, 170, 203
quotas, 130, 147, 275; *see also* voluntary export restraints

R and D, *see* research and development
racial discrimination, in education, 184
racial segregation, 196
Reagan, President Ronald, 24, 25, 37, 51, 57, 87–89, 93–96, 100, 109, 111, 113, 117, 119, 121, 122, 144, 147, 181, 190, 231, 233, 249
recession
  and government countercyclical policy, 6–8, 63, 85, 86, 100, 113
  of 1974–75, 24, 36, 229
  of 1980–82, xvi, 22, 25, 89, 107, 156, 175, 231
  of 1990–91, 91, 92
Reconstruction Finance Corporation (RFC), 132, 143, 166, 168
Republican party, 111, 255
research and development (R&D), 127–29, 131–34, 145, 158, 162–63, 169, 204, 224, 241
research and development consortia, 145, 241
Research Triangle, 241
restructuring, through industrial policy, 127, 130–32, 138, 140–43, 163, 166, 167, 201, 246, 251, 272, 278; *see also* corporate restructuring; global restructuring
revenue bonds, 254, 255, 264; *see also* tax-exempt bonds
Rhode Island, economic conversion planning in, 260
right-to-work states, 11, 227
Rochester, school system, 189
Roosevelt, President Franklin D., 6, 8, 205, 229, 254
Rustbelt, loss of manufacturing jobs in, 223

S & L, *see* savings and loan industry
Sacramento, economic development policies of, 272
sales taxes, 55
Samsung company, 167
San Diego, and U.S.–Mexican trade, 224
Santa Monica, economic development policies of, 227, 266
savings and loan industry, 88, 91, 92, 110, 114
Say, Jean Baptiste, 84
Scholastic Aptitude Test (SAT), 185, 195
school-business partnership, *see* business-education partnership
scientific socialism, 74, 75
Sears company, location incentives paid to, 240
Seattle, business-education partnership in, 190
second-chance training programs, 191, 200; *see also* workforce training
Second World War, *see* World War II
secondary labor market, 27; *see also* labor market segments
Securities and Exchange Commission, 10
Sematech, R&D consortium, 145
service sector
  employment in, 27, 28, 175, 223, 236, 268
  productivity in, 156, 169
services, producer, 223, 225, 233
shared foreign sales corporations (SFSCs), 243
Shearson-Lehman-Hutton company, location incentives paid to, 235
Silicon Valley, 241, 264
Singapore, as U.S. competitor, xv, 1, 18, 20, 125
skills shortages, 186, 213
Smith at home and Smith abroad, 277
Smith at the federal level and Keynes at the state level, 248
Smith at the federal level and Smith abroad, 247
Smith-Lever Act of 1914, 204
Smithian versus Keynesian policy, 30, 260
social democracy, 67, 69, 115
Social Security, 24, 25, 65, 86, 93, 113
Social Security Act of 1935, 9
social welfare
  policy, 16, 23, 24, 36, 247
  programs, 35, 88, 89, 93
  spending, 1, 6, 24, 93, 96, 118
South Africa, state and local disinvestment from, 248
South America, and global trade, 153

South, the
  economic conditions in, 223, 264
  tax-exempt bonds, 228, 234, 254, 257
South Korea, as U.S. competitor, xv, 1, 19, 20, 35, 104, 125, 146, 275
Southeast Asia, as U.S. competitor, 167
Soviet Union, see U.S.S.R.
speculation, in currency markets, 21, 22, 103–6, 121
spillovers, 132, 133, 148, 152, 158, 177, 179
stagflation, xvi, 23, 24, 57, 87, 98, 100
Stanford University, 203
strategic planning, 245, 246, 259, 265, 271, 273
sub-Saharan Africa, in the global economy, 276
subsidies, of business investment, 3, 106, 125–26, 131–34, 137, 139, 142, 146, 149, 150, 153, 155, 160, 165, 179, 227, 228, 232, 235–38, 241, 246, 257, 268–71
sunrise industries, 133, 134, 137, 163
sunset industries, 138
Super 301, U.S. trade law, 147, 153
supply-side fiscal policy, see fiscal policy, supply-side
surplus value, 60–62, 65, 76
Sweden
  economic growth of, 141
  social democracy, 67, 115
Switzerland, economic growth of, 141
  education spending of, 213

Taft-Hartley Act of 1947, 134, 139
Taiwan, as U.S. competitor, xv, 1, 18, 20, 104, 125
target zones, in currency values, 105
Targeted Jobs Tax Credit program of 1978, 11, 184, 198
tariffs, xvi, 3–5, 108, 124, 125, 130, 153, 154, 275
tax
  abatements, 233, 234, 237
  burden, distribution of, 270
  credits, 87
  incentives, 234, 249, 271
  subsidies, 268, 271
tax-base sharing, 236, 238
tax-exempt development bonds, 231–34; see also revenue bonds
Tax Reform Act of 1986, 94, 112
Taylorist management, 197
Tennessee Valley Authority, 229
third wave in economic development, 244, 245

Third World debt, 99, 103–6, 108, 116–20, 122
Tokyo, impact of globalization on, 263
tourism promotion, for economic development, 243
tracking, in education, 10, 32, 183, 184
trade deficit, U.S., xvi, 25, 30, 90, 91, 94, 97, 100, 103, 104, 117, 120, 125, 126, 128, 151, 180, 181, 224
trading blocs, 153, 154, 180, 276
transnational corporation, 5, 17, 19, 39
transportation/communications revolution, 19, 39
Truman Commission, on higher education, 10
Turkey, postwar reconstruction of, 5
two-tier wage structures, 37

unemployment insurance, 9, 24, 65, 83, 93, 101
unions and unionization, xvi, 11–13, 28, 29, 32–34, 37, 41, 52, 70, 79, 100, 101, 129, 130, 134, 137–40, 153, 160, 171, 174, 194, 216, 227
United Auto Workers, 194
United Kingdom, G-5 member, 105; see also England; Great Britain
university-industry cooperation, 201–3, 222, 250; see also business-education partnership
up-skilling, 193, 208
urban renewal program, 229, 230, 255
Urban Development Action Grant (UDAG), 229–31
Uruguay Round, of GATT negotiations, 152, 177, 248
U.S.–Canada Free Trade Agreement (FTA), 126, 153, 179, 180, 224
U.S. Constitution, conflict with state and local policies, 248
U.S. Department of Housing and Urban Development, 230
U.S. Economic Development Administration, 230, 231
U.S. Employment Service, 11, 206
U.S. Export-Import Bank, 249
U.S. Federal Reserve, see Federal Reserve Board of Governors
U.S. Food and Drug Administration, 10
U.S. Foreign and Commercial Service, 249
U.S. House Committee on Ways and Means, 121
U.S. Interstate Commerce Commission, 10

Subject Index 329

U.S.-Mexico free trade agreement negotiations, 153, 254
U.S. Small Business Administration (SBA), 230, 231, 241
user fees, 112
U.S.S.R. (Union of Soviet Socialist Republics), 83, 91

Versailles Peace Treaty of 1919, 2
Vietnam War, 5, 8, 20
Virginia
  defense spending in, 224
  student learning assessment policy of, 202
Virginia Center for Innovative Technology, 242, 244
vocational-technical education, 10, 183, 184, 192, 194, 201
Volcker, Paul, 88
Volkswagen company, Pennsylvania's subsidies to, 233
voluntary export restraint (VER), 125, 130, 146, 147, 152; *see also* quotas
vouchers, in education, 189, 190, 196, 212, 218

wage-price controls, 96, 100, 113
Wagner Act of 1935, 11
Walras, Leon, 79
Walsh-Healy Act of 1936, 9
war between the states, for investment and jobs, 236, 237, 271

War on Poverty, 15, 87, 229
Washington, economic conversion planning in, 260
Washington, D.C., economic conditions in, 224, 262, 263
Washington, Harold, Chicago Mayor, 267, 270; *see also* Chicago
welfare, 2, 9, 65, 68, 83, 87, 95, 98, 113, 114, 117, 119, 122, 191, 220, 250, 251, 266; *see also* social welfare
welfare state, 23, 24, 36, 56, 78, 118–20
West Germany, *see* Germany
Western Europe, *see* Europe
worker cooperatives, and worker ownership, 67, 140, 161, 174, 227, 278
worker participation, in decision making, 70, 170, 172, 174, 215, 220
workforce training, 1, 2, 6, 10, 13, 28–30, 70, 108, 129, 132, 182–85, 194, 198, 203, 214, 216, 219, 220, 222, 226, 232, 239, 251, 268, 269, 271–273
workplace democracy, 138, 139, 172, 174, 278
World Bank, 32
world trade center (WTC), 243, 273
World War II, xv, xvii, 1–5, 8, 12, 13, 19, 24, 33, 39, 64, 66, 93, 98, 106, 117, 118, 120, 129, 145, 155, 172, 173, 176, 206, 276, 277

John J. Accordino is associate professor of urban studies and planning at Virginia Commonwealth University in Richmond, where he teaches courses in economic development policy, planning and finance, and strategic planning. He holds a Ph.D. in urban and regional planning from the Massachusetts Institute of Technology.

The editor of the series, John H. Whaley, Jr., has a master's degree in library science and a Ph.D. in history. He has been a librarian since 1974 and has had ten years' experience in reference. At present he is Head of Special Collections and Archives at Virginia Commonwealth University in Richmond.